Henry IV

HENRY IV

DAVID BUISSERET

Director of the Hermon Dunlap Smith Center for the History of Cartography at the Newberry Library, Chicago; formerly Professor of History, University of the West Indies, Jamaica Campus

London
GEORGE ALLEN & UNWIN
Boston   Sydney

George Allen & Unwin (Publishers) Ltd,
40 Museum Street, London WC1A 1LU, UK

George Allen & Unwin (Publishers) Ltd,
Park Lane, Hemel Hempstead, Herts HP2 4TE, UK

Allen & Unwin, Inc.,
9 Winchester Terrace, Winchester, Mass. 01890, USA

George Allen & Unwin Australia Pty Ltd,
8 Napier Street, North Sydney, NSW 2060, Australia

First published in 1984

British Library Cataloguing in Publication Data

Buisseret, David
   Henry IV.
1. Henry IV, *King of France*
2. France—Kings and rulers—Biography
I. Title
944'.031'0924   DC122.8
ISBN 0-04-944012-8

Library of Congress Cataloging in Publication Data

Buisseret, David.
   Henry IV.
1. Henry IV, King of France, 1553–1610. 2. France—
History—Henry IV, 1589–1610. 3. France— Kings and
rulers—Biography. I. Title.
DC122.B88   1984   944'.031'0924   83-22464
ISBN 0-04-944012-8 (cased)

Set in 10 on 12 point Bembo by Computape (Pickering) Ltd
and printed in Great Britain by
Mackays of Chatham

For Mark and Paul

A Note on Henry's Ciphers

Henry's ciphers survive in a variety of places. On the parts of the Louvre for which he was responsible we find both 'HDB', for Henri de Bourbon, and an interlaced 'HG', for Henry and Gabrielle. A most interesting account of these ciphers has been given by Jean-Pierre Babelon in the *Commission du Vieux Paris. Procès-verbal de la séance du lundi 2 avril 1979*.

Sometimes the king signed his letters with a sort of monogram in which two 'M's, for Marie de Medici, are combined with an 'H' (see, for example, BN Collection Rothschild, A XVI 144). On the binding of some of the books from his library we also find a cipher, normally a crowned 'H'. For the dust jacket of this book we have chosen an example of the latter cipher, taken from the magnificent atlas preserved in the Musée Condé, Chantilly (MS 534).

Contents

Preface   *Page*   xiii
Acknowledgements   xv
Abbreviations   xvi
List of Plates   xvii
List of Maps and Plans   xviii

Prologue   1

1 A Prince of Great Promise, 1553–84   3

   (i)   Birth and Infancy, 1553–7   3
  (ii)   Troubled Boyhood, 1557–67   4
 (iii)   Formative Years with Jeanne, 1567–72   5
 (iv)   At the Royal Court, 1572–6   7
  (v)   The Governor of Guyenne, 1576–80   9
 (vi)   Henry's Growing Influence, 1580–4   12

2 An Almost Incomparable Vigour of Body, 1584–8   15

   (i)   The War of the Three Henrys, 1584–9   15
  (ii)   The King Allies Himself with Navarre, 1584–5   17
 (iii)   The King Allies Himself with the Guises, 1585–8   18
 (iv)   The War of Pamphlets   18
  (v)   Military Operations, 1586   21
 (vi)   Coutras, 20 October 1587   21
 (vii)   The Climacteric Year: 1588   25
(viii)   The Empty Throne: 1589   26

3 A King without a Kingdom   28

   (i)   The New King's Supporters   28
  (ii)   Retreat from Paris, August 1589   29
 (iii)   Arques, 21 September 1589: 'Ils ne se sont gueres bien servys
      de leur avantaige'   29
 (iv)   The First Attack on Paris, September–November 1589   31
  (v)   Ivry, 14 March 1590: 'Dieu nous a bénis'   32
 (vi)   The Second Attack on Paris, May–September 1590   35
 (vii)   The Struggle in the Provinces 1589–90   37
(viii)   Venus and Mars, February–April 1591   37
 (ix)   The Siege of Rouen, November 1591–April 1592   38
   (x)   The Struggle in the Provinces, 1592   40
 (xi)   Relations with Rome, 1584–92   41
 (xii)   The Troubles of the League, 1589–92   41
(xiii)   The Estates-General of 1593   42

4 The Perilous Leap, 1593–4   44
 (i) The Desired Instruction, July 1593   44
 (ii) The Necessary and Customary Ceremonies, 25 July 1593   44
 (iii) The Falling Out of Faithful Friends, 1593–4   45
 (iv) 'To Condemn the Treason, and Reward the Traitor', 1593–4   46
 (v) The King as *Sacerdos*, February 1594   50
 (vi) The Joyous Entry, 22 March 1594   51
 (vii) The Paternal Blessing, 1593–5   54
 (viii) The *Croquants* of 1594   54

5 'La guerre au roy d'Hespaigne', 1595–7   56
 (i) Châtel and the Jesuits, 1594–5   56
 (ii) The Eastern Campaign, 1595   57
 (iii) The North-Eastern Frontier, 1596   58
 (iv) The Assembly of Notables, 1596–7   62
 (v) An Interval of Peace, 1597   63
 (vi) Amiens Lost and Amiens Regained, 1597   65

6 'L'heureuse saison', 1598   69
 (i) The Brittany Voyage: 'Mercure ou Mars', February–May 1598   69
 (ii) 'The Affairs of Those of the Religion', April 1598   70
 (iii) A Small Town Called Vervins, February–May 1598   74
 (iv) 'Mon humeur mélancolique', June–December 1598   75
 (v) 'Partagés ma couronne', 1598–9   77
 (vi) Savoy, December 1599–June 1679   79
 (vii) Theological Interlude: 'Le sieur Duplessis sacrifié au Pape', April–May 1683   81
 (viii) 'Mon premyer metyer', August–December 1600   83
 (ix) 'Quelque princesse digne de la moitié de son lict', October 1600–January 1601   86

7 'The Hercules That Now Reigns',1600   88
 (i) The King's View of France   88
 (ii) The King's Household   94
 (iii) The Great Officers and Their Charges   96
 (iv) The King's Daily Round   101

8 The Consolidation of the Dynasty, 1601–2   106
 (i) 'Monsieur de Rosni Doth Promise Millions'   106
 (ii) 'Pour visiter les fortifications que j'y fais faire'   107
 (iii) 'Puer natus est nobis', September 1601   108
 (iv) 'Both in Watch and Warde Attending the Opportunity'   110
 (v) 'If He Comes He Deceaves the World'   111
 (vi) 'The Opinion Is, That Hee Shall Dye'   112
 (vii) 'If Bouillon Comes, His Doom Is Already Geeven'   114
 (viii) 'Le nombre de tels larrons n'est ja que trop grand'   115
 (ix) 'To Hold in Bridle the Gallies of Spain'   115

Contents

9 'A Confused Labyrinthe', 1603–4   118

    (i) 'On est paisible en mon royaume'   118
   (ii) 'Le bon Dieu veut disposer de moy'   119
  (iii) 'La reine d'Angleterre est décédée'   120
  (iv) 'These Jesuits Having Now the Liberties of France'   121
   (v) 'Nous avons descouvert force trahisons'   125
  (vi) The Cold War Continues   126
 (vii) 'No Places Should Be Fortified but the Frontiers'   127
(viii) 'This Town Is Growing Much Fairer than You Have Seen It'   128
  (ix) 'L'honorable passion . . . d'embellir son royaume de toutes
     sortes d'artifices'   133

10 'Un malheur inconnu', 1605–6   136

    (i) 'Souvent d'une estincelle il s'allume un grand feu . . . '   136
   (ii) 'Ceux de la Religion de Guyenne et de Languedoc y font rage'   137
  (iii) 'We Have Been Advised of the Opposition . . . to the Sieur
     de Monts'   138
  (iv) 'Il me tint continuellement la main'   139
   (v) 'The King Rejoyceth Much in His Dolphin'   140
  (vi) 'Tant j'estois amoureux de Sedan'   141
 (vii) 'The Princes of Germany Begin to Bristle Themselves'   141
(viii) 'The Placing of These Waters, for the Transporting of
     All Her Commodities'   142
  (ix) 'Great Multitudes of Irishmen'   144

11 The Halcyon's Nest, 1607–9   146

    (i) 'The Great Mortification of His Natural Vivacity'   146
   (ii) 'His Majesty Was Magnificently and Sumptuously Arrayed'   146
  (iii) 'Tandem arbiter orbis'   148
  (iv) 'The Greatest and Goodliest Palace of Europe'   149
   (v) 'Spunges to the King'   151
  (vi) 'Someone of Proven Quality, Capacity and Fidelity'   156
 (vii) 'The Greatness of His Governors'   159
(viii) 'L'insolence de ceux dudict parlement'   161
  (ix) 'Je vous prie que ce soit Lecomte'   163
   (x) 'J'estime que ce ne soyent que querelles particulières'   167

12 'L'infortune de cet abominable jour'   168

    (i) 'Things Were Now Tending to an Universall Peace'   168
   (ii) 'The Matter of Cleves Is Growen Hote Again'   171
  (iii) 'The Noise of Warre'   173
  (iv) 'La main de cet esprit farouche'   174
   (v) 'C'était un roi, celui-là'   176

Conclusion: 'Un roy pour estre grand ne doit rien ignorer'   178

Notes 186
Sources and Bibliography 203
Chronological Table 217
Glossary 220
Index 225

Preface

What, the reader may justly expostulate, another book on Henry IV? It would be difficult to make a full catalogue of all the biographies of the *Vert Galant*, and yet, as was written on the first page of the short-lived *Revue Henri IV*, in 1905, his epoch remains 'plus célèbre que connue'. This is partly because, as will be seen in Sources and Bibliography, the period witnesses a sort of 'information explosion' in comparison with what survives from previous periods in France, so that the very bulk of the material prevents any one person from ever mastering all the documents pertinent to the reign. It is also because the king had a very strong and generally attractive personality, around which clustered many savorous anecdotes, from which it is very difficult for the biographer to free himself. So there have been many histories recounting again and again the old *histoires* about the peasants he met while he was out hunting, or his exploits with Gabrielle d'Estrées, or remarks like the one about the 'poule au pot'.

I hope to have moved away from an excessive preoccupation with these pleasing stories, and have tried as well not to see the reign too much through the eyes of Sully, whose often mendacious memoirs continue so largely to form our view of the period. My plan is largely chronological, as seems inevitable in dealing with a life, but the emphasis falls differently from that of most previous biographers. They have nearly always devoted at least half of their books to the period before Henry's accession, in 1589 (he was then 36, and had twenty-one years to live). I have dwelt much less fully on this early period which takes up only a sixth of my *Henry IV*. Some readers will be disappointed by that; I have concentrated instead on Henry's activities as king. Others will surely protest at the prominence accorded to military events, giving equal weight to both words. But Henry was above all a *military* man, as I hope to show, and had any one of half a dozen *events* gone the other way, then he would not have reached the throne or retained it and, I venture to say, the history of France in the early seventeenth century would have been quite different.

So, although it is the story of a man, it is also, especially in the latter pages, the history of a reign, and the two are quite inseparable. As far as possible, I have let the king speak for himself, so that the source most frequently quoted is his *Lettres missives*; although these have now been published for well over a century, they still contain some surprises. Other fresh material comes from the 'Papiers de Sully', acquired by the Archives Nationales in 1955, and from the inexhaustible correspondence-series of the Bibliothèque Nationale, particularly manuscrits français 23195−8. I have also made extensive use of the English diplomatic dispatches, preserved mainly in the Public Record Office. They have the advantages not only of containing interesting information, but also of expressing it in a particularly pungent way.

The list of sources, *pace* Marc Bloch, will be found at the end of the book. I have noted there certain archives which it has not been possible fully to investigate, and ought to add that there are even some secondary sources which I have not been able to track down, particularly in the older French provincial reviews. In the notes, references to printed works have been abbreviated as far as possible, because the full reference will be found in the bibliography. In the hope of leaving the text uncluttered, I have relegated the explanation of certain technical terms to a glossary. The first time such a term occurs, it is marked by an asterisk. Generally, I have translated quotations from the French, but where the language was particularly apt I have left it as it was written.

If there is one single impression which I should like the reader to carry away after reading this book, it is that of the reign's paradoxical nature, or of the reluctance of actual events to fit the mould into which we too easily cram them. Thus we have a king who is concerned to educate the *noblesse d'épée*★ and to involve its members more closely in running his state. We have the *premier président*★ of a *parlement*★ who in the absence of the governor makes military decisions concerning the province. We have a proto-*intendant*★ who vociferously takes the part of those local communities whom he was supposed to be crushing. We have a monarch who grants ecclesiastical benefices to his bastards and mistresses, and yet is in the forefront of the Catholic renewal. We have a minister who, himself an obdurate Protestant, yet seeks out good Catholic preachers for the king. Everywhere we look, when we look closely, the old easy generalisations collapse, and the reality of things is seen to defy categorisation. But that is how it actually was.

Acknowledgements

This book has now been more than twenty years in the making, and during that time I have incurred debts of gratitude to many people in many places, of whom I can name only a few. At Cambridge, my choice of thesis-subject and early experiments were guided by Patrick Bury, of Corpus Christi College, and by Professor Charles Wilson. In Paris, my constant friend and critic has been Bernard Barbiche; we were students of Professor Roland Mousnier in the late 1950s, and have worked together with his encouragement ever since then, particularly on our edition of the memoirs of Sully. The late Professor Michel François also helped us a good deal, and I have had fruitful meetings with Jean-Pierre Babelon and with the late Père François de Dainville.

Much of this work was written while I was teaching at the University of the West Indies, where my students forced me to explain myself carefully about a period and place so foreign to most of them. It has been finished at the Newberry Library, Chicago; after working here twice as a Fellow, I have now joined the Library as a member of its staff, grateful for the opportunity to try out new ideas on my colleagues and on our rich flow of readers.

DAVID BUISSERET
Chicago, September 1981

Abbreviations

AAE   Archives du Ministère des Affaires Etrangères
AC   Archives Communales
AD   Archives Départmentales
AM   Archives Municipales
AN   Archives Nationales
BN   Bibliothèque Nationale

Cal. MSS de L'Isle   *Report on the Manuscripts of Lord de L'Isle and Dudley Preserved at Penshurst Place*, 6 vols (London, 1926–66)

Cal. MSS Salisbury   *Calendar of the Manuscripts of the Most Honourable the Marquis of Salisbury at Hatfield House*, 24 vols (London, 1883–1976)

CSP Foreign   *Calendar of State Papers, Foreign Series of the Reign of Elizabeth*, 23 vols (London, 1863–1950)

CSP Venice   *Calendar of State Papers and Manuscripts . . . in the Archives and Collections of Venice*, 3 vols (London, 1864–1940)

Lettres missives   *Lettres missives de Henri IV*, ed. B. de Xivrey and J. Guadet, 9 vols (Paris, 1843–76)

Palma-Cayet   Pierre-Victor Palma-Cayet, *Chronologie novenaire* and *Chronologie septenaire* in *Choix de chroniques et mémoires sur l'histoire de France*, ed. J. A. C. Buchon, Vols I and II (Paris, 1836)

PRO SP   Public Record Office, State Papers

Valois, *Inventaire*   Noël Valois (ed.), *Inventaire des arrêts du conseil d'Etat (règne de Henri IV)*, 2 vols (Paris, 1886–93)

Winwood, *Negotiations*   *Memorials of Affairs of State in the Reigns of Queen Elizabeth and King James I . . .*, ed. Edmund Sawyer, 3 vols (London, 1725)

List of Plates

1   East front and entrance to the *château* at Pau
    Arch. Phot. Paris/S.P.A.D.E.M.
2   Portrait of Henry at the age of 3
    Private collection/photo. Giraudon
3   Drawing of Henry at the age of about 18
    Bibliothèque Nationale
4   German engraving of Parma's relief of Paris in September 1590
    Bibliothèque Nationale
5   Engraving of Henry IV touching for the King's Evil
    Bibliothèque Nationale
6   Engraving of Henry's entry into Paris in March 1594
    Bibliothèque Nationale
7   Engraving of Henry's entry into Lyon in September 1595
    Bibliothèque Nationale
8   Engraving by Claude de Chastillon of the siege of La Fère in January 1596
    The British Library
9   Detail from the engraving of the siege of La Fère
10 Drawing of the siege of Amiens in September 1597
    The British Library
11 Engraving by Claude de Chastillon of the artillery magazine in Metz
    The British Library
12 Detail from the engraving of Paris in Caspar Merian's *Topographia Galliae*
    (1655–61)
    The Newberry Library
13 View of the Pont Neuf
    Author's photograph
14 Engraving by Claude de Chastillon of the Hôpital Saint-Louis
    The British Library
15 Engraving by Jean Le Clerc of the baptism of the dauphin in September 1606
    Bibliothèque Nationale
16 Engraving of Henry IV as the Gallic Hercules
    Bibliothèque Nationale
17 The Porte Dauphine at Fontainebleau
    Arch. Phot. Paris/S.P.A.D.E.M.
18 Dutch engraving of the assassination of Henry IV
    Bibliothèque Nationale
19 Bust of Henry IV
    Musée Jacquemart-André/ photo. Giraudon

List of Maps and Plans

1	The basis of Henry's power about 1583	*page*	13
2	Areas under the control of the Guise family		16
3	Towns surrendered to the League in 1585		19
4	The battle of Coutras, 1587		23
5	The battle of Arques, 1589		30
6	Henry's attack on Paris, 1589		32
7	The battle of Ivry, 1590		34
8	Henry's track after Ivry		35
9	Henry at Chelles in 1590		36
10	Parma at Caudebec in 1592		40
11	Towns which came over to Henry in 1594		47
12	Henry's attack on Paris, 1594		52
13	The north-eastern frontier 1594–6		59
14	Towns granted to the Protestants by the Edict of Nantes		71
15	The Savoy campaign, 1600		84
16	Henry's travels in France before 1600		89
17	The fortifications and governors of north-eastern France		93
18	Plan of the royal quarters at the Louvre		102
19	General plan of the Louvre		102
20	Henry's works at Paris		132
21	Canals undertaken by Henry and Sully		143
22	Fortifications constructed by Henry and Sully		153
23	Roads and bridges constructed by Henry and Sully		155
24	The site of the duchy of Jülich-Cleves-Berg		172

Prologue

France about 1550 was coming to the end of a long period of economic growth and political consolidation. Agricultural production had been increasing steadily since about the middle of the fifteenth century,[1] and this had given rise to a substantial volume of trade, both internal and external. Many internal market-towns had emerged and developed in order to meet local demand, and the great commercial cities had grown rich exporting wine, salt and textiles. Some, like Paris and Lyon, had also developed into great banking centres.

The pattern of political consolidation went back at least to Louis XI, in the latter part of the fifteenth century. Around the Ile-de-France had slowly clustered the great French-speaking provinces – whether of the *langue d'öil*★ or of the *langue d'oc*★ – until by 1550 the hexagon was virtually complete, except along its eastern frontier. Within the country there was a well-defined system of provinces, each with its *gouverneur*,★ and at the centre was the king and his council, supported by a developing fiscal system. The process of monarchical centralisation had not gone without opposition, but on the whole the theory of emergent absolutism – powerfully argued by the Roman Law theorists of François I (king 1515–47) – was successfully translating itself into practice.

By the middle of the sixteenth century, though, there were sharp signs of contradiction in this general picture of economic growth and political consolidation. The population had reached a size at which it was threatening to outstrip the supplies of food, given the inflexible techniques of agricultural production. Just as in the early fourteenth century, more and more marginal land had to be put under the plough, making the equation of people to land ever more precarious. To this long-term, Malthusian imbalance would be added in the late 1550s the 'accidental' collapse of the Lyon money-market; in 1550 it could be said that France's economic structure looked strong, but was in fact vulnerable.

The same might be said of the political situation. The monarchy of François I and Henri II (king 1547–59) was apparently powerful, and had largely succeeded in thwarting the wider political ambitions of the Emperor, Charles V. But the long series of wars, spread over four decades, had resulted in heavy taxation, and in growing discontent against the Crown among those who paid the *taille*,★ that is, all sections of society except the clergy and the nobility. Here and there were rumblings of peasant revolt, and in the towns there were many who regretted old

1

municipal liberties. To these fiscal discontents were added religious divisions. Even before Luther's outburst, in 1517, there had been people in France who thought like him, and their numbers grew in the 1520s and 1530s, in spite of savage repression after 1534. In the 1540s and 1550s a new form of Protestantism, defined by John Calvin, emerged in Geneva and rapidly penetrated France. It was francophone and highly organised, and soon succeeded in establishing itself over wide areas of the country.

At first these religious movements appealed primarily to clerics and intellectuals, but as time went by Calvinism penetrated the ranks of the nobility, and then in some areas the mass of the peasantry. The ancient nobility was, of course, far from reconciled to the progress of royal absolutism, and to the pre-eminence of the house of Valois. Three other great noble houses claimed the allegiance of a substantial part of the French nobility. In the east there was the redoubtable Guise family, still headed in 1550 by the ageing Duke Claude, whose sons François (1519–63) and Charles (1524/5–74) were able and ambitious. In the south-west there was the Montmorency dynasty. Duke Anne (*sic*) would live on until 1567, leaving his formidable sons François (1530–79) and Henri (1534–1613). Finally, scattered over central and south-western France were the domains of the house of Bourbon-Vendôme, whose leader in 1550 was Antoine de Bourbon (1518–62).

Antoine fought against the armies of Charles V for François I and then for Henri II; he was a brave and capable soldier, famous for his calm under fire and his impetuosity in attack. He was also a lively correspondent, with a particular gift for the telling phrase. He had a constant need for violent exercise, and was markedly licentious. In 1537 he became governor of the frontier province of Picardy, enjoying the favour of François I. The year after Henri II came to the throne of France, in 1547, Antoine took a wife; he was thirty years old. She was Jeanne d'Albret, daughter of Henri d'Albret, and heiress not only to that duchy but also to the kingdom of Navarre. Jeanne, twenty years old, was a highly intelligent princess, who already showed a certain gift for administration.[2] Her father Henri was a skilful ruler, of sanguine temperament, but a very licentious king, whose latter days were plagued by gout and venereal disease.

Antoine and Jeanne lost no time in starting a family, but their first child died just before his second birthday, perhaps because of the incompetence of his nurse. Jeanne had been following Antoine in his travels between the province of Picardy, the Bourbon estates in central France, and her own country in the south-west, but when she found herself pregnant for the second time she returned to her father's *château* at Pau. There, on 14 December 1553, the future Henry IV was born.

1 A Prince of Great Promise, 1553–84

(i) Birth and Infancy, 1553–7

According to legend, the little prince's early days were largely regulated by his grandfather Henri, who wanted to bring him up as a true *Béarnais*,★ away from the debilitating influences of the Valois court.[1] His nurse was a certain Jeanne Fourcade, chosen after seven others had been found wanting; her young master never forgot her, and retained contact with her even after he became king of France. His governess was Suzanne de Bourbon-Busset, who brought him up largely at her *château* of Coarraze. Alas, nothing remains of it today but a single tower, and most of the furniture in the *château* at Pau, which would have been familiar to Henry, has long since been removed.[2] Still, it is easy at Coarraze for us to imagine the little prince's childhood, playing with the village boys alongside the Gave de Pau, the small river which flows down from the direction of Lourdes.

For most of this time, Jeanne was absent from Béarn, following her husband to the wars and to the royal court. When Henri d'Albret died, in May 1555, she came back to Pau; so did Antoine, but he soon left again for the north-eastern frontier. Jeanne probably took over part of Suzanne de Bourbon-Busset's duties at this time. It must have been a difficult juncture for Jeanne personally, since she was in the process of adopting Protestantism, which was then making rapid progress among the French nobility. In November 1556, Antoine rejoined her in Béarn, and together with Henry they made a journey northwards to the court of Henri II. They arrived in February 1557, and were welcomed by the king, who playfully asked the little prince if he would like to be his son. In reply, Henry turned to his father Antoine and replied, in his *Béarnais* patois, 'Quel es lo seigne pay' – 'Here is my father'. The king, amused by this composed answer, then suggested that, if he could not be his son, he might like to be his son-in-law, to which Henry replied 'Obé', or 'Yes'.[3]

He was already impressing adults by his presence of mind and sturdy independence. There are several versions of a very charming portrait of him at this age (Plate 2) as well as a marble bust. Already we can see what Vaissière calls his 'regard éveillé et malicieux', and a remarkable combination of determination and intelligence for so young a child. After that

3

visit to court, Jeanne took him back to Béarn, where Antoine joined them in October 1557. But his parents soon left again, and this time Henry was moved from Coarraze to Pau, where Suzanne de Bourbon-Busset continued to be his governess, joined now by the Bishop of Lescar as tutor.

(ii)   Troubled Boyhood, 1557–67

The next three years were relatively calm ones, as Henry grew up in Pau, visited as her duties permitted by Jeanne and, more rarely, by Antoine. But then in August 1560, when the prince was nearly seven, his mother took him back to the French court and to a situation which soon became disastrous for the unity of her family. Antoine had never been faithful to her, and he now began to act with spectacular infidelity. He was, as Montaigne put it, extremely 'ondoyant', incapable for long of sustaining a fixed course or policy. As we shall see, this trait of *ondoyance* was strong in his son.[4] He also quarrelled with Jeanne over religious matters for, although he had leaned towards Protestantism even earlier than she, he had never summoned sufficient willpower to make a clean break with the ancient church; of course, his behaviour was largely influenced by considerations of political advantage. The quarrels between the couple became more and more scandalous until, in March 1562, Antoine ordered Jeanne to return to Béarn.

At the age of 8, Henry was thus separated from his mother, and left to fend for himself at court. Not content with that, his father began an assault on the prince's religious beliefs, which he had acquired from his mother; his Protestant tutor was sent away and a Catholic one replaced him. For some weeks, Henry held out against this assault, earning the unwilling admiration even of the Spanish ambassador. But on 1 June 1562 he capitulated, accompanying his father to Mass and there swearing to observe the ancient faith.

Meanwhile Jeanne was making her way back to Béarn, through territory made increasingly dangerous by the outbreak of armed conflict between the religious factions. Henry's thoughts must often have been with her, to judge by this letter, written to one of her retainers on 26 September 1562:

> Larchant, write to me and tell me about my mother, for I am so afraid that she will come to some harm on the journey which you are taking, that the best way to please me would be to write often with her news. . . .[5]

To crown this year, so disastrous for the young prince, came news that his father had succumbed on 17 November to a wound which he had received at the siege of Rouen on 16 October. Six weeks before that, on 31 August, Antoine had seen his son for the last time. Henry would now be at court by himself for the next two years, for his mother could not venture up from Béarn to fetch or comfort him. However, he does seem at this juncture to have been kindly treated by the queen mother, Catherine de Medici, who saw to it that he got back his former Protestant tutors and other household officers; he was also now allowed to have Protestant services in his rooms, and was not required to attend Mass.

The chief business of 1563 must have been Henry's schooling, which has been described by Palma-Cayet, a member of his household. The prince's tutor was François de La Gaucherie, who taught him Latin and Greek 'par forme d'usage sans préceptes, comme nous apprenons nos langues maternelles'. Henry would have enjoyed that, and in particular relished a number of Greek phrases; Palma-Cayet affirms that his favourites were 'Sedition must be banished from the city' and 'Either conquer or die'.[6] The prince also enjoyed reading Plutarch, who, he affirmed in 1601, had been like a conscience to him and had 'whispered into his ear much good advice and excellent maxims for his personal conduct and the regulation of public affairs'.[7]

Henry seems to have been an ebullient child, and probably recovered quite fast from the news of his father's death. He had many playmates at court, including Prince Henri d'Anjou, later Henri III, and also Henri de Guise; the foremost adversaries in the struggles of the 1580s and 1590s had thus known each other as children. In March 1564, Henry left Paris with the rest of the court, at the beginning of a great tour which Catherine de Medici was then making to acquaint Charles IX with his kingdom. The court reached Mâcon at the end of May and, on 1 June, Jeanne came there, and was reunited with her son. She soon quarrelled with Catherine, however, and left the grand tour, which pressed on southwards. They reached Salon de Crau, in Provence, on 17 October 1564, and here Henry had the interview with the soothsayer Michel de Nostredame which is reported by L'Estoile.[8] Nostredame came to the prince's bedroom early in the morning, and after gazing at him for a while remarked to his tutor that Henry would 'have all the inheritance', and that the tutor himself, if he lived that long, would have for his master a king of France and of Navarre. Catherine's reaction to this prophecy is not recorded.

(iii) Formative Years with Jeanne, 1567–72

The grand tour then swung westwards to Bayonne, and finally northwards to Paris, which was reached in May 1566. By then Jeanne had rejoined the court, and showed an inclination to take her son's education

5

in hand. Thus they were often together in 1566, as with Catherine's permission they visited Jeanne's estates in Picardy and Vendômois. Back in Paris, Henry joined the other princes in boisterous games and jousts. But then, in January 1567, Jeanne and Henry left to go to La Flèche, for which they had permission, and simply kept going until they crossed the Garonne and reached safety. Henry was now thirteen, and for the next year accompanied Jeanne as she travelled through her domains, continuing his studies but no doubt learning more about the kingly craft from his mother's life than from his books. There is an interesting assessment of the young prince at this time, written by a member of the *parlement* of Bordeaux:

> We have here the prince of Béarn; it must be confessed that he is a charming youth. At thirteen years of age, he has all the riper qualities of eighteen or nineteen; he is agreeable, polite, obliging and behaves to everyone with an air so easy and engaging that wherever he is there is always a crowd. He mixes in conversation like a wise and prudent man, speaks always to the purpose, and when it turns out that the court is the subject of discourse it is easy to see that he is perfectly well acquainted with it, and he never says more nor less than he ought, in whatever place he is.[9]

With due allowance for writer's hyperbole, we can surely see here the man emerging from the child, no doubt in part because of that long and sometimes brutal spell at the royal court between 1562 and 1567. In February 1568, Jeanne sent him off for the first time in an independent capacity, when he went to 'pacify' the formerly rebellious subjects of Basse-Navarre at Saint-Jean-Pied-de-Port. This was to be the first of many such tasks, and his style was already there: 'charm, flattery, appeals to personal loyalty, magnanimity and wit sweetened the dose to be swallowed'.[10] But the position of Jeanne and Henry in Béarn became dangerously isolated at the start of the so-called Third War, and so in September 1568 they moved to La Rochelle, the Protestant headquarters.

Here the young prince came under the tutelage of his uncle Louis, prince de Condé, and began seriously to develop his military skills. However, he was only fourteen, and still prone to foolish pranks, as when he was narrowly rescued from the sea after venturing too far out along one of the dikes at La Rochelle. The tutelage of Condé did not last long, for in March 1569 he was killed at (or, rather, after) the battle of Jarnac. Henry now became titular head of the Protestant cause, and as such was formally presented to the Protestant army by his mother. In the public library in Geneva is a portrait of him at this age; the childish charm of the earlier paintings has quite disappeared, and now we see a lean and austere-looking young man, whose prominent nose alone reminds us of the mature Henry IV.

The next sixteen months were spent with the Protestant armies, in the campaign which ended with the signing of the Peace of Saint-Germain in August 1570. This treaty allowed considerable concessions to the Protestants, including four *villes de sûreté*,* or cautionary towns: La Rochelle, Montauban, La Charité and Cognac. In January 1571, Henry rejoined his mother in La Rochelle, and they spent the next year doing what they could to restore things to normal in Béarn and Guyenne. Jeanne again took in hand Henry's education. Books were bought for him in La Rochelle – Froissart, Pliny, Guicciardini and Appian Alexander[11] – and he began to acquire considerable proficiency at tennis. Jeanne also received several emissaries from Catherine de Medici, who was now anxious to arrange a marriage between Henry and her daughter Marguerite. Catherine's motives have often been analysed in an unfavourable way, but she probably wished chiefly to establish some form of closer relationship with Henry, and also of course to calm the rival religious groups by this symbolic union.[12] By the end of the year Jeanne had been won over, and in December 1571 she left for the royal court; Henry remained behind until the final details had been agreed.

(iv)   At the Royal Court, 1572–6

By March 1572, Jeanne was in the Loire valley, where she had many meetings with Catherine. Their negotiations were arduous, but by the beginning of April the marriage contract had been agreed; Jeanne sent for Henry to come to court, and herself went on towards Paris to make preparations for the marriage. Henry could not come at once, as he was ill; meanwhile Jeanne, too, sickened, and on 9 June 1572 she died, of a tubercular pleurisy. By 13 June, Henry had reached Chaunay, in Poitou. There he learned that his mother was dead, with the shock which we can easily imagine. Then he continued on his way to Paris, very slowly, as if he were not looking forward to his marriage. He entered the city in mid-July, with the young Henri de Condé and François de Conty and a great train; as an English observer wrote, 'here are now the princes of the Religion, who are worth the seeing'.[13]

The marriage took place on 17 August 1572, with five days of festivity to follow. However, this time of rejoicing ended in a great tragedy. There had long been rumours of a Catholic plot to exterminate the Protestants, and on 22 August 1572 a hired assassin, Maurevert, shot at the Protestant leader Gaspard de Coligny and wounded him, setting in train the course of events which led to the Massacre of Saint Bartholomew. As the massacre

7

was beginning, on the night of 23–4 August, Henry of Navarre and Henri de Condé were called to the royal chamber, and there held under guard; the Protestant gentlemen who had accompanied them were among the first victims. Others included Henry's tutor, Louis Goulard, sieur de Beauvoir, his private secretary, Caboche, Coligny himself and many of the other Protestant nobles who had trustingly accompanied their young prince to Paris. Even their wives and children were cut down unless, like the future duc de Sully, they could find some ruse to save their lives.[14]

To Henry and Condé the king offered a simple choice: conversion to the ancient church or death. Henry met this demand with a skilful and evasive commentary which in effect asked for time to think; Condé replied with a violent denunciation of the shameful deeds. It is said that Henry at this juncture was 'gentle as a lamb'; he did not believe in futile heroic gestures, and on 26 September 1572 he was re-admitted to the ancient church. The Bibliothèque Nationale has a portrait of him made about this time, and it is certainly possible to imagine this disabused-looking young man playing a double game (Plate 3). On 3 October he had to write a letter imploring the Pope's forgiveness, and on 16 October signed an edict re-establishing Catholicism in Béarn.

Thereafter he behaved as if the Massacre had never taken place. He walked and talked at the Louvre with the Protestants' murderers, including notably Henri, duc de Guise. When a royal army was sent to besiege La Rochelle, where Henry had served his military apprenticeship not so long before, he went along, albeit under guard. When his viceroy in Navarre, the baron d'Arros, imprisoned the Catholic comte de Grammont, who had been a scourge of the Protestants during the war, Henry ordered Grammont's release.[15] Arros was hurt and bewildered at his young lord's inconstancy, but other observers were not surprised. Was he not the son of the *ondoyant* Antoine de Navarre?

Peace came in July 1573, and Henry continued to amuse himself at the royal court. He went hunting with the duc de Guise and completed his amorous conquest of Madame de Sauve. Catherine de Medici must have felt that the pleasure-loving and libidinous elements of his ancestry had finally gained the upper hand. However, Henry was at the same time involved in several plots with François, duc d'Alençon, the queen mother's youngest son, against the king and the queen mother herself. Of course, he did not confess to this, and in March 1574 went so far as to publish a declaration denying all knowledge of the conspiracy attempted against the king in Saint-Germain-en-Laye, and announcing his intention to devote life and property to the preservation of the king and the realm.[16]

Late in May 1574, Charles IX died, and thereafter both Alençon and Henry were closely guarded by the queen mother, until the new king, Henri III, could return from Poland to take up his throne. Once Henri III had been established, Henry seemed to fall back into his old easy ways, consorting with the Guises, lying abed with Madame de Sauve, ignoring his wife and in general behaving as if he had forgotten all Jeanne's teaching and advice. From this time dates a curious incident related by the English agent in Paris; while he was talking with Catherine, Alençon and Henry, the two latter constantly affirmed that they wanted nothing but to love and serve the king and the queen mother, 'but in the meantime, whiles they told their tale, Monsieur held me fast by the hand, and the king of Navarre jogged Mr Leighton by the elbow, to give us to understand that their meaning was not as they spoke'.[17] The king showed little judgement of the balance of forces in his new kingdom, for with quite insufficient military power he attempted to crush all his enemies. The consequence was that many moderate Catholics were alienated from the Crown; at court there were fearful quarrels between the king and Alençon, and in September 1575 the latter fled from Paris and raised an army of his own.

(v) The Governor of Guyenne, 1576–80

Five months later Navarre followed suit. As the English agent Valentine Dale wrote at the time, 'he was nothing mistrusted at this time because he had been divers times a-hunting eight or nine days together and used to return on the sudden and sometimes in the night when he was least looked for'.[18] So with three or four close friends he left early on the morning of 3 February 1576 from Senlis, and instead of going hunting galloped off towards Pontoise. The little band was soon joined by others as they passed swiftly south-westwards, reaching the safety of the town of Alençon on 7 February. After a pause of four days they went on to Saumur, where they arrived on 26 February and decided to stay for a while.[19]

Henry's reception by his Protestant brethren was not encouraging. They had heard of his apparent fondness for the Guises, and some had even seen him in the Catholic ranks at the siege of La Rochelle. Many preferred the leadership of the young Condé, who lacked the embarrassing association with the Guises. Nor could Henry hope easily to win the allegiance of Catholic nobles, after his flight from the court and various plots against the Crown. The king, faced with the possibility of an alliance between Condé, Henry and Alençon, now hastened to patch up some kind of understanding, and early in May 1576 the Edict★ of Beaulieu was promulgated. The Protestants this time secured eight *places de sûreté*,★ as well as special courts; Condé received the *gouvernement*★ of Picardy, Alençon was granted Anjou, and Henry was confirmed in his *gouvernement* of Guyenne.

After his flight from the court in February 1576, Henry had to choose what religion to adopt. He had been forcibly 'Catholicised' after the Massacre, and it might have been expected that once at liberty he would loudly return to Protestantism. However, he wavered for some time before coming to this decision, which he sealed by formally abjuring Catholicism at Niort on 13 June 1576. A fortnight later, on 28 June, he entered La Rochelle. The Rochellais had last seen him among their besiegers in the spring and early summer of 1573, and their welcome was far from enthusiastic. However, his sister Catherine rode at his side, and with her intransigently Protestant spirit she seemed a kind of guarantee of his future conduct. With this necessary pilgrimage to the heart of French Protestantism behind him, Henry then rode south into his *gouvernement* of Guyenne, arriving at Agen in August 1576.

Up to this point in his career, Henry had shown merely promise, which in many instances had been belied by events. He was plainly intelligent, as many observers had noted from his childhood onwards, and he was courageous, as he had shown more than once. But he also seemed excessively fickle, both in his public and in his private life, a true son of the *ondoyant* Antoine. It remained to be seen if he could apply himself to the business of consolidating his power and winning followers among those who – very reasonably – mistrusted him.

From the time of his entry into Guyenne in the summer of 1576 we begin to see a different prince, plainly foreshadowing both in his strengths and in his weaknesses the future king. In the many pronouncements dated from Agen at this time his constant appeal is to patriotism rather than to religious loyalty, and to tolerance rather than to a resumption of hostilities. His attitude is equally far removed both from the intransigent Protestantism of Condé and from the aggressive Catholicism emanating from the estates-general* of Blois, which sat between November 1576 and January 1577. Following a closely defined code of military law, his regulations promise to run down all those who disturb the public peace, and thereafter to hold the balance between Protestants and Catholics. For, as he wrote at this time to one of his Catholic captains,

> those who unswervingly follow their conscience are of my religion, as I am of all those who are brave and virtuous . . . . And I shall soon be able to see my true-hearted followers who wish to acquire honour with me, among whom I hope always to find you.[20]

When, early in 1577, the representatives of the Blois estates-general came to Agen, with their programme for re-establishing Catholicism, he explained with regret that he could not adopt this policy, which had proved to be impractical; as he put it, he could not 'think that the request they have made to the King to allow exercise of only one religion in France will bring peace, but rather plunge the kingdom into fresh troubles'.[21] However, when war broke out shortly afterwards, he refused to join with Condé in a general offensive, and insisted to the Protestants that the Treaty of Bergerac, signed in September 1577, though less favourable to them than previous treaties, was nevertheless preferable to a continuation of the war.

He now established himself in Nérac, which he used as a base from which to promote this kind of even-handed compromise, constantly travelling through his *gouvernement* and gaining an easy familiarity with his subjects. From this period we begin to hear the stories about peasants whom he met while hunting and questioned incognito about the state of the province (sometimes receiving startling answers), or about legendary feasts with country gentlemen, or, indeed, about amorous adventures with their wives and daughters. Some were deceived by his casual style and, as late as October 1580, Henri III is reported as discounting him as an 'homme qui ayme trop son plesir'.[22] But he was in fact developing his own distinctive style of governing – and of publicising it – which he would one day practise on a larger scale.

He still had many difficulties, even in Guyenne. Among his entourage the Protestants and Catholics tended to quarrel, and it needed all his tact to reconcile them. Some towns remained very hostile; he was refused entry to Bordeaux in December 1576, and almost murdered in Eauze in March 1577. Meanwhile Catherine de Medici was becoming increasingly nervous about the way in which he was consolidating his power in the south-west, and resolved to visit him there, partly to settle certain problems arising from the Treaty of Bergerac, and partly in the ever-present hope that she might be able to draw him back to Paris. Between September 1578 and April 1579 she was in the province, and there were many conferences, in Nérac and elsewhere. But Henry was more than a match for Catherine in duplicity; as the English ambassador Amyas Paulet reported to Walsingham in February 1579, the queen mother and her best councillors were 'at the end of their Latin', finding Henry to be 'furthest out of their danger' just when they thought that they had snared him.[23] In the end all that was achieved was some clarification of the treaty provisions; Henry had no intention of being drawn back into Catherine's net.

When Catherine moved on, she left behind her Henry's wife Marguerite, and for the next two or three years they were often together in Guyenne. Pau proved altogether too Calvinist for Marguerite, but she was fond of Nérac, and spent some happy months there with Henry between August 1579 and May 1580. In the latter month, however, Henry went back to war and led his forces in a famous raid to capture Cahors. It was a hand-to-hand battle over four days, in which the prince conclusively demonstrated his ability to rally his followers in the most adverse

11

circumstances: house-to-house fighting with no quarter asked or given. He also showed that he could sustain extraordinary bouts of intense activity; as he characteristically wrote in January 1580 to the sieur de Saint-Geniés, 'nobody who likes to relax inside his armour should trouble to make war'.[24] After this tactical victory, however, Henry had little idea of what to do next; as would often be the case, he seemed to lack any wider strategy.

(vi) Henry's Growing Influence, 1580–4

All the same, within the Protestant ranks he was increasingly recognised as the leader of the reformed church in the whole of the south of France. At the Nérac conferences he had come to speak for the deputies of the churches not only of Guyenne, but also of Languedoc, and now at the end of 1580 he was approached by François de Bonne, sieur de Lesdiguières, head of the Protestants in Dauphiné, and asked to take up their case in negotiations with the queen mother. So in May 1581 he felt strong enough to call a general assembly of the churches in Montauban, and this assembly in general endorsed his policy of toleration. Meanwhile Marguerite had been getting tired of her long exile from the French court, and in the spring of 1582, when her mother came south into Poitou, she went back to Paris with her. This separation was not too painful for Henry, who was nothing if not unfaithful. His reputation as the *Vert Galant* was by now well established, earning him about this time from the faithful but virtuous Philippe Duplessis, sieur de Mornay, the following appeal:

> Sire, pardon yet another word from your faithful servants. These
> open and time-consuming love-affairs no longer seem appropriate.
> It is time for you to begin loving all Christianity, and specially
> France herself.

Needless to say, Henry did not, perhaps could not, follow this good advice. But at least he did not let his *amours* distract him from wider political considerations. From infancy onwards he had been signing letters to foreign princes – part of the perennial Protestant efforts to obtain foreign aid – and now in 1583 he began to play that game with a vengeance, sending ambassadors from the Nérac court to virtually all the Protestant courts in Europe. About this time, too, he received a message from an unexpected quarter, when Philip II of Spain tentatively solicited his alliance.[25]

   Inside the realm, the childlessness of the king and of Alençon necessarily drew him forward as a possible successor; as an English intelligence report noted in the spring of 1583: 'all the good Frenchmen begin to cast their eyes upon him, and to try more and more to gain his favour'.[26] The same report gives an interesting 'state of the king of Navarre and his party in France'. The heart of his power lay in his hereditary lands in Albret, Basse-Navarre, Béarn, Bigorre and Foix, though he also held substantial areas to the north (see Map 1). It was from these areas that the main core of his support came, as well as the legendary swaggering Gascons who filled

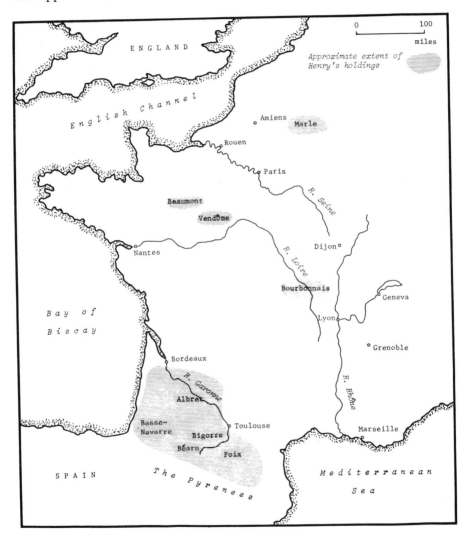

Map 1   *The basis of Henry's power about 1583*
Sources: Maps in Roelker, *Queen of Navarre*, and *CSP Foreign 1583*, art. 734.

his cavalry. He also, of course, inherited the full apparatus of a royal household: chamberlains, chancellors, secretaries, almoners and all the rest. On the whole, these early supporters did not find posts with him when he became king of France; the only exception seems to be Paul Choart, sieur de Buzenval, who served him as ambassador in the 1580s and survived on as a diplomat for France in the early seventeenth century.

On the other hand, there was a small group of nobles in constant attendance upon him, and many of these stayed with him all along.[27] Four were particularly close, having like their master survived the Massacre of Saint Bartholomew. They were: Philippe Duplessis (usually known as Duplessis-Mornay) (1549–1623); Henri d'Albret, sieur de Miossens; Maximilien de Béthune, sieur de Rosny (1560–1641) (the future duc de Sully); and Jacques Nompar de Caumont, sieur de La Force (1558–1652). With them we should include the lieutenant-governor★ in Périgord, Jean de Gontaut, sieur de Salignac (1533–1610), and Antoine de Roquelaure (1543–1625).

Apart from these members of his immediate entourage, and his *serviteurs*★ in his domains, Henry could by 1583 rely on a number of powerful allies. In Poitou there was Henri, prince de Condé (1552–88), and in Limousin there was Henri de la Tour d'Auvergne, vicomte de Turenne (1555–1623). Down in Languedoc, Henri de Montmorency had been governor since 1563, and aligned with Henry since about 1575; he was supported by François de Châtillon (1557–91) and Charles de Châtillon-Coligny, marquis d'Andelot (1564–1632). Finally, away in the east, Dauphiné was still held by the redoubtable Lesdiguières (1543–1626).

By 1583, then, Henry could rely on support from a substantial area of southern France, and had opened negotiations with several foreign princes. In June 1584, Alençon died, and as heir apparent Henry's strength steadily grew during the next few years.

2 An Almost Incomparable Vigour of Body, 1584–8

(i) The War of the Three Henrys, 1584–9

The period between 1584 and 1589 is confused and confusing, but a mastery of its main political events is essential to an understanding of Navarre's position, when in August 1589 he became titular king of France. In 1584 there were three main political groups: that of the king, that of Henri, duc de Guise, and that of Henry of Navarre. The course of the ensuing struggle between the 'three Henrys' was largely determined by the vacillating policies of the king, and by the fact that the Protestants and Guises could never become allies. At first, Henri III seemed to wish to ally himself with Navarre; and at that stage, between May 1584 and June 1585, Henri de Guise was their common enemy. After July 1585, however, the king was forced into an uneasy alliance with the Guises, until in December 1588 he rid himself of Henri and his brother the Cardinal Charles by murdering them. In the spring of 1589 he made a formal alliance with Navarre, and these two Henrys were campaigning together at the time of Henri III's murder in August 1589.

The strength of the king lay in his undisputed right to the crown, but he had frittered away this commanding advantage by his personal eccentricities and his slovenly administration.[1] Moreover, he had been unable to produce an heir, so that Frenchmen who in the normal course of events might have put up with another 'bad king', hoping for a better in the successor, had to decide which of his potential successors to support. One alternative royal house could be seen in the Guise family. It had an ancient lineage, with royal connections, but its great strength lay in the extraordinary abundance of able leaders, through whom the family or, rather, dynasty held enormous areas of land. Duke Henri himself had extensive lands in Champagne, and Cardinal Charles held the archbishopric of Reims and other benefices. Their brother Charles, duc de Mayenne, was strong in Burgundy. One cousin, Charles, duc d'Aumale, was powerfully based in Picardy; another cousin, Charles, duc d'Elbeuf, controlled much of Normandy. In Brittany the duc de Mercœur was their distant relative and close ally; one way and another, they controlled a large part of northern and eastern France (Map 2).

In December 1584 this powerful territorial dynasty entered into a

15

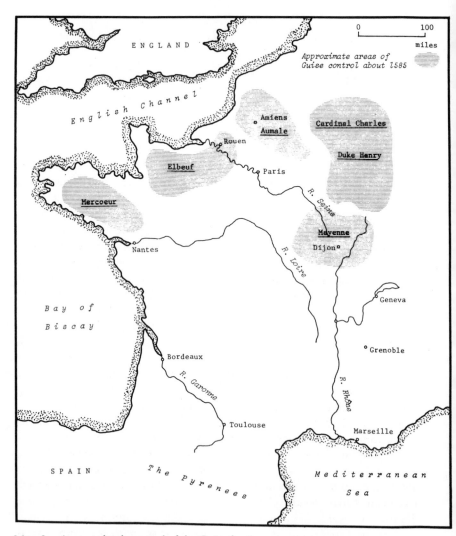

Map 2 *Areas under the control of the Guise family*
Source: Poirson, *Histoire*, i 134.

formal alliance with the king of Spain, by the Treaty of Joinville. The chief Guise leaders here signed an agreement with the agent of Philip II to form a Holy League. The king of Spain would supply a substantial annual subsidy and would recover the town and citadel of Cambrai; both parties pledged themselves to extirpate heresy in France and the Netherlands, and to exclude the house of Navarre from the succession. This Hispano-Guisard league was soon aligned with another Holy League, which with the same objectives had emerged in many of the French towns as soon as

Navarre had become heir apparent.[2] By the end of 1584 these redoubtable forces held not only the northern and eastern part of France, but also most of her great towns.

(ii) The King Allies Himself with Navarre, 1584–5

The first reaction of Henri III, after the death of Charles IX, had been to attempt to persuade Navarre to reconvert to Catholicism. In May 1584 he sent Jean-Louis de Nogaret, duc d'Epernon, down into Guyenne, where in August 1584 he met Henry. Once again the king of Navarre had to subject his religious loyalties to the test and temptation of political advantage. There were those who, like Henry's Catholic follower Antoine de Roquelaure, saw it as a choice between 'the crown of France on one hand and a pair of psalms on the other'.[3] But this was a simplistic view; Henry well knew that if he went over to Catholicism he might cement his alliance at court with the king, but he risked losing his solid base of Protestant support. He also seems to have had properly religious scruples about a conversion; as he wrote in March 1583 to the Archbishop of Rouen, 'Tell those [who advocate my conversion] that religion, if they have ever known what it is, is not something you discard like a shirt, for it dwells in the heart'.[4]

So he declined Epernon's persuasions, while re-affirming his loyalty to the Crown, and even offering 'to be instructed in a free and properly established council, in which religious controversy might be duly debated and decided'.[5] Meanwhile the position of the king was becoming desperate, for he was unable formally to ally himself with the heretic Navarre, and yet was in mortal danger from the ever-increasing forces of the Guises. In November 1584 he issued an edict against the League, but this could not win over even moderate Catholics, who saw that he lacked the will and the power to enforce either his threats or his fair words.

By the spring of 1585 it was apparent that the Guises would soon launch an offensive throughout France. In March 1585, Navarre met with Montmorency and Condé in Castres, where the three signed a declaration condemning the Guises' attempt to usurp the Valois throne, and accusing them of fomenting civil war. At the end of that month, the Guises themselves issued the Declaration of Péronne, arguing that because of bad government France was on the brink of anarchy, and pledging the Holy League to bring peace by eradicating the Huguenots and establishing the Guise candidate as heir apparent. Passing from words to deeds, in April and May the Guises formally consolidated their power by levying troops and occupying several towns which still held out for the king. By the end of June a still larger area of northern and now central France was in their hands. The king retained only parts of western France and one or two of the great towns of the south; the Navarre–Condé–Montmorency coalition held firm in Guyenne and Languedoc, while Lesdiguières remained strong in Dauphiné.

(iii)   The King Allies Himself with the Guises, 1585–8

At this juncture Henri III tried a new tactic. In the hope of taking over the Guise war-machine, he signed the Treaty of Nemours (July 1585), which rescinded all previous edicts granting some degree of recognition to the Protestants. But he had miscalculated if he thought that he could now control the Catholic tide; in addition to this humiliating concession, he was obliged to surrender key towns to the League: Soissons to the Cardinal of Bourbon, League pretender; Rue to the duc d'Aumale; Beaune and the keep at Dijon to Mayenne; Dinan and Le Conquet to Mercœur; Verdun, Toul, Saint-Dizier and Châlons-sur-Marne to Guise himself (Map 3). In effect, the Crown was now allied to, or rather absorbed by, the League, and pledged to the eradication of Protestantism.

(iv)   The War of Pamphlets

Navarre later claimed that when he heard of the Treaty of Nemours half his moustache turned white with 'appréhension des maux que je ressentis pour mon pays'.[6] Earlier in the year, he had been writing to the Protestant powers of Europe – England, Scotland, Sweden, Denmark and some German princes – trying to drum up help. But it was slow in coming, and for the time being the best he could do was to consolidate his power in the south-west. In August 1585 he met near Toulouse with Montmorency, and they drew up a document 'concerning the peace made with the House of Lorraine, the chief instigators of the League, to the prejudice of the House of France'.[7] This powerful appeal to monarchical sentiment was followed shortly afterwards by another document condemning the Treaty of Nemours as

> a peace made with foreigners at the expense of the princes of the blood; with the House of Lorraine at the expense of the House of France; with rebels at the expense of obedient subjects; with agitators at the expense of those who have brought peace by every means within their power. . . . I intend to oppose it with all my heart, and to this end to rally around me . . . all true Frenchmen

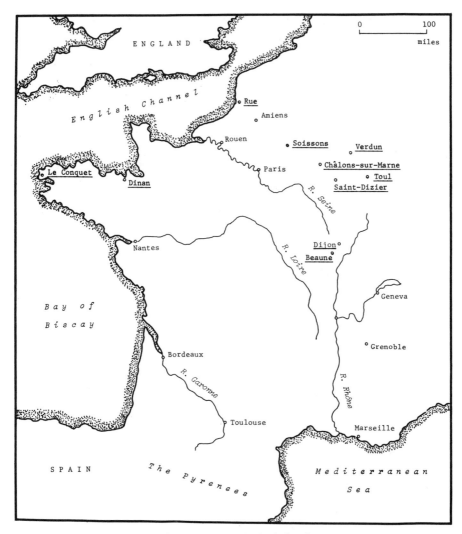

Map 3   *Towns surrendered to the League in 1585 (underlined)*

without regard to religion, since at this time it is a question of the defence of the state against the usurpation of foreigners.[8]

The drafting of these manifestos – largely, it would seem, the work of Duplessis-Mornay – was very astute. Even if the king of Navarre's military position seemed nearly hopeless, he was more than holding his own in the battle of propaganda and, as the English agent observed, 'many good Catholics flooded to his standard'[9] after these declarations.

19

Meanwhile the rest of 1585 and the beginning of 1586 were consumed in military preparations. The Leaguers and the king consolidated their power in the north and east, levying troops, stocking strongholds and concerting their plans within the wider aims of Spanish foreign policy.[10] Navarre arranged for the defence of Guyenne as best he might, and then in June 1586 moved to La Rochelle. This was part of a strategy worked out in the summer of 1585, if we are to believe Sully,[11] by which Navarre would himself carry the war nearer to the League's own territory, having left Turenne in charge of Guyenne, Montmorency in control of Languedoc, and Lesdiguières in Dauphiné. In fact, this was the same appreciation of the situation as that reached in 1583 by an English report, which suggested that 'one thing would greatly increase his power, if it could be done; that the king of Navarre might approach the centre of France, being a prince agreeable, skilful and endowed with all the parts required to attract the hearts of the nobility'.[12]

The material preparations went along with continuing psychological warfare. Early in 1586, for instance, Navarre published another set of appeals, this time addressed to the three orders of the realm. The ones to the clergy and the nobility are particularly remarkable for the skill with which Navarre's case is put, rallying moderate opinion and seeking to separate 'true Frenchmen' from the rest. To the clergy he wrote:

> God saw that I was born a Christian prince, and I desire the strengthening, growth and peace of the Christian religion. We believe in one God, we recognize Jesus Christ, and we draw on the same Gospel. . . . I believe that the war which you so ardently pursue is unworthy of Christians, unworthy among Christians and especially those who call themselves Doctors of the Gospel. If you like war so much, if a battle pleases you more than an argument, a bloody conspiracy more than a council, I wash my hands of it. May the blood which will be spilt be upon your heads.[13]

His aim was to show that he was not an obdurate heretic, but open to the persuasions of 'douces voyes', by which he meant a national council. This, of course, was just what the League leaders – and particularly the Spaniards – most feared. To the nobility he wrote rather differently:

> The French princes are the heads of the nobility. I love you all, and feel myself weakening and dying in your blood. A stranger cannot have this feeling. A stranger has no sympathy with this loss. I could complain about some of you, but I prefer to commiserate with you. I am ready to embrace you all. What displeases me is that in the press of battle I cannot distinguish those whom I know to have been

deceived, but God knows the secret of my heart. May the blood fall upon the authors of these miseries.

As Lavisse remarks, 'this thirty-year-old king instinctively found the right tone and the telling word'; the appeal was to those led astray by foreigners. The League's counterblast was Louis d'Orléans' *Warning from the English Catholics to the French Catholics*, in which he argued that if Navarre became king of France, then the Catholics of France would suffer the fate of those of England under Elizabeth. Four hundred years later, this argument may not seem very convincing, but it exactly reflected the fears of many adherents of the League, and helps to account for the extraordinary savagery of the impending struggle.

(v)   Military Operations, 1586

For the 1586 season, the king sent three armies southwards. One, under Armand de Gontaut, maréchal* de Biron, entered Poitou during May, in order to attack Navarre in La Rochelle. A second, under the duc de Mayenne, cut down into Guyenne, and a third under Joyeuse carried the war into Gévaudan. But these campaigns were directed with a certain lack of enthusiasm. Biron, after capturing half a dozen towns in Saintonge, found it impossible to penetrate the defences which Navarre had organised around Marans. Mayenne and Joyeuse also began by taking some Protestant towns, but soon found that their offensives, too, were bogged down. By the end of the year, Navarre could with justice boast that he had 'victorieusement resisté à trois armées fraisches et bien payées'.[14]

That December he met again with Catherine de Medici at Saint-Brice, near Cognac. As always, Catherine hoped to persuade him to abjure Protestantism and come to the royal court. But the time was long past when that might have been a possibility, and Catherine had to return with nothing accomplished. By this time Navarre's propaganda seems to have been telling, for in the years 1585 to 1587 several powerful nobles came over to his side, bringing with them their networks of clientage. They included Claude, duc de La Trémoille (1566–1604), Charles de Bourbon, comte de Soissons (1566–1612), and François de Bourbon, prince de Conty (1558–1614);[15] they were followed some time in 1588 by the famous 'bras de fer', François de La Noue (1531–91).

(vi)   Coutras, 20 October 1587

Meanwhile the agents of Navarre had succeeded in raising an army of Germans and Swiss, partly funded from England. For the 1587 season, his

21

object would be to combine this army with his forces round La Rochelle, so as to carry the war northwards. The king was well aware of this danger, and took the dispositions necessary to fend it off; Guise was assigned to guard the eastern frontier against the Germans, Henri III himself patrolled the Loire, and Joyeuse led a fresh army southwards into Poitou.

In the spring and early summer of 1587, Navarre was busy extending the area he controlled around La Rochelle by capturing little towns like Chizé-sur-Boutonne, Sanzay, Saint-Maixent and Fontenay-le-Comte. His energy was extraordinary and the way in which he escaped serious injury little short of miraculous. After the capture of Sanzay, for instance, he remarked that he had not slept in his bed for fifteen days.[16] At the siege of Chizé, a messenger coming from the French agents to the German princes just had time to say: 'Sire, messieurs de Clervant et Guitry m'ont depesché de Heidelberg pour lui faire entendre . . .', when he was shot through the head and fell back dead.[17]

It was Navarre's desire to join up with his German mercenaries which led to the decisive battle of 1587.[18] As the army of Joyeuse moved southwards into Guyenne, Navarre tried to slip away across its front in a south-easterly direction, from La Rochelle towards Périgueux and Brive. On 10 October the Protestant and Catholic armies were at La Rochelle and Vouzailles respectively; on 17 October at Montguyon and Chalais, and on the evening of 19 October their advance-guards met in the long street of Coutras, situated in the neck of land between the Dronne and the Isle (Map 4). At that time the bulk of Navarre's troops were crossing the Dronne at Gué-de-Sénac, while the forces of Joyeuse were quartered about ten miles to the north, at La Roche-Chalais. Both commanders therefore knew for the first time of each other's proximity at about eight o'clock in the evening. For Joyeuse, the next decision was easy; he would advance at midnight, and attack at dawn. For Navarre, it was not so easy; his three pieces of artillery had just crossed the Isle, in the direction of Bergerac, and he must have been tempted to follow them and so get out of what could be a trap, with the enemy to the north, and escape in other directions blocked by the rivers. But he must have calculated that such a course might leave him open to attack at a vulnerable time, before all his army could get clear across the Isle. So he recalled the artillery – Sully (who was still the baron de Rosny) recounts what a time the gunners had getting their weapons back across the river[19] – and established a defensive position just to the north of the town of Coutras.

Here the guns arrived well after first light, but in time to be set up on the left of the line, on a little hill called the Butte aux Loups. They were protected by a body of infantry, and their flank was secured by the stream called the Pallar and by the Dronne. On the right, stretching away in a slightly concave line, were the squadrons of cavalry: Soissons', Henry's

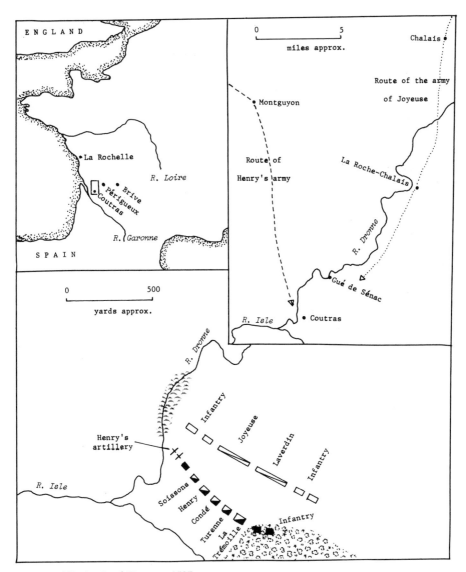

Map 4   *The battle of Coutras, 1587*
Source: Oman, *The art of war*, p. 477.

own, Condé's, Turenne's and La Trémoille's. In between them were
arquebusiers, and to the right of them, half hidden in a ditch and among
the trees of a park, were the rest of the infantry. Navarre was able to take
his time about disposing his troops – and some accounts say that he
radically corrected the original dispositions of his commanders – because

the forces of Joyeuse were slow in deploying from the line of march into a linear formation. Eventually they came to be stationed much as Navarre's army was, with strong infantry forces on each flank, and the cavalry in the centre. Joyeuse had perhaps 2,000 horse and 5,300 foot, against Navarre's 1,600 horse and 4,000 foot. However, whereas Navarre's cavalry was grouped into the five squadrons, drawn up six deep with a front of about fifty, the horse of Joyeuse – 'the most resplendent ever assembled in France' – was arranged in a long line only two deep. Theoretically, the extra length of Joyeuse's line ought to have allowed him to envelop the Huguenot horse. But in practice what usually happened when formations disposed like this clashed was that the long line was broken, and the possibility of control lost.

It is not certain where the Catholic artillery was sited, but we do know that it was not sited well, and could not do much damage. The Protestant guns, on the other hand, started the battle by wreaking great havoc among the infantry on the right of Joyeuse's line. His captains then urged him to attack without delay, and the whole line moved forward. It was a little after nine o'clock in the morning, and as the Protestant army saw the gorgeously appointed line roll towards them they broke into their battle-hymn:

> La voici l'heureuse journée
> Que Dieu a faite à plein désir. . . .

On each flank, the infantry was soon skirmishing furiously. On Navarre's right, the light squadron of La Trémoille was the first to be attacked by the approaching cavalry; this was well led by Jean de Beaumanoir, sieur de Laverdin and the Protestants were soon in full flight. A few rejoined Condé's squadron, but most were scattered and cut down. In the centre it was different. Here Navarre waited until the last moment, when the long advance had considerably disordered Joyeuse's extended line, and then charged at a steady trot. His solid squadrons broke through at every point, and soon the cavalry of Joyeuse was in hopeless disorder. There was nothing for them to do but flee, and many were cut down in the process, including Joyeuse himself. At the end of the day, the Catholics had lost about 2,500 men to the Protestants' 500 or so. It had been a crushing victory for Navarre, whose dispositions had proved greatly superior to those of Joyeuse. The Protestant artillery was better sited, the cavalry was better grouped, and the infantry posted so as to maintain a particularly murderous fire. While Navarre had made the best use of his force and the ground, Joyeuse had made imprudent dispositions which prevented him, for instance, from exploiting his considerable advantage in numbers of infantry.

Navarre had thus proved, as he remarked at the time, that the Protestants knew how to win a battle. But when it came to exploiting the victory it was a different matter. His intention had originally been to join up with the German army of invasion, and theoretically he ought now to have done that. Instead, he let his army break up, and went down into Béarn to lay the twenty-two captured Catholic standards at the feet of his mistress, Corisande d'Andoins. As Sully put it, 'all the advantage of so famous a victory floated away like smoke on the wind'.[20] Navarre had shown himself to be a fine cavalry leader, with a marvellous eye for the right moment to attack. But he was a poor strategist, as he would show on other occasions.[21] The Germans whom he had intended to meet were poorly led, and after reverses at Vimory (26 October 1587) and Auneau (24 November 1587), where the duc de Guise showed his skill at shadowing a force and then picking his moment, they withdrew in confusion.

(vii)   The Climacteric Year: 1588

The prestige of the duc de Guise grew still more after his defeat of the Germans, particularly in contrast to that of the king, whose favourite's army had been so terribly routed by the Protestants. As the League consolidated its power in the towns of northern France, Guise and his Spanish advisers saw that the moment had come for a showdown with Henri III. Early in May, in defiance of the king's explicit orders, Guise came to Paris, where he was greeted by the populace as a hero – their deliverer from a feeble king and from the threat of his heretical heir. Meeting Henri III, Guise demanded the exclusion of Navarre from the succession and his own appointment as *lieutenant-général*.* The king at first resisted, but then after the Day of Barricades, when the Paris mob rose against him, was forced to flee the city. Paris was left in the hands of the Guises, though the king lived on in freedom, which had not been part of the League's original plan.

However, Henri III could not rally enough support to offer serious opposition to the League, and in June 1588 he was obliged to sign the Act of Union, which confirmed the terms of the Treaty of Nemours and provided for the extirpation of heresy and the exclusion from the succession of Henry of Navarre. The latter watched these remarkable events from the security of south-western France. In March he had lost his great ally Condé, poisoned, it would seem, by his wife, but this had in some ways strengthened Navarre's position, since he was now the undisputed leader of the Protestants. In October 1588 two assemblies opened: the estates-general at Blois, and a Protestant gathering at La Rochelle. The

Blois estates were fiercely Leaguer, and confirmed the Act of Union; the assembly at La Rochelle sent a message to the king requesting religious liberty, after it had become clear that Navarre now enjoyed even the support of the zealots, who had formerly favoured the implacable Condé. The king now found himself in an *impasse*, from which he attempted to escape on 23 December 1588 by having both the Duke of Guise and his brother the cardinal murdered.

Henri III had hoped that by cutting off the beast's head he might kill the League. But he was wrong; Guise's brother Mayenne was elected *lieutenant-général* and more towns than ever fell under the control of the Sainte Union, as it was called. Associated with this popular and sometimes even republican movement were the nobles; Mayenne had the difficult task of driving this ill-assorted but powerful tandem, listening all the time as well to the advice of his Spanish paymasters.

(viii)   The Empty Throne: 1589

Early in 1589, Catherine de Medici died, worn out and shattered by the failure of all her schemes. Navarre very nearly followed her to the grave, for he, too, had spent many months under terrible strain, and in January 1589 broke down at a little village near Niort. He had ridden a long while on a very cold day, and when he dismounted felt thoroughly chilled. He stamped about a bit and felt better, but then after eating felt chillier yet. Soon he was in a fever, and after that it became plain that he had pleurisy – of which his mother Jeanne had died. Henry had already had three attacks, and this one looked like carrying him off, in spite of the skill of Nicolas Dortoman, his doctor. However, he narrowly held out, and after a few days was able to write this characteristic letter to Corisande d'Andoins:

> Surely, my love, I saw the sky open, but was not ready enough to enter in. God still has something for me to do. Twice in twenty-four hours, I had to be turned in winding-sheets; you would have found me pitiable, and if the crisis had been delayed two hours, the worms would have had me. . . .[22]

After his recovery, he took the military initiative, pushing out his position in Poitou by capturing Loudun, Mirebeau, Vivonne and l'Isle-Bouchard. By 4 March he was at Châtellerault, where he issued a famous manifesto to the three estates of the realm.[23] As usual, he knew just the right note to strike:

> Is it not miserable that while we all can see the cure for this state's long and mortal fever, nobody has opened his mouth to recommend

26

the remedy? That in the whole estates-general at Blois not a single person dared pronounce the holy word of 'peace', in which the whole salvation of this realm will be found? We have all done and suffered evil long enough. We have been mad, senseless and furious for four years. Is that not enough?

Meanwhile his agents had been negotiating with Henri III, and in April 1589 the two parties agreed on a truce, confirmed at Plessis-lès-Tours on 30 April when the two kings met. Many of Navarre's advisers had been unwilling to let their king put himself in the hands of the last perfidious Valois, but Navarre had insisted on going, and nobody could miss the significance of the occasion. It seemed to promise a way back to peace; a great crowd surrounded them, 'and nothing was heard anywhere but joyful cries of "Long live the king"; some also cried "Long live the kings"...'.[24]

Now the two surviving Henrys joined their forces and marched on Paris. They made good progress, and soon had established a noose of cities around the capital. By the end of July the royal army had seized the town and bridge of Saint-Cloud, while the Protestants had advanced as far as Meudon. Then Jacques Clément struck. At first it was thought that Henri III had survived his dagger-blow, and Navarre remained in his quarters at Meudon. Soon, however, the king's condition worsened, and before Navarre could reach his bedside Henri III died.[25] As the new king approached the old royal quarters, the Swiss guard came out and threw themselves at his feet. 'Sire,' they said, 'you are now our king and master.'

3 A King without a Kingdom

(i) The New King's Supporters

The reaction of the Swiss guard was also that of many members of the nobility. Before he died, Henri III had solemnly recognised Navarre as his successor; he was indeed the claimant with the best case, and this recognition was sufficient to ensure much support. The three royal captains of the guard, Nicolas d'Angennes, sieur de Rambouillet, Joachim de Châteauvieux and Jean d'O, sieur de Manou, now looked after their new master's personal safety. Armand de Gontaut, maréchal de Biron, assured him of the support of the Swiss, and Nicolas de Harlay, sieur de Sancy, saw to their payment. The *grand écuyer*,★ Roger de Saint-Lary, sieur de Bellegarde, spoke for the loyalty of a large part of the royal household.[1] Finally, several leading nobles came forward to pledge the support of, at any rate, part of the nobility of extensive regions: Jean d'Aumont for Champagne; Henri d'Orléans de Longueville and Charles d'Humières for Picardy; Anne d'Anglure de Givry for the Ile-de-France; and Henri de Bourbon, duc de Montpensier, for Normandy.

These declarations of support were significant, but so were the defections. The Keeper of the Seals,★ François de Montholon, withdrew from the court. So did the duc d'Epernon and Louis de Gonzague, duc de Nevers, as well as a considerable number of petty nobles like Louis de l'Hôpital, sieur de Vitry. The royal army, which had numbered 40,000 men, rapidly fell to about 18,000. As before, in 1576 and 1584, Henry had to subject his religious loyalties to political pressures. A deputation of nobles headed by François d'O came to tell him that with the kingdom he should embrace its religion, or at least promise to take instruction within a few days. The king, 'going pale from fear or anger', rejected this unreasonable ultimatum. But his position was very difficult, just as it had been in 1584. So he took much the same line as he had then, declaring on 4 August 1589 that he would 'maintain and conserve within the realm the catholic, apostolic and Roman faith in its entirety, without altering anything', and that he was 'ready and desired nothing more than to be instructed in the said religion by a good, legitimate and free general national council, so as to follow and observe whatever might be concluded there'; he also agreed to convoke such a council within six months.[2] It was a cunning compromise, which cost him the minimum possible loss, but, even so, La Trémoille left for Poitou with many

Protestants from that province, and several more Catholic nobles also left the court.

(ii)   Retreat from Paris, August 1589

With such diminished forces, the king could not maintain the siege of Paris. Indeed, outside the Protestant areas of the south, only eight large towns held for him – Caen, Châlons-sur-Marne, Clermont, Compiègne, Dieppe, Langres and Tours[3] – and several of his advisers thought it best to retreat again south of the Loire. But the weakness of this course was well exposed by Givry, one of the king's new subjects, who is said to have remarked to him, 'Who will believe that you are king of France, when he sees your edicts dated from Limoges?' and the king had no hesitation in rejecting it.

So he himself moved north into Normandy, while the duc de Longueville and La Noue went into Picardy, and Jean d'Aumont into Champagne. He had heard that several towns might declare for him if he came in person, and he also wished to establish relations with England by sea. Meanwhile he sent the various authorities of the different provinces a strong appeal for them to declare their loyalty, which was the 'duty of all good people, of all true and natural Frenchmen'. He also confirmed Henri III's establishment of the 'corps et services du gouvernement' in Tours,[4] where the royalist *parlement* operated in rivalry with the League *parlement* in Paris. Another one was established at Châlons-sur-Marne, and similar royal courts emerged in Caen, Carcassonne, Flavigny and Pertuis, as against the League ones in Rouen, Toulouse, Dijon and Aix respectively.

(iii)   Arques, 21 September 1589: 'Ils ne se sont gueres bien servys de leur avantaige'

The duc de Mayenne followed Henry into Normandy, announcing that he would either throw the king into the sea or bring him back to Paris in chains. Henry reached Dieppe on 26 August, and was well received by the inhabitants; he then fell to fortifying not only the town, but also its eastern suburb, Le Polet, across the River Béthune. Mayenne, moving slowly as usual, reached Le Polet on 13 September, and for three days tested the king's new system of earth bastions and ditches. He then withdrew to the south-east, in order to force a crossing at Arques. Here, too, the king had prepared fortifications, chiefly consisting of two parallel trenches, the latter of which was covered by the guns of the *château* at Arques. The forces were very unevenly matched, for against Mayenne's 4,000 cavalry

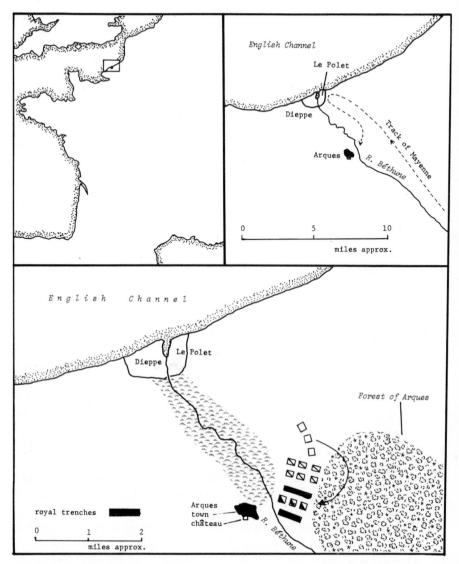

Map 5   *The battle of Arques, 1589*
Source: Oman, *The art of war*, p. 487.

and 20,000 infantry the king had only 1,000 cavalry and 4,000 infantry. But his defensive position was tactically very strong, since Mayenne could bring only part of his overwhelming force to bear at a time (Map 5).

Battle was joined at daybreak on 21 September 1589. The king and his cavalry were stationed between the two trenches, ready to offer support where it might be needed. Mayenne sent a powerful force of German infantry through the forest on the left of his line, and these soldiers succeeded in outflanking the king's first trench. The infantry holding it fell back in considerable confusion, whereupon the League cavalry charged through the undefended centre, and a furious battle ensued. The outcome was by no means certain, for the king's men were outnumbered four to one. But the Swiss in the second trench held astonishingly firm, and at the crucial moment the early fog lifted, so that the cannon in the *château* of Arques could fire. They did great damage, and eventually Mayenne was obliged to withdraw.

He had not made very intelligent use of his greatly superior force but, even so, it had been a close-run thing. The king's tactical dispositions had again been very skilful, but might not have been sufficient without the courage and skill of the Swiss in the second trench. In fact, Mayenne did not withdraw fully until 6 October, after making a probing attack on Dieppe from the south-west.

(iv)   The First Attack on Paris, September–November 1589

Meanwhile the king had received substantial reinforcements from England, and this encouraged him to make a quick dash on Paris. Leaving Dieppe on 19 October, he was joined by the forces of the duc de Longueville and Jean d'Aumont; this combined army of about 15,000 men reached Mantes on 28 October, Saint-Cloud on the 29th, and on 1 November, early in the morning, assaulted the suburbs of Paris from the north and the south simultaneously. These suburbs were only lightly fortified, and the royal troops quickly penetrated them at several points. But then they came up against the fortifications of the city proper, on the line of Philippe-Auguste's wall, and were everywhere checked (Map 6).

During this time Mayenne had been returning from Picardy as fast as he could. The king had ordered the bridge over the Oise at Pont-Sainte-Maxence to be broken, but this was carelessly done, with the result that Mayenne was able to repair it, and on the afternoon of 1 November began filtering his troops into the city. By 2 November there were 20,000 of them within its walls, and the king's chance was lost. In fact, even if the royalists had pierced the major fortifications on 1 November, they would have been in serious trouble, with a fanatical citizenry practised in street-fighting to contend with inside the city, and the superior army of Mayenne rapidly approaching. The stakes were high, and the bid worth making, but this was a *coup de main* which had very little chance of coming off. So Henry withdrew to the south-east, and reached Tours, the seat of his govern-

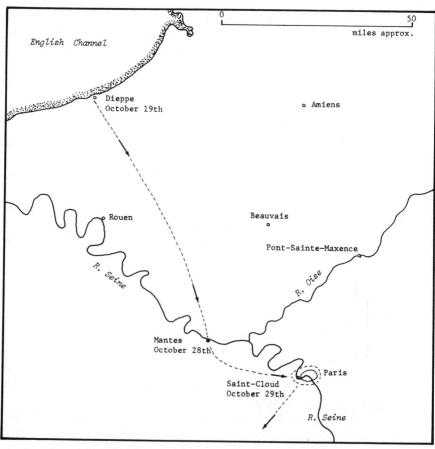

Map 6 *Henry's attack on Paris, 1589*

ment, late in November; along the way many of his noble supporters returned to their estates, which they could not afford to leave for too long.

Shortly after he arrived in Tours, the king received the welcome news that the Venetian Senate had decided to recognise his rule and to maintain at his court their ambassador to Henri III, Giovanni Mocenigo. Venice was the first Catholic power to recognise the heretic prince, and this act, by a state renowned for its political sagacity, dismayed Henry's enemies as much as it encouraged his friends.

(v) Ivry, 14 March 1590: 'Dieu nous a bénis'

The king did not go into winter quarters, but straightway began a campaign designed to recover Normandy. It was astonishingly success-

32

ful; as he himself immodestly wrote, 'mes faicts sont des miracles',[5] and in rapid succession he took Le Mans, Laval, Alençon, Falaise, Lisieux and Honfleur, until the only League strongholds left in Normandy were Rouen and Le Havre.

Philip II could not remain indifferent to this energetic offensive, and sent Mayenne a contingent of 500 arquebusiers and 1,200 cavalry, chosen from his Walloons* and commanded by Philip, Count of Egmont. Mayenne added these to his army, and marched out from Paris towards the north-west, into Normandy. The king was outnumbered, with 3,000 horse against 5,000, and 8,000 foot against 12,000. But he was resolved to give battle, and on 13 March drew so close to the League army that a conflict became inevitable. This time he was not fighting an essentially defensive battle, using natural obstacles, as at Coutras or Arques, but a conflict in the open, which he had freely sought. In fact he altered the defensive disposition adopted by his commanders, remarking that 'le champ de bataille auquel nous combattons sera le lieu de notre retraite'.[6] In other words, to recall the motto which had pleased him as a child, he was determined this time to 'either conquer or die'. On the Plaine de Saint-André, south-east of Evreux (Map 7), his army was drawn up in the usual way: six cavalry squadrons in line, with some infantry screening them in front and other groups of infantry in between the squadrons. The guns were roughly in the centre of the line, and behind it the maréchal de Biron commanded a very small reserve. Opposite the royal army, that of the League was arrayed in much the same way.

The king's plan was to smash the left of the enemy's line with his own redoubtable squadron, supported by Swiss infantry. As usual, his artillery had the better of the opening exchange, while the opposing squadrons manœuvred a little, like boxers sizing each other up. Suddenly both lines advanced, and clashed. For some time it was unclear who had the advantage. D'Aumont's squadron put the opposing light horse to flight, but Egmont did the same to the light horse opposing him. Between the squadrons of Montpensier and Nemours the struggle was very equal, but on the right the king crashed right through Mayenne's arquebusiers and cavalry, totally breaking them up. The squadron of Egmont was routed in its moment of victory by a flank charge led by the maréchal de Biron at the head of the royal reserves, and soon the Leaguers were in full flight. Their cavalry had been severely mauled, and their infantry virtually annihilated.

It had been essentially a cavalry action, with very little contribution either from the infantry or from the artillery. The king's old Protestant captains – La Trémoille, Duplessis-Mornay, Rosny, Aubigné and the rest – had led the crucial charge and proved again their virtual invincibility, particularly against opponents still encumbered with the lance.* Henry

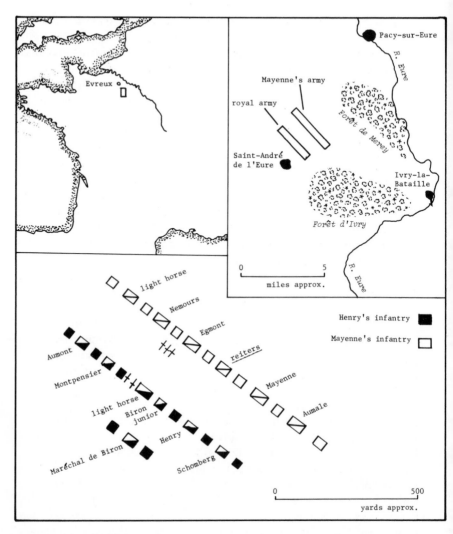

Map 7   *The battle of Ivry, 1590*
Source: Oman, *The art of war*, p. 501

was in his element, rallying the captains round his famous white plume, and orchestrating the tactic, first developed by him, known as the *pistolade*, in which the royal cavalry came to close quarters before discharging their pistols, and then charged with the sword.[7] It is noteworthy that all his squadron commanders were men who had come over since the death of Henri III; clearly this battle marked a stage in the process by which Henry was uniting the realm under his leadership.

(vi) The Second Attack on Paris, May–September 1590

However, after the battle came his usual indecision. Instead of marching straight on Paris, only thirty-six miles away, he set out on a leisurely curve of conquest through Mantes, Melun, Corbeil, Provins, Bray-sur-Seine and Montereau, coming to a halt before Sens (Map 8). Meanwhile the Parisians had gathered their wits and recovered their morale, so that when the royal army attacked the Faubourg Saint-Martin on 12 May it was repulsed. The king therefore decided on a siege. He already held many of the towns which normally supplied Paris with grain and other provisions, and now began seizing the suburbs: Saint-Denis in the north and all of the ring in the south. Conditions soon became very difficult in the city, even though the king had a formidable task in trying to close a perimeter of about thirty miles with only 20,000 men. What made his task more difficult was that he recoiled before the idea of inflicting the full

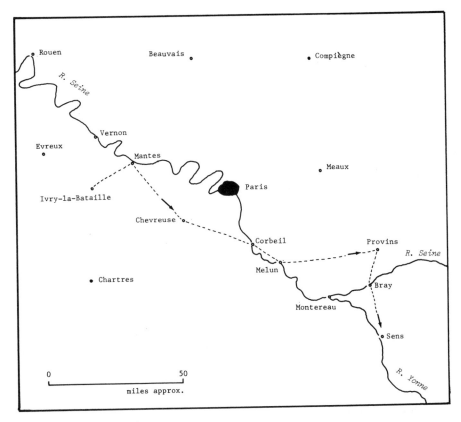

Map 8   Henry's track after Ivry

35

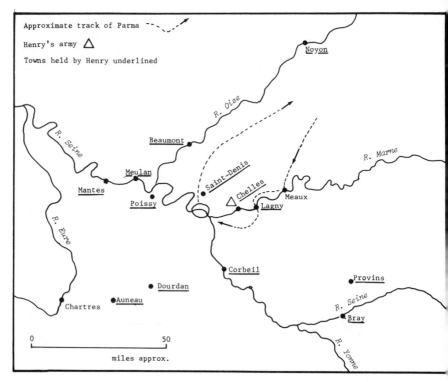

Map 9   *Henry at Chelles in 1590*

and ultimate rigours of a siege on the women and children of Paris. On 15 June he wrote a letter to the inhabitants assuring them of his parental concern for their well-being, and on 24 July demonstrated it by allowing 3,000 of them to leave the city.[8]

That was a blunder, from the military point of view, but even so it was clear by the beginning of August that, unless some outside force intervened, Paris would soon fall. Philip II therefore ordered the Duke of Parma, commanding the Spanish troops in the southern Netherlands, to make a diversionary expedition into France. Parma crossed the frontier in mid-August, and on 23 August joined Mayenne and the League forces at Meaux. Their combined army numbered about 24,000 men, which was just about the number now under the king's command, as his forces had been swollen by soldiers anxious to help in the looting of Paris.

By the end of August the king had decided that he would have to fight Parma's force. So he withdrew his blockading detachments, and with 7,000 horse and perhaps 20,000 foot posted himself at Chelles, on the north bank of the Marne (Map 9). Here he hoped to bring Parma to battle, and duly set out his army in the usual way. Each day the king hoped for an engagement, and as usual bustled round his detachments to be sure that they were well sited; here the English ambassador Sir Edward Stafford found him, 'eating of a morsel in an olde house'. But Parma had other ideas; declining to impale himself on the royal army, as Joyeuse had done at Coutras and Mayenne at Arques, he protected his force by cautious manœuvres and the extensive use of earthworks. Then he seized the town of Lagny, which permitted him to revictual Paris (Plate 4), and having achieved his objective drew away to the north, leaving Mayenne in charge. The king had suffered a serious reverse, and he withdrew to the north-west, after making one last lightning raid on Paris. Soon his nobles began to go home, and eventually the army virtually broke up. The campaign of 1590, which had begun so brilliantly, had faded out. But at least the king retained most of his positions around Paris, and could return at leisure to tighten the noose.

(vii)   The Struggle in the Provinces, 1589–90

Meanwhile in the rest of France the struggle between royalists and Leaguers was very equal. In Auvergne, on the very day of Ivry, the royalists decisively defeated the Leaguers at Issoire. But in Brittany the duc de Mercœur received a force of 3,000 Spaniards and consolidated his hold on the province. In Berry, the maréchal de La Châtre had the better of the royalists, and in Dauphiné and Provence the royalist leaders, Lesdiguières and La Valette, had to struggle not only against the Leaguers, but also against the Duke of Savoy. At the end of 1590, things were still very evenly balanced.

(viii)   Venus and Mars, February–April 1591

After the failure to take Paris, many of the king's advisers counselled an attack on Rouen; it was said to be feebly defended, it was the League's greatest stronghold in northern France after Paris, and its seizure would add to the supply problems of the capital. However, in November 1590 the king had met Gabrielle d'Estrées at Cœuvres, in Picardy, and his political decisions at this juncture were greatly influenced by his desire to please her and to buy off her rapacious relations.

So, instead of proceeding against Rouen, the king laid siege in February 1591 to Chartres, which was a town of modest strategic importance – it did contribute to the food-supply of Paris – but central to his amorous campaign. For its governor had until 1588 been François de Sourdis, uncle of Gabrielle; the governor of the surrounding *pays chartrain* had been

Philippe Hurault, sieur de Cheverny, the lover of Sourdis' wife, Isabeau Babou de La Bourdaisière. We cannot here go into the many affairs which had linked the La Bourdaisière women for a hundred years to the kings of France; suffice it to say, in the sober words of the *Dictionnaire de biographie française*, that 'la beauté très accessible de plusieurs membres de la famille ne paraît pas avoir été sans efficacité'. By his passion for Gabrielle, the king now found himself caught up in the intrigues of this very extended family.

Guided, then, by his amorous designs, Henry besieged Chartres between February and April 1591. As Vaissière observes, 'we are unfortunately less well informed about the surrender of Gabrielle than about that of Chartres'. But we may assume that both sieges were successful more or less at the same time; Sourdis and Cheverny were reinstated, and Gabrielle became the king's constant companion. After capturing Chartres, he went on to Noyon, and having captured that town he installed Gabrielle's father as its governor and one of his sons as bishop. Not for the first or last time, Henry showed that when Venus was in the ascendant his judgement was defective.

Meanwhile substantial reinforcements were coming in from England and Germany. About 4,000 English troops, under the command of the Earl of Essex, reached Dieppe in mid-August, and about the same time in Frankfurt there was a final muster for 6,800 German horse and 10,000 foot, which then took the road for France, under the command of Christian of Anhalt. Much to the disgust of Sir Henry Unton (the English ambassador), of Queen Elizabeth, and of Henry's advisers, the king still showed little inclination to get down to business.[9] But in September he went to meet his German allies at Sedan, and returning with them joined in the siege of Rouen, which had been begun in November 1591 by the maréchal de Biron.

(ix) The Siege of Rouen, November 1591–April 1592

The royal forces threw a cordon round Rouen, and slowly pushed their siege-works closer to its defences. The king was prominent in all the action; as the Bohemian volunteer Charles de Zérotin wrote on 11 January 1592:

> I go nearly every day with the king to the trench and to the batteries, and wherever I may learn and observe something, not only during the day but also at night. The king takes me to the very front line, where bullets whizz past all the time, for this lord never stays still, sees to everything himself, goes everywhere, wants to know about everything, and exposes himself to every danger. His activity is

admirable, and those who wish to obtain his favour have to do as he does, without sparing themselves.[10]

However, all this expenditure of energy did not produce the desired result. The royalists had decided first to assault the Fort Sainte-Catherine, and this was a hard nut to crack, defended with great skill and bravery by André de Brancas, sieur de Villars. In any case, the king was soon diverted, for about the middle of January 1592 the Duke of Parma re-entered France, at the head of an army of 5,000 horse and 18,000 foot. The king had to make the same kind of decision as had confronted him during the siege of Paris in August 1590. This time he left his infantry at the siege, and about 26 January took a force of 7,000 horse off to harass Parma and Mayenne. The two armies met first at Folleville, on 29 January; thereafter the king constantly shadowed Parma's army, attacking it when he could. This was not very often, for Parma maintained a defensive oblong formation even on the march. On 5 February the king seems to have miscalculated one of these attacks – it must have been a matter for very nice judgement, that business of pecking away at Parma's flank – and at Aumale was wounded and very nearly captured. However, he could not prevent Parma from relieving Rouen, which towards the end of February received reinforcements of 1,200 men; by the end of April, Biron had to abandon the siege.

With Rouen delivered, Parma's main objective was accomplished, but before leaving for the Netherlands he decided to capture Caudebec, which had been intercepting supplies destined for Rouen. He duly took the town, but the king took advantage of the delay to mobilise a fresh army and place himself across Parma's line of retreat, at Yvetot (Map 10). Parma was now in a tricky position, with his back to the sea and his escape-route apparently blocked by an army of 8,000 horse and 18,000 foot, decidedly superior in numbers to his own. However, at this juncture he showed why he was regarded as one of the best generals in Europe; on the night of 16 May he put a large part of his army across the Seine,[11] so that when the king's scouts reconnoitred his camp on the next day they found it empty. This feat, the transporting of 15,000 men across a tidal river at least 300 yards wide under pressure from an enemy, was of course far beyond the capacity of most sixteenth-century armies; once on the south side of the Seine, Parma made off to the Netherlands by way of Saint-Cloud and Château-Thierry.

Henry might now have re-opened the siege of Rouen. But his army was breaking up, with his nobles wanting to go home and the foreign auxiliaries coming to the end of their term of service. So he left the lower Seine, and marched to the siege of Epernay, which fell on 8 August. At the end of the year he was hardly any closer to his objective, the capture of

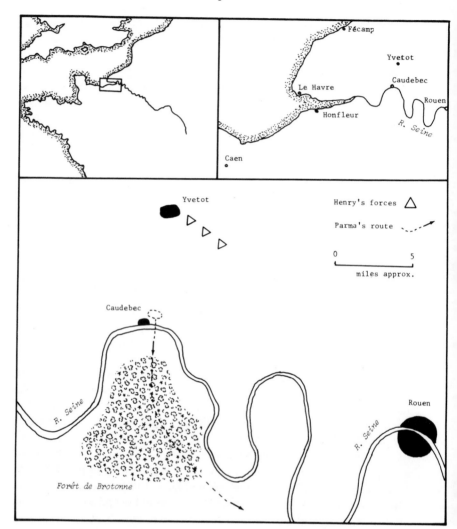

Map 10 *Parma at Caudebec in 1592*

Paris, in spite of the help of his English, Dutch and German allies. The king had shown that his cavalry could beat any other, and could control large areas of countryside; but horses were no use for street-fighting, and the capture of great towns like Rouen or Paris continued to elude him.

(x) The Struggle in the Provinces, 1592

Meanwhile in the provinces the struggle between royalists and Leaguers continued to be indecisive, as neither party could develop an ideology sufficiently attractive to win over the uncommitted. In Brittany, the royalists were beaten at Craon in May 1592, and the power of the duc de Mercœur was confirmed. In Languedoc, on the other hand, the Leaguers were severely defeated at Villemur in September 1592; in Provence and Dauphiné, Lesdiguières held his own against both the League and Charles-Emmanuel of Savoy. The stalemate reached by the king in Normandy was thus a reflection of the situation in the country as a whole.

(xi)   Relations with Rome, 1584–92

At the beginning of his pontificate, in September 1585, Sixtus V had issued a powerful bull excommunicating Navarre (who, of course, was anyway a Protestant) and also declaring him excluded from the line of succession. This latter provision infuriated many churchmen in France, whose Gallican★ principles could not accommodate papal interference in a French constitutional issue. It also infuriated the very Catholic *parlement* of Paris, which issued a protest at these ultramontane★ claims. As time went by, Sixtus himself came not only to have a certain admiration for Henry of Navarre, but also to fear that if he were crushed, then Philip II would become excessively dominant; as J. H. Elliott puts it, he feared that 'a Spanish victory in France could mean the end of papal independence'.[12]

So towards the end of the 1580s his policy came increasingly to aim not at the exclusion of Navarre, but at his conversion, which would keep France Catholic but also ensure the exclusion of Spain. However, Sixtus died in August 1590, and in March 1591 his successor, Gregory XIV, issued a bull reaffirming Henry's exclusion. The king was able to use this imprudent attack to rally to his side Gallicans who feared the extension of papal power; in July 1591 he issued the Edict of Mantes, which by revoking the anti-Protestant edicts of 1585 and 1588, and re-establishing the terms of the Edict of Poitiers (1577), emphasised his claim that the papacy had no authority in France to override monarchical jurisdiction. Clement VIII succeeded to the pontificate in January 1592, and began slowly to feel his way back towards a policy less committed to Spanish interests. But this took time, and for the next three years Henry could expect little support from Rome.

(xii)   The Troubles of the League, 1589–92

The king's position was therefore difficult, with a military stalemate and a hostile papacy. But, in some ways, the position of Mayenne was more difficult still. From the time that he inherited the leadership of the Guise

41

faction, in 1588, he had had to rely on the Spaniards not only for constant subsidies, but also for actual armies in 1590 and 1592. There had been many differences between Mayenne and Parma during the campaigns, which was not surprising as these allies had conflicting aims. Both wished France to remain Catholic but, while Philip sought a ruler whom he could dominate, Mayenne rather fancied himself as king, sooner or later.

In this way he came into conflict with the other members of his dynasty, some of whom also had claims to press; that was why he supported the candidature of the feeble cardinal de Bourbon, under whose nominal rule as Charles X he would be *lieutenant-général*. If his relations with the high League nobility were marked by mistrust, those with the towns, and particularly with Paris, were often frankly hostile. The Spanish ambassador, Bernardino de Mendoza, had been exceptionally skilful in organising the League in Paris, where he had agreed on a programme of action with the revolutionary 'Sixteen' which left little room for Mayenne.[13] In November 1591, bereft of Mendoza's guiding hand, the Sixteen had moved against some of the moderates in the Paris *parlement*, and had hanged three of them. Mayenne was obliged to respond by seizing and hanging the ringleaders, and imprisoning other members of the Sixteen.

In May 1590 the cardinal de Bourbon, 'Charles X', died; he had been a very unconvincing candidate for king, but now there was none at all, and the various factions of the League could not agree upon his successor. Some of the nobles, who were busy consolidating their power in the provinces, did not care who was king as long as he was weak; the same might be said of some of the towns, which might be either republican- or independent-minded or both. The Spaniards, however, had a decided preference for some arrangement which would include the Infanta, Isabella Clara Eugenia, married to some convenient French noble. During 1592 they brought pressure to bear on Mayenne for the calling of an estates-general, which they hoped would ensure such an election. Mayenne long opposed the idea, but eventually capitulated, and in December 1592 sent out the letters convoking the members of the three estates to a meeting in Paris in January 1593.

(xiii) The Estates-General of 1593

The various representatives had a good deal of trouble in getting to Paris, through the complicated network of royalist towns and territories. However, by the end of January 1593 a total of 128 deputies – not nearly as many as usual – had assembled in Paris, where the habitual opening ceremonies took place in the Louvre. Mayenne, as *lieutenant-général*, on 26 June gave the initial speech, emphasising that the purpose of the meeting was to find a Catholic king for France. There was a symbolically empty chair at Mayenne's side; on the other side of it sat Cardinal Nicolas de Pellevé, who in effect spoke for the papacy and for Philip II.

The king did not let this opening go unopposed, but on 27 January promulgated two acts. The first denied the validity of the assembly, illegally convoked and consequently guilty of *lèse-majesté*.* The second suggested that, since peace could only come through consultation and compromise, it would be useful to have a series of conferences in which delegates from the estates might meet with royal representatives. This suggestion was bitterly opposed by Cardinal de Pellevé and by the extreme Leaguers, but was accepted on 9 March by the body of the estates; twelve persons were therefore named from this assembly, and eight by the king, and they met for the first time in Suresnes on 29 April. The royal eight were of course all Catholics, and mostly recent adherents: Renaud de Beaune, Archbishop of Bourges; Pomponne de Bellièvre; Nicolas d'Angennes, sieur de Rambouillet; Gaspard de Schomberg, sieur de Nanteuil; François Le Roy, sieur de Chavigny; Geoffroy Camus, sieur de Pontcarré; Jacques-Auguste de Thou; and Louis Revol. To be chosen for this crucial assignment, they must have enjoyed the king's special confidence; as we shall see, several continued to serve him in delicate affairs.

A truce was at once agreed upon for ten days in the surrounding region and, in spite of the efforts of the extreme Leaguers, the populace eagerly took advantage of this respite. Meanwhile negotiations went forward, chiefly between the Archbishop of Bourges (Renaud de Beaune) for the king, and the Archbishop of Lyon (Pierre d'Epinac) for the Leaguers. There was also a good deal of 'corridor diplomacy', in which Villeroy, the very experienced *secrétaire d'État** was prominent.[14] It soon became clear that Epinac and his colleagues would not contest the constitutional right of Henry IV, but only his religion; Beaune was thereupon able on 17 May to top this argument by announcing the king was now resolved upon a reconversion, 'pour avoir cogneu et jugé estre bon de le faire'.

This announcement was soon widely known, and caused consternation among the diehard Leaguers. On 2 April the Spanish ambassador extraordinary, the Duke of Feria, had arrived to put his master's case to the estates. He arrived too late to oppose the initial concession which had led to the Suresnes conference, but he now put forward various proposals intended to advance the case of the Infanta. It was too late. The estates replied that 'our laws and customs prevent us from calling forward as king any prince not of our nation',[15] and on 28 June even the Paris *parlement* reiterated this position. Meanwhile the delegates at Suresnes had several times extended the truce; it became clear that no diplomatic improvisations could prevent the eventual recognition of Henry IV, and on 8 August most of the members of the estates-general went home.

43

4 The Perilous Leap, 1593–4

(i) The Desired Instruction, July 1593

From the start of his reign, Henry had suggested that he might be converted following the deliberations of 'a good, legitimate and free general national council'. Now, late in July 1593, he went to Saint-Denis to receive instruction from such a collection of prelates and doctors; they included not only Renaud de Beaune, leader of the royalists at Suresnes, and Jacques Davy du Perron, who would become one of the most prominent bishops at court, but also René Benoist, the celebrated Leaguer and *curé* of Saint-Eustache.

The discussions began on 23 July, between the king and four of his instructors. According to L'Estoile, the king rapidly took the offensive, questioning the four until they were 'astonished and unable to give sensible answers to his questions'.[1] But L'Estoile's version is not corroborated either by Palma-Cayet or by the *procès-verbal*★ of the proceedings.[2] What really seems to have happened is that after five hours of discussion, covering tricky points like the Pope's authority in France and the reception of the decrees of the Council of Trent,★ a preliminary form of abjuration was agreed upon. Rereading it the following day, the king found some of its points unacceptable, and so on the 24th signed a revised version of it.

(ii) The Necessary and Customary Ceremonies, 25 July 1593

All was then ready for the ceremonial abjuration, which took place on Sunday, 25 July 1593. This was the first major ceremony of the reign, and showed the king's masterly use of symbolism.[3] It was a very hot day, and the streets of Saint-Denis were hung with tapestries and strewn with flowers. In front of the king marched a large number of princes and nobles, followed by the Swiss guard with their drums beating, the Scots and other guards, and finally twelve trumpeters. The king himself was magnificently dressed in white satin with a black cloak and hat, and as he slowly paced through the streets found a great crowd – many of whom had come out of Paris – constantly shouting 'Vive le roi'. When he came to the basilica of Saint-Denis, the Archbishop of Bourges was waiting for him, seated on a throne of white damask, adorned with the arms of France and of Navarre. The following exchange then took place:

Archbishop: Who are you?
Henry: I am the king.
Archbishop: What do you ask?
Henry: I ask to be received into the communion of the catholic, apostolic and Roman church.
Archbishop: Do you truly desire it?
Henry: Yes, I wish and desire it.

Then the king knelt and made his profession of faith in these words: 'I protest and swear, in the presence of almighty God, to live and die in the catholic, apostolic and Roman religion, to protect and defend it against all comers at the risk of my life and blood, renouncing all heresies contrary to this catholic, apostolic and Roman church.' Then, after giving the Archbishop a signed copy of this profession, he kissed his ring and received the Archbishop's absolution and blessing. Rising to his feet, he made his way through the great crowd into the church, and falling to his knees before the high altar repeated his profession of faith, while the people never ceased from crying 'Vive le roi'.

He then went to a special *prie-Dieu*, covered in velvet and embroidered with green *fleurs de lis*,★ under a similarly decorated canopy. High Mass was sung, during which the king performed the traditional acts, kissing the proffered Gospels, beating his breast at the Elevation, and receiving the kiss of peace. The Mass over, he returned to his lodgings in a similar procession, with the streets again ringing to cries of 'Vive le roi'. It must have been an extraordinarily moving occasion, and Henry made the most of it.

(iii) The Falling Out of Faithful Friends, 1593–4

That very night, he sent out a circular letter to all the provinces of France: 'Recognising the catholic, apostolic and Roman church to be the true church of God, full of truth, unable to err, we have embraced it and have resolved to live and die in it.'[4] Letters also went to the Catholic rulers like the Duke of Tuscany, expressing the hope that this news would give them 'beaucoup de contentement'.[5] It was not so easy to write to Protestant rulers like Elizabeth and the German princes. Maurice of Hesse, for instance, had been particularly active in trying to prevent Henry's conversion,[6] and from Elizabeth of England Henry received a letter beginning:

Ah! Que [*sic*] douleurs, oh! quels regrets, oh! que gemissements je sentois en mon ame. Ah! c'est dangereux de mal faire pour en faire du bien. . . .[7]

Equally tricky was the task of explaining his conversion to the king's old Protestant friends. In May 1593 he had received a deputation of ministers, and had had to listen to their remonstrances over his rumoured conversion.[8] The following July, immediately before the ceremony of the abjuration, he had taken a tearful farewell of Antoine de La Faye and the other ministers, assuring them that he would never allow anybody to trouble them because of their religion.[9] But it was impossible for him to maintain his former relations with the Protestants. In August and September of 1593, for instance, he wrote three letters to Duplessis-Mornay, begging him to come to court;[10] Duplessis-Mornay stayed down in Saumur. Then in November 1593 he received a deputation of Protestants, who hoped to receive a new and more favourable edict; they had to disperse to their provinces on 12 December 1593 with their *cahiers*★ unanswered.[11]

Duplessis-Mornay finally came to court in February 1594, with another delegation. They hoped the king would revive the relatively favourable edict of 1562, but were again disappointed.[12] In November 1594 he did renew the edict of 1577, but when a further delegation protested at this, requesting special courts and a 'protector', he rebuffed them with some asperity, and with the scathing comment that their kingdom had now 'tombé en quenouille'.[13] So the Protestants were increasingly thrown back on their own resources, and began making political arrangements for their defence if necessary. In March 1594, for instance, the king wrote to Duplessis-Mornay that he

> finds the recent assembly at Fontenay very strange, because it did not concern itself solely with religion, but with several other things, against my service. You well know that I know the difference between a synod and an assembly. See that it does not happen again. . . .[14]

Eventually, a considerable number of Protestants like Agrippa d'Aubigné, the duc de Bouillon, Duplessis-Mornay himself and the duc de La Trémoille were more or less permanently estranged from the king, even if others, like the sieur de La Force, the sieur de Lesdiguières, and the future duc de Sully, continued to serve him.

(iv)   To Condemn the Treason, and Reward the Traitor', 1593–4

The king's abjuration was the signal for many town governors to declare, or rather sell, their loyalty to Henry IV.[15] During 1593 the chief towns to

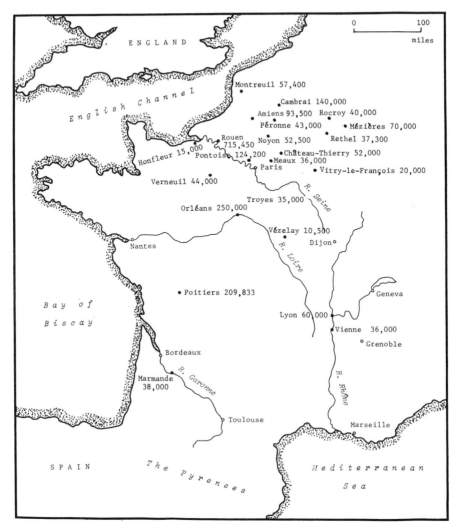

Map 11   *Towns which came over to Henry in 1594 (solid circles, with price in écus).*

come over were Lillebonne and Fécamp, under Jean (or Charles) de
Goustemesnil, sieur de Boisrozé, and Cambrai, under Jean de Monluc,
sieur de Balagny. Then, in January 1594, Louis de l'Hôpital, sieur de
Vitry, surrendered Meaux, and that was the beginning of a year of such
capitulations, summarised in Map 11. There does not seem to be any
particular chronological pattern to these surrenders, except of course that
those of the north-eastern towns, under the control of the Guise family,
were bunched together at the end of the year.

The question of how much the king paid for these new loyalists is a

47

difficult one. There are six main sources of information, two printed and four manuscript: (1) the *Mémoires* of Claude Groulart, *premier président* of the Rouen *parlement*; (2) the *Oeconomies royales* of Sully; (3) Manuscrit français 6411 of the Bibliothèque Nationale, a collection of documents concerning French political history (1478–1619); (4) Manuscrit français 10884 of the Bibliothèque Nationale, the journal of the Assembly of Notables (see below for details of this); (5) Manuscrit Dupuy 549 of the Bibliothèque Nationale, a collection of documents relating to the reigns of kings between François I and Louis XIII; (6) the 'Papiers de Sully', preserved in the Archives Nationales. In one of the appendixes to his *Histoire du règne de Henri IV*, published in 1856, Auguste Poirson tried to reconcile sources (1), (2) and (5). In general, his finding was that Groulart's figures were much lower than those of Sully and the Dupuy manuscript, who more or less confirm each other. Then, in 1905, Georges Boussinesq published a short note on the question, pointing out that the Groulart figures were roughly comparable with manuscripts (3) and (4).[16]

Neither of these historians was able to use the figures contained in (6), the 'Papiers de Sully', which have become available in the Archives Nationales only since the late 1950s. These new documents include the *acquits de comptants*★ from the year 1593, and they ought to be the most reliable sources, since they are derived directly from the original receipts. It might be expected that these documents, found among Sully's papers, would confirm the figures which he gives in his *Oeconomies royales*. But such is not the case, as these specimen figures show (payments are in *écus*★):

Person paid	Groulart	Oeconomies royales	Papiers de Sully
Duc de Lorraine	900,000	1,255,608	922,000
Maréchal de Brissac (Paris)	482,000	565,133	492,000
Sieur de Balagny (Cambrai)	140,000	276,310	139,666
Duc de Guise	629,500	1,296,276	629,600
Duc d'Elbeuf (Poitiers)	209,833	323,608	209,833
Sieur de Libertat (Marseille)	102,000	135,333	102,000

Usually, it is Groulart's figures which correspond most closely with those of the *acquits de comptants*. The figures given in Sully's *Oeconomies royales* are nearly always much larger, so that his total comes to 10,714,327 *écus* as against 6,467,596 *écus* for Groulart. Poirson argued that this was because Sully was able to take into account various secret payments, but we may suspect that it was also because he had an interest in inflating the figures. All in all, it seems best to base our calculations on Groulart's figures.

These are summarised in Map 11, which of course can include only those payments for which a geographical locality is indicated. It thus excludes the enormous sums paid to the duc de Lorraine (900,000 *écus*), the duc de Guise (629,500), the duc de Mayenne (820,000), the duc de Nemours (220,000) and the maréchal de Joyeuse (372,000). But the distribution of monies is, all the same, suggestive. The old Protestant areas are excluded, as in Brittany, still stubborn under the duc de Mercœur. Apart from these regions, it is the great commercial centres which command the highest prices, corroborating the theory of Martin Wolfe that these payments were really indemnities, to compensate League leaders for the loss of revenues illegally withdrawn from the Crown during the wars.[17]

Some contemporaries felt that Henry was demeaning the monarchy by these payments; Queen Elizabeth, for instance, 'thought that [he] dealt too basely in making composition with his subjects, and buying peace'.[18] But to Sully the king is said to have remarked that it would have cost him ten times as much to recover them by the sword; he was probably correct. Other foreign observers were less critical than Elizabeth; in January 1594, for instance, Giovanni Mocenigo, Venetian ambassador, wrote to the Doge and Senate that 'the conditions on which [Henry] receives even those who have most deeply injured him are taken to be the result of an indescribable clemency and extraordinary humanity'.[19]

As well as recovering the great towns and magnates, the king was also working on the League captains. In October 1594, for instance, he wrote to François de Saint-Jean, sieur de Moussoulens, in these terms:

> Monsieur de Moussoulens, although you have so far followed the party of my enemies, I all the same value the good qualities which I hear that you have, and am sorry to see them used other than in my service. That is why I wish to exhort you henceforward to return to your duty, like most of the respectable members of the League. You have no further excuse for holding out, since the religious pretext, through which you were for so long exploited, is no longer relevant; do not think that your return to obedience will be less agreeable to me just because it has been so long delayed.[20]

It must have been difficult to resist such appeals. Of course, different people could be attracted in different ways. For some, money or loyalty were not the prime considerations. As Jean de Vernyes, president of the Montferrand *cour des aides*,* advised the king in 1593, 'the sieur de Saint-Hérem is very rich and so may be seduced by honours and high office; for the other person money will be best'.[21] One way or another, the king worked at it.

(v) The King as Sacerdos, February 1594

If, as some historians argue,[22] the kingly craft in early modern Europe may be analysed under the qualities of *rex*, *dux* and *sacerdos*, then Henry now lacked only the third attribute. He was fully *rex* by hereditary right, and amply *dux* by his military skill, but he could not yet claim the priestly qualities of the *sacerdos*. Normally, he would have been consecrated in the cathedral at Reims, but that city was in the hands of the duc de Guise. So, relying on several historical precedents, he decided instead to hold the ceremony at Chartres.

He came quietly into the city on 17 February 1594, and was lodged at the Bishop's palace. The next week was taken up with preparations, meaning not only the decoration of the streets and cathedral, but also the final assembly (and sometimes fabrication) of the various symbolic objects: the crown, sceptre, cloak, sword and so forth. These were normally kept at Saint-Denis, but some had been destroyed during the wars.[23] On 26 February, a Saturday, the king went as usual to Mass and heard a sermon given by René Benoist on the significance of the consecration and unction.

On the next day, a Sunday, the lay and ecclesiastical lords made their way very early in the morning to the cathedral, where according to the traditional form they chose two of their number to go and fetch the king.[24] They found him lying on a bed, wearing the special consecration-robe, and with him formed a procession to return to the cathedral. First came the archers, then the cathedral clergy and choirboys, followed by the Swiss guard, the trumpeters, the heralds, the knights of the Holy Spirit and the Scottish guards. Immediately in front of the king marched the maréchal de Matignon, deputising for the *connétable*,★ and bearing aloft a naked sword; behind were the four great household officers, the Chancellor (Philippe Hurault, sieur de Cheverny), the Chamberlain★ (duc de Longueville), the *grand maître*★ (comte de Saint-Pol) and the *grand écuyer* (Roger de Saint-Lary, sieur de Bellegarde).

As this great procession approached the cathedral, the choir sang the appointed chants, and the traditional ceremony began. Soon the king had to take the oath, promising not only to keep the peace and dispense justice, but also to 'chase out of all lands under my jurisdiction all heretics denounced by the church'. Then followed the actual anointing, followed by the consecration of sword, ring, sceptre and staff. These ceremonies complete, the Chancellor called upon the lay and ecclesiastical peers present to bear witness to the event, using these words as each answered in turn: 'Monsieur le comte de Soissons, deputising for the Duke of Normandy, present yourself!'

Then the king was crowned, and after receiving the homage of his lords, and hearing Mass, he left the church bearing the sceptre and staff and wearing the ring. The crowd broke into great shouts of 'Vive le roi', and the heralds scattered *largesse*.★ It had been a marvellously effective piece of propaganda, which was soon known throughout France, and surely accounted for many of the defections from the League during 1594. For his part, Henry took his functions as *sacerdos* seriously, as we shall see; he often, for instance, carried out the tiring and disagreeable ceremony of touching for the King's Evil,★ with such efficacy that even Spaniards came to him to be cured (Plate 5).

(vi)   The Joyous Entry, 22 March 1594

In January 1594, mistrusting his predecessor, the duc de Mayenne appointed as governor of Paris Charles de Cossé, comte de Brissac. In spite of the surveillance of the Sixteen and of the Spaniards, Brissac soon began plotting with the king. Early in March a plan was worked out for the capture of the city, and Mayenne may have got wind of it, for he himself left Paris on 6 March with his wife and children. By the 19th preparations were sufficiently advanced for Brissac to hold a secret assembly at the Arsenal, where no doubt the final arrangements were discussed.[25] Meanwhile the king was organising his forces around Senlis, whence on 17 March he wrote to Sully that he should come to Saint-Denis on the 21st, 'so as to help cry "vive le roi" in Paris'.[26]

Astonishingly enough, firm news of the preparations did not reach the Leaguers and Spaniards in Paris. On the evening of the 21st, it is true, the Duke of Feria confronted Brissac with a rumour that a *coup de main* was intended,[27] but Brissac so succeeded in calming the Spaniards' apprehensions that by 3 a.m. on the 22nd they and the representatives of the Sixteen had mostly gone to bed. The plan of Henry IV was then put into effect. Three forces had been converging on the city from west, north and east, and at 4 a.m. they reached their respective gates, on a morning of mist and driving rain very suitable for their purpose. Brissac and Lhuillier, *prévôt des marchands*,★ opened the Porte Neuve for Timoléon d'Espinay, sieur de Saint-Luc, and François d'O. The leading *échevin*,★ Martin Langlois, opened the Porte Saint-Denis for the sieur de Vitry, and in the east the sieur de La Chevalerie raised the chain on the Seine so that royal troops from Melun and Corbie could enter the city (Map 12).

These forces met very little resistance, and soon joined up in the centre, at the Grand Châtelet. By 6 a.m. the king himself was able to enter, through the Porte-Neuve (Plate 6). He made his way past the Louvre, and went to the cathedral of Notre-Dame, where about 8 a.m. he heard Mass. Meanwhile his heralds and troops were circulating in Paris, giving out

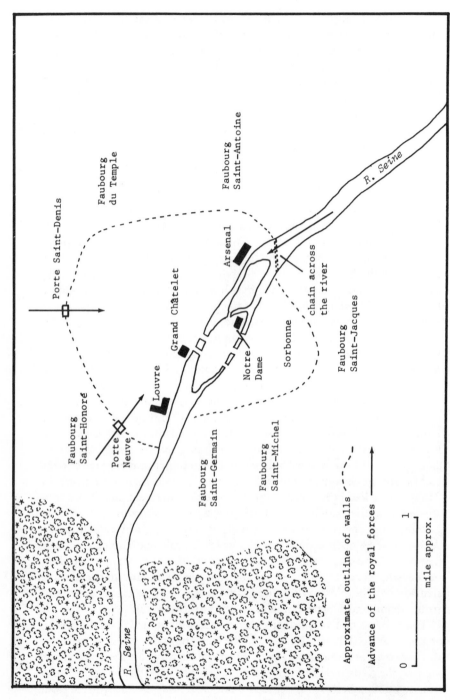

Map 12 *Henry's attack on Paris, 1594*

Porte Saint-Denis

Faubourg du Temple

Faubourg Saint-Antoine

R. Seine

Arsenal

Grand Châtelet

chain across the river

Louvre

Notre Dame

Sorbonne

Faubourg Saint-Jacques

Faubourg Saint-Honoré

Porte Neuve

Faubourg Saint-Germain

Faubourg Saint-Michel

R. Seine

Approximate outline of walls - - - -

Advance of the royal forces ⟶

0   1

mile approx.

leaflets which assured the citizens of his peaceful intentions.[28] He had wisely not attempted to enter by the southern side, where resistance might have been encountered around the Sorbonne.★ Some Leaguers now tried to whip up resistance in that *quartier*,★ but they were soon suppressed by men like the *parlementaire* Guillaume du Vair, supported by citizens like Pierre de L'Estoile, who gives us an interesting account of his own preparations for the *coup de main* and action in it.[29]

While he was at Notre-Dame, Henry's officers had been assuring potential leaders of resistance like the Duke of Feria, the papal legate, Madame de Nemours (Mayenne's mother) and Madame de Montpensier (Mayenne's sister) that this would be futile and that pardons would be widely granted. In effect, none of them stirred, and soon the king was able to go back to the Louvre, which we are assured by Chancellor Cheverny was in such good order that it seemed as if the king had only just left there.[30] After lunch he went out again into the streets, surrounded as before by cries of 'Vive le roi', and rode to the Porte Saint-Denis. Here, about 2 p.m. he was able to watch the retreat of the 3,000 foreign troops which had been garrisoned in Paris. First came the Neapolitans, and then the Spaniards, followed by the Walloons. Among them were the Duke of Feria and other Spanish leaders, to whom according to legend the king gaily cried: 'My compliments to your master, but do not come back.'[31] It had been a marvellously joyful and miraculously almost bloodless day, thanks to good fortune and careful preparations, and on the 22nd the king made sure that the good news was spread to the four corners of the kingdom.[32]

There was indeed a 'désir presque général' among the Parisians to recognise the king, and the number of those now proscribed was astonishingly small, about 120.[33] Only the most inveterate and furious Leaguers received their *billets*, as the phrase went. Brissac became *maréchal de France* and received, as we have seen, an enormous indemnity; François d'O succeeded him as governor of Paris. Most of the members of the Paris *parlement* retained their offices, and were joined in Easter week by their colleagues from the exiled royal offshoots in Tours and Châlons-sur-Marne.[34] By now the king was drawing in all those who had for so long sat on the fence; as he remarked when a certain *robin*★ sought audience about this time: 'Show him up here, for if *he* is coming it's a sure sign that I am winning'.[35] On 28 March letters-patent were formally verified reestablishing the Paris *parlement* and also the other sovereign courts: the *chambre des comptes*,★ *cour des aides* and *cour des monnaies*.★[36] Then on the 30th a solemn *arrêt*★ was promulgated to cancel all legislation enacted after 29 December 1588 'to the prejudice of the authority of our kings and royal laws'.

At this Easter season the king went out of his way to demonstrate his

53

orthodoxy, washing the feet of the poor on Maundy Thursday, visiting the sick in the Hôtel-Dieu, freeing some prisoners on Good Friday, and on Easter Sunday touching 660 persons for the King's Evil. Robiquet, who gives a good account of these events, calls them a 'comédie',[37] but they were much more than that: an outward sign that the king had come into his own and would not let his orthodoxy be challenged. Soon even the Sorbonne was won over; a deputation came to see him on 2 April, leaving well satisfied, and on 22 April a general assembly at the Collège de Navarre formally passed a decree recognising Henry IV as 'légitime et roi très-chrétien'.[38]

(vii)   The Paternal Blessing, 1593–5

The Sorbonne's decree of April 1594 had to admit that 'our Holy Father the Pope has not yet publicly admitted and recognised King Henry as eldest son of the church'. It was not for want of trying, on the part of the king. After his abjuration in 1593, he had sent first Brochard de La Clielle and then Louis de Gonzague, duc de Nevers, to Rome. But neither could make much impression on Clement VIII; the excommunication of 1585 still stood. In 1594 the Pope was assailed by a barrage of conciliatory letters from Henry; His Holiness was showing some signs of yielding, when in December 1594, following the assassination attempt of Jean Châtel, an edict expelling the Jesuits from much of France was promulgated by the *parlement* of Paris.

This made the task of Henry's representatives more difficult but, in July 1595, Jacques Davy du Perron, one of the king's instructors of July 1593, went to Rome with Arnaud d'Ossat, and by September 1595 agreement had been reached. In exchange for the papal absolution, the French representatives agreed on Henry's behalf to recognise the insufficiency of the Saint-Denis abjuration, to publish the decrees of the Council of Trent in France, to re-establish the Catholic church in Béarn and certain other places, and to appoint only Catholics to high office. Clement must have known that some of these provisions would not be enforced, but he probably hoped that over the years he could insist on them. There was a magnificent ceremony in Saint Peter's, and the final excuse for Frenchmen to belong to the League had been swept away.

(viii)   The Croquants of 1594

Some Frenchmen, though, had during 1593 been driven to insurrection by a different kind of discontent. The early 1590s had seen an intensification of peasant resistance to the levying of *tailles*, and to the depredations of some of the lesser nobles.[39] Now, in the spring of 1594, there was a widespread uprising in central south-western France, by peasants who came to be known as *Croquants*. Some historians have seen in this insurrectionary movement a phase of the 'class struggle', but this is surely a misunderstanding. From the start the *Croquants* protested their loyalty to the Crown, and they had no ambitions for radically changing the structure of society; what they wanted to do was to put a stop to the illegal extortions of nobles and others who were taking advantage of the endemic state of anarchy. Sometimes, indeed, they were led by their *seigneurs*, and the movement was to some extent one of local communities banding together in self-defence.[40]

Henry himself showed a good deal of sympathy towards the *Croquants* and, indeed, is said to have remarked that he would have become one himself, if he had had a little more time.[41] By the end of July 1594 their numbers had become formidable, but in writing to the sieur de Bourdeille, governor in Périgord, the king insisted that the 'disorder should be ended by gentle means if that is possible'.[42] He also appointed Jean-Robert de Thumery, sieur de Boissize, to go to the south-west as *surintendant en la justice et police*★ with the mission of restoring order. Boissize arrived in July 1594, and in collaboration with the sieur de Bourdeille succeeded in persuading the peasants to lay down their arms, in return for assurances that the noble extortions and abusive taxes would be curbed.

In a sense, the revolt of the *Croquants* may be seen as part of the general *ralliement* by which Frenchmen of all kinds reasserted their allegiance to the Crown. There have been attempts by historians to explain this movement in more or less elaborate ways. For Roland Mousnier, the restoration of Henry IV was largely the work of rich officeholders, anxious once again to have a stable government to back their investment.[43] For Fernand Braudel, the crucial winning-over of the towns after 1593 came because they 'desperately needed access to the rest of France'.[44] For Boris Porchnev, the nobles rallied to the Crown after 1594 because the 'masses populaires françaises' had now been roused in their class-consciousness.[45] To each his own, but it hardly seems necessary to invoke such elaborate explanations; once Henry had made his perilous leap, and shown his ability to maintain some degree of order, rich and poor alike had every interest in rallying round him, to put an end to four decades of civil strife.

5 'La guerre au roy d'Hespaigne', 1595–7

(i) Châtel and the Jesuits, 1594–5

From now onwards, Henry made his base at Paris, as the life of his kingdom slowly returned to normal. Usually he was sanguine, as he always had been, but, on 2 January 1595, Madame de Balagny (sister of Gabrielle d'Estrées) noticed that he was looking very depressed. She asked him why he was unhappy, and received this vehement answer:

> Ventre-Saint-Gris,* how could I be happy? To see a people so lacking in gratitude towards its king ... as to make constant attempts upon his life. For since I have been here I hardly hear anything else spoken of.[1]

No doubt the king was particularly thinking of Jean Châtel, who six days earlier had tried to stab him in the throat, and had succeeded only in knocking one of his teeth out. But the whole of his reign was a nightmare from this point of view. Twice in 1593, three times in 1594, twice in 1595, twice in 1596 and at least nine times after that there were attempts upon the king's life.[2] Usually they involved a single person with a knife, but sometimes there was more than one person involved, and sometimes ingenious devices were to be used. In November 1594, for instance, a band of eight robbers was arrested and hanged in Saint-Germain-en-Laye, where they were making inquiries about the king's movements.[3] In April 1603 a priest and a gentleman were arrested at Bordeaux in possession of a murderous device. As the English ambassador Sir Thomas Parry then wrote to Sir Robert Cecil: 'Th' engine is of steele about a span long, and doth shoote poisoned needles which of a reasonable distance will pierce a corcelet....'[4] Three years later, in June 1606, Parry's successor, Sir George Carew, reported to Cecil that 'I learned of late of a powder treason, intended against this King, to have been executed by laying powder under a gallery that passeth through the Louvre to the lodging of the comtesse de Moret, his last mistress....'[5] These constant threats must have been very trying, even for a man as naturally sanguine as Henry IV. He always rode with a pair of pistols to hand,[6] and did his best to forget the ever-present danger. But in times of depression he would reflect on what he saw as the ingratitude of his subjects. The Châtel incident of December 1594, like many of the others, was widely thought to have been inspired by the Jesuits, and two days after it the *parlement* of Paris promulgated an *arrêt* giving the members of the order three days to leave Paris and fifteen days to quit the region. The Jesuits did not receive any trial, and in any case shared the same point of view concerning Henry's kingship as that of virtually all the other religious orders.[7] But they were old enemies of the Gallicans in the *parlement* of Paris and at the Sorbonne, and so they (mostly) had to go. As we shall see, it was not for long.

(ii) The Eastern Campaign, 1595

The Spaniards had been behind much of the opposition to Henry, but he had until the end of 1594 preferred not to enter into open hostilities against them. In January 1595, however, he felt that the time had come to make a declaration of war,[8] and moved early in June into Burgundy. There the inhabitants of Dijon had shut the pro-Spanish garrison up in the *château*, and called him to their aid. He rushed swiftly southwards, establishing his troops among the Burgundian royalists, and himself advanced to meet the Spanish general, Luis de Velasco, governor of Milan, who had crossed the Alps in order to come to the aid of the League in Burgundy.

On 5 June the royal cavalry under the maréchal de Biron encountered the vanguard of Velasco's cavalry near the village of Fontaine-Française. Biron thought that the enemy squadrons were merely outriders, far from the main body of Velasco's army, but having attacked them found to his consternation that the whole Spanish army was almost upon him. He had also drawn the king forward into this attack, in which the royal cavalry was outnumbered about five to one, with a powerful hostile infantry to hand. It was a situation in which reckless courage was needed, and Henry showed again that he did not lack this quality. Although he had come ill prepared to fight, lacking proper armour,[9] he led two furious charges which in the end forced the enemy cavalry to draw off. Mayenne saw better than Velasco how weak Henry's position was, and urged an attack. But the Spanish general could not believe that Henry would be operating in this way, without a powerful force to hand, and so withdrew across the Saône, leaving the king in possession of the field. It was a famous victory, which halted the Spanish advance and so disgusted Mayenne with his allies that he resolved to come to terms with the king. For his part, Henry was in high spirits. This comes out well from the letter which he wrote to Jean d'Harambure, one of his boon hunting-companions: 'Hang yourself for not having been with me in a fight which we had against the enemy, in which we really cut loose, though not all who were with me. . . .'[10]

Among his squadrons by now were virtually none of his early Huguenot officers, if we except La Trémoille and Sully;[11] almost all were now Catholics, many of them recently converted to Henry's cause. One of those who particularly distinguished himself at Fontaine-Française was Guillaume Fouquet, sieur de La Varenne, whom we shall meet in a variety of roles. According to the *brevet*★[12] which was published two days after the battle and appointed La Varenne a *chevalier de l'accolade*,★ he had accompanied the king at Coutras, Ivry, Arques and Rouen, and at Fontaine-Française had given His Majesty a pistol when he most needed one. This battle was not only a tactical triumph, but also had important strategic consequences, for the royalists were now able to consolidate their hold over Burgundy, formerly so hostile to them. The king now continued southwards to Lyon, where early in September 1595 he made a splendid entry. Plate 7 gives us some idea of what it looked like.

The procession is winding its way from the bottom left-hand corner of the engraving, where Henry is visible under a canopy, back and forth across the middle ground, and ending up in the top left-hand corner, where the Archbishop is waiting with his clergy, under the arms of France and of Navarre. Each of the arches, obelisks and so forth has a symbolic significance. The king has just passed, for instance, between altars marked for Piety and Clemency. The great central arch is inscribed with the names of 'Arques', 'Ivry' and – surprisingly – 'Dijon', which must have been the first way in which the victory of Fontaine-Française was known.[13] Entries of this kind were designed to impress the population with the royal authority and power.

(iii)   The North-Eastern Frontier, 1596

Meanwhile on the north-eastern frontier things had been going badly. Already in May 1594 the Spanish captain, Count Charles de Mansfelt, had captured La Capelle, and now in 1595 Pedro Enríquez de Guzmán, Count of Fuentes and the new governor of the Spanish Netherlands, began a new offensive. Le Catelet, adjacent to La Capelle, fell on 25 June 1595, and then he quickly turned on Doullens, one of the key strongholds north of the Somme (Map 13). By the end of June this town had been captured, with severe loss of life by the French, including the son of our chronicler Pierre de L'Estoile.[14] Fuentes was a brutal and able commander, whose Walloons and Neapolitans were able to sow a kind of panic among the French. As the English agent Ottywell Smith wrote to the Earl of Essex on 24 July from Dieppe:

Them of Abbeville and Amiens do demand garrisons, they fear so far the Spaniards. The taking of Dorland [Doullens] so furiously

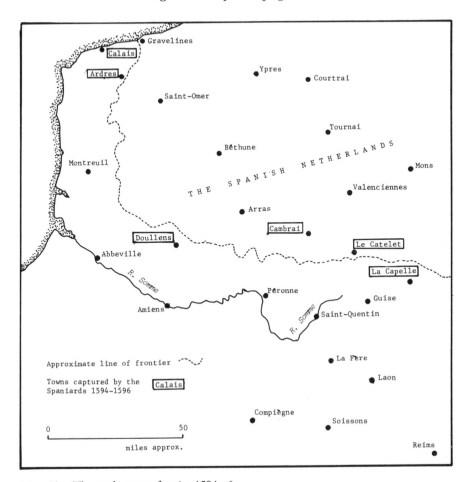

Map 13   *The north-eastern frontier 1594—6*

maketh them all to tremble, it is to be feared that if the King come not into Picardy all stands in great danger to be lost. The enemy is 16,000 men strong and yet looketh for more forces daily. This Compte de Foyentes is cruel. . . .[15]

The cruel count now turned on Cambrai, to consolidate his hold on the region and the headwaters of the Somme. Henry was still down in Lyon, but he recognised the urgency of the situation and on 12 September wrote from there to Urbain de Laval, sieur de Boisdauphin, cavalry captain and a recently repented Leaguer, that he was resolved to save Cambrai or perish in the attempt.[16] He appealed desperately to the United Provinces for troops,[17] and to the *parlement* of Paris for the verification of his fiscal edicts.

59

But the *parlement* was stubborn, and the foreign troops were slow in coming. The governor of Cambrai, Jean de Monluc, sieur de Balagny, was unpopular with the inhabitants, and early in October, tired of being bombarded by seventy Spanish cannon, they opened one of the gates. Balagny retired to the citadel, but surrendered this on 7 September 1595. L'Estoile's comment is that this engagement brought as much honour to Fuentes as it did shame to Balagny;[18] certainly the French forces had put up very little resistance during this campaign by the Spanish general.

Having eventually assembled a large army, Henry decided to lay siege to La Fère, which was the last remaining Spanish outpost south of the Somme. Strongholds like this were a thorn in the flesh of the surrounding countryside, because of the wide area which their cavalry could ravage. The Leaguers in Soissons, for instance, at the beginning of 1595 made a raid as far as Paris itself, a distance of about sixty miles.[19] To besiege La Fère the king had by January 1596 assembled:

> ... 2,000 horses, 3,000 Swiss, 2,500 landsknechts,* 4,000 French picorreurs,* ill pay'd and dayly disbanding, and 1,800 French well armed and disciplined under the command of M. de La Noue (pay'd by the States), besides the forces which the admiral Nassau hath, being above 2,000....[20]

Many of these units are mentioned by name on the original of Plate 8; it is an engraving whose finest print is very hard to reproduce. But Henry did not long remain with his troops at La Fère. After setting out the general dispositions of the siege in October and the early part of November 1595, he left for Folembray, eight or ten miles to the south. Here there was an ancient *château* with excellent hunting in the forest of Coucy; Gabrielle joined him and they spent Christmas there.

However, this was not a time merely for amusements. By late September 1595 negotiations with Mayenne had gone far enough for the king to write to Savary de Brèves, his ambassador in Constantinople, that he had 'obliged the duke of Mayenne to recognise me';[21] early in 1596 the Duke came to Montceaux, fifty miles or so south of Folembray, and there he was personally reconciled with Henry. Sully tells an amusing story of how the king took his vengeance on the fat Duke by walking him very briskly about the park until Mayenne, 'red in the face, very hot, and panting hard', asked him for pity. 'There,' replied the king, 'let us shake hands on it, for that is all the harm which you will ever receive from me.' In fact, Mayenne's opposition had been curiously half-hearted; unlike Mercœur in Brittany, Mayenne in Burgundy neglected to build up a sound provincial base, preferring to dabble in political combinations at the national level. Here, too, he proved oddly ineffectual; as Henri Drouot

60

puts it, he was 'un aventureux qui hésite'.[22] All the same, his submission was a notable event; the dukes of Joyeuse and Epernon soon followed suit and, as the young Charles de Lorraine, duc de Guise, had come over to Henry the previous January,[23] now only the duc de Mercœur among the greater nobles remained intransigent.

In the spring of 1596, however, with Henry's main army immobilised before La Fère, the Spaniards opened a new campaign, this time in the far north of the region. Cunningly disguising their intentions,[24] they suddenly appeared before Calais, seized an outlying fort, and by the end of April were able to take the city by assault. Its defenders reacted slowly and at first without much conviction. Henry was committed at La Fère, but there was a powerful English fleet in the Straits of Dover and he had begged Elizabeth to send it to reinforce the French defences. The English queen having answered that she would only do so if she could then keep the town, the negotiations ended, Henry remarking that he would as soon be bitten by a lion as by a lioness.[25] Elizabeth's policy in this emergency was not that of a friend; as Henry put it, she had 'measured her friendship by the profit she could make from it'.[26] Secure in Calais, the Spaniards turned south-east to Ardres, which they quickly took. It did not have formidable defences, but there was a general feeling that the governor (Jean-François de Belin, League governor of Paris) had not done his best. When Henry heard of the loss he burst out with a furious 'My cowards do me more harm than the enemy ever could do',[27] and Belin was for a while deprived of some of his posts.[28]

At La Fère things went better for the French. Plate 8, reproduced from a drawing by Claude de Chastillon, one of Henry's engineers, gives a very good idea of the site of the town, with the village of Beautor on the left margin and the king's quarters at Travecy in the middle at the top. Slanting across the left-hand side of the plate is the dike by which the royalists hoped to contain the River Oise (coming in at the top right) and so flood the town out. Plate 9 is a detail of Plate 8, showing in more detail the 'logis du roy' (left centre) and behind it the 'cartier des marchands' who supplied the army. Behind these little huts are the tents of the various regiments, with the troops themselves drawn up as if ready for action, their lances* forming the familiar dense hedge. At the top we can see the regiments of Navarre, of the guards, and of Montigny; away at the bottom right, behind a wood, is the 'regiment de Champagne'. It was not a particularly glorious siege, but at least it was successful, for the town surrendered late in May 1596. Henry had shown that he could mobilise a powerful army, with the accompanying artillery (top left in Plate 8), and hold a substantial town blockaded while simultaneously preventing its relief by groups of hostile cavalry.

The situation in the north-east had now reached a stalemate, even though the season was far from over. The Spaniards were content with their acquisitions of Calais and Ardres, and the king with his recovery of La Fère; neither wished to undertake a fresh siege, which might lead to the defeat of the besiegers by the enemy's mobile army.

(iv)   The Assembly of Notables, 1596–7

During the siege of La Fère the king had to write letter after letter to his councillors in Paris, asking them to send him money and supplies; as he said to the assembled members of the *parlement* of Paris in October 1595, 'tout ira bien sy j'ay de l'argent'.[29] Now, in the late summer of 1596, he thought that he had found a way to solve this problem. Earlier in the year the assembly of the French clergy had requested an estates-general in order to get the decrees of the Council of Trent applied. In spite of his agreement with the Pope in September 1595, Henry had no intention of applying the Tridentine decrees in France, for they might infringe royal jurisdiction in areas like the appointment of bishops; nor was he keen on calling an estates-general, which might turn out to resemble those of the League. But he did seize the opportunity to call an Assembly of Notables, chiefly with the aim of tackling his fiscal problems.[30]

Such assemblies had been called in the past, most recently in 1583; they were normally smaller than an estates-general, though their general composition was not dissimilar. From the king's point of view, they had the advantage that he nominated the members; letters of convocation were sent about the end of June 1596. At first the Assembly was due to meet at the end of the following August, but the opening was eventually deferred until the beginning of November, in Rouen. At the appointed time about 'eleven bishops, twenty-six nobles, twenty-four members of the sovereign courts, eighteen *trésoriers-généraux***** and deputies from fifteen towns' were present. Henry made an opening speech which was generally judged to be appropriate, even if, according to the *premier président* of the Rouen *parlement*, it rather smacked of 'son accoutumée façon militaire'.[31] The original is preserved in the Bibliothèque Nationale with the king's manuscript alterations,[32] which allow us a rare glimpse into the way that he was thinking. On the whole, his corrections aim to make the speech more concise – he hated long speeches – and to give it more flow; as it came out, it was brief, in short sentences, and to the point.

The members soon decided to sit in three chambers, each containing representatives of the three estates, instead of by separate estates, as at an estates-general. Then some weeks followed in which quarrels over precedence and over the existing fiscal structure threatened to bring the proceedings to a fruitless end. On 1 December the English ambassador Sir Anthony Milday wrote to Cecil that

> The assembly of our deputies here hath not yet brought forth anything in parfet shape, but only affordeth matter of discourse and expectation, and every daie more and more discovereth the disagreinge humours, factions and povertie of this state, some seekinge to defend their owne faultes by way of a diversion upon others, many practising to dissolve ye assembly, and all labouring to make this reformation serve their owne termes.[33]

However, towards the end of December the deputies began to pull some constructive ideas together, and on 26 January they presented a *cahier* containing their proposals. Their chief recommendations, intended to bring the budget into balance, were that the expenditure on the royal household and on governors should be cut, and that a tax of one *sol pour livre* (commonly called the *pancarte*,* after the poster on which the rates were set out) should be imposed on all merchandise sold in the towns. The first of these measures would have cut into the nobles' allowances, and the second would have transferred some of the fiscal burden from the peasantry to the townsfolk; both therefore met stiff resistance and both had to be abandoned. As Mildmay wrote to Cecil in February 1597, concerning the *pancarte*,

> They of Paris and the King agree not well, especially about ye taxation of five in ye hundred of all merchandise sold there, to which they oppose themselves resolutely. The King threatens to bring them to itt by force, unless they yeild thereto willingly; it is thought following ye course here [there] will be another barricadoes. . . .[34]

This conflict was very acute in the *cour des aides*, which had to be coerced at the end of April 1597 into registering the edict establishing the *pancarte*.[35] However, by then Amiens had fallen to the Spaniards and Sully had achieved virtual supremacy in the *conseil des finances*;* soon it would become much more difficult to resist the demands of the Crown.

(v) An Interval of Peace, 1597

In Henry's tumultuous life there were intervals, as at Nérac between August 1579 and May 1580, when for the time being his nervous energy seemed to be exhausted, and he gave himself over to idle pleasures. One such interval occurred towards the end of 1596, after the exceedingly

63

arduous two years of struggle against the Spaniards. Now Henry seemed to have time only for Gabrielle; or, as the censorious English agent Thomas Edmondes put it, 'The King was never a more superstitious servant to his mistress, and doth whollie emploie his spyrittes in that affection'.[36] During the five years following their meeting at Cœuvres in November 1590, Gabrielle had snared the king's heart ever more tightly. At first it was merely as the latest in a series of mistresses; as one of the archers on guard at the Louvre replied to a foreigner who inquired of him whom this fine lady might be, 'Mon ami, ce n'est rien qui vaille, c'est la putain du Roi'.[37] Gradually her role changed. In January 1596 she had received Mayenne at Montceaux, when he came for his reconciliation,[38] and by October 1596 an Italian observer could write that 'among the French nobility people begin to suspect that the king intends to name as his successor the natural son born of Gabrielle'.[39] All the king's advisers realised that this would open the way to a disastrously disputable succession, but Henry seemed bent on it and, as the Cardinal of Florence wrote in March 1597, 'nobody dares to speak to him about it'.[40] So, as the months went by, the king manœuvred himself into a potentially disastrous situation with Gabrielle.

His other amusements, during the winter of 1596–7, were less dangerous. He had acquired a good friend in 1594, when Sébastien Zamet the banker had first made his acquaintance, as an envoy from Mayenne.[41] Zamet was to become his inseparable companion in financial and amorous adventures, lending him great sums of money and making his house available for dubious pleasures. Zamet was also a gambler, a taste he shared with the king. In September 1594, for instance, Henry spent one afternoon playing tennis and the whole night dicing with M. d'O. Tennis had long been one of his favourite distractions, and he was often seen playing in the 'jeu de paume de la Sphère'.[42] This love of exercise also found expression in frequent hunting excursions, on which by the end of the day he was often lost. A good many of these occasions are recounted by L'Estoile in his *Journal*, whose accuracy we might doubt were it not that they are sometimes confirmed by foreign observers. On 3/10 October 1596, for instance, the Earl of Shrewsbury wrote to Cecil[43] that 'yesterday [the king] went a–huntynge ye stagge (as was said), and perhaps lost himselfe in ye woode, for to Gallion [Gaillon in Normandy, where he was staying] he returned not ye night . . .'. In fact, his hunting around Rouen during the Assembly of Notables was particularly successful; of thirty–two stags hunted, he killed thirty–one.[44]

Soon he had a rude awakening from this pleasant round. On 12 March 1597, after dancing until about three in the morning, he received news that the Spaniards had suddenly captured Amiens. This almost unthinkable disaster seems to have shaken him back into reality. Sully describes how he rapidly began formulating plans for its recovery,[45] and the Venetian ambassador affirmed to the Doge and Senate that 'two hours after receiving the news of the fall of Amiens, the King set out on horseback for those parts'.[46] For his part, L'Estoile puts the usual *mots justes* into Henry's mouth, claiming that after a little thought the king cried, 'C'est assez faire le roi de France; il est temps de faire le roi de Navarre',[47] before galloping off to Picardy. Whatever the truth of these various accounts, it is certain that the king received a rude shock and that he responded to it by rediscovering his old dynamism. As the English ambassador put it,[48] 'this accident, though it be greatly prejudicial unto him, yet in respect that it will awake him from his pleasures, wherein he is too much drowned, may turne to his great advantage, if from henceforth he take another course'.

(vi) Amiens Lost and Amiens Regained, 1597

The seizure of Amiens by Hernantello Portocarrero was a classic example of the use of surprise. A small party of Spaniards secured a gate by deception, and then called up the main force before the urban militia could respond. According to Sir Anthony Mildmay, the king lost twenty-six cannon, 40,000 shot, 8,000 *milliers*★ of powder, 8,000 *setiers*★ of wheat and 'six score thousand crowns in ready money';[49] Amiens had in fact been the bulwark from which Henry intended to attack the Spaniards in 1597.

For the remaining three weeks of March he was in Picardy, taking the measures necessary to ensure that other towns did not go the way of Amiens. His resources were stretched to breaking-point, and his letters show an altogether uncharacteristic note of despair at this time. To Gaspard de Schomberg, for instance, he wrote on 31 March that 'I am not only unwell, but also assailed by so many problems and burdens that I hardly know which saint to invoke in order to lead me out of this unfortunate situation'.[50]

An assault on Arras failed, and the members of the council left in Paris seemed incapable of getting adequate supplies of money and munitions up to Picardy. The Protestants, meeting in Châtellerault, refused to send any help,[51] and to crown Henry's misfortunes the *parlement* of Paris decided to '[faire] les fols', by refusing to register those fiscal edicts through which money could be raised.[52] Returning to Paris on 21 May, the king addressed them in terms which show how vexed and frustrated he must have been:

I am extremely displeased, gentlemen, that the present subject should be what brings me into my *parlement* for the first time. I would have preferred to come and hold my *lit de justice*,★ talk about your duty, and recommend to you in its discharge both your

65

consciences and mine. But the misfortunes of the time have prevented that, so that I have been obliged to come here by your delays, stubbornness and disobedience, for the safety of the state, whose imminent peril does not trouble you. . . . Now I shall fall silent and require my chancellor to let you know what my wishes are.[53]

Meanwhile letters of recruitment were going out all over France. As yet the French kings had no better means of mobilising the bulk of their forces than by asking the leading nobles to 'assemble as many of your friends as you can, and come to [the rendezvous]'.[54] Of course, Henry as usual couched these letters in his own style, which must have made them unusually effective. To the sieur de Saint-Germain-Beaupré, for instance, he wrote at the beginning of June:

> I know that you have too much courage to remain at home while I am on campaign with all my good *serviteurs*, to oppose my enemies and make assaults upon them . . . [when you come] you will find a goodly number of *gens de bien* who wish to acquit themselves well, and I am sure that you would regret missing this opportunity to serve me when I most need help from those who love this state and wish to preserve it.[55]

Slowly, then, the royal army assembled. During his first visit to Picardy the king had given orders for the investment of Amiens, so that when he returned there at the beginning of June the various forts and trenches had largely taken shape. It seems to have been the engineer Jean Errard who designed a whole series of forts with linking trenches, running round the perimeter of Amiens to the north of the Somme. To man this extensive line, the king had at first too few soldiers; by the end of May there were still fewer than 10,000 infantry (including 2,500 English and 2,000 Swiss), and this number increased only slowly during June.[56]

On 17 July the Spaniards made a furious sortie, killing about 500 of the besiegers[57] and ruining part of the works by which the French artillery was slowly approaching the town walls. Even Sir Arthur Savage, commander of the English force, had to admit that the sortie was largely successful:

> . . . the enemy's purpose was to have cloyed our ordinans [spiked our guns], and came provided for the same with hammers and great spikes, of which they fayled hardly thereof, for they had wonn the trenches of ye places of batterye, with the losse of much bloude on our side, and many good men. . . .[58]

Slowly, though, numbers began to tell. By the end of August the besiegers numbered something like 20,000 infantry, with 3,000 horse and forty-five cannon; inside the town, Hernantello Portocarrero had fewer than 4,000 infantry and 1,000 cavalry. The Spanish commander himself was killed on 3 September, and about the middle of the month a relieving force led by Cardinal-Archduke Albert from Brussels was forced to withdraw. That marked the end of Spanish resistance; surrender terms were agreed on 19 September, and on the 25th the survivors of the garrison marched out of the town. They passed through the middle of the French army, and as each captain came to Henry he dismounted and kissed the king's boot; 'His Majesty spoke to them very courteously'.

By then the royal army had reached the size shown in Plate 10. Notice, in the right foreground at A, the king's headquarters in 'La Madelayne', a ruined abbey. Just in front are the tents (B) of the maréchal Biron, the king's deputy, and just behind (2) are the tents and huts of the merchants supplying the army. Immediately to the south (the view is oriented southerly) is the quarter of the grand-master of the artillery, with the munition-park (C). The various regiments stretch in a circle round the north-west perimeter, each side of the headquarters. The core of the infantry was formed by the *Quatre Vieux* (regiments), of which we can identify the regiments of the guards (D), of Picardie (M) and of Champagne (O); the *régiment de Piémont* was no doubt engaged on the south-eastern frontier with Lesdiguières. Henry's own *régiment de Navarre* is at L; these four regiments had just come from La Fère, as had the regiments of Cambray (F), Flessan (F), Montigny (H) and Regnacq. The Swiss (E) and the English (N) had their own quarters; all were protected from attack by a trench-line supported by frequent forts (I). Supplies came down the Somme from Abbeville (19, top right), and the river was blocked each side of the town by fortified bridges of boats (8 and 18). A mile or two away to the north-west (20) at Longpré a field-hospital had been organised, and was greatly praised at the time for its efficiency.[59] Finally, the system of 'approaches' is shown by the various trenches leading diagonally up to the town walls; it was here that each regiment served in its appointed place, and into these trenches that the Spaniards stormed their way in the sortie of 17 July.

With the town recaptured, Henry heard a Mass of thanksgiving in the cathedral (58), and then went to challenge the Archduke under the walls of Arras.[60] But the Archduke was no longer in a fighting mood, and the king soon found that he had no army left to fight with. As he wrote on 28 September 1597 to his sister Catherine: 'On Thursday evening I had 5,000 gentlemen; on Saturday at midday I have less than 500. Among the infantry the loss through disbanding is less, though very great.'[61]

Apart from the foreign auxiliaries, his army had been raised, as we have seen, through the feudal method of calling on his greater retainers and captains to come and help him; once the obvious need was past, they tended to go home again. But the king had shown, even more convincingly than at La Fère, that this method could still give remarkable results. Moreover, the technical arms were making considerable progress. His artillery was more numerous and better served, his sappers were skilful at constructing extensive fieldworks, and the hospital service had emerged. As we shall see, these arms would continue to develop during the rest of his reign, marking a decisive improvement over the improvisations of the Valois kings and their predecessors. All these more complex services demanded great sums of money, which were raised through the domineering energy of Sully, who emerged at this time as the hard-driving and authoritarian fiscal chief; here, too, the siege marked a decisive stage in the development of the power of the Crown.

The remaining problems were considerable. The Protestants had been conspicuous by their absence from the siege, during which they stubbornly negotiated with Schomberg, the royal emissary, for an edict giving them extensive concessions over the matters of special courts and *places de sûreté*. In Brittany, too, the duc de Mercœur remained intransigent, so that the king would have to come to a reckoning with both him and the Protestants before he could call the kingdom his own. But enough progress had been made for one year, and Henry could now turn his mind to these remaining matters. As he wrote on 22 September 1597 to Duplessis-Mornay: 'We have recovered Amiens by the grace of God and the help of so many *gens de bien* who have served me there. Now we must recover Brittany, turning in that direction our wishes and our forces, with our persons and our blood. . . .'[62]

6 'L'heureuse saison', 1598

(i) The Brittany Voyage: 'Mercure ou Mars', February–May 1598

The year 1598 was for Henry an *annus mirabilis*, when Mercœur ended his stubborn resistance, the Protestants accepted an edict of compromise, and an honourable peace was concluded with Spain. The king had written in September 1597 that 'we must recover Brittany', and the winter of 1597–8 was spent in preparations for this. Henry took the forthcoming campaign seriously, raising supplies from the towns and even requesting fourteen ships from the United Provinces, to keep the Loire blockaded.[1] He sent the usual letters to his friends, asking them to turn out in the spring. Late in January, for instance, he wrote:

> Brave Grillon, it would be too much to have been absent from the siege of Amiens and to miss that of Nantes [Mercœur's stronghold]. The sieur de Pilles, who saw the first of these, will tell you what happened there and how I longed for you; if you miss the second, there are no more friends. . . .[2]

So at the end of February he set out with a considerable force for Brittany. Mercœur, though, was no longer able to resist. He had held the province since 1582, establishing a ducal court in Nantes and defeating various attempts to oust him. But he had never succeeded in consolidating an autonomous Breton power, and by inviting the Spaniards to establish themselves in Blavet in October 1590 he had alienated many of his followers.[3] So, when Henry appeared in February 1598 at the head of his troops, Mercœur sent his wife to meet the king, just outside Angers, and an agreement was rapidly concluded. Mercœur agreed to recognise the king's authority, surrendering Nantes and the other towns which he held; of course he received suitable compensation. It was also agreed that Mercœur's daughter should marry Henry's bastard son, César de Vendôme, offspring of Gabrielle. The happy pair were very young and, as two English observers wrote at the time,[4] 'many a good Frenchman laughed, to see a couple of puppies, that knew not the difference between a contract and a botterfly, should be putt together with such an assembly'.[5] However, this precocious alliance served its political purpose.

The king remained in Angers from the early days of March until the middle of April, and then moved on to Nantes itself – busy, as he wrote, 'mopping up and recovering'[6] his province. He remained at Nantes until the beginning of May, when he returned to Fontainebleau. Mercœur could not easily reconcile himself to the loss of his independence; as he remarked, it may only have been a dream, but it had lasted for ten years. So he went off to serve the Emperor in the Christian army on the Danube, and after some distinguished exploits died in 1602 at Nuremberg on his way back to France.

(ii) *'The Affairs of Those of the Religion', April 1598*

During his stay in Mercœur's former capital, the king signed the document which has become celebrated in French history as the Edict of Nantes, regulating for the rest of the reign his relations with the Protestants; as he wrote on 13 April, 'I have now settled the affairs of those of the Religion'.[7] This edict had been long in the making. From the time of his abjuration, in July 1593, Henry's relations with his former companions had deteriorated. Successive assemblies at Sainte-Foy (1594), Saumur (1595) and Loudun (1596)[8] had seen the development of an ever more intransigent group among the Protestants, who received no easy answers from the king, while he was desperately fighting the Spaniards. By 1597, as we have seen, they were so far alienated as to deny him help during the grave crisis which followed the Spanish capture of Amiens.

By the spring of 1598 the king's position was much stronger, with Mercœur out of the running and negotiations for peace with Spain going well. So the Protestants were induced after hard bargaining to accept what is called the 'Edict of Nantes', but what is in fact four separate documents: ninety-two general articles, fifty-six secret articles and two royal *brevets*.[9] The main body of ninety-two articles generally re-affirmed the provisions of previous edicts like those of 1562, 1570 and 1577. Liberty of conscience was conceded, Protestant services were permitted in many towns and *châteaux*, full civil rights were granted, and extensive judicial protection was offered by special courts. On the other hand, the imposition of taxes was forbidden, as were the construction of fortifications, the levying of troops and the holding of political assemblies.

The fifty-six secret articles mostly consisted of elucidations and explanations of tricky points among the ninety-two general articles, but the *brevets* dealt with more significant matters. One arranged the payments of stipends for pastors from public funds, and the other not only agreed that the Protestants might hold for eight years all the towns which they occupied in August 1597 (see Map 14), but also arranged for annual royal payments for their garrisons. These payments were faithfully made (see

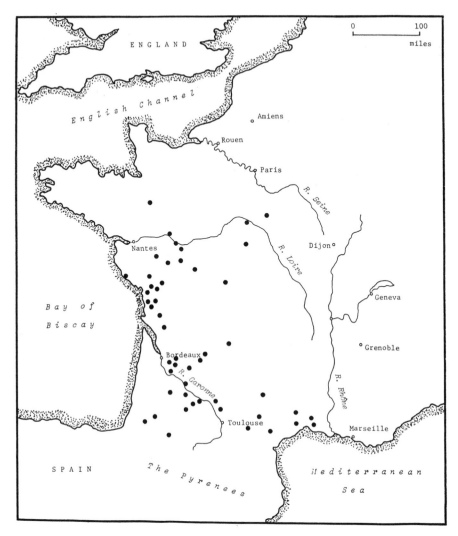

Map 14   *Towns granted to the Protestants by the Edict of Nantes. Not including towns in Navarre or Dauphiné, or those controlled by individual Protestant nobles.*
Source: Anquez, *Histoire des assemblées politiques,* p. 162–5.

Chapter 11, section v), and the *brevets* were in general a considerable concession, since they in some sense endorsed the idea of the Protestants as a separate political entity.

Once its main provisions were known, there was widespread opposition to the implementation of the Edict. In order to spare the sensibilities of the papal legate, in France to help the negotiations for peace with Spain, Henry did not attempt to get the Edict registered by the *parlements* until

71

September 1598. Then he came up against difficulties which called for all his powers of persuasion. The *parlement* of Paris having proved stubborn, the king called its members to the Louvre on 7 February 1599 and made to them a speech so memorable, and so characteristic, that it deserves to be quoted extensively:

> Before talking to you about the matter for which I have called you here, I should like to tell you a story.... Immediately after the Massacre of Saint Bartholomew, four of us playing dice at a table saw drops of blood on it, and after seeing that after being wiped off twice they appeared again a third time, I said that I would play no more, and that it was a bad omen against those who had spilled the blood. M. de Guise was one of the party.
>
> You see me in my study, where I have come to speak to you not in my royal garb or with sword and cloak, like my predecessors, nor like a prince speaking to foreign ambassadors, but like the father of a family speaking informally to his children. What I want to say is that I wish you to verify the edict granted to the Protestants. What I have done is for the sake of peace; I have established it outside my kingdom and now wish to ensure it inside. You ought to obey me if only because of my position, and the obligation which is shared by my subjects and particularly by you of my *parlement*.
>
> I have restored some of the homes from which they had been banished, and have restored faith to others who had lost it. If obedience was due to my predecessors, still more is it due to me, because I have restored the state, God having chosen to establish me in the kingdom which is mine both by inheritance and by acquisition. The members of my *parlement* would not be in their seats without me; I do not want to boast, but I wish to insist that I myself have set you an example.
>
> I know that there are intrigues in the *parlement*, and that seditious preachers have been stirred up, but I shall attend to that without your help. That is what led to the barricades and eventually to the assassination of the late king. I shall see to all that, cutting all factions and seditious preaching off at the root.... I have stormed plenty of town walls and shall surely storm barricades, too, if necessary. Do not speak to me of the Catholic religion; I love it better than you. I am more Catholic than you; I am the eldest son of the church, which none of you is or can be. You are deceiving yourselves if you think that you are well in with the Pope; I am better in than you, and if I wish shall have you all declared heretics for disobeying me.
>
> I am better informed than you; whatever happens, I know what each of you will say. I know what is in your houses, I know what

you are doing and everything that you say, for I have a little devil who reveals all to me. . . . I am now king, and speak as king. I wish to be obeyed. The men of the law are indeed my right arm, but if the right arm becomes gangrenous, then the left must cut it off. . . .

Yield up to my entreaties what you would not have given up by threats, for you will have none from me. Do what I require of you at once, I beg you; you will be doing it not only for me, but for the sake of peace.[10]

It was the usual masterly blend of command and entreaty; three weeks later, the Edict was registered by the Paris *parlement*. Some of the other *parlements* were also stubborn, and these, too, evoked memorable harangues from the king. The deputies from Bordeaux came to Saint-Germain on 3 November 1599, and found the king playing with his children. He began by addressing them kindly, but ended on a very authoritative note:

I have made an edict and wish it to be kept. In any case, I wish it to be obeyed, as it will be good for you. My chancellor will let you know more fully what is my desire.[11]

The same day, the deputies from Toulouse received rougher treatment:

It is strange that you cannot cast out your ill-will. I see that you still have Spanish notions in your bellies. Who, then, can believe that those who have exposed their life, property and honour for the defence and preservation of this state are not worthy of honourable public posts in it? . . . But those who have done their very best to wreck the state are to be seen as good Frenchmen, worthy of such posts! I am not blind; I see through all this, and wish that those of the Religion should be able to live at peace in my realm and be eligible for all posts, not because they are Protestants, but because they have faithfully served me and the French crown. I wish to be obeyed, and that my edict shall be published and implemented throughout my kingdom. It is high time that all of us, drunk with war, sobered up.[12]

So the most tenacious opponents were gradually won over; the *parlement* of Toulouse registered the Edict on 19 January 1600, that of Dijon the same month, that of Bordeaux on 7 February 1600, and that of Rennes on 23 August 1600. As the *parlement* of Grenoble had conformed on 27 September 1599, that left only the *parlement* of Rouen, which held out on certain details until 1609. The registration of the Edict had been very important for Henry not only as a political necessity, but also as a matter of personal honour; he had put all his rhetorical skill and the power of his personality into this struggle, and had finally triumphed. As we shall see, the result was that many Protestants were induced again to participate in the mainstream of French political and economic life.

(iii)   A Small Town Called Vervins, February–May 1598

While the king was in Brittany, dealing with Mercœur and the Protestants, two of his most trusted agents, Chancellor Bellièvre and Nicolas Brûlart, sieur de Sillery, were in the little town of Vervins, up by the border with the Spanish Netherlands, where they were negotiating with the representatives of the king of Spain, under the encouraging eye of the papal legate, Alexander de Medici, Cardinal of Florence. Both France and Spain needed peace, and since the recapture of Amiens there was no immediate quarrel to prevent its conclusion. During April 1598 the negotiations went well, so that on 2 May the treaty could be signed.[13] It was in effect yet another statement of stalemate in the long struggle which had begun when the French invaded Italy in 1494; its first article provided that the terms of the Treaty of Cateau-Cambrésis (1559) should again prevail, and that all towns captured since that time should be returned.

This meant that France had to return Cambrai, but in exchange she recovered Ardres, Blavet, Calais, Doullens, La Capelle, Le Catelet and Monthulin. Henry was exultant; as he wrote to the Duke of Piney-Luxembourg,[14] 'they are to return my towns. . . . I shall not spend a *sou* for them.' Now the only French territory still in foreign hands was the marquisate of Saluzzo, seized by the Duke of Savoy in 1588; at Vervins it was agreed that this territory would be the subject of papal arbitration within a year.

The English and Dutch had done all they could to impede the negotiations, both going so far as to send special envoys to Nantes in order to dissuade the king from peace.[15] But neither Justin of Nassau nor Robert Cecil could sway Henry from his decision. Cecil took it badly, writing back to England about the end of April[16] that 'the King hath sent tonight to my lodging to courte me, and hath intreated me that I will go tomorrow a-hunting with him, to kyll a wolfe and play the good fellow and not be melancholy. I have absolutely denied him, and made him a sullen answer. . . .' Sullen answer or no, the time of formal hostilities with Spain was now over; as we shall see, it was succeeded by what can best be called a period of cold war. The king formally swore to observe the terms of Vervins at a magnificent ceremony in Notre-Dame on Sunday, 21 June 1598.

On the following Tuesday, there was another splendid occasion when, as a sign of peace, the various instruments of war – drums, trumpets, lances, swords and so forth – were formally burned in front of the Hôtel de Ville* in Paris. We may suppose that these instruments were no longer serviceable, but the symbolism was there; afterwards a splendid feast was held in the Hôtel de Ville. Gabrielle was prominent at this feast, as L'Estoile recounts it:

> ... the duchess of Beaufort [Gabrielle, was] seated in a chair, and Madame de Guise brought her the various dishes with great ceremony. Gabrielle took what she most liked with one hand, and gave her other to be kissed by the king, who was near her. ... [17]

It is a delightful vision; Gabrielle playing the dizzy blonde, while the ladies of the court scurry round entertaining her. Three weeks later, on 12 July, the Archduke Albert (ruler of the southern, Spanish, Netherlands) also swore to observe the treaty, in Brussels. Here the French representative was the maréchal de Biron, now made a duke. According to Sully, it was on this occasion that Biron began making those advances which eventually led to his disgrace and death. [18]

(iv) 'Mon humeur mélancolique', June–December 1598

In June 1598 the king returned to Paris, which he did not leave for the rest of the year, except to visit his palaces at Fontainebleau, Montceaux and Saint-Germain. In Paris he fell back into the routine of pleasures and duties which would be his for the next ten years; playing tennis and hunting, but also meeting each day with his councillors and carrying out his religious duties, like touching for the King's Evil. At the end of September, tragedy struck the old Constable, Henri de Montmorency, when his young and beautiful wife died horribly of eclampsia, during an unsuccessful pregnancy. The king's letters on this occasion show his rare gifts as a writer; a quick letter of commiseration (28 September) was followed by another designed to rally Montmorency's spirits:

> You have some reason to indulge your pain, since even those whom it does not directly touch feel it, and sympathise with you. But if on the one hand it is painful, on the other hand age has brought you the long experience needed to put up with it, and you ought yourself to be able to console somebody else in the same position, keeping yourself yet to serve me and this state, without giving way to sadness, and so following rather the weakness of women and not of a man such as you should be and appear to be.

That is why, my old friend, I beg you, for the love both of me and of yourself, to console yourself that it was the will of God, to which we all must conform; it is my care for you which makes me speak in this way. If soon, to try to banish your sadness, you want to come and see me here with a few friends, please believe that you will be very welcome, and that I shall do my best to divert you. . . .[19]

Later that month, the king himself had a brush with death. It began at Montceaux on 11 October 1598, when he became very hot playing tennis, and that evening developed a high fever due to an inflammation of the bladder. For the previous twenty years he had been paying for his various amatory escapades by venereal infections,[20] but this one was exceptionally sharp and stubborn; as the king wrote to Sully, he had not had such a fever since his pleurisy at La Mothe-Fénelon in January 1589 (see above, Chapter 2, section viii). Eventually it left him, but towards the end of the month he had another attack of gonorrhoea, which gave rise to a temporary but alarming heart condition. He slowly emerged from this crisis in early November, but it had shaken him; writing again to Sully on 6 November, he remarked that it 'has made me very depressed [*tout chagrin*], and I do everything that my doctors recommend, so keen am I to get better'.[21]

The summer of 1598 was in fact the first occasion on which he was able to think of planning for the future, without immediate problems from the Spaniards, Leaguers and Protestants. Late in August, Claude Groulart, *premier président* of the Rouen *parlement* and a trusted friend, visited the king at court; Henry took him into the Louvre and showed him the great chamber and gallery which he was building. Groulart remarks in his *Mémoires* that there will be nothing like it in Italy, and that it will excel even the works of the Ancients;[22] this was surely excessive praise, but the king certainly did show his breadth of vision in turning so soon to the peaceful works which would fill his last decade.

Another preoccupation was the fortification of the frontiers. Towards the middle of October 1598, just before his illness, he called to court one of his chief engineers, Claude de Chastillon, who was to bring 'the plans of all my frontier towns, so that I can see where work is needed'.[23] Chastillon, who had been serving the king since 1580, first as *topographe du roi*,* and then after about 1591 as *ingénieur du roi*,* no doubt brought the plans on which he and his fellow-engineers were then working, and which were eventually combined with their maps to provide a renewed cartography of France.[24] As we shall see, this 1598 conference was the first of many, out of which a great work of frontier-fortification emerged.

(v) *'Partagés ma couronne'*, 1598–9

By the beginning of 1599 Henry's political position was relatively strong. But he was already 46 years old, and had no recognised heir. The obvious first step in correcting this weakness was to obtain an annulment of his marriage to Marguerite de Valois, whom he had not seen since 1582. Marguerite had seemed inclined to be helpful when he was inquiring about this in 1593–4,[25] but it was not until February 1599 that she actually agreed to refer the case to Rome.[26]

Meanwhile the king was more than ever infatuated with his delicious blonde, as somebody has called her. His closest friends hesitated to interrogate him about his intentions, but by the beginning of 1599 most were convinced that he was seeking his divorce in order to marry her. They would have been even more certain had they been able to read the poem he sent her about May 1598,[27] whose fourth verse begins:

> Partagés ma couronne
> Le prix de ma valeur. . . .

By the early spring of 1599 the matter was settled; according to the *premier président* of the Rouen *parlement*, 'the king meant to marry the Duchess about Quasimodo [which is the Sunday after Easter]'.[28] To Henry, the advantages seemed considerable; not only would he marry the woman he most (and most often) loved, but he would also be able to have her two sons legitimated, and so acquire instant heirs. Such were his fantasies. In fact, this arrangement would never have been approved by the Pope, and surely would have aroused such controversy among the French nobles that civil war might have followed Henry's death. All the same, during February and March preparations were going on in Paris for the impending ceremony and, on Mardi Gras, Henry put on Gabrielle's finger the diamond ring with which he had symbolically married France on the day of his anointing in 1593.

With Holy Week approaching, Henry and Gabrielle were at Fontainebleau; Gabrielle was well advanced in her fourth pregnancy. Partly as an exercise in propaganda, they decided that it would be better if they carried out their Holy Week devotions separately. So on Holy Tuesday they parted at Melun, the king returning to Fontainebleau and Gabrielle continuing by the Marne to Paris. She felt rather unwell that night, and on the Wednesday, after attending the service, was seized by frightful pains. However, these passed over and on Holy Thursday she was well enough to hear Mass at Saint-Germain-l'Auxerrois. That afternoon, though, she was suddenly racked by even more furious pains, and these hardly left her before her death on Holy Saturday. Then and afterwards, people said that she had been poisoned,[29] but she had in fact died of convulsions resulting from an aborted pregnancy. The young wife of the Constable had met the same frightful death the previous September.

Henry allowed himself to be dissuaded from hurrying to her bedside; in truth, he could have done nothing for her. Now for a short while he seemed grief-stricken, but this unfamiliar emotion soon left him, perhaps because to himself he half acknowledged that he had been spared from a political disaster. Most of his friends expressed nothing but heartfelt relief. The English agent Edmondes wrote to Cecil that this event 'is by all men acknowledged to be a spethiall favor of God towards him [the king]',[30] and a fortnight later he explained that there was general satisfaction,

> ... and the King himselfe doth freelie confesse it, that albeit her death is a great grief unto him, in regard that he did so dearlie love her, and intending as he acknowledgeth to have married her, but that God having directlie manifested that he would not suffer him to fall into the danger of so great an error and inconvenience to himselfe and to his state, that he will not faile to make his lesson thereof. . . .[31]

Poor Gabrielle was duly buried in style; the secret accounts show that 415 *écus* went on the 'linge de Madame la Duchesse', 421 *écus* on 'plomb acheté à Rouen pour ladite dame', and 6,000 *écus* pour les obseques et funerailles de ladite dame'.[32] Alas, the same accounts show how short-lived was Henry's grief, for quite soon afterwards 'Mademoiselle d'Entragues' received 50,000 *écus*, and towards the end of 1599 payments began to be made as well to 'Mademoiselle des Fossez'.[33]

Even by Henry's standards, he seems to have indulged in a remarkable bout of wenching after Gabrielle's death. Only a month later, the English ambassador Sir Henry Neville, arriving in Paris, found him 'in secret manner at Zamet's house',[34] where he was presumably being entertained by 'la belle garce Claude'.[35] The following June he began to chase Henriette d'Entragues in earnest; as Neville wrote early in August, 'the King rode post yesterday to Paris, upon no occasion but to see Mademoiselle d'Entragues'.[36] However, for a long time Henry was unable to do anything more than admire the new object of his desire, for Henriette and her relatives (like Gabrielle and hers) were very skilful at extracting the maximum possible advantage from the wilful king.

In October 1599, Henry was actually reduced to giving Henriette's father a written promise that if Henriette were allowed to become his 'compagne', and if she then became pregnant and bore a son within a certain time, then the king would take her as 'femme et legitime épouse'.[37] Of this arrangement Charles Merki, Henriette's biographer, remarks that Henry was 'médiocrement scrupuleux, dépourvu même de toute sens moral à certains égards', and it is hard to disagree with him. Shortly after this promise, the English ambassador was able to report to Cecil that 'the King hath now at length wonne the Fort at Malesherbes which he hath so long laid siege to; the conditions are 100,000 crowns in ready money and an yearly pension'.[38] Malesherbes (Loiret) was the site of the Entragues *château*; as we shall see, it now became a centre of intrigue against the king. Meanwhile he won various other forts, including those of Marie Babou de la Bourdaisière, Madame Quélin, who was the wife of a *conseiller*★ at the Paris *parlement*, and Isabelle Potier, wife of a *président* of the same court.

He was insatiable, but he had still not succeeded in siring a legitimate heir. In October 1599 the *parlement* of Paris deputed the sieur de La Guesle to seek audience with the king, and to beg him to marry some princess 'digne de la moitié de son lit'.[39] According to an undated English document of this period, 'there are named the sister of the king of Denmark and Poland, and two daughters of the house of Brandenburg, and Saxonie . . .'.[40] But Henry did not feel drawn towards these eastern princesses, in spite of the enthusiasm of the French Protestants for such a marriage; according to Sully, the king said that if he married a German princess he would feel as if he had a wine-barrel in bed with him.[41]

From as early as 25 April 1599 one of the candidates had been 'the princess Maria, niece of the Grand Duke of Tuscany'.[42] At first Henry's overtures were not warmly received in Florence, but he persisted in his suit, for Maria was very rich. The negotiations for the king's divorce, well advanced in February before Gabrielle's death, now went ahead fast, so that on 17 December the nullity of the 1572 marriage could be pronounced by the Archbishop of Arles. It was 'grounded upon these three pointes: that they were too neere of kynne, being in the third degree, and that the Queen's father Henri II was godfather unto the King, which is spirituall alliance, and that she was inforced to the match by her mother'.[43] By January 1600 the French and Florentine negotiators had agreed on the marriage contract, which was signed the following April. It consisted essentially of an enormous dowry of 600,000 *écus*, 250,000 of which were used to wipe off Henry's debt to the Grand Duke. Henry and Maria were formally married in Florence in October 1600, with the sieur de Belle-garde acting as proxy for the king. But in pursuing Henry's marital adventures we have run ahead of the rest of our story, and must now return to the end of 1599.

(vi) Savoy, December 1599–June 1600

One of the terms of the Treaty of Vervins had been that the marquisate of Saluzzo, seized by the Savoyards in 1588, would be the object of papal arbitration. But Clement VIII was not equal to the task of reconciling the two parties, and after some rather feeble efforts said that he would no longer meddle in that affair.[44] So towards the end of 1599 Charles-Emmanuel, Duke of Savoy, decided to take affairs into his own hands, and to come in person to negotiate with the French king.

Charles-Emmanuel set out from Chambéry about 1 December 1599, and after a formal reception at Lyon made his way to Roanne and thence to Orléans. On the way from there to Fontainebleau, he had a first meeting with the maréchal de Biron.[45] He arrived at Fontainebleau at eight o'clock in the morning, just as Henry was emerging from Mass with the intention of meeting the Duke on the road. This irregular manner of proceeding was characteristic of the Duke, who was not only a very cunning schemer but also very disorganised in his daily round, doing what he liked when he felt like it, without regard for protocol or, indeed, for other people.[46] He remained at Fontainebleau for six days, well entertained by the king. But people noticed that whenever the question of Saluzzo came up 'he replied in France just as if he had been in his citadel at Turin', affirming that he had not come to surrender the Marquisate.

On 21 December he came to Paris, where he would remain for the next ten weeks. During this time, the king went out of his way to impress the Duke with the grandeur of the French monarchy. On 2 January 1600, for instance, they went to Saint-Germain, to see the *château* and the fine houses in the neighbourhood. On 17 January they attended the *parlement* of Paris, where the leading barristers were pleading an interesting case.[47] According to Sully,[48] on 24 December they visited the Paris Arsenal, where Sully had established himself as *grand maître de l'artillerie** some weeks earlier. The Duke apparently asked to see the magazines, which were in fact empty; instead Sully took him to see the foundry and workshops, where forty or so cannon were being cast and mounted.

Meanwhile the Duke was busy with his own programme, giving out lavish presents on New Year's Day,[49] and using Jacques de La Fin (Biron's agent) to get into contact with various malcontents at the French court.[50] When the king came to discuss Saluzzo with him, the Duke took a high line, saying that rather than surrender the Marquisate he would 'make it the tombe of himselfe and all his Race'. So the matter was referred on 24 January to a council of eleven, consisting of five from each side, with Bonaventura da Caltagirone, patriarch of Constantinople, as mediator.[51] The going was slow, but on 27 February an agreement was signed which provided that the Duke would either surrender Saluzzo to Henry by 1 June or else at the same date cede to him Bresse and certain other territories.[52] So the Duke left Paris at the beginning of March, protesting his desire to observe the treaty. In fact, even before getting back to Savoy he sent emissaries to Brussels and to Madrid, claiming that the treaty was broken, and asking for help to defend Saluzzo.[53]

On 7 March, Henry wrote to his ambassador in Constantinople that since the Duke had 'pledged his faith we have no cause for contention, each of us being satisfied to hold what belongs to him'.[54] All the same, towards the end of the month he made plans, which he communicated to the Duke,[55] to go to Lyon during May, so as to be at hand when 1 June approached. The agreed date came and went without word from the Duke, so that, on 26 June, Sully was ordered to send the regiment of guards, some cavalry and his artillery to Lyon. On the same date even the pacific Villeroy was writing that he was not optimistic about the Duke's intention of keeping his word,[56] and by early July the king was convinced of the Duke's bad faith.[57] On 12 July, Henry reached Lyon and, on 14 July, Sully, who had been with the king there, went quickly back to Paris to put the final touches to his preparations.

Earlier in the year, following the Duke's visit to the Arsenal, contracts had been signed for the delivery of at least 63,000 cannon-balls, as well as large quantities of powder and accessories for the cannon.[58] Now, on 26 July, three watermen received contracts to transport 525 *milliers* of cannon, powder and shot from the Arsenal's quay on the Seine to Nogent-sur-Seine and Troyes.[59] Other contracts went to various *voituriers par terre*★ for the transport of this and other equipment, mostly to an assembly-point at Chalon-sur-Saône. At the same time, further artillery supplies were levied from Châlons-sur-Marne,[60] Grenoble, Lyon and Valence, so that by the middle of August fifty-seven guns, 500 *milliers* of powder and 30,000 cannon-balls were available in Lyon.[61] All this equipment was handled by about 2,000 *pionniers*,★[62] for whom levies were made during July around Paris, Chartres, Orléans and Lyon itself. Meanwhile the king had been attending to the recruiting of infantry and cavalry, so that by the beginning of August he had enough men to move against the Duke's forts.

(vii) Theological Interlude: 'Le sieur Duplessis sacrifié au Pape', April–May 1600

Before describing how the campaign went, we should relate a curious but significant event which took place in May 1599, when the king was still hoping that the Duke would observe the treaty agreed the previous April. It all began when Duplessis-Mornay, Henry's old but now somewhat estranged companion, published a work called the *Institution de la Sainte Eucharistie*,[63] in which he tried to show, using the writings of the Church Fathers, that the Protestant communion rite more closely resembled the original eucharist than did the Catholic one. This book was of course fiercely assailed by the Catholics, but Duplessis-Mornay at first replied that he did not intend to enter into a dispute with 'monks, Jesuits and other pedantic or insubordinate persons'.

Considering the weakness of his case, he would have done well to maintain this unreasoning but unassailable stance. However, about the middle of March 1600 some Protestant friends persuaded him that he ought to make some reply to his critics, and so on 20 March he issued a formal challenge to Jacques Davy du Perron, Bishop of Evreux, who had severely criticised his book. The matter now came before the king, who had been requested by Duplessis-Mornay to name *commissaires** before whom he would defend his book against Du Perron. Henry must have known that the Huguenot nobleman, though a notable amateur scholar, would be no match for the Catholic theologian, and that his old comrade-in-arms was risking a public humiliation. Nevertheless, he agreed to a confrontation, and on 10 April named six persons, three Protestant and three Catholic, to act as *commissaires*.

Du Perron arrived at Fontainebleau on 27 April 1600, and Duplessis-Mornay the next day. On 2 May the six *commissaires* arrived, and after some initial fencing the great debate was set for 4 May. Du Perron had sent Duplessis-Mornay a preliminary list of sixty passages which he alleged to be incorrect in one way or another, and the Huguenot chose nineteen of these to defend. So at one o'clock on the 4th the debate opened, with the king sitting at the end of a long table, Du Perron on his right and Duplessis-Mornay on his left, the *commissaires* down the right-hand side and the secretaries at the bottom. There were also some bishops, some princes, the secretaries of state, and about 200 spectators.

During the afternoon and early evening nine of the passages were examined, and in almost every case Duplessis-Mornay was found to be in error, even according to the judgement of the Protestant *commissaires*.[64] It was not so much a contest as an intellectual massacre, which came to an end about seven o'clock. The debate ought to have continued on the following day, but when the king's doctor, La Rivière, went to see Duplessis-Mornay he found that he was ill, vomiting and trembling uncontrollably. As this condition got no better, at the end of the day the proceedings were indefinitely deferred, and the *commissaires* dispersed. Duplessis-Mornay had indeed shown himself to be 'as bad a doctor [of theology] as he is a brave soldier', and had been totally vanquished. The king now sent the duc d'Epernon a letter which was also printed and widely disseminated;[65] in it he remarked that

the diocese of Evreux has beaten that of Saumur [where Duplessis-Mornay was governor], and the fairness of the proceedings is such that no Huguenot can say that anything but the truth prevailed. The present bearer was there, and will tell you how I achieved wonders. Certainly it is one of the greatest blows for the church of God which has been struck for a long time. . . .

Why the king chose thus to humiliate the man who had been at his right hand for so many years is a mystery, unless we admit that Henry could be singularly forgetful of past services when future advantages seemed to offer themselves. Perhaps, too, he was tired of the obstructive attitude shown by the Protestants since his conversion, and wished to give a striking demonstration of his new loyalties. At any rate, the so-called 'Fontainebleau conference' marks a decisive stage in Henry's personal and political move away from the reformers. Duplessis-Mornay returned sadly to Saumur, and Du Perron soon afterwards became a cardinal, giving rise to the following characteristic exchange between the king and Sully:

Henry: Well, what do you think now of your Pope [Duplessis-Mornay]?
Sully: I think, sire, that he is more of a pope than you realise. For do you not see that he has conferred a red [cardinal's] hat upon M. d'Evreux?[66]

(viii) 'Mon premyer metyer', August–December 1600

In describing the progress of the preparations against the Duke of Savoy, we left the king in Lyon towards the beginning of August 1600. Having spun affairs out until then, the Duke no doubt calculated that winter would come before Henry could mobilise his forces. However, this was to reason without the energy of Sully, who as we have seen had been furiously assembling guns, powder and shot since the beginning of July. Thus as soon as Henry declared war, on 11 August, his armies were ready to move. On the 13th a northern army under Biron took the town of Bourg,[67] and on the 14th a southern army under Lesdiguières captured the town of Montmélian;[68] in each case the citadel was invested. The king then passed on to Chambéry, taking the town on the 20th and the citadel on the 21st.[69] From there he moved north-east to Conflans, which fell on the 27th.[70] The Duke had barely had time to move any forces for the defence of these towns, and already on the 30th Henry was attacking Charbonnières, the key to Maurienne (for this campaign, see Map 15).

Charbonnières was a serious proposition; it was well gunned and provisioned, and situated on a steep rock commanding the valley of the Arc. However, the gunners directed by Sully had become expert in handling their heavy weapons. Using twenty pioneers for each gun

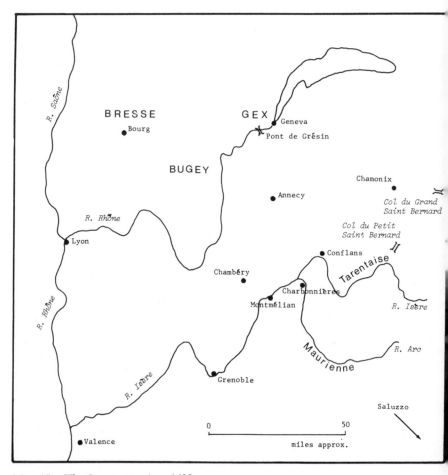

Map 15   *The Savoy campaign, 1600*

(instead of the usual six), they hoisted the great cannons and their equipment up a neighbouring hill, and after firing 600 rounds convinced the defenders that resistance was futile. Charbonnières capitulated on 10 September,[71] and Lesdiguières mopped up the remaining resistance in Maurienne and Tarentaise. By 16 September the king could write to Princess Maria of Tuscany that he had run out of enemy forces;[72] only the citadels of Bourg and Montmélian were still holding out by then.

Montmélian was another difficult proposition, on a strong site commanding the valley of the Isère about thirty miles north of Grenoble: 'a place in the estimation of men almost imprenable', as Ralph Winwood, secretary to the English ambassador, wrote to Neville on 5 September 1600.[73] However, here again the French artillery was fully equal to its task;

twenty cannon were soon in position in seven batteries, and after a brief bombardment the citadel agreed to a capitulation which took effect on 16 November.[74] Towards the end of October and during the first weeks of November, the Duke had organised a relief force which actually made contact with the most advanced royal troops, up by the Saint-Bernard pass, but he must have calculated that having lost all his strongpoints his case was hopeless, particularly with winter coming on; he did not attempt to press the offensive.

Meanwhile Henry moved northwards, to where the Duke's Fort Sainte-Catherine held the Protestant city of Geneva in check. Early in December the garrison of this stronghold surrendered, whereupon the fort was razed by Sully. From about the first week in October,[75] the king had had news of the imminent arrival of a papal emissary, Cardinal Pietro Aldobrandini, sent to negotiate peace between the two parties; negotiations began in Lyon about the turn of the year, and on 17 January 1601 a treaty was signed.[76] Henry gave up the marquisate of Saluzzo, but received instead not only Bresse, as agreed on 27 February 1600 (chapter 6, section vi) but also Bugey, Valromey and Gex, the last in lieu of an indemnity for the expenses of the war. The treaty was concluded after considerable arguments within Henry's council, for Villeroy and some others thought that it would have been better to have retained Saluzzo; Lesdiguières, indeed, remarked a little later that the Duke had made peace like a prince, while the king had made it like a merchant. According to Winwood, 'they which are almost all of what quallitie or condition soever, which more regard the honour of France than the proffit of the King's purse, doe terme it a shamefull and dishonourable treaty . . . '.[77] Sully, on the other hand, was in favour of the acquisition of Bresse and the other territories, which were four times as valuable in fiscal terms as Saluzzo (especially once Sully went to work on them) and usefully extended France's territories to the Rhône.[78]

Modern historians have been equally divided on the case. For Poirson, it was 'impossible to bring the struggle to an end more gloriously or more advantageously'.[79] For Nouaillac and Rott,[80] however, the loss of Saluzzo was a fatal blunder, which effectively deprived France of the possibility of counterbalancing Spain in the affairs of northern Italy. Henry regarded the treaty as 'ceste rhubarbe au cœur savoyard',[81] but the haste with which the Spaniards obliged the Duke to ratify it suggests that Philip III and his councillors were not displeased by it.[82] One point about the treaty merits close attention, and that is the first clause, by which the Duke resigned his rights to the *pont de Grésin* (see Map 15). This bridge and adjacent corridor, passing through what was now French territory, were part of the vital Spanish passage from northern Italy to the Netherlands, the 'Spanish road'.[83] From now on, the French could cut it almost at will, which is why the Spaniards eventually sought another passage north, through the

Grisons, the area which would come into such prominence under Richelieu.

(ix) 'Quelque princesse digne de la moitié de son lict', October 1600–January 1601

While Henry was waging war against the Duke, he was also co-ordinating the arrangements for his marriage with Maria de Medici. As we have seen, the formal union had taken place in Florence in October 1600, with the sieur de Bellegarde acting for the king. From the end of May 1600 onwards, Henry had been writing letters at roughly fortnightly intervals to his future wife, assuring her of his devotion; he kept up this correspondence even during the problems and diversions of the Savoy campaign.

Alas, he also maintained his liaison with Mademoiselle d'Entragues, who in the spring of 1600 became marquise de Verneuil. So, after assuring Maria on 30 September that he wished to kiss her lovely mouth 'cent mille fois', on 11 October he wrote two similarly loving letters to the marquise, ending the second with the phrase, 'je te baise et rebaise un million de fois'.[84] Meanwhile Maria was setting out on her journey. She embarked at Livorno (Leghorn) on 19 October, travelling in a splendidly decorated galley belonging to the Grand Duke. This galley was escorted by five papal ones, five from Malta and six others belonging to the Grand Duke, for the king of France had no naval forces worth mentioning, and the Turks were very active even in the northern Mediterranean.[85]

The squadron reached Marseille on 3 November 1600, and late that afternoon Maria disembarked, to a splendid reception and address by Guillaume du Vair, humanist and *premier président* of the *parlement* of Provence.[86] Some days were spent recovering from what had been a stormy voyage, and then, on 17 November, Marie (as we now may call her) and her suite went to Aix. Her reception there was described in this way by Winwood:

> There she was solemnly received by the court of Parlament. In the middle of the High Street there was erected an Arch Triumphant, wherein were painted the conquests of Savoy, and under was written *Sabaudia redacta*; there was the picture of the King on horseback triumphing over a centaure reversed presenting up a crown, with this word, *opportune*.[87]

A few days earlier Winwood had sent back a judicious account of how Marie struck observers: 'she is of a comely stature, and for her beauty, the commendation which she seemeth most to affect (for she doth use no Artifice) is to be *forma uxoria*'.[88] From Aix she progressed on 19 November to Avignon, where there was another splendid reception, with seven triumphal arches echoing many other Avignon 'sevens'; the symbolism was designed to show that seven was a propitious number for Henry as well as for Avignon.[89] On 3 December she entered Lyon, where there were still more splendid processions and ceremonies, with '. . . the streets carpeted, the main squares embellished with arches, porticoes and pyramids, and a great green canopy over the middle of the bridge over the Saône, with niches containing twelve statues of princes of the house of Medici'.[90]

Meanwhile the king was finishing off his business in Savoy, and on the evening of 9 December came incognito to Lyon, where he found the queen at supper. He observed her for a while, and then when she retired to her chamber went to find her:

> She met him at the door, and offered to kneel down, but he took her in his arms, where he held her embraced a long time. . . . He doth profess to the World the great Contentment he finds in her, how that for her Beauty, her sweet and pleasing carriage, her gracious behaviour, she doth surpass the Relation which hath been made of her, and the Expectation which he thereby conceived.[91]

On the 16th, legate Aldobrandini came to Lyon, and presided over the conclusion of the treaty; there was also a further marriage ceremony, very splendidly conducted.[92] In the latter part of January 1601 the royal pair left for Paris; he went swiftly ahead, and the queen followed more slowly, entering the capital on 7 February. The previous day he had written to Montmorency to say that the queen was pregnant;[93] she lodged the first few nights at the house of Jérôme de Gondi, the next with Zamet, and on the 15th moved into the Louvre.[94] This she found so delapidated that she at first thought Henry must be making fun of her, but on the 17th he took her to Fontainebleau and Saint-Germain, so that she could appreciate 'the magnificence of these truly royal houses'.

Henry had greatly improved his position during 1600. The kingdom was at last fully under his control, with the last foreigners ousted from its soil. The religious quarrels had been calmed by the widespread acceptance of the Edict of Nantes, and for the time being there seemed to be no plots among the great nobles. Most important of all, the question of his marriage had been settled, and it looked as if that of the succession might soon be solved. One way and another, at the end of 1600 Henry was entering on a new and more settled phase of his life.

7 'The Hercules That Now Reigns', 1600

(i) The King's View of France

At the end of 1600 the king celebrated his forty-seventh birthday. Thirty years of constant exertion had transformed the smooth youth of Plate 3 into a rather care-worn man. And yet he remained lively and vivacious, with a light step and a quick mind. As the English observer Robert Dallington put it: 'this king . . . is about 48 years of age, his stature small, his haire almost all white, or rather grisled, his colour fresh and youthful, his nature stirring and full of life, like a true French man'.[1] He made a good recovery from the various illnesses of 1598, and remained relatively free from further venereal and pulmonary complications. His teeth continued to torture him, as they long had done, and he had to use glasses for reading, but he seems otherwise to have suffered from nothing worse than severe colds, before his gout began about 1602. He also had frequent bouts of indigestion, but these were inevitable, given his amazing eating habits, which included gorges of melons and oysters.[2]

This was just one aspect of his tumultuous nature, which had to express itself in constant, preferably violent action: hunting during the day, gambling in the evening, and wenching at night. Unlike his father, he had absolutely no vanity concerning his appearance, and used to appear at court in clothes which were decidedly the worse for wear; dirty, tattered and holed.[3] This carelessness extended to other areas, and he became famous for his strong smell, which Marie de Medici did her best to blot out by the lavish use of perfume.

These undomesticated habits were no doubt the result of his long years in the saddle and in the field. But, if they had given him a rather uncouth appearance and smell, they had also equipped him with an unrivalled knowledge of his kingdom. As Map 16 shows, there was hardly an area of France in which he had not made long stays, in the course of the wars, and this gave his economic projects and political manœuvres a rare authority and practicality.

When he thought about his kingdom, he no doubt used the geographical framework with which we are familiar, for quite accurate maps had been printed from the middle of the sixteenth century onwards, and during Henry's reign very detailed and accurate ones were produced for military use. But his concept of the realm would have been a very unquantitative one; he thought not in terms of resources and production figures, but

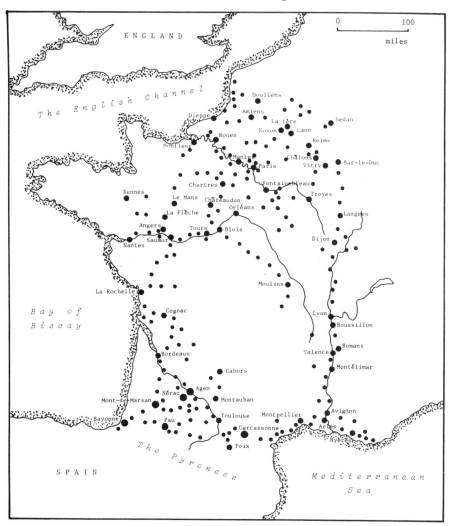

Map 16   *Henry's travels in France before 1600. This is a map which minimizes the evidence, in the sense that it notes only identifiable places where Henry spent at least one night (●), or more than five (⬤), and wrote letters which have been preserved in the* Lettres Missives. *A fuller map would be more complex, but would probably indicate much the same coverage.*

Source: the 'séjours et itinéraires' in Lettres Missives.

in terms of people, most of whom he knew well. In Normandy, for instance, one of his main contacts was Claude Groulart (1551–1607), *premier président* of the *parlement* in Rouen since 1585. This magistrate visited the king at court almost every year between 1590 and 1604, and enjoyed Henry's particular trust. Groulart described these visits in some detail in his 'voyages par lui faits en cour', which are a precious source for the king's views on a variety of subjects;[4] back in Normandy, he used his extensive influence in Henry's cause. The governor of the province was Henri de Bourbon, duc de Montpensier (1573–1608); he had fought both for Henri III and for Henry IV, but without great distinction. Normandy contained the two considerable ports of Le Havre and Dieppe, whose governors were respectively Georges de Brancas, sieur de Villars, and Aymar de Chaste. Georges de Brancas and his more famous brother André had been leading members of the League in Normandy, but having come over to Henry served him loyally; André, indeed, was killed in his service at Doullens in 1595. Aymar de Chaste had welcomed Henry to Dieppe at the time of the Arques campaign, in 1589, and continued to provide a centre for royalist forces there. As we shall see, he was also involved in colonial ventures in North America. He died about 1603, and was succeeded as governor by Charles Timoléon de Beauxoncles, sieur de Sigogne (c.1560–1611). The latter had been an ardent Leaguer, but after being captured at Ivry by Sully came over to the king, and served him in his amorous intrigues, particularly with the marquise de Verneuil; he also wrote bad verse.

To the west of Normandy lay Brittany, a province which had been the last to acknowledge Henry's rule. With Mercœur banished after 1598, the governorship fell into a kind of interregnum, theoretically filled by César de Bourbon, duc de Vendôme, son of Henry and Gabrielle. When the king wanted news of Brittany he wrote to the governor of Brest, René de Rieux, sieur de Sourdéac (1558–1628), who was one of the few members of the Breton nobility not to have supported the League. Sourdéac was particularly concerned with attempts to organise an Atlantic fleet. In the very south of the province was Nantes, in the charge of Hercule de Rohan, duc de Montbazon (1568–1654), who was often at court and had a reputation for stupidity.[5]

Angers, the next large town up the Loire, had for its governor Guillaume Fouquet, sieur de La Varenne (1560–1616), who had distinguished himself at Fontaine-Française and in other battles. The king was particularly fond of him, often saw him at court, and made him *contrôleur-général des postes de France*★ in 1594.[6] Just upstream from Angers was Saumur, governed since 1589 by the redoubtable Duplessis-Mornay. Saumur was the northernmost protestant town of any significance, and even after the lamentable controversy of 1600 (above, Chapter 6, section vii) Duplessis-Mornay remained on quite good terms with the king, who used him as one of his chief intermediaries with the Protestants. Further still up the Loire was Orléans, commanded by Claude de la Châtre. He had been one of the League's leading generals, but after surrendering Orléans and Bourges in 1594 (for a large sum; see Chapter 4, section iv) had become a loyal subject of Henry.

To the south of the Loire lay the turbulent province of Poitou, for many years a lively theatre of warfare and still a seed-bed for all kinds of plots. In 1600 its governor was Jean de Chourses, sieur de Malicorne, but in 1606 he was replaced by Sully, better able to survey and control the discontented Protestant nobles. Apart from Bordeaux and La Rochelle, the main Atlantic ports were Blaye, Brouage and Bayonne. At Blaye the governor was Jean-Paul d'Esparbez, sieur de Lussan, captain of the Scottish guards, who was often on duty with the king. Brouage was guarded by Timoléon d'Espinay, sieur de Saint-Luc; he was an old companion-in-arms of the king, and responsible for privateers operating off the mouth of the Gironde. At Bayonne the governor was Antoine de Grammont, another old friend of the king; he, too, directed privateers preying on Spanish vessels in the Bay of Biscay, and in general watched France's south-western frontier.

The lieutenant-governor of Guyenne was Alphonse d'Ornano (1547–1610), who had been among the first to rally to Henry in 1589, and had been made *maréchal de France* in 1596. Ornano had the difficult task of keeping an eye on the numerous and discontented Protestant nobles of Guyenne; he was by nature rather quarrelsome, and did not enjoy the king's full confidence. His counterpart in Navarre was Jacques Nompar de Caumont, sieur de La Force (1558–1652).[7] He had been with Henry in Paris at the time of the Massacre of Saint Bartholomew, and having escaped on that occasion had served the king ever since. In 1593 he was appointed governor of Béarn and viceroy of Navarre, but much of his time was spent at court, since in 1592 he had become one of the four *capitaines des gardes*.* His role in the south-west was essentially to guard the land frontier with Spain, and to direct covert French activity across the Pyrenees.

In Languedoc the governor was Henri, duc de Montmorency (1534–1614). He had held that post since 1562, and had been *maréchal de France* since 1566. Henry appointed him *connétable* in 1593, and frequently consulted him over military matters. The Languedoc *parlement* sat in Toulouse, and its *prémier president* after 1602 was Nicolas de Verdun. He was not so closely associated with the king as Groulart of Rouen, but he did make frequent reports to him on the state of the province.[8] Across the Rhône, in Provence, his counterpart was the celebrated Guillaume du Vair, who had played a prominent part in the Suresnes conference of 1593, and now maintained a constant correspondence with the king concerning political affairs in the province. Du Vair was an outstanding humanist, and a great friend of the poet Malherbe. The governor of Provence, who worked closely with Du Vair, was young Charles de Lorraine, duc de Guise; he was also *amiral des mers du Levant*.* After making his peace with the king in 1594, he had served him very faithfully, and in the early seventeenth century was largely responsible for the French Mediterranean fleet, based on Toulon.

To the north, in Dauphiné, the governor was the redoubtable François de Bonne, duc de Lesdiguières (1543–1626). He had played a leading part in consolidating Protestant power there during the religious wars, and was now responsible for guarding the Alpine passes against the Duke of Savoy. At Grenoble he held almost independent sway, and was building himself a splendid *château* at Vizille, a few miles to the south of the town. North again of Dauphiné lay the provinces of Burgundy and Bresse, which in 1600 were governed by the maréchal de Biron. He had served the king well in the 1590s but, as we shall see, had to be removed and executed in 1602 for plotting with the Spaniards. He was then replaced by Roger de Saint-Lary, sieur de Bellegarde, who had been one of Henri III's favourites and remained high in the favour of his successor. His task as lieutenant-governor of Burgundy was to guard the eastern frontier, and in particular to monitor the passage of Spanish troops along the route between Italy and the Netherlands – the 'Spanish road'. A key town in this sensitive area was Langres, whose mayor, Jean Roussat, often corresponded with the king.[9] The *premier président* of the *parlement* in Dijon was Denis Brûlart, a former Leaguer in whom Henry had little confidence; he relied instead on Pierre Jeannin, who was often consulted by the king, and spent much time on diplomatic missions.

In Champagne the governor in 1600 was Louis de Gonzague, duc de Nevers; he, too, had as his chief task the protection of the eastern frontier. This was not very well defined, but consisted essentially of a series of strongholds like Saint-Dizier, Vitry-le-François, Troyes and Châlons-sur-Marne. In each of these towns Henry had a reliable governor; in Troyes, for instance, he was Charles de Choiseul, sieur de Praslin, one of the king's four guard-commanders. To the north, in Picardy, the fortresses were more numerous yet, following the dangerous westward curve of the frontier from Rocroi to Doullens (see Map 17). On the northern end of the line was Calais, governed by Dominique de Vic, who had been prominent in the king's campaigns of the early 1590s. The key town of Doullens was held by Charles de Rambures, who had been wounded both at Ivry and at the siege of Amiens, and was known as 'Rambures the brave'. Anchoring the southern end of the line was Saint-Quentin, whose governor was Eustache de Conflans, sieur d'Auchy, nicknamed 'la grande barbe'. In charge of Picardy itself was François d'Orléans, comte de Saint-Pol, who had come over to Henry after his accession, but proved to be a rather uncertain governor.[10]

So we come back to the Channel coast. Of course, Henry's own view of France and her constitutional structure was enormously more complex than the one we have sketched in. He had to know where the most refractory nobles were, and how to curb them. He had to keep in touch with the moderate Protestants, so as to learn about the activities of the

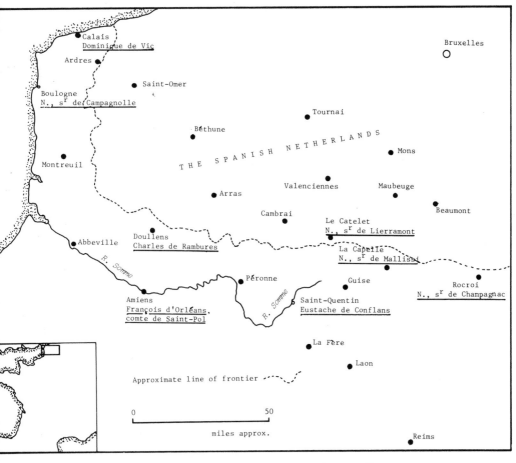

Calais
Dominique de Vic
Ardres

Saint-Omer

Boulogne
N., s^r de Campagnolle

Béthune

THE SPANISH NETHERLANDS

Tournai

Mons

Montreuil

Arras

Valenciennes

Maubeuge

Beaumont

Cambrai

Le Catelet
N., s^r de Lierramont

Abbeville

Doullens
Charles de Rambures

La Capelle
N., s^r de Mallisui

R. Somme

Péronne

Guise

Rocroi
N., s^r de Champagnac

Amiens
François d'Orléans,
comte de Saint-Pol

R. Somme

Saint-Quentin
Eustache de Conflans

La Fère

Laon

Approximate line of frontier

0   50

miles approx.

Bruxelles

Reims

Map 17   *The fortifications and governors of north-eastern France*

wild men. He had to watch all the towns, for many of them had during the wars developed aspirations towards independence. He had to send his representatives to the meetings of the provincial estates,★ so as to make sure that they voted at least part of what he had requested. Finally, he had to direct as far as possible the proceedings of the *parlements*, using his friends among the *premiers présidents*. In short, he had to be like a spider at the centre of his web, constantly surveying the distant fringes, and ready if necessary to rush out in person to resolve a problem.

(ii) The King's Household

At court he was served by a large number of *officiers domestiques*, amounting in all to about 1500 people, without counting the guards. The best way to describe this massive household is by adopting the order of contemporary documents.[11] In the first group come 400 or so ecclesiastics, headed until 1607 by the *grand aumônier* Renaud de Beaune, and after that by Jacques Davy du Perron. Among the 300 or so *aumôniers sans gages*★ we find nearly all the French bishops, normally resident in their dioceses. Roughly twenty-five chaplains looked after the royal chapel, and until 1608 the king's confessor was René Benoist, so prominent at the time of his conversion; after Benoist's death the office was held by the Jesuit Père Coton.

After the ecclesiastics comes a smaller group, mostly nobles concerned with the immediate running of affairs around the king. The *grand maître* was Charles de Bourbon, comte de Soissons; he was in charge of the whole household. The *grand chambellan* was Mayenne until 1600, and after that his son the duc d'Aiguillon. The two *premiers gentilhommes* were Roger de Saint-Lary, sieur de Bellegarde, and Henri de La Tour, duc de Bouillon. Bellegarde, who was also *grand écuyer*, long remained a boon companion, but Bouillon, as we shall see, quarrelled with the king and left his court. The *maître de la garderobe*★ was Antoine de Roquelaure, a former Protestant companion-in-arms, and the *premier maître d'hôtel*★ was first Nicholas de Harlay, sieur de Sancy (1594–6), and then Robert de Harlay, sieur de Montglat (1596–1607). These, together with Guillaume Fouquet, sieur de La Varenne (who was first *huissier du cabinet* and then *portemanteau ordinaire*), were the men closest to the king in his everday round; what an English report calls 'les compagnons du roy'.[12]

Another group of nobles saw to his ceremonial needs (the *premier pannetier*,★ *premier tranchant*★ and so forth), and after them came a large group of *secrétaires*, numbering about 240. Heading these were the seven *secrétaires de la chambre*, among whom we find the four *secrétaires d'état*, whose functions we shall analyse later on. Then came five *secrétaires du cabinet*, including the enigmatic Raymond de Viçose, who seems to have enjoyed the king's particular confidence (see Chapter 11, section vi).

Among the *autres secrétaires* and *secrétaires sans gages* we find many of the most important functionaries of the various fiscal sub-units: Florent d'Argouges, *trésorier-général des gabelles*,★ François Hotman, *trésorier de l'épargne*,★ Gilles Maupeou, *intendant des finances*,★ Michel Sublet, *trésorier des parties casuelles*★ and so on. Finally in this section come the *secrétaires interprètes*, of whom Jacques Bongars became a distinguished ambassador to the German princes.

In the next major group were the doctors, numbering eighty or so. Until 1594 the *premier médecin* was Jehan d'Ailleboust, or d'Alibour, who had accompanied the king at the siege of Paris (1590). After his death the post was held by Jehan Ribit, sieur de La Rivière, who had been prominent in the examination in 1599 of the supposed sorceress Marthe Brossier,[13] and who treated Duplessis-Mornay when he fell ill during the Fontainebleau conference with Du Perron. When La Rivière died, in 1606, he was succeeded by André du Laurens (1558–1606), who had been a professor at Montpellier as a young man, and had assisted La Rivière in the Marthe Brossier affair. He was a prolific author, and his *Discours de la conservation de la veue* ... (Paris, 1597) in particular was often reprinted. Du Laurens and La Rivière were very close to the king, and the former apparently used to read to him when he had insomnia.[14] There were some interesting characters among the 'autres médecins'. Jehan Héroard, for instance, became physician to the dauphin and left a *Journal* concerning his upbringing which is a treasury of information about the rearing of children at that time.[15]

Théodore Turquet, sieur de Mayerne (1573–1655) also wrote a good deal, concerning not only the practice of medicine but also the reunion of the churches.[16] Michel Marescot wrote a *Discours véritable sur le fait de Marthe Brossier* (Paris, 1599), which has often been used by scholars investigating medical attitudes towards sorcery. Henry thus had an abundance of general physicians; there were also several specialists. Claude Charpentier, for instance, was his *opérateur oculiste*, Jehan Robin his *herboriste* (he wrote *Le Jardin du roy très-chrétien Henri IV* in 1608), and Séverin Pineau his *opérateur pour la pierre*.[17] Like all doctors, these ones no doubt sometimes did more harm than good to their patients, but their combined efforts provided something like a health service at the court, from which they were often detached when great nobles and ministers, or their wives or children, required attention.

After the doctors came a group of thirty or so officers concerned with ensuring that the court ran smoothly during its frequent travels. These were the *mareschaux des logis*,★ of whom the most prominent was Pierre Fougeu, sieur d'Escures. He had a wide variety of responsibilities, for he was also *intendant des turcies et levées sur les rivières de Loire et Cher*,★ responsible for floodworks on those rivers, and *lieutenant du grand voyer*★ in the generalities of Moulins and Orléans,[18] a task which chiefly involved looking after the many bridges in that area. The king seems to have used him as well in delicate negotiations like the ones leading to the arrest of Biron (1602) and Auvergne (1604); he eventually became *maréchal-général des camps et armées du roi.*★ He had a house in the Place Royale, where the dauphin visited him informally in April 1610;[19] clearly he enjoyed the king's special confidence.

There were of course a large number of court servants concerned with particular aspects of the king's comfort: *coureurs de vin, paticiers, lavandières, parfumeurs* and so forth. There was a 'plumassière ordinaire', who at least once supplied the king with 'quatre grands pannaches touts blancz'.[20] Among these servants were some who became celebrated in their own right: the riding master, Antoine de Pluvinel, for instance, who wrote a widely used treatise on the handling of horses; or the gunsmith, Marin Bourgeois, who invented an air-gun and built sporting flintlocks for the king;[21] or the *tailleurs* Isaac and Barthélemy Laffemas, who as we shall see won fame far beyond their tailoring circles.

There was also a final group concerned with what we might call cultural affairs. Heading these was the *maître de la librairie*, who from 1593 onwards was Jacques-Auguste de Thou (1553–1617), author of the great *Histoire universelle* and one of those Catholics who had most helped the king in the difficult years after 1589. Traveller, diplomat, humanist and lawyer, Thou played a part in almost all the important events of the 1590s, including especially the conference at Suresnes and the negotiations leading to the Edict of Nantes. After him come the *tapissiers*, concerned with preserving and hanging the great tapestries which accompanied the king in his travels; the families of Herbannes and Gaboury monopolised these posts. Among the *peintres et gens de mestier* were the painters Martin Fréminet, Martin Foullon and Claude Douet; we shall describe their work on the royal palaces later on. With them were grouped the sculptors Mathieu Jacquet, Barthélemy Prieur and Pierre Biard, and also the *graveur* Philippe Danfrie. Eventually, once the building was ready, most of these artists were actually accommodated by the king in the *grande galerie du Louvre*, as we shall see.

Of course, not all of these officers were at court all the time. Many of the ecclesiastics and financial officials were at their posts in the provinces, and a good many of the others served only one out of the four quarters of the year. Even so, the royal court at any given time offered a rich concentration of varied talents, particularly in medicine and the arts. We shall see how, in the years after 1600, the king used these talents.

(iii)   The Great Officers and Their Charges

In medieval times, the 'great officers of the Crown' had all been household officers: the Chancellor responsible for the dissemination of laws, the

Constable for the good running of the stables, the *grand maître* for the organisation of the household, the *grand écuyer* for the hunt, and the *chambellan* for the affairs of the bedchamber. As we have seen, the last three offices continued to exist within the household. But those of the Chancellor and Constable had grown into much wider functions. The Chancellor by 1600 was responsible for overseeing the whole judicial system in France; since 1599 the office had been held by Pomponne de Bellièvre, succeeded in 1607 by Brûlart de Sillery. The Constable was the duc de Montmorency, and he was responsible for everything to do with military affairs. In 1601, Henry raised the office of *grand maître de l'artillerie* to the rank of 'great office of the Crown'; this continued to be occupied by Sully.

The Chancellor, Constable and *grand maître de l'artillerie* – Bellièvre, Montmorency and Sully – were three of the leading members of the king's highest and most informal council, the *conseil des affaires*. The fourth member was Villeroy, who was one of four secretaries of state. This was an office which had emerged during the sixteenth century, and by 1600 had taken on something like its definitive shape.[22] Villeroy was the secretary responsible for foreign affairs and war; other functions were divided among the three other secretaries: Martin Ruzé, sieur de Beaulieu (royal household), Pierre Forget, sieur de Fresnes (Protestants and the south-western provinces), and Louis Potier, sieur de Gesvres (the western area). While Villeroy was normally present in his own right at the *conseil des affaires*, the other secretaries were called only when affairs in their area of competence were being discussed. After the necessary letters or instructions had been written, it was the duty of the appropriate secretary to sign under the 'signature' of the king, which might in fact have been executed by one of the *secrétaires de la main*.

Of course, there were ideological and personal differences among the members of the *conseil des affaires*. On the whole, Sully stood for the authoritarian, centralising approach to problems, while Bellièvre, supported by Villeroy, believed that 'one must act gently and after due thought'[23] – and, it might be added, through the time-honoured institutions rather than through novel agents of the central power. The king held the balance between these views, though after 1605, when Bellièvre retired, Sully's intemperate policies increasingly prevailed. The *conseil des affaires* usually met every day, and often deliberated as the king walked about; its sessions were frequently ambulant. Once it was over, each of its members would have to implement its decisions in his own realm.

Chancellor Bellièvre, for instance, would return to his chancery, where he would attend to the promulgation of the necessary edicts, validating them with his seal. The edicts would then be sent to the *parlement* of Paris and to the provincial *parlements* for verification and registration. Sometimes the *parlement* would raise objections or suggest amendments, but once the edict had been formally approved it would be promulgated and enforced in the jurisdiction of the *parlement* in question. Occasionally this routine judicial procedure needed supplementing, when an edict was encountering resistance in the provinces, or when there was discontent of some kind. Then special *commissaires* might be appointed, often with the title of *intendant de justice*.★ In 1598, for instance, after the promulgation of the Edict of Nantes, special *commissaires de l'édit* were sent out to supervise its application in the provinces. In 1604, as we shall see below, there was an edict banning commerce with Spain; it met with much resistance in the south-west, and Etienne de La Fond was sent down there to enforce it. But these were special occasions, and most legislation simply passed through the *parlement* for its verification and enforcement.

After the *conseil des affaires*, Sully would normally return to his base at the Paris Arsenal. His responsibilities were very complex, for he eventually held five key posts as: (1) *surintendant des finances*, from about 1599; (2) *grand voyer*, from 1599; (3) *grand maître de l'artillerie*, from 1599; (4) *surintendant des bâtiments*, from 1600; (5) *surintendant des fortifications*, from 1600. The first of these posts was crucial to all the rest, for as *surintendant des finances* he was responsible for all collection and disbursement of royal funds.[24] He inherited a relatively coherent and well-understood fiscal structure, operating in much of France (though not, generally, in the ancient frontier provinces) through the fifteen *bureaux des finances* and their attendant *trésoriers de France*. At the Arsenal, he was building up a central secretariat – something very new – which, working through these *bureaux*, succeeded in making the old methods work much more efficiently, so that there was eventually a yearly surplus and a growing treasure laid up in the Bastille. However, the *bureaux* did not cover the whole of France, being generally absent from provinces which still held their own provincial estates; thus large areas tended to escape Sully's full attention.

As *grand voyer* he was responsible for all roads, bridges and canals in France, and soon set up an organisation whereby he had fifteen *lieutenants* in the key areas, who identified projects, gave contracts and supervised the work according to strict rules. He established much the same kind of organisation to carry on the work of the *grand maître de l'artillerie*; here again he appointed *lieutenants*, to the number of fifteen or sixteen, who in the provincial arsenals got on with the same work as that undertaken in Paris: founding cannon, ordering powder and shot, training gunners and so on (Plate 11). His work as *surintendant des bâtiments* was less exacting, consisting of the direction of all works on the royal palaces. Here he introduced the same methods of identifying projects and giving contracts as applied to the work of the *grand voyer*. Finally, as *surintendant des fortifications* he was responsible for the strengthening of France's frontiers; here again he introduced a provincial sub-structure, in which the essential elements were the *ingénieurs du roi*,[25] whose task was to collaborate with the provincial governor in organising work on fortifications, and to send back to the king frequent reports, accompanied with maps, on the state of the works.

Constable Montmorency attended the *conseil des affaires* much less often than Bellièvre or Sully; normally only in time of war or rumour of war. As we saw in discussing the French forces at the siege of Amiens in 1597, most of his troops were levied only when hostilities had broken out. The five main infantry regiments – Guards, Picardie, Piedmont, Champagne and Navarre – retained only skeleton cadres in time of peace, and almost all the cavalry returned to their normal occupations on their estates. As a bodyguard the king retained about 1,400 soldiers, organised in four companies and clad in the royal uniform of blue, white and red. The quarterly commanders of these guards were highly trusted and prominent men. First was the sieur de La Force, whom we have already met as governor of Navarre. Towards the end of the reign he often complained to his wife about having to spend three months every year up in Paris, but he served on until 1610. Then there were Charles de Choiseul, sieur de Praslin, who was governor of Troyes; Louis de l'Hôpital, sieur de Vitry, governor of Meaux; and Joachim de Châteauvieux, who was also captain of the Scottish guard. As we shall see, these guard-commanders played crucial roles at such times as the arrest of Biron or the flight of Louise de Montmorency.

The fourth member of the *conseil des affaires* was Villeroy, 'dean in chapter of all the statesmen in Christendom', as the English ambassador Carew called him.[26] Villeroy had become *secrétaire des finances* in 1559, on the eve of the wars of religion, and had been appointed secretary of state in 1567. He thus had an unrivalled knowledge of the workings of the government, both at home and abroad; during the reign of Henry he became in effect minister of foreign affairs. In this capacity he maintained a constant correspondence with the French ambassadors at foreign courts, roughly nine in number.

The ambassador to the English court in 1600 was Jean-Robert de Thumery, sieur de Boissize, whom we encountered with the *Croquants* in 1594.[27] The routine business of his mission involved endless complaints to Queen Elizabeth about English pirates, and a perpetual delaying action to avoid the English requests for the repayment of sums borrowed by Henry during the 1590s. The queen had been very displeased when France made peace with Spain at Vervins in 1598, and continued to urge on France the desirability of weakening Spain – by aiding the rebels in the Low Countries, for instance.

In Amsterdam, French affairs had for some time been in the hands of Paul Choart, sieur de Buzenval (1551–1607), who was a Protestant and an old councillor of Navarre. The Dutch had been as displeased as the English by the conclusion of the Treaty of Vervins, but Buzenval and Henry, as we shall see, found ways to continue French support to them. Towards the end of the reign this support waned, as the inherent rivalry between France and Holland in commercial affairs began to become more apparent.

In the southern, Spanish, Netherlands there had of course been no ambassador until the Treaty of Vervins, and the position was now held by Antoine Le Fèvre, sieur de La Boderie. His task was to explain away the various French infractions of that treaty, which Henry committed by continuing to send aid to the Dutch. The 'archdukes', Albert and Isabella, were not entirely free agents, but had more or less to follow the line set down by Madrid. In that capital, too, there was a French ambassador after April 1600: Antoine de Silly, sieur de La Rochepot. He seems to have had a difficult time at a court where only the papal nuncio and the Venetian ambassador showed him any friendship, and in a country whose inhabitants sometimes went so far as to attack members of his staff.[28] But he stuck to his job of informing Henry about Spanish affairs, and succeeded in persuading Philip III to ratify the Treaty of Vervins. However, the new king (1598–1621) proved no more friendly towards France than his father, Philip II.

The chief French diplomat at the courts of the German princes was Jacques Bongars (1554–1612), a Huguenot who had been in Henry's service since at least 1586. Bongars had to deal with the inquiries of creditors like the Duke of Würtemberg, the Prince of Anhalt, and the Elector Palatine. He also eventually worked towards the formation of a new league of Protestant princes.[29] His counterpart down in Vienna was the sieur de Baugy, who kept Henry informed about developments in the Holy Roman Empire, and tried to give the king good advice about his chances of succeeding to that dignity.

In Switzerland, so important both as a part of Spain's route to the north and as a source of mercenary soldiers, the chief French agent in 1600 was Méry de Vic. His chief task was to retain the friendship of as many cantons as possible, so that their soldiers would enter French pay if required. It was also in his time that the struggle began for the control of the Valtelline, that pass which was to play so important a part in French foreign policy in the time of Richelieu.[30]

South of the Alps, Henry retained permanent representatives in Venice and in Rome. In the Serene Republic his ambassador from 1601 was Philippe de Canaye, sieur de Fresnes, and in the Holy See from the same date it was Philippe de Béthune, Catholic brother of Sully. From Venice,

Fresnes advised the king about affairs in the whole of north Italy, including the Spanish Milanese, and also sent him news coming from the eastern Mediterranean. In Rome, Béthune found French influence at a low ebb, and began building up again in the College of Cardinals a party which would be favourable to French interests.[31]

The other ambassador with whom Villeroy maintained a constant correspondence was François Savary, sieur de Brèves, in Constantinople. Brèves was in constant rivalry and even conflict at the Porte with the English ambassador there, Henry Lello. Each sought to become the protector of the Dutch, and each protested constantly about the depredations of the other's pirates; this was a rivalry which would last until the end of the reign.[32]

With this summary of the network of ambassadors about 1600, we end our attempt to give a general view of the main posts in Henry's kingdom and of the men who held them. In the next section we shall try to reconstruct the events of a single day in Henry's life about 1600, and then in succeeding chapters we shall see how between 1600 and 1610 the king used these men and institutions to effect various changes in his kingdom.

(iv) The King's Daily Round

As we have seen in Chapter 6, the new queen reached Paris early in February 1601. After she joined the king there, Henry remained in Paris until about the middle of April, when he went to Fontainebleau. The king's days in Paris followed a well-established pattern. On 3 March 1601, for instance, he would have woken up in the Louvre at about seven in the morning. At this stage of his marriage there was no question of his sleeping apart from the queen, and she would be at his side, in the great curtained bed of the 'petit cabinet de la Reine' (see Map 18).

The gates of the Louvre, shut at eleven the previous night, had been opened at five o'clock so that the various members of the household staff could begin their work. Very few of them remained in the palace overnight, when it was guarded by a detachment of fifty or so soldiers from the Swiss or French guards. Entering, then, at five o'clock, the servants would go to their tasks, clad in the splendid red, white and blue livery of the French Crown. Some would clean the rooms, courts and staircases, others would open all the windows, and others would light the fires. At six o'clock in winter they would light the various flambeaux and candles, for by then the first courtiers would be arriving.[33]

Only the most favoured, like Sully, would be admitted to the royal bedchamber, and there they would have to make the required bows before the curtained bed. Eventually the king would rouse himself and draw back

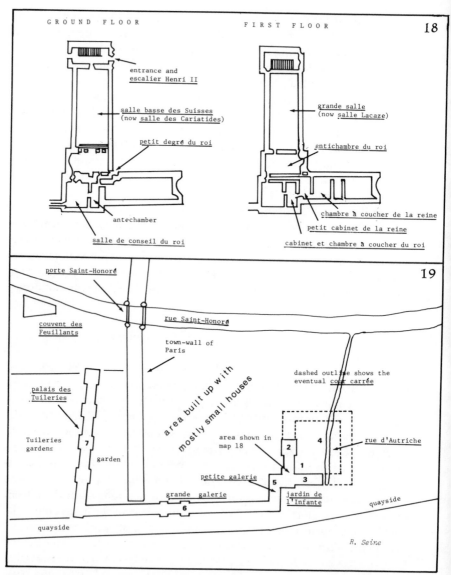

GROUND FLOOR   FIRST FLOOR   18

entrance and
escalier Henri II

salle basse des Suisses
(now salle des Cariatides)

petit degré du roi

grande salle
(now salle Lacaze)

antichambre du roi

antechamber

salle de conseil du roi

chambre à coucher de la reine

petit cabinet de la reine

cabinet et chambre à coucher du roi

19

porte Saint-Honoré

rue Saint-Honoré

couvent des
Feuillants

town-wall of
Paris

palais des
Tuileries

area built up with
mostly small houses

dashed outline shows the
eventual cour carrée

Tuileries
gardens

garden

area shown in
map 18

rue d'Autriche

petite galerie

grande galerie

jardin de
l'Infante

quayside

quayside

R. Seine

Map 18   *Plan of the royal quarters at the Louvre*
Sources: Batiffol, *Le Louvre* and Berty, *Topographie historique.*
Map 19   *General plan of the Louvre*
Sources: Batiffol, *Le Louvre* and Berty, *Topographie historique*

the curtains, other courtiers would come in, and a general conversation
would get under way. Towards seven o'clock the king would finally get
out of bed, and would call for his *bouillon*. This was of beef tea, eaten with

bread, the whole thing ceremoniously borne in by two gentlemen of the bedchamber, preceded by two guards. After this light meal, typical of breakfast before the days of coffee, Henry would wash himself rather perfunctorily and dress. His clothes were usually simple, and often very old and even torn; he seems to have made a kind of virtue of this unkingly appearance.

Then he would leave his bedroom and pass into the antechamber, where a crowd of courtiers would be in attendance. Evading their importunities as best he might, he would hurry downstairs to the council-room, where most days his ministers would be waiting for him. When it was fine, he would go out into the gardens and discuss the affairs of state as he walked with Sully, Bellièvre, Villeroy and whomever else had been called that day. When it was wet, he would hold his peripatetic court in some large room, like the grande galerie, where he could pace up and down. The ministers had to have their facts at their fingertips for this kind of discussion; once a conclusion had been reached, one of the four secretaries of state would be called up to take the necessary instructions for action.

On 3 March 1601 the deliberations must have borne mostly on foreign affairs.[34] There was no fresh news from England, where the Earl of Essex had been executed a week or so earlier, and not much from Germany, where the Emperor was preoccupied with his astrological studies. The news from Rome was that the Spanish party seemed in no hurry to ratify the peace of Lyon, and that no doubt was why the fortifications of Provence, Savoy and Dauphiné were discussed. The duc de Guise and Guillaume du Vair had reported on the state of the defences of Provence, and the duc de Lesdiguières was attending to those of Dauphiné; at the council meeting the previous day, final arrangements had been made to cover this work. The archdukes in Brussels had sent an envoy, Don Roderigo Lasso, captain of the guard, who had an audience on the 2nd; no doubt this also was discussed. Finally, arrangements would have been made to receive the maréchal d'Ornano, who was soon to come to Paris concerning the affairs of Guyenne. Once the decisions had been taken, the secretaries of state were called up and Villeroy, for instance, was instructed to tell Montmorency what had been decided.

Once this formal meeting of the conseil des affaires was over, the king would attend to those courtiers who were able to catch his ear with their requests. Sometimes this was impossible, if Henry really did not wish to see the person concerned. Often suppliants had to be ready to spend days in the antechamber before the king 'saw' them; amusing cases of this kind of siege of the king's good nature are recounted by Nicolas de Brichanteau, sieur de Beauvais-Nangis, and by the Protestant minister Daniel Chamier.[35] Once an interview had been granted, the king would at once decide on the merits of the case, and if some action were required would at once command it from the relevant secretary. If a prince of the blood were present at these informal sessions, he would be specially called up afterwards as a mark of consideration, and the king might well spend some time walking and talking with him. Once he had attended to this business, he would be free to go to Mass, which normally involved a walk through the Tuileries to the abbey of the Feuillants on the rue Saint-Honoré (see Map 19).

Of course, he was often late for Mass, as there was no way of knowing how long these interviews would last; the monks were used to this. One of his servants followed him to the Feuillants, and when he came out of Mass inquired what time he wished to dine; his meal had theoretically to be ready any time after half-past nine. So the king came back to the Louvre, mounted the *petit degré du roi* (see Map 18) and dined in his antechamber. In ceremonial principle, he had to dine alone, but in fact he often invited visitors to join him at table, as we know from Claude Groulart's accounts of his visits to court. The menus were extensive but varied little from day to day; each dish was ceremoniously brought in and ostentatiously tasted before it was served.[36] The wine, too, was tasted, using the king's own glass. Often, it would seem, bystanders talked to the king as he ate; sometimes the musicians from the royal chapel came and played.

Once the meal was over, the king retired to his study and chatted for a while with such old friends as were there. Then he was ready for the afternoon's entertainment. Quite often, the king and queen would walk together to the Tuileries, where they would listen to a concert given by the royal musicians. Sometimes foreign singers would come, like the Spanish Isabelle de la Camere, on her way to Flanders, or Giulio Romano, specially sent from Italy.[37] Presumably these concerts were normally given in the summer months; in March 1601 it is more likely that the royal couple would have called up one of their carriages to drive and see some friend in town. One of their favourite distractions was the Arsenal, where Sully would show them some cannon being founded, or plan with them the organisation of a ballet. The king sometimes went out alone, hunting in the Pré-aux-Clercs, just across the Seine from the Louvre. But the Louvre was no longer as well sited for hunting as it had been in medieval times, and Henry looked to Fontainebleau or Montceaux for long days in the saddle.

At the end of the afternoon, he would sometimes retire to the Louvre, where supper would be served at any time after six o'clock, following the same routine as at midday. But he often liked to invite himself out to dinner, with Madame de Guise, with Sully at the Arsenal, or with Sébastien Zamet in the rue de la Cerisaie. It was something of an ordeal to entertain the king, for the usage was that he would fix the names of the guests whom his host had to invite; normally the host had also to taste each dish before the king ate it. After the meal six pages would come from the Louvre to escort the royal carriage back again. This was rather a perilous procedure, in a city as tumultuous as Paris, but the king seems to have disliked the idea of having his carriage properly escorted. In fact, his movements about the town were often very informal, to such a degree that once, as he was hurrying out of the Louvre by the dark corridor of the main entrance (see Map 18), an incoming courtier almost knocked him down. Once the king was back at the Louvre, towards eight o'clock, he would normally spend the evening playing either at cards or at dice with a number of old friends. Bassompierre was usually one of the group, and so were La Varenne and Roquelaure. Sometimes, too, they would be joined by Bellegarde, the duc de Guise and the duc d'Epernon.[38] They were often on the losing end of games of dice, perhaps because these were (literally) loaded. There is curious evidence to suggest that Bassompierre introduced to the royal circle a certain Edouard Fernandez, 'portugais', who had been associated with Manuel Pimentel, a crooked dice-maker.[39] Certainly Bassompierre made a great deal of money at this gaming, and the king lost a good deal.[40]

The king very rarely gave dinner-parties in the evening, but he would quite often organise a ballet, or a dance, or the visit of some troop of comedians. Ballets often started at midnight, and shortly before then the king would enter the *grande salle* on the first floor and would act the part of the host, seeing to it that everyone was properly seated and that the room was properly set out. Then the musicians would enter, and after them the ballet proper would begin. Although Henry and Marie were less enthusiastic for ballets than the Valois had been, they did organise a considerable number of them, in which the leading members of the court appeared dressed as nymphs, camels, Turks, and so forth.[41] Close to the ballet as a form of amusement was the dance; in the time of Henry IV the court dances still reflected their peasant origins, with names like *branles*, *courantes*, *gaillardes* and so on.

Henry quite enjoyed dances, but he was not so keen on the performances of comedians, which Marie liked. Indeed, he had an embarrassing tendency to fall asleep during theatrical performances;[42] no doubt he found it difficult to stay awake when he was obliged to remain still, a thing he never liked doing. Once the performance was over, nearly everybody would leave the palace. The *flambeaux* and candles would be snuffed out, and the gates would be shut one by one back to the main gate on the rue d'Autriche. Then that great gate would also be shut, and its key given to the captain of the guard. Henry, disregarding the elaborate rules of the *coucher*, would rapidly dress for bed, with or without the queen. The curtains would be pulled across, and he would fall asleep.

8 The Consolidation of the Dynasty, 1601–2

(i) 'Monsieur de Rosni Doth Promise Millions'

As we have seen in Chapter 5, the Assembly of Notables of 1596–7 had approved the imposition of a tax of one *sol pour livre* on all merchandise sold in the towns. The *déclaration*★ providing for this tax had been promulgated in May 1597,[1] and in 1601 the king and Sully decided to begin serious efforts to collect it. In the previous March, the scale of contributions in force for Paris had been published,[2] and in spite of the resistance of the *cour des aides*[3] an *arrêt* of February 1601 decreed that all towns without exception should be liable to the tax, 'recognised as just by the Assembly of Notables'.[4]

By the autumn of 1601 a good many towns had fallen into line; these included Bourges, Limoges, Lyon, Moulins, Orléans, Riom, Soissons and Tours.[5] But Poitiers was strongly resistant, and from the start towns like Angers, Caen, Châlons-sur-Marne and Reims had been allowed to pay a *subvention* in place of the hated *pancarte*. The king had long mistrusted Poitiers, a strong centre of League activity, and he seems to have decided to make an example of it over this issue. In May 1601, Pierre d'Amours, *conseiller d'Etat*,★ had been sent to the town with some other officers, to establish the tax there. But, as the English agent Winwood wrote, 'The people did mutiny against [the *commissaires*] and assailled the house where they were retyred, from whence to save themselves they were forced to escape by a postern doore ...'.[6]

The king was furious at this daring resistance, and was all for harsh measures. But several of his councillors argued that it would be necessary to tread warily, so as not to arouse the same kind of disobedience in other towns.[7] On 28 August 1601, Henry wrote to the Constable that he was 'extremely dissatisfied, and even more determined to enforce [my] will by one way or another. To that end, I have ordered up some military forces ... so as to prepare what will be necessary to punish this disobedience.'[8] By the following July, Winwood was reporting that 'Poytou hath received the Pancharte, and the town of Poytiers hath composed for 2,000 ducats the year'.[9] Similar forceful measures were taken against Brittany, Gascony and Guyenne, and by the end of the year most of the towns had come to heel.

106

In 1602, the main centres of disobedience were at first the towns of the west. On 9 March 1602, the mayor of La Rochelle wrote to the king that his town had decided that the imposition of the *sol pour livre* would 'entirely subvert the privileges which you have granted to us, and would entirely banish that little trade which now remains'.[10] According to the papal nuncio, it was to crush this Protestant municipal resistance that the king made his journey to the south-west in August 1602.[11] But it was not only the Protestants who were discontented; there was widespread resistance in Auvergne[12] and Limousin, so that in May 1602 the mission of Antoine Le Camus, sieur de Jambeville, to Limoges had to be supported by military force.[13] In Limoges, Jambeville eventually got his way by replacing the six erring *consuls*★ by fresh ones obedient to the king;[14] as we shall see, this was a frequent royal tactic.

However, very often during 1602 the king accepted the *subvention* which towns offered in place of the hated tax. In September 1602, for instance, Bourges, Limoges, Poitiers and Riom all sought this way out,[15] and on 10 November 1602 an edict suppressing the *pancarte* was promulgated. What had happened in effect was that the king had allowed himself to be bribed into abandoning the tax.

Very much the same thing happened in the case of the various *chambres de justice*.★ In August 1601 an edict was published creating such a *chambre royale*, composed of seventeen royal officers, whose function would be to investigate the 'malversations des financiers',[16] or peculations of the *trésoriers de France* and tax-farmers. Such a chamber had already been set up in May 1597, and after sitting for about a month had been suppressed on receipt of the appropriate sum by the king. The *chambre royale* of 1601 sat until September 1604, when it received such handsome propositions from the leading 'financiers' – a 'loan' of 600,000 *livres* for the king – that it, too, was revoked.[17] These *chambres de justice* thus met the same fate as the *sol pour livre*; in each case a promising and desirable reform was transformed into a fiscal expedient.

(ii) 'Pour visiter les fortifications que j'y fais faire'

About the middle of April 1601 the king went to Fontainebleau, to take advantage of the spring hunting. By 10 May he was beginning to think about a trip which he wanted to make in the summer, to visit the fortifications of Picardy.[18] Later that same month he was looking to the fortification of Antibes; 1601 was in fact the year during which most money was spent on this work, as Table 11.1 shows.

At the end of May he was still at Fontainebleau where, as he wrote, 'the weather is so fine and I am enjoying myself so much that I cannot leave.'[19] He was still there on 9 June, but shortly afterwards went to Paris, where he remained until the end of August, with excursions to Saint-Germain and Montceaux. By 31 August he was at Montreuil, and on 2 September in Calais. He inspected the fortifications of these two towns, and also visited Boulogne and Ardres; presumably he had passed through Abbeville and Beauvais on his way northwards.[20] While he was in Calais, he sent the maréchal de Biron to visit Queen Elizabeth, who characteristically greeted him with these words: 'Ho, monsieur de Biron, how is it that you take the trouble to visit a poor old woman, in whom nothing remains alive but her affection for the King, and her judgement in recognising his good servants, and in prizing cavaliers like you?'[21] In fact, Elizabeth had at first suspected that Henry was involved in the Essex rebellion, which broke out just as the king set out northwards.[22] But Biron's embassy went off well, with feasting and mutual congratulations. Better founded were the suspicions of the archdukes, who feared that Henry's visit to Calais was part of a scheme to intervene in the siege of Ostend,[23] which had started the previous July (and would last until September 1604). The king was well aware of the importance of this siege,[24] but had no intention of intervening in it. By 10 September, Henry had seen all that he needed of the state of the fortifications; the queen was due to give birth very soon, and so he hastened back to Fontainebleau. For had he not written to her on 6 September that he was resolved 'to be one of your midwives'?

(iii) 'Puer natus est nobis', September 1601

Henry's relations with Marie, from the time that she entered Paris, had been complex. He had made it clear from the start that she was not to concern herself with affairs of state. When, at her first coming, she had asked him, as a special favour to her, to accept in France the decrees of the Council of Trent, he had replied something like this: 'Just look after yourself; you shall have all the pleasures and delights that a queen of France could desire, but I beg and command you not to meddle in affairs of state.'[25] Marie could perhaps have accepted this advice with good grace, but she found it hard to come to terms with Henry's mistresses. Very soon after her arrival he had presented the marquise de Verneuil (Henriette d'Entragues) to her, thus causing a famous scene in which, judging that Verneuil's curtsey was unsufficiently low, he had personally forced her into a lower obeisance.[26] After that, though,

The Queen did kindly entertain her, and since all three have dined on Sunday together in publick. He hath provided a house for her hard by the Louvre, and will follow the track of Henry the Second, who did keep Madame Valentinois in court, in presence of the Queen-Mother. . . .[27]

But this bold public front must have concealed the most bitter disappointment for the Tuscan princess, unaccustomed to Henry's ways. Not only did he continue to visit Verneuil,[28] but in June he took up with 'a new Mistress, called La Boidissière',[29] while still continuing to frequent Zamet's house, where the 'belle garce Claude' awaited him. He was incorrigible, and yet when he went to Calais in September he wrote back the most tender letters to Marie, assuring her that he could not wait to see her again; in fact, as we have seen, he hurried back so as to be present at her delivery.

Henry arrived at Fontainebleau in mid-September, and it was at midnight on 26 September that he had to send for the midwife, Louise Bourgeois, since the queen was feeling uneasy.[30] Soon it was clear that the labour pains had begun; Henry was constantly at her bedside, holding Marie and comforting her. The labour was very long, lasting nearly the whole day of the 27th, but eventually Marie gave birth to a fine son. Henry had insisted that three princes of the blood – Conty, Soissons and Montpensier – attend the delivery, even though he feared that Montpensier might faint. Once the child had been wrapped in swaddling-clothes a crowd of spectators was allowed in to see him; the joy was great, for, as Henry said, it was eighty years since a dauphin had been born in France. He moved his bed alongside the queen's lying-in bed, and slept there until she was quite recovered.

Meanwhile messengers were sent to speed the good news all over France and Europe, and after a week or so the dauphin began to receive visits from ambassadors and other notables. The English agent Winwood was among these; he reported that the baby was 'strong and a goodly prince, and doth promise long life'.[31] Towards the end of October, young Louis was taken from Fontainebleau to Saint-Germain, passing by Paris where he had a jubilant reception.[32] Marie, who had said in September that if she bore a son she 'would begin to be a queen',[33] must have felt that her fortunes had turned, but it was not to be expected that this happy event would cure her husband of his philandering.

Early in November, indeed, the marquise de Verneuil also gave birth to a son. Henry seems to have been at Verneuil for the birth and, according to L'Estoile, made a great fuss over the baby, saying that he was more handsome than the dauphin, who was swarthy and fat like the rest of the Medici.[34] Could the king really have said something so horribly wounding for his wife? It is, alas, quite possible, for the dark side of his ready wit was that he sometimes let his tongue run away with him. At all events, Marie did not need this further evidence of his infidelity; the royal couple was well embarked upon nine years of mutual recrimination and misunderstandings, in which the main fault plainly lay with the king.

(iv) 'Both in Watch and Warde Attending the Opportunity'

On 2 December 1601, Henry formally swore the peace with the Duke of Savoy,[35] which might suggest that relations with Spain were improving. In fact, the contrary was the case, for the year had seen a series of minor aggressions by both French and Spaniards, and these would long continue. Spanish agents were constantly active among the French nobles, and received an exceptionally favourable reception from the maréchal de Biron. He first seems to have been approached by them in July 1598, when he went to Brussels for the installation of the Archduke Albert.[36] No doubt he remained in touch during 1599, and even during 1600, when he was waging Henry's war against the Duke of Savoy. The king had some notion of his treachery, and in January 1601 denied him the key governorship of Burgundy, which made Biron very discontented.[37] By August 1601, Biron was dealing directly with the Count of Fuentes, Spanish governor in northern Italy;[38] as we shall see, his negotiations turned out disastrously for him. But he was by no means the only great French noble in Spanish pay; about July 1599 the duc de Guise was well hooked, and in 1601 the duc de Bouillon was also negotiating with Spanish representatives.[39]

The French do not seem to have enjoyed a comparable success among the Spanish grandees, but as early as 1601 they were encouraging a movement of resistance among the Moriscoes.*[40] Henry also carried on a more conventional diplomatic offensive. In May he received the visit of two ambassadors from Venice;[41] the Serene Republic had been the first power to recognise him, in 1589, and was valued by France as a counterpoise to Spanish influence in northern Italy. In March he received a visit from an ambassador of the 'Grand Seigneur', the Sultan of Constantinople.[42] The Franco-Turkish connection was seen by him as a means of keeping up pressure on the southern and eastern flanks of the Habsburgs; indeed, in January 1601 he wrote to Savary de Brèves, French ambassador in Constantinople, that he should secretly encourage the Grand Seigneur to attack the coasts of Calabria and Sicily.[43] This policy, not entirely consistent with Henry's title of Most Christian King, went back to the time of François I and the Franco-Turkish alliance of 1536.

In the north, too, France kept up the pressure on Spain, by subsidising the rebels in the Netherlands. From 1598 onwards they received substantial sums, remitted as secretly as possible through Dieppe.[44] Some-

1   East front and entrance to the *château* at Pau

In its external appearance, this building has not changed much since Henry's day. It stands on a small spur above the Gave de Pau, and away to the south (left on the photograph) enjoys a splendid view of the Pyrenees.

HENRI PRINCE DE NAVARR
AGE   DE 5 AN
EN   1556.

2 Portrait of Henry at the age of 3

In this charming portrait, Henry's large eyes and prominent nose are already evident.

3 Drawing of Henry at the age of about 18

This crayon, whose attribution is rather dubious, seems to catch something of Henry's volatile charm in his early manhood.

4 German engraving of Parma's relief of Paris in September 1590

Parma may be seen almost in the middle ('P. von Parma'), surrounded by his infantry (with lances) and his cavalry (some with lances, others with fire-arms). At the head of the column a single supply-wagon is just entering one of the gates of Paris; behind it is the artillery, and behind that more supply-wagons. In the top right-hand corner, the operation is disconsolately watched by 'Des Königs Navarre Folck': the king of Navarre's people.

5 Engraving of Henry IV touching for the King's Evil

The patients are each being presented by a sponsor, perhaps an *aumônier* in the royal household. The King slowly works round the circle, touching each sick person; in the background, his guards maintain order.

6   Engraving of Henry's entry into Paris in March 1594

The side of the narrow street is crammed with spectators, and the middle occupied by Henry's fully-armed soldiers. The King himself, wearing the hat with the white plume, is accompanied by two other riders; in the distance may be seen Notre Dame.

7   Engraving of Henry's entry into Lyon in September 1595

The procession, which winds its way from bottom to top, is headed by drummers and standard-bearers. The King may be seen riding on a horse and sheltered by a canopy, lower left.

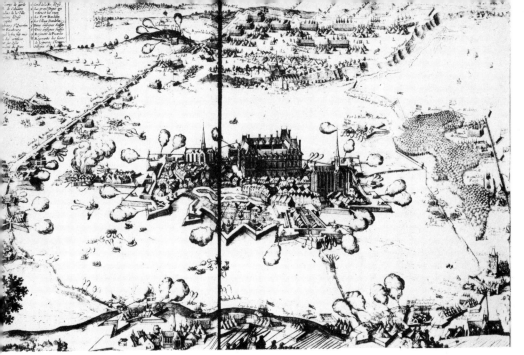

8 Engraving by Claude de Chastillon of the siege of La Fère in January 1596

This general view gives a good idea of the complexity of a siege-operation of this kind. The town has been entirely surrounded by an earthen rampart, broken by forts, and the royal camp itself (top centre) has had to be fortified with equal care.

9 Detail from the engraving of the siege of La Fère

This detail has been chosen to show the royal camp more closely; notice the several regiments on parade, the triangular tents, and the King's own quarters.

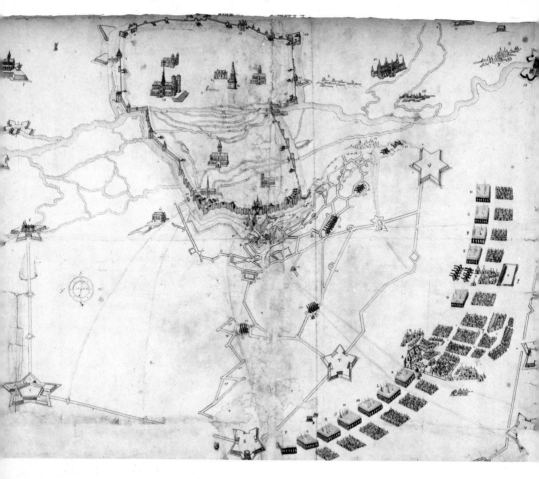

10 Drawing of the siege of Amiens in September 1597

Another complex siege-operation: note the royal army drawn up in a crescent on the lower right, with some of its guns in the artillery-park, and others in batteries in the approach-trenches. These temporary trenches and forts have proved remarkably permanent, for they may still be identified on aerial photographs.

11 Engraving by Claude de
Chastillon of the artillery
magazine in Metz

This engraving gives us a good idea
of the scale of the work undertaken
by Sully. In the vaulted cellar,
gunpowder is stored, in barrels of
different size according to its nature:
fine for muskets and coarser for
heavy weapons. On the other floors
there would have been armour and
equipment for the cannon; the latter
were too heavy to be stored off the
ground.

12 *Right* Detail from the
engraving of Paris in Caspar
Merian's *Topographia Galliae*
(1655–61)

This detail, which should be
compared with map 19, shows the
Louvre from the west. In the
foreground, behind the bastion, is
the new garden, and behind that the
Tuileries. On the right, alongside
the river, is the *grande galerie* linking
the Tuileries with the main body of
the Louvre; as yet only one part (an
eighth) of the *cour carrée* has been
completed. Note also the triangular
Place Dauphine on the point of the
Ile de la Cité.

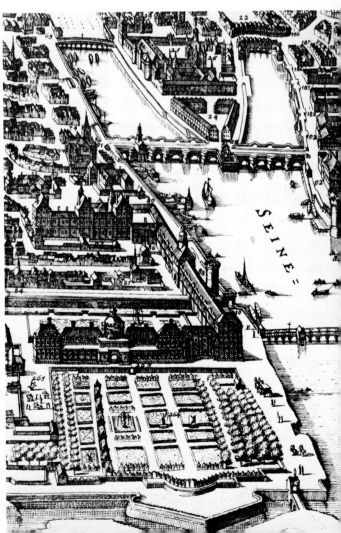

13   View of the Pont Neuf

In this corner of Paris, we can still feel the robust style of Henry's architects. In the foreground, looking north-east, is the southern arm of the Pont Neuf, with its turretlike refuges for pedestrians and its marvellously solid arches. Behind are the two buildings forming the apex of the Place Dauphine. Generations of greedy landlords have ruined the symmetry of the rest of the square, but these two buildings give us an idea of how it once was.

14   Engraving by Claude de Chastillon of the Hôpital Saint-Louis

This fine engraving shows us the Hôpital Saint-Louis in the foreground. Then, looking south, we see the western half of Henry's Paris, from the Louvre on the right to Notre Dame on the left. Note that the hospital lay clear outside the city, on one of whose bastions windmills apparently stood.

15   Engraving by Jean Le Clerc of the baptism of the dauphin in September 1606

The dauphin is seated at a table, attended by the great nobles who are carrying the various implements needed for the christening. In the foreground are the royal guards; the King and Queen look on through the open windows.

HERCVLI · SACR · GALLICO

16 Engraving of Henry as the Gallic Hercules

A typical propaganda engraving. Notice, in the small *cartouches* at the top, scenes of Henry's coronation and (on the right) of one of his victorious battles

17 The Porte Dauphine at Fontainebleau

This remarkable entrance-arch, which would have been even more elaborate had it been finished, breathes the spirit of Italy and of the baroque, with its curvilinear lines, scroll-work and elaborate medallions.

18 The assassination of Henry IV

Ravaillac has just stabbed the poor King, whose hat has fallen off as he slumps back. La Force is detaining the assassin, while all around the people begin to realize that a catastrophe has taken place (even the people in the upper windows!). The carriage-curtains are now open; soon they will be closed for the journey back to the Louvre.

19 Bust of Henry IV

This spirited bust seems to catch many of Henry's qualities; a lively intelligence, but also a slightly faunish look. In general outline, his face has not changed much since early manhood (plate 3).

times, too, the king allowed the recruitment of French soldiers to serve the Orangist* cause. In July 1600 the Spanish ambassador, Juan Bautista de Tassis, protested against these levies, which were contrary to the Treaty of Vervins, and received the enigmatic answer that Henry would gladly forbid them, since he foresaw that he would need the troops elsewhere (i.e. in Savoy).[45] In fact, the French seem from start to finish to have turned a blind eye to these illegal levies, which also served the purpose, in the language of the time, of purging the kingdom of turbulent humours.

The Spaniards were unable to offer much opposition to the French on the Channel and Atlantic coasts, controlled by the ships of England and the Orangists. But they were constantly active on France's other frontiers, along the Pyrenees, on the Mediterranean seaboard, and all along the sinuous route from Spanish Italy to the Spanish Netherlands. In January 1601, for instance, Guillaume du Vair reported the presence of a fleet of twenty-five ships at Antibes; the governor, Charles de Guise, was absent at the time, and so the *parlement* ordered the nearest gentlemen to proceed to Antibes 'with what forces they can raise' so as to oppose the expected landing.[46] This 'invasion' came to nothing, but was part of a long series of such alarums. The previous year there had been rumours of Spanish plots in Narbonne and Leucate,[47] and, as we shall see, there were constant alerts as parties of Spanish soldiers made their way north along the 'Spanish Road', just off France's eastern frontier.

In 1601 the government of Philip III showed its malice more spectacularly than by these mere demonstrations. That July in Valladolid there was a quarrel between certain members of the suite of La Rochepot, French ambassador, and some local Spaniards. Philip III ordered the *alcalde** to enter the ambassador's lodging and seize the persons concerned, which he did. This violation of diplomatic immunity – which has become a classic case in international law – greatly angered the French king, who put an embargo upon French trade with Spain.[48] Martin Philippson thought that 1600 marked a turning-point in French diplomacy, in the sense that in that year a formal programme of French diplomatic aggression began.[49] But it would be nearer the mark to conclude, with the English agent Winwood, that there never had been any sincere peace between the two countries after 1598, 'both in watch and warde attending the opportunity who can first get the start of the other'.[50]

(v) 'If He Comes He Deceaves the World'

As we have seen, the maréchal de Biron had been in contact with Spanish agents since at least 1598. While the king was in Lyon, in January 1601, the maréchal had come to him and had confessed some of these evil practices;[51]

111

Henry had pardoned him, hoping that he would avoid them for the future. But Biron was by nature 'ambitieux sans mesure',[52] and found it impossible to withdraw from the conspiracy into which he had already deeply entered.

At the beginning of 1601, this plot had consisted essentially of a combined operation, using Fuentes' army and Spanish gold to support a rising of French nobles. Biron was to organise this rising, in collaboration with the Constable, the comte de Soissons, the comte d'Auvergne and the prince de Joinville.[53] In fact, the conclusion of the Treaty of Lyon made it impossible to carry out the project in this form. But during 1602 Biron continued to organise a conspiracy, so that in February 1602 we find the English agent Winwood reporting to Cecil about a certain 'practize' in Auvergne and Gascony;[54] 930 gentlemen of the region were said to 'hold intelligence with the Duke of Savoy and King of Spaine', and to be directed by Biron, the Constable, the duc de Montpensier, the comte d'Auvergne, the duc d'Epernon and the duc de Bouillon.

One of Biron's chief agents for these arrangements was a certain Jacques de La Fin. After a quarrel with Biron, La Fin came to Fontainebleau in March 1602 and revealed the entire conspiracy to the king, with supporting documents.[55] He was handsomely paid for this act,[56] and remained at court, while the king and his council digested the information. They continued to write to Biron about routine administrative matters as if nothing were amiss,[57] and Henry went through in the usual way with a long-planned visit to Blois and Poitou. It was from Tours that the king wrote on 14 May asking Biron to come to court so as to clear himself of various calumnies.[58] The next day Henry wrote to his old friend and guard-commander La Force, who was Biron's brother-in-law, advising him that 'every day I discover the greatest evil-doings, perfidies, ingratitudes and plots against me which you could ever believe'.[59] However, the king was careful not to alarm Biron himself, and on the last day of May wrote him two letters,[60] saying how glad he was that the maréchal would soon be able to explain himself. Biron still did not know of La Fin's treachery, and so agreed to come back to court at Fontainebleau with the king's emissaries, president Jeannin (of the Dijon *parlement*) and the sieur d'Escures.[61]

(vi) 'The Opinion Is, That Hee Shall Dye'

He arrived very early in the morning of 12 June,[62] and the king at once went walking with him through Fontainebleau's gardens, admiring the new buildings as they strolled.[63] Biron had seen La Fin upon his arrival, and his former servant had whispered to him: 'Courage, master, they know nothing.' So, when Henry told him of the rumours which he had heard, Biron denied any guilt, and affirmed that he needed no pardon, since he had committed no fault. Again after lunch their conversation reached the same stalemate, and when after supper the comte de Soissons (a fellow-conspirator?) spoke to Biron the answer was the same.

Henry rose early on the 13th, and had a final talk with Biron. When this proved fruitless, it was decided at the council meeting that afternoon that Biron and the comte d'Auvergne would have to be arrested. The king sent for the guard-commanders on duty, and gave them their instructions; fortunately, La Force was not serving that quarter, so that the task fell to Vitry and Praslin. As Biron left the king's chamber that night, Vitry arrested and disarmed him; Praslin did the same a little later to Auvergne. On the 14th, the council met in the morning, and it was agreed to take the prisoners to the Bastille; they were accordingly escorted there on Saturday, 15 May. Meanwhile letters had been sent out, announcing the arrest and explaining the reasons for it. There was a general circular, of which seven original copies have survived,[64] and also special letters to people like the duc d'Epernon and the sieur de La Force. The towns were enjoined to keep special watch against tumults, and the maréchal de Laverdin was sent into Burgundy, Biron's province, to make sure that there was no trouble. Laverdin met with no resistance as he secured the key towns in that province, and then for some weeks kept his forces on the alert to shadow a Spanish army which was due to make its way up the Spanish Road.[65] Henry believed, and he may well have been right, that this army was ready to strike into France, if Biron had been able to put his plan into effect.

The king returned to Paris on the 15th, some hours after Biron and Auvergne; on the 18th, he received a deputation headed by La Force, imploring mercy for the maréchal. But it was too late, and that same day the case was referred to the *parlement* of Paris.[66] La Fin had submitted a most damning deposition, of which the five chief charges were that Biron had: (1) engaged a certain Picoté to take messages to the archdukes; (2) offered to help the Duke of Savoy in 1599; (3) arranged for the capture of Bourg in 1600; (4) tried to get the king killed at the Fort Sainte-Catherine; (5) sent La Fin to deal with Fuentes.[67] Until this stage, Biron still imagined that La Fin had destroyed the incriminating correspondence. Now, when the two were brought together and La Fin substantiated his points, Biron 'showed so little moderation in the violence of his passions that he attempted divers times to take him by the throat'.[68] Biron's behaviour at this time was truly remarkable, more like that of a demented beast than that of a noble who had been charged with high treason. There seemed a good chance of a rescue-attempt, but Sully was captain of the Bastille and took such stringent measures that none was made.[69] Biron and Auvergne were lodged apart, in cells for which special furniture had to be bought; as Sully wrote on the account for this purchase, 'we must keep this furniture for another time'.[70]

So the trial went through to its inevitable conclusion, and on 31 July 1602 Biron was decapitated in the Bastille. He died as violently and irresolutely as he had lived, several times putting off the moment of laying his head upon the block, so that in the end the executioner had to take him by surprise.[71] Biron's capture, trial and execution were extraordinary and dramatic events, which is why they have been described in such detail. But they also demonstrate a remarkable weakness in the France of Henry IV, when so many of her leading nobles were willing to sell themselves to Spain. And, even with Biron gone, the king must have lost some of his old confidence in figures like the Constable, let alone in Bouillon and Epernon.

(vii) 'If Bouillon Comes, His Doom Is Already Geeven'

What had been the precise role of the Spaniards in the affair? It was proved beyond doubt that Fuentes, governor of the Milanese, had been involved, and the whole affair had of course been orchestrated by the Duke of Savoy. But Henry at first tried to believe that Philip III had known nothing of the plot to assassinate his fellow-sovereign.[72] Alas, as the weeks went by, and more evidence came in, it became clear that 'the said king had known and ordered everything which the others did and negotiated with Biron'.[73] Worse, it became increasingly clear that the rumours of complicity among the highest French nobles were probably true. It hardly seemed politic to bring charges against the Constable, Epernon or Soissons, and even the comte d'Auvergne was released, in order to please his sister, the marquise de Verneuil. But Henry did not feel that he could overlook the evidence against the duc de Bouillon, whom he invited in November 1602 to come and explain himself.[74] Bouillon, temporarily safe in his *château* of Turenne (Corrèze), at first gave an evasive answer, but then towards the end of 1602 went down into Languedoc, where he held 'quelques assemblées',[75] trying to drum up support, and finally in December appealed (as a Protestant) to the *chambre mi-partie**★** (established by the Edict of Nantes) in Castres. Receiving no favourable response, he fled France altogether, first to Geneva and finally to Sedan. Here, as we shall see, he formed a focus of discontent against Henry. He was probably right in thinking that a return to court would have been perilous, for the marquise de Verneuil remarked about this time to the Princess of Orange that Biron's room in the Bastille was being kept ready 'to entertaine one of her best friends' (meaning Bouillon),[76] and

Winwood expressed the view that if he fell into the king's hands 'his doom is already geeven'.[77]

(viii)   *'Le nombre de tels larrons n'est ja que trop grand'*

The arrest and execution of Biron was the major political event of 1602 in France, but there was another arrest, much less well known, which also throws light on the king's problems and intentions. This involved François Jusseaume, receiver-general for the *bureau des finances* of Tours. The fiscal system of *bureaux* covered a large part of France (broadly speaking, outside the provinces which had their own estates), and each *bureau* had a receiver-general who was responsible for receiving and disbursing monies; needless to say, they were often suspected of peculation.

Jusseaume seems to have been a particularly unsatisfactory officer, for as early as December 1600 a royal *arrêt* commanded the *trésoriers de France* in Tours to explain his accounts.[78] After that we hear nothing more of him until December 1601, when a further *arrêt* orders his arrest, since he has fled, carrying with him the generality's funds.[79] Tours is, of course, about as far in France as anywhere could be from the country's frontier, but Jusseaume safely made his way to the south-east, eventually seeking refuge in the Duchy of Savoy, at Turin. No doubt he counted on the Duke's recent hostilities with Henry to keep him safe.

In February 1602 the king wrote to 'mon frère le duc de Savoye', asking him to hand Jusseaume over to a certain Jehan Flament, sent to escort him back to France.[80] At first the Duke demurred, trying to win a grace for Jusseaume, but after another letter he agreed to return the errant financier. It is not quite clear whether the initiative in this matter had come from the king or from Sully,[81] but we know that Jusseaume did come back, and that he then had to stand trial. On Friday, 20 September 1602 he was hanged and strangled in the courtyard of the *palais de justice*,[82] for having stolen monies from his account. It may seem rather unjust that a king and minister who were willing to be bribed over affairs like the *pancarte* and the various *chambres de justice* should proceed with such brutal severity in this case, but it also illustrates their determination to wipe out certain kinds of unofficial peculation.

(ix)   *'To Hold in Bridle the Gallies of Spain'*

The year 1602 was not solely remarkable for its trials. It was also the year in which the king at last began to make some progress with his project for

115

a Mediterranean galley-fleet.[83] From 1597 onwards we find mention in his correspondence of the need to have galleys to patrol the Mediterranean coast, for the magnificent fleet of Henri II had entirely wasted away during the civil wars. This need was strongly felt in the spring of 1600, when Spanish vessels were very active off Toulon, carrying reinforcements from Barcelona to the Spanish army in Flanders. Both Guillaume du Vair and the duc de Guise wrote at length of the need for a fleet, which could also deter English and Moorish pirates.[84]

Nothing much had been accomplished by the end of 1600, when Maria de Medici had to use Tuscan, papal and Maltese galleys on her way from Livorno to Marseille. During 1601 some progress was made, so that by January 1602 Winwood could write that there were five galleys in preparation at Marseille, of which one was ready for the sea.[85] These vessels had probably been constructed through an agreement with the Genoese Ambrogio Lomellini, who in 1597 had become *gentilhomme ordinaire de sa chambre* to Henry.[86] In February 1603 a further contract was signed with Lomellini,[87] stipulating that the Genoese would construct and maintain six galleys for 30,000 *livres* each; the king would provide the oarsmen (mostly from condemned criminals), and Lomellini could use each vessel for two months each year for private trading. About half a dozen other galleys were built under individual contracts by officers of the *marine du Levant*,* so that by 1610 Henry could count on about a dozen of these vessels.

The French galleys were rather larger than the normal Italian or Barbary ones,[88] and had about 200 oarsmen, forty-seven seamen and sixty soldiers; they were roughly 180 feet long, and so lightly balanced that a single man in the wrong place could spoil their balance.[89] Their guns and pyrotechnics came from the Marseille Arsenal, controlled by Sully as *grand maître de l'artillerie*; their captains had often been Knights of Malta.* Jacques Vincheguerre, for instance, came into French service from the Maltese after a conversation with Guillaume du Vair; other officers from Malta included Claude Douet, Philibert de Foissy and also probably the Genoese captain Vassallo. Marseille was the traditional galley-base, but it had several disadvantages; the port had to be shared with commercial vessels, and the captains of these, fearful of reprisals, were often opposed to attacks on the Turks. Also, the inhabitants of Marseille had been spectacularly unruly during the religious wars, and unrest continued at a high level. So the king began looking for a new base. About 1606 he was considering Hyères,[90] but he eventually chose Toulon, which incidentally had been loyal to him during the League. A whole new naval installation was built there, under the direction of one of Sully's *ingénieurs du roi*.[91] In the accounts, work like this on constructing and fortifying Mediterranean ports is combined with expenditure on the galleys in the rubric *marine du*

Levant; this prevents us from getting any clear idea of the annual expenditure on the fleet proper. However, we may judge that something approaching 200,000 *livres* was yearly spent on the galleys between 1600 and 1610.

The result of this expenditure was that from about 1604 onwards the king was able to protect his Mediterranean coast. In August 1604, for instance, the galleys captured a Savoyard brigantine which had been ravaging French ports,[92] and in 1609 they escorted the sailing-ship *Lune* during her Mediterranean exploits.[93] Of course, these sailing-ships, or *vaisseaux ronds* as they were called, were the ships of the future, even in the Mediterranean. But Henry's galley fleet did attain local control of French waters, and eventually played an important part at the battle of Saint-Martin-de-Ré in 1622.[94]

9 'A Confused Labyrinthe', 1603–4

(i) 'On est paisible en mon royaume'

The king had several reasons for visiting his eastern frontier in the late winter of 1602–3. The most pressing was that he needed to regulate the affairs of Metz, where Roger de Comminges, sieur de Sobole, had as governor for the duc d'Epernon hopelessly alienated the inhabitants of the town. Another matter which needed his attention was the succession to the bishopric of Strasbourg; he also wanted to be close to Heidelberg when the German princes had their assembly there, beginning in February 1603.

Leaving Paris about the end of February, he rapidly regulated the affairs of Metz, dismissing Sobole and establishing Antoine de La Grange, sieur d'Arquien, in charge of the citadel there. On the way to Metz, early in March, he passed through Verdun, and there received a deputation of Jesuits who, as we shall see, induced him to consider the question of their return to France. While he was at Metz he received a group of German princes, come to solicit his intervention in the disputed succession to the bishopric of Strasbourg.

Henry's relations with the Protestant princes had been equivocal since his conversion in 1593. Before that, many of them had helped him with loans; after it, they became very mistrustful – refusing, for instance, to help him during the Amiens crisis of 1597. Many of them felt that the peace of Vervins had been concluded to their disadvantage, and consequently when Bouillon fled to his brother-in-law in Heidelberg he was well received by the assembled princes.

Some of this enmity towards the French king began to be dissipated after Maurice the Wise, landgrave of Hesse, visited France in October 1602.[1] Maurice came to talk to Henry about the money he owed the German princes, and about the Strasbourg problem; for his part, the French king was anxious to encourage an alliance of German Protestant princes against the Emperor, and indeed for a time to promote his own candidacy for the Empire. This latter aim did not long survive the pressure of hard facts; when in April 1600 the Venetian ambassador in Rome, Giovanni Mocenigo, assured the Doge and Senate that negotiations for Henry's election as Holy Roman Emperor were well advanced,[2] he surely overstated the case. But the project for an alliance like the one concluded at Chambord in 1552 between the French King and some German princes was more hopeful, and seems to have failed in 1603 only because of Bouillon's hostility and the support he aroused. As for the question of the Strasbourg succession, Henry wished to offend neither Protestants nor Catholics, and so engineered a compromise.[3]

In fact, Henry's policy towards Germany suffered from inherent paradoxes and contradictions, well illustrated by his reaction to the news of a Turkish victory in Hungary in 1594. On that occasion he is said to have remarked: 'God knows how these misfortunes afflict me, but the ambition of Christian princes wills it so; the League made me King, [and] the Turk may make me Emperor.'[4] He could not, all the same, adopt a resolutely anti-Catholic policy in Germany or indeed elsewhere, since the basis of his power lay in his reconciliation with the ancient church. In that respect his origins kept him on a leash; it was left to Richelieu to carry through the logic of Henry's foreign policy, by using his religious credentials to disregard the religious element in France's external relations.

(ii) 'Le bon Dieu veut disposer de moy'

The king left his eastern frontier in the early days of April 1603, and by the middle of the month was at Fontainebleau. He always enjoyed the springtime there, but on 17 May 1603 suddenly and unexpectedly fell very ill. As he himself wrote: '. . . about 7 in the morning I was taken by a colic which lasted all day and night, with pain greater than I have ever known, and a fever which made me very apprehensive.'[5] A week later, the Venetian ambassador Marin Cavalli gave this account to the Doge and Senate:

> The King has had a brief but very severe attack; they called it colic, but it really was pain in the kidneys with retention of urine for some hours. So intense was the pain that he twice fainted. There remained a slight tertian fever, from which he is now free, and as there is nothing the matter except the exhaustion caused by his malady, he will soon be in his wonted health.[6]

Henry did in fact make a full recovery, but it had been a close call; he had at one stage bitterly lamented that he would leave the dauphin so young, and had called for Sully and Villeroy to give them his last instructions.

By the time Sully came, he was already feeling much better, and was lying peacefully in bed with Marie in a chair at his side, holding one of his hands in hers. Before Sully was allowed to leave, the king insisted on demonstrating how well he could now pass water.[7] But the doctors were not so easily impressed, and prescribed that if he wished to avoid grave danger he should give up women for three months, stop hunting and eat more moderately.[8] Needless to say, Henry paid these sensible instructions no heed, and does not seem again to have suffered from urinary disorders. What did begin seriously to trouble him in 1603 was gout. He had had a first minor attack at Blois in April 1602, when it was confined to the big toe, but in September 1603 had a very painful swelling on the knee for three days;[9] as he then wrote to the Constable, a fellow-sufferer, he had 'joined the brotherhood'. Eventually, as we shall see, this tedious complaint came to be a serious nuisance to the king.

(iii)   *'La reine d'Angleterre est décédée'*

On his way back from the eastern frontier, on 11 April 1603, Henry had learned of the death of Elizabeth of England.[10] The king must have had some regret, for in spite of their quarrels she had helped him from the time when he was a mere claimant to the throne. However, he had early recognised that James of Scotland would one day succeed her, and now sent Sully as extraordinary ambassador to the new king. Apart from congratulating James on his accession, and confirming all former alliances, Sully had also to try to persuade him to continue the war with Spain, to complain about English piracy, to press for more favourable conditions for English Catholics, and to dissuade James from supporting Bouillon.[11]

Sully soon established a friendly relationship with the English king, who shared his rather ponderous taste in humour. After exchanging pleasantries about Henry's prowess as a hunter, and about the health of Duplessis-Mornay, they soon agreed on minor points like the suppression of piracy (a hopeless quest), more advantageous conditions for the English Catholics (reviewed after the Gunpowder Plot), and the problem of Bouillon (James detested unruly subjects). But on the substantive question of war with Spain there was little meeting of minds. Basically, Sully had to answer the tricky question put by James: 'How can you ask me to go to war, in order that you may live in peace?'[12] There really could be no satisfactory answer for a king as pacifically minded as James, but Sully found a compromise, whereby half the annual French subsidy to the United Provinces would count towards repaying the sum owed by Henry to England for help during the 1590s. It is not quite clear whether James fully agreed to this arrangement or not, but the French certainly claimed that he did, and so by 1613 reckoned that the debt had been paid off. Henry was well content with the embassy,[13] but his relations with

England continued to be unsatisfactory, especially after the Anglo-Spanish treaty of 1604; as we shall see, he also had a strong personal antipathy for James.

One curious incident during the embassy concerned the loss of one of Sully's confidential letters back to the king. According to Sully, his courier, 'homme simple mais fort fidèle', had delivered it to one of Villeroy's clerks; Sully went so far as to add, for the king's benefit, that 'there has to be somebody in that office who is betraying Your Majesty'.[14] Villeroy did the deciphering work himself,[15] but there were occasions on which his office seemed prone to leaks; in April 1603, for instance, the English ambassador Parry, in reporting on some secret French negotiations in Rome, wrote to Cecil that 'I may not tell you that it comes from Villeroy's papers'.[16] All this was explained in April 1604, when Villeroy's confidential secretary Nicolas L'Hoste was discovered to be a Spanish agent, and was drowned in the Marne as he was fleeing to the Spanish Netherlands.

Generally speaking, the Venetian diplomats seem to have been the most skilful at this time in discovering the secrets of their host countries. In 1598, for instance, Francesco Contarini knew the provisions of the Treaty of Vervins before he should have done,[17] and in 1603 Giovanni Scaramelli was able to give an account of Sully's most private negotiations.[18] Later that year, Angelo Badoer made friends with the English ambassador, Sir Thomas Parry, and succeeded in reading the dispatches he received from the secretary of state.[19] By the side of the Venetians, Henry's diplomats were decidedly amateurish, and the French king relatively ill-informed. In January 1603, for instance, he believed that the English agent Winwood had written to London that the French king 'wished to make a second massacre' (after Biron).[20] But there is no sign of such a letter in Winwood's correspondence.

(iv) 'These Jesuits Having Now the Liberties of France'

As we have seen, in March 1603 the French king had received a deputation of Jesuits. Theoretically, the Society of Jesus had been expelled from much of France in December 1594, after the Châtel incident. But several *parlements* had failed to follow the condemnation of the *parlement* of Paris, and so the Jesuits survived in places like Bordeaux, Limoges and Toulouse. They were naturally anxious to have the prohibition of 1594 lifted, and the king had shown himself favourable to approaches like that made by the Père Maggio in Lyon in August 1600.[21] Indeed, as time went by the king more and more saw the advantages which the Jesuits could bring to France, so that in September 1601 his ambassador

121

in Rome, Philippe de Béthune, had instructions to negotiate for their recall.

Consequently, he gave a friendly reception to the deputation of March 1603, and after that invited the Pères Armand and Coton to visit him at Fontainebleau the following May. At the royal court Coton's influence rapidly increased; the king took a particular liking to him and very often insisted upon his company.[22] Sometimes they would talk theology; as Coton himself wrote, 'I once was with the king and Du Perron for more than two hours, discussing holy and useful things, which very much interested the king'. Small wonder, then, that on 1 September 1603 the king promulgated in Rouen an edict recalling the Jesuits to France. The conditions imposed might seem harsh: all Jesuits residing in France had to be native Frenchmen, for instance, and they had to swear an oath not to impede the king's service or trouble the public peace. But these were conditions which time could modify; the essential thing was that the ban was lifted, in spite of many protests from the *parlement* of Paris and elsewhere.[23]

Meanwhile Coton went from strength to strength at court, and even for a while seems to have persuaded the king to give up the marquise de Verneuil, and to acquaint the queen more closely with the routine of government. According to Coton, in October 1603

> [the king] daily grows in piety, acknowledging that he owes every-thing to God. The queen says that every morning he prays for half an hour before speaking to anybody, and does the same at night. He has given up all his *fols amours*, banished sin and loose women from the court, and cannot tolerate swearing there....[24]

We may doubt if the good father was aware of how Henry really spent his days, but it may truly be that about this time the king had an access of piety. Certainly he retained his fondness for Coton, whose name gave rise to all kinds of puns, mostly around the theme that Henry's ears were now blocked with cotton-(wool).

The 'recall' of the Jesuits had profound effects on the country at large. Just five years earlier, in 1598, their *ratio studiorum* had received its final approval, and this subtle yet powerful scheme of study soon enabled them to win many students to their high schools.[25] All over France in the early seventeenth century their colleges were proliferating, until eventually it seemed that every Frenchman of consequence in every field of human activity had been one of their pupils. Symbolically enough, two of the earliest pupils at the newly founded college of La Flèche were Marin Mersenne and René Descartes.[26] Henry can hardly have foreseen how widely the Jesuits' influence would spread – and it extended far outside

France as well, to Canada and Constantinople – but there is no doubt that he prized them as educators, 'better and abler than the others for instructing the young'.[27]

The Jesuits were not the only order which the king tried to encourage. According to the *oraisons funèbres* recently analysed by Jacques Hennequin,[28] he introduced the reformed Augustinians, the reformed Franciscans, the Capucin sisters and the Thérésiennes (Carmelites); to this list Poirson would add the Brothers of Charity, the Barnabites, the Capucin brothers, the Feuillants and the Minimes.[29] How are we to discern, amid such a welter of claims, what the true and personal action of the king was? As far as the Barnabites are concerned, it was in 1608 that this order, founded in Italy, was invited to France by Henry, specifically to work among the Protestants of Béarn.[30] The reformed Augustinians received the king's prolonged support, and he gave them permission to establish houses in Paris and elsewhere. The Carmelites were established chiefly through the efforts of Madame Acarie, but she enjoyed constant support from Coton, who in turn relied on the king.[31] The first French Ursulines were encouraged both by the king and by Marie de Medici, receiving royal letters-patent in 1608. In the end, it is almost impossible to discern the personal action of the king in each case; we are reduced to noting, with Bremond, that 'the creative and well-thought-out sympathy of the king went along with all these works'.[32]

True; but the same king could show an astonishing insensitivity in his treatment of some monasteries. Tiring of the charms of Mademoiselle de La Haye, in 1605, he sent her to Fontevrault until a vacant abbey could be found for her. Wishing to repay Sully for certain services, he gave two abbeys to this Protestant minister. In short, Henry was – even more than most people – an incongruous mixture of the disinterested and of the corrupt. This was amusingly demonstrated when he visited certain abbesses. Renée de Lorraine, abbess at Reims, hearing that he intended to pass her way, asked her mother to keep her company, 'fearing to be left alone with that monarch'. The abbess of Chelles, Marie de Lorraine, went one better, receiving the king at the head of her whole company.[33]

Sometimes it was not a whole order which the king tried to encourage, but a single churchman of whom he had heard good things. He had a particular appreciation for skilful preachers, and used to call them to Paris so as to enjoy their oratory. In 1602, for instance, he called Pierre de Besse from Limousin to preach at Saint Séverin.[34] A few years later it was the turn of André Valladier, who came from Burgundy, was named *prédicateur* in 1608, and went on to become vicar-general at Metz.[35] About this time, too, the Dominican Nicolas Coeffeteau was summoned from the provinces, and also became preacher to the king, as well as a noted controversialist. Indeed, Henry and Sully seem to have compared notes on the comparative excellence of preachers rather as other people might compare actors, or singers. In March 1605, for instance, Sully wrote to the king that, following his recommendation, he had been to hear a sermon by the 'doctor' preaching at Saint-Benoist, and that this preacher (whose name we do not know) 'will be a great person, [as] I have never heard anyone who orders his material better, or who argues more clearly and intelligibly'.[36] Preachers who caught the royal ear in this way might be taken on among the twenty-one household *prédicateurs* (see Chapter 7, section ii), and from there be promoted to high office in the church.

The French kings at this time enjoyed the right of nomination to bishoprics, and the use Henry made of this right has recently come under scrutiny by historians. According to Michael Hayden, Henry appointed many more members of the third estate and of the 'new nobility' than had been the custom until 1589 – or would be usual after 1610.[37] Frederick Baumgartner, while not disagreeing with this general argument, adds that the process had to a large extent already begun under Henri III.[38] Certainly the king himself boasted, speaking to the deputies of the clergy in 1605, that he had appointed bishops 'very different from those of the past'.[39] By 'different', of course, he meant better, and on the whole, as Hayden argues, his appointments *were* more zealous in carrying out their pastoral duties. It looks from the household lists as if Henry kept a roster of *aumôniers sans gages*, among whom were to be found not only most of the serving bishops, but also young men of promise who might hope to succeed them.

It would be tedious to enumerate the activity of Henry's nominations all over France, especially as these Counter-Reformation prelates acted in rather similar ways: visiting their dioceses, holding synods with their clergy, establishing seminaries, setting up schools and so on. But we have to imagine a few of them in specific terms.[40] At Troyes, René de Breslay (1604) was introducing a variety of orders and founding hospitals. At Auxerre, François de Donnadieu (1598) began his episcopate with a thorough visitation, and then plunged into a frenzy of reforming activity, holding synods, founding schools, and introducing orders – Capucins, Jesuits and Ursulines. At Mâcon, Gaspard Dinet (1599) was almost equally active, adding the Oratorians to the list of orders introduced. At Montpellier, Pierre de Fenouillet (1607), who had been called to the royal court in 1606, introduced the same furious burst of reforms: organising missions into the countryside, introducing the Capucins and Jesuits, and establishing a faculty of theology.

All over France it was the same story, as Henry's bishops began making up for the sloth and neglect which had characterised the pre-Tridentine church. There were, of course, some disappointments. Saint François de Sales came to Paris in 1602, but could not be tempted into leaving Annecy to accept a bishopric in France.[41] There were, too, still some rank abuses. Charles de Levis was nominated to Lodève in 1604 when he was four years old, and Henri de Verneuil to Metz in 1607 when he was six.[42] But these aberrations cannot justify Mariéjol's curiously harsh judgement that in his episcopal appointments the king 'normally catered to his passions and his interests';[43] on the whole, Henry clearly aimed to raise the pastoral level of the episcopate, and largely succeeded in doing so. Indeed, the whole life of the ancient church largely revived during the latter years of his reign, in part through his policies. It is one of the ironies of history that this great renewal should have taken place under a king who was long a heretic, and remained a person of scandalous private life.

(v)   'Nous avons descouvert force trahisons'

On the whole, 1603 had been for the king a year of tranquillity and achievement, both at home and abroad. But in 1604 he again became the target of a dangerous conspiracy. This time it revolved around the ambitions of the marquise de Verneuil, who had also been compromised at the time of Biron's plot. Henriette's father, the sieur d'Entragues, and brother, the comte d'Auvergne, had come to an agreement with Tassis, the Spanish ambassador, that the young Henri (Henriette's son by the king) would be recognised as heir; the king and the dauphin would be suppressed, and the new royal house would be established with the help of Spanish money and arms.[44]

As usual, many French nobles allowed themselves to be drawn into the plot; not only eternal malcontents like Bouillon and La Trémoille but also, it would seem, Lesdiguières and Duplessis-Mornay. On 22 June 1604 the king wrote to Sully that 'many treacheries have been discovered', and during the following days the full ramifications of the plot became clear. The king was brilliantly served on this occasion by N. Defunctis, *grand prévôt,*★ and by the sieur d'Escures, who had been prominent in the arrest of Biron. Defunctis succeeded in capturing Entragues in his *château* at Malesherbes, where compromising documents with the Spanish king's cipher were seized. Escures had the more difficult task of seizing Auvergne, a wily bird well aware of his peril. Escures waited until the Count was attending a review of soldiers near Clermont, and then had him seized as he waited watchfully on his swift horse; Auvergne was quickly removed to the Bastille, and shut up in the quarters which Biron had occupied.

The trial of the conspirators began in November 1604, and at the beginning of February 1605 the *parlement* of Paris gave its verdict: Auvergne and Entragues, guilty of *lèse-majesté*, were condemned to death, while Henriette was sentenced to seclusion in the convent of Beaumont-lez-Tours. Needless to say, the king could not bring himself to go through with these just and salutary punishments. In the end, in spite of the unanimous advice of his council, he allowed Henriette to retire to Verneuil, and Entragues to return to Malesherbes; Auvergne paid for all the conspirators by remaining in the Bastille until 1616. The court poet Jean Bertaut claimed that in this affair 'l'amour avait vaincu la mort', but in truth the king's lust for Henriette had led him into an unjust and foolish clemency. As usual, his judgement failed him, once Venus was in the ascendant. But the whole lamentable business showed more than the king's own weakness; it also demonstrated again the vulnerability of a France in which so many nobles were ready to conspire with the foreigner against the Crown.

(vi)   The Cold War Continues

The year 1604 was a difficult one for Franco-Spanish relations. Early in 1603, partly as a protest against continuing French aid for the Dutch, Philip III had imposed a levy of 30 per cent on all goods coming into his dominions from abroad. Henry had tried to persuade the Spaniards to remove this damaging imposition and, when his negotiations had failed, in February 1604 himself declared a general interdict on trade with Spain and her overseas territories.[45]

Of course, it was difficult to enforce this prohibition, particularly in south-western France, where many merchants relied on the Spanish trades. So on 24 April 1604 the king wrote to Sully, in whose *gouvernement* most of the infractions were taking place, instructing him to 'send down there a good man with a commission',[46] to seek out the lawbreakers and punish them as necessary. Sully chose Etienne de La Fond, who after serving the League in Normandy had been undertaking fiscal work there for the Crown.[47] La Fond received a commission for the coastal area between the mouths of the Loire and the Gironde, and by late June had done his best to enforce the interdict there, punishing a number of lawbreakers. There was some local complaint about his lack of judicial competence, but Henry was well pleased with his work, and a few months later appointed him *intendant des meubles de la Couronne.** However, the suspension of trade was beginning to damage both France and Spain, and in October 1604 the French interdict was raised,[48] as was the Spanish levy of 30 per cent.

Another incident marring Franco-Spanish relations during 1604 was the treachery of Villeroy's secretary, Nicolas L'Hoste, which has been briefly mentioned above.[49] Nicolas was the son of Pierre L'Hoste, one of Villeroy's oldest retainers. He had accompanied the sieur de La Rochepot to Spain on his embassy there, and had been recruited as a Spanish spy, though we do not know with what inducements. From 1601 onwards, he informed the Spaniards of virtually all French diplomatic negotiations, including of course the secret agreements to support the Dutch, and no doubt the arrangements with the Sultan.

His career as a spy might have continued indefinitely, but for a certain Raffis, a Frenchman who had had to take refuge in Spain after the religious wars. Raffis wanted to return to France, and saw in the uncovering of L'Hoste an opportunity to win the French king's favour. So, after a series of nerve-wracking interviews in Spanish churches and other secluded places, he was able to convince the sieur de Barrault, French ambassador in Madrid, of L'Hoste's perfidy. Even after that the affair was bungled, for L'Hoste got wind of his betrayal and fled before he could be arrested, drowning himself in the Marne on his way to the Spanish Netherlands, in April 1604. Villeroy was distraught, as well he might be, but the king continued to trust him, expressing regret chiefly that the Spaniards must now know how hard-pressed the Dutch were.[50]

Of course, Spain's corruption of L'Hoste was just one incident in the long cold war with France. As early as 1587, Henry had had discussions with the Moriscoes of Spain, and from that time onwards it was La Force who dealt with them.[51] In 1602, there were specific requests for support from the Moriscoes of Valencia, Aragon and Castille, and Henry sent a certain Panissault into Spain to concert their resistance. This action was duly reported in January 1603 by the Spanish ambassador Tassis, who of course received copies of all Villeroy's interesting correspondence through L'Hoste.[52] At least one French agent was captured and tortured, but in 1604, after the flight of L'Hoste, a further emissary came to Pau. This time La Force was enjoined to ensure the strictest secrecy, no Moriscoes being allowed to come to the French court 'avant le temps de l'execution'.[53] In fact the plot never came to a head, no doubt because the agents of Philip III had too thoroughly infiltrated the whole Morisco community. For a while, though, it did seem as if an overt resistance could be fomented in the peninsula; there is no doubt that the existence of the Moriscoes was 'a definite danger to the [Spanish] state',[54] and their expulsion in 1609 entirely justifiable in political terms.

(vii) *'No Places Should Be Fortified but the Frontiers'*

As we have seen, the French king did his best to counter Spanish plots by fortifying strongpoints along his frontier. The internal counterpart to this programme was the destruction of all unauthorised fortresses in the interior of the country. In 1604, for instance, the king gave orders for the demolition of the *château* at Craon (Mayenne).[55] The Brittany estates were asked to pay for this work, but they requested to be spared such an expense, having, as they said, already paid for dismantling fortifications at Douarnenez (Finistère), Blavet (Morbihan), Primel (Finistère), Crozon (Finistère) and Hédé (Ille-et-Vilaine).[56]

Of course, there were bound to be many razings of this kind in Brittany, where Spanish and League resistance had been strong and long-lasting. But there were others throughout France, in obedience to a decision of the 1597 Assembly of Notables that 'all ye citadels within ye body of this realm' should be destroyed;[57] in many cases the local inhabitants were glad to see the destruction of castles which had been in effect robber strongholds during the civil wars. So in 1598 the *château* of Rochefort-sur-Loire was pulled down, followed in 1603 by those of Carlat, Fécamp and Rennes.[58] The work was normally undertaken by the *lieutenants* of the *grand maître de l'artillerie*, though the local estates often paid for it.[59] It is impossible to say how many citadels were thus dismantled, but the number probably ran to at least two dozen.[60]

(viii) 'This Town Is Growing Much Fairer Than You Have Seen It'

While he was thus destroying unauthorised castles in the provinces, in Paris the king had ever since 1594 been putting up buildings; in the words of the *Mercure françois* for 1610, 'as soon as he was master of Paris, you saw masons at work everywhere'.[61] By the end of 1604, this work had transformed the appearance of large parts of the city; in the words of the English agent Tobie Mathew:

> This town is growing much fairer than you have seen it. The key between the bridge and the palace is almost finished. The long gallery is within forty paces as far as it shall goe in length; at the corner near the river by the Tuileries the King hath given order for a very great pavillion to be erected. Queen Margaret is making a young towne on the other side of the water, with a garden whereof I measured one of the alleys the other day to be 12 hundred paces long. You know the King gives her a CM crownes towarde the building, and shee hath instituted M. le Dauphin her heire.
>
> But the wonder of a buildinge is that of the old Marché aux Chevaux, now call'd the Place Royalle, which is already half built with galleries to walk drye round about, a goodly fountaine in the midst, and a pavillion on one side of the square to lodge the Kinge. The buildinge all of bricke and free-stone; the place must all be pav'd. This must be destined to the sale of those stuffs of silke and

golde which are already made in great abundance by Dutch and Italians who dwell nearby. I forgot to tell you that this costs the Kinge nothinge; men builde to have the profit that will grow of it, and pay the K. a rent besides.

I must fetch you back to the new bridge, to shew you a street they are making from the end thereof, that must pass through the garden de l'Hostel de St-Denis and render at the Porte Bussy. The pompe or waterwork is goinge, but castes not enough to cleanse so foule a towne as Paris.[62]

In this long extract we surely catch something of the wonder which Henry's works aroused in both visitors and Frenchmen. The 'key between the bridge and the palace' probably refers to what is now the quai du Louvre (Plate 12); in fact, all along this northern bank of the Seine the king saw to the rebuilding of the embankment, so as to protect from flooding the area round the Hôtel de Ville and the rue Saint-Antoine.[63] He also began the four main quays around the Ile Saint-Louis – Bourbon, Anjou, Béthune and Orléans – and saw to the extension of the embankment each side of the Pont Neuf. This, of course, is Mathew's 'new bridge'; it had been begun under Henri III, and from 1599 onwards the work of completing it went on. By June 1603 the king was able to cross the bridge in its unfinished state.[64] The crossing was still hazardous, and several people broke their necks doing it, but then, as Henry remarked, none of them was a king like himself. By 1609 the bridge was finished, and proved a great success, for it had no encumbering houses upon it, and was wide enough for carriages to cross with ease (Plate 13).

Toby Mathew's 'long gallery' is the extension to the Louvre which ran alongside the Seine. From 1594 onwards Henry had been working on this palace, which he inherited in an unfinished and delapidated state (Map 19). At its heart was the medieval courtyard (1), whose western (2) and southern (3) sides had been rebuilt under François I and Henri II by Pierre Lescot; these marvellous wings – described by Dallington as 'new and princelike'[65] – still survive. Late in the reign of Henri III, Lescot drew up what became known as the 'grand dessin du Louvre', involving a great extension of the original courtyard (4), a 'petite galerie' to the south (5), and a 'grande galerie' (6) linking the Louvre to the Tuileries (7). After the death of Henri II the work went on more slowly, but Catherine de Medici saw that Lescot was able at least to complete the ground floor of the 'petite galerie', to set out the foundations of the 'grande galerie', and to make a good start on the Tuileries.

When Henry IV became king, he decided to carry on with Lescot's plan. Between 1596 and 1605 the 'petite galerie' was completed by adding the first floor and decorating the interior with paintings and the exterior with sculptures. From 1594 onwards, we find contracts for work on the 'grande galerie', and by 1606 or so the Dauphin was able to use this route to pass from the Louvre to the Tuileries; hence Mathew's report in 1605 that it was 'within forty paces of completion'. During the rest of the reign, sculptors and painters worked to complete this section, so that by 1610 it formed a coherent link between the Louvre and the Tuileries, where work had also been going on from about 1594 (Plate 12). If we have described this work only in the broadest outline, it is because little that is definitely attributable to the artists of Henry IV survives in its original form: just a few sections of the 'petite galerie', and one room in the 'grande galerie'.

Henry's personal influence is more evident in the work on the gardens. When he was king only of Navarre, he had seen to the development of the gardens at Pau,[66] and as early as January 1597 was sending there for fruit-trees for Fontainebleau, Saint-Germain and the Tuileries.[67] As Plate 12 shows, there was a small 'old garden' behind the Tuileries. But the 'new garden' on which Henry lavished his care was to the west of the Tuileries, between that building and the new bastion of the town wall. Here Pierre Le Nôtre – grandfather of Louis XIV's great gardener – laid out extensive flower-beds, and Pierre Tarquin planted trees, particularly mulberry-trees to feed the silk-worms. Here, too, Etienne du Pérac built an *orangerie*, and the Flemish engineer Jean Lintlaer dug several great ponds with their attendant canals. Plate 12 gives a good idea of the flower-beds and groves of trees, though for some reason it does not show the water-works.

Beyond this garden, to the west, were the marshes and woods of the Champs-Elysées. In a sense, the whole concept of the Louvre–Tuileries complex was absurd. The original Louvre had been built just outside the wall of Philippe-Auguste, and then the Tuileries had been constructed just outside the wall of Charles V. After that came the idea of joining them, even though they were not parallel to each other, and were indeed separated by a substantial wall. Of course, once the southern connection (the 'grande galerie') had been made, it was inevitable that the northern one would one day be made as well. Indeed, according to Malherbe, Henry himself had the idea of building this northern wing and then clearing all the ground between it and the 'grande galerie'.[68] So there developed under the Napoleons a massive palace, which in our day has a rather unfinished look, owing to the destruction of the Tuileries in 1871.

The 'young towne' which 'Queen Margaret' was building on the 'other side of the water' was Marguerite de Valois' mansion on the rue de Seine, where Henry had given her a large parcel of land opposite the Louvre.[69] But Mathew was right in suggesting that 'the wonder of a buildinge is that of the old Marché aux Chevaux', for this was surely the most remarkable and original of Henry's works. In one sense, its history goes back to

Catherine de Medici, for when in the early 1560s she decided to abandon the Hôtel des Tournelles she provided that any persons buying lots there should be obliged to construct houses to a common plan 'pour la decoration de la ville'.[70] However, the civil wars prevented this project from getting under way, and the site of the Hôtel des Tournelles fell into neglect, eventually becoming a horse-market (the 'Marché aux Chevaux').

Early in the seventeenth century, Sully had had the idea of constructing workshops there for the production of silks and tapestries, and these workshops seem actually to have been built, about 1604. However, in 1605, following a decision by the king, the whole area was divided into lots, around a great square, and these lots were sold over the next few years by the *trésoriers de France*. Their twenty or so purchasers, as may be seen from the lot-plan,[71] were nearly all royal officials or financiers, many of whom we have already encountered in the royal household: Pierre Fougeu, sieur d'Escures, Etienne de La Fond, Pierre Jeannin, Barthélemy de Laffemas and so on. In the centre of the north and south sides of the square, Henry reserved lots for the Crown; here were built the *pavillon du roi* and the *pavillon de la reine*, a little larger than the adjacent *pavillons*. These were all of the same size, with an arcade facing on to the square, brick walls, stone quoins and courses, and high-pitched slate roofs with dormer windows. When the square was complete, about 1611, it was very striking both for its size and for the originality of its appearance. Quite unlike previous royal structures, it owed nothing in style to Italy, but was a synthesis of traditional French and Netherlandish features. It seems to be impossible to discover who designed it,[72] but we may be sure that it conforms to the ideas and taste of the king himself, for he took a keen interest in the work, and had other sections of the city rebuilt in a similar style.

One of these sections was Mathew's 'street they are making from the end [of the Pont Neuf]'. This is the rue Dauphine, about which Henry wrote very specifically to Sully in 1607:

> [having learned that they are beginning these buildings] I should be very glad if you would ensure that those who build here construct the façades to a common plan [d'un mesme ordre], because it would be very fine to look down the street from the bridge and see the uniform fronts. . . .[73]

In fact, the rue Dauphine was not completed for some years, but it is clear what the king's ideas were. Just by the Pont Neuf itself, on the Ile de la Cité, he was able to carry through a plan for another square. This time – contradiction in terms – it was triangular (see Map 20), in order to give a good view of the equestrian statue on the point of the island to the west. In May 1608 the king was harassing Sully for him to see to the allotments of

131

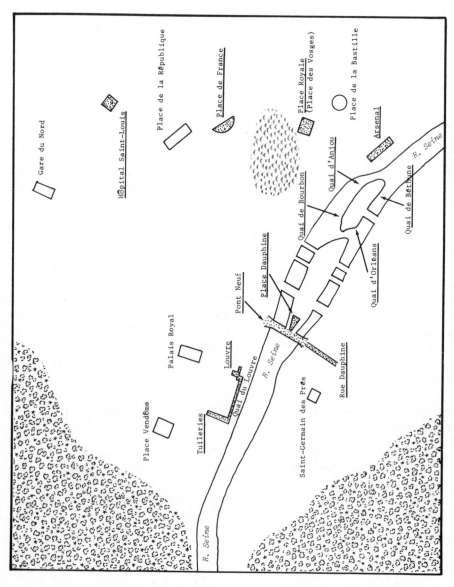

Map 20 *Henry's works at Paris. The names of buildings undertaken during the reign are underlined; a few more recent monuments have been included so as to orient the reader.*

this square, which like the Place Royale was to be built by private individuals.[74] Later that year, Malherbe wrote to Peiresc that work was going on at the Place Dauphine, and it may well have been largely finished by 1610 (Plate 12). Its houses resembled those of the Place Royale, with their walls of brick, in which the quoins, courses and window-surrounds were picked out in stone (Plate 13). Clearly, this was the style which the king liked, and according to L'Estoile he planned it himself.[75] However, it is impossible to say how far he took the lead in the actual designing, and how far he was influenced, for instance, by the suggestions of Sully.

Towards the end of his reign, he undertook three other major projects in Paris. In July 1607 he laid the first stone of what was to become the Hôpital Saint-Louis.[76] There has been much speculation about who actually designed the building, but this imposing and harmonious structure, which still stands on the rue Bichat, clearly shows many of the characteristics of the two great squares; in particular, its style owes nothing to Italy (Plate 14). In the north-eastern part of Paris, the king began a project to be known as the 'Place de France'. This great square, whose first survey on the ground was personally supervised by the king,[77] was to have taken the form of a semi-circle, pierced by streets bearing the names of the greatest French provinces: Picardy, Dauphiné, Provence and so on.[78] It would have been an architectural celebration of French unity, but on the king's death it was abandoned, and only a few street-names today remind us of it.

Finally, there was the plan to build a royal college. On 23 December 1609, according to the *Mercure françois*, the king sent Sully, Thou, Du Perron and some others to report on the site of the former colleges of Triquet and Cambray. Here he planned to build four great lecture-rooms, lodgings for the professors, and accommodation for the royal library. But his death cut the project short, and it was never completed in the way that he had planned.

In spite of these disappointments, in sixteen years the king had left an indelible mark on the outward appearance of Paris. If the work at the Louvre and Tuileries was relatively conventional, carrying on the plans of previous sovereigns, many of the other constructions were highly original: the Pont Neuf with its wide carriage-way clear of houses, the rue Dauphine with its unified façades and, above all, the two great *places* with their uniform houses in the distinctive brick-and-stone style which has taken the name of the king – the *style Henri IV*.

(ix) 'L'honourable passion ... d'embellir son royaume de toutes sortes d'artifices'

After describing some of these buildings, in his *Chronologie novenaire* for 1604 Palma-Cayet goes on to write about the industrial ventures which

133

the king was fostering at that time. In these affairs, Henry's chief adviser was Barthélemy de Laffemas (1545–1611), *tailleur ordinaire*. At times the king seemed to find it odd that his tailor should meddle with affairs so far from his trade, and on one occasion, when Laffemas had presented him with a work on industrial policy, remarked that since his tailor composed books he would be glad if for the future his chancellor would make his shoes.[79] There was in fact a slightly ludicrous, feckless aspect to Laffemas,[80] but he was also a tireless propagandist for the development of various French industries, and in 1597 proposed to the king a general programme of industrial development.

Henry received this programme with interest, for like all France's rulers at that time he was concerned by the way in which foreigners had invaded French markets for manufactured goods; the English with their cloth, the Dutch with their tapestries and, above all, the Italians with their silks and other fine, expensive goods. The Assembly of Notables of 1596 had advocated the encouragement of native industries to challenge these imports and so preserve French supplies of bullion; in 1602 Henry therefore authorised the establishment of a 'conseil de commerce', whose members essentially deliberated upon subjects submitted to them through Laffemas. Their meetings were frequent in 1602, 1603 and 1604,[81] and the council acted as a sort of clearing-house for deciding which schemes deserved support and how it ought to be given. Often they went to see the king or Sully, and sometimes Henry would personally decide on some question which was in doubt.[82]

Their deliberations covered a very wide range of industrial enterprises, and it would be tedious to enumerate them all, for they numbered over two hundred. However, we may examine the fortunes of a few of them, so as to assess how successful Henry was in these mercantilist ventures. The industry on which he lavished most attention was the production and manufacture of silk. Between 1602 and 1604 the *conseil de commerce* engaged contractors who distributed mulberry-plants and silk-worms in many generalities, including particularly those of Lyon, Orléans, Paris, Poitiers and Tours. Henry's ambition was for all the 36,000 parishes of France to have their own rearing-houses for silk-worms; he hoped like this not only to save foreign exchange but also to offer intensive employment. Of course, before his time there already were some such enterprises in many southern provinces: Provence and parts of Dauphiné and Languedoc, for instance. The result of his efforts, supported by many nobles but on the whole disregarded by the peasantry, was to extend northwards the limit of silk production. Ventures in Brittany, Normandy, Picardy and Poitou were failures, but a lasting expansion took place in the silk production of areas like Touraine, Lyonnais and the Vivarais.

The success of silk manufacture was similarly mixed. The projects in Paris, including those at the Place Royale, were only limping on by 1610, and those in Troyes failed altogether. On the other hand, the factory founded at Mantes in 1604 for producing light silks (*crêpes*, or crapes) was very successful, and flourished long after the end of Henry's reign. This factory seems to have been under the particular care of Sully, governor of Mantes; it would appear that such ventures often thrived when some great noble took them under his wing.

Another industry which the king wished to stimulate was tapestry production, where again there was a great loss of currency to the Italians and the Dutch. Factories were founded under his protection in Amiens, Calais, Paris and Tours, and several of these prospered. The one in Paris, in the old dye-works known as the 'Gobelins', acquired a strength and reputation which have lasted down to the present day, and it seems that Henry was also responsible for the beginning of the tapestry-works known as the 'Savonnerie'. In tapestry, then, he was remarkably successful, and some progress was also made in the production of morocco leather, paper and fine glass, under royal encouragement.[83] On the whole, ventures in the metallurgical industries were much less successful, and Henry had no effect on the large-scale linen and cloth industries. In general, his efforts naturally were concentrated on industries producing small quantities of fine-quality goods, and it is plain to us now that the great advances – precursors of the 'industrial revolution' – would be made not here but in the industries of mass-production. However, in order seriously to increase production in those areas, the king would have had to be able to change not only guild practices and traditional economic relationships, but also existing technologies, including those of agricultural production. Such a programme – which has baffled many governments of our day – was manifestly beyond the capacity of any government of the *ancien régime*; what is remarkable is not that Henry did not attempt it, but that he was so successful in his relatively limited economic ventures.

10 'Un malheur inconnu', 1605–6

(i)   'Souvent d'une estincelle il s'allume un grand feu . . .'

As we have seen in Chapter 9, section v, the year 1604 was marked by the plot organised by Entragues and Auvergne. Although its leaders had been disciplined, very little had been done about the lesser conspirators, and in 1605, to judge by alarming reports sent from central France by Queen Marguerite,[1] the embers of this conspiracy seemed about to burst into flame. So, about the middle of July, the king asked La Force, governor of Navarre, to go down into Périgord and do what he could to counter various 'plots and secret assemblies'.[2] La Force did his best, but at the beginning of September Henry had as well to write to Epernon, governor of Limousin, and to Ornano, lieutenant-governor of Guyenne, asking them to assemble the loyal nobles of their *gouvernements* and to root out the conspirators.

The king cannot have expected much of the efforts of Epernon, who had himself been implicated in so many rumoured plots, and the *remuements* did not seem to be abating. So in late September the king himself left for Limoges, an event marked by Malherbe's *Prière pour le roy Henry le Grand, allant en Limousin.* As it turned out, the fears of Malherbe were entirely belied by the course of events; Henry made a leisurely progress to Limoges, whence he was able to report in mid-October that all the strongholds had been surrendered and that nearly all the nobles had assured him of their loyalty.[3] After his departure, the governor of Quercy saw to the rounding-up of a dozen or two of the most stubborn conspirators, of whom five were beheaded;[4] the plot was over.

This agitation, typical of those with which the king had to deal, had its roots in previous conspiracies; to judge by Henry's correspondence, he suspected that it ran back to Bouillon's agents, or Biron's plots, or perhaps to the ducats of the king of Spain. These rebellions were not in any sense 'class conflicts', even though the nobles sometimes pretended to be acting for the common good. As the *Mercure françois* puts it, the rebels used their 'normal pretext' that they were acting for the relief of the people, and for the better administration of justice, but the real motive of the turbulent nobles of Limousin and Périgord was 'to fish in troubled waters, and while seeming to act for the public good to grow fat upon the spoils of the poor people'.[5] Henry's great achievement had been to put an end to a situation of civil war, in which these noble acts of violence were only too common; there was no general support for a return to the days of pillage and disorder.

(ii) *'Ceux de la Religion de Guyenne et de Languedoc y font rage'*

Intermingled with this conspiracy was a slightly different movement, one of resistance among the Protestants. After the promulgation of the Edict of Nantes, various problems had arisen in its application, and many of these issues had been resolved by an assembly which the king allowed the Protestants to hold at Sainte-Foy in 1601.[6] During the ensuing years, though, Henry's increasingly favourable attitude towards the ancient church led to a growing distrust among the Protestants, and in October 1604 the king felt obliged to consent to a further general Protestant assembly for 1605.

In Henry's view, such an assembly ought not to have any concern with political matters, but ought simply to elect two deputies who could thereafter represent Protestant grievances to him at court.[7] Of course, such a limited function was not acceptable to the party zealots, and it became clear, when the assembly met in July 1605 in Châtellerault, that they would try to force further concessions. The royal representative in Châtellerault was Sully, evidently chosen because he was a Protestant who enjoyed the close confidence of the king. His instructions clearly reveal Henry's fears and preoccupations. First of all, he was to prevent any attempts to rally support for Bouillon. Then he was to suggest that six deputies might be elected, so that the king could choose two of them. He was to turn the Assembly away from any discussion of the difficult problem of whether the Pope was in fact Antichrist or not, and in general was to hustle the Assembly through as fast as possible, without giving any guarantees for a further reunion.

On the whole, Sully was successful in these aims, no doubt in part because the deputies were meeting in the province (Poitou) of which he was governor. No support was evident for Bouillon, and two acceptable deputies were chosen. No untactful references to the Pope were published, and the Assembly broke up after just two weeks.[8] On the surface the Protestants seemed content. However, the continuing favour shown by the king towards the leaders of the Catholic Reformation in France kept the Protestants mildly apprehensive, and led to further protests when they met again in Jargeau in 1608.

(iii) 'We Have Been Advised of the Opposition . . . to the Sieur de Monts'

When the dauphin was at Saint-Germain in November 1605, he was taken to see two strange sights: a large and unfamiliar animal, and a small boat, covered with tree-bark and painted red, which three sailors rowed for him at an incredible speed.[9] The large animal was probably a moose, and the boat was of course an Indian canoe; both were the tangible evidence of the French expedition to Canada in 1604–5.[10]

From about 1598, Henry seems to have been interested in encouraging the settlement of what became known as New France.[11] In that year he delivered a commission to the marquis de La Roche to establish himself in Canada; La Roche having failed, in 1599 the king concluded a contract with a certain Pierre de Chauvin, sieur de Tonnetuit, of Normandy. The latter made two voyages, but it is clear that he was more interested in making a quick profit than in establishing French power. In January 1603, therefore, Henry set up a commission of inquiry in Rouen to discuss the whole question of whether such a monopoly should be granted, and of how a colony could be established.[12] The commission seems to have decided – against the opposition of the merchants of several French ports – in favour of a monopoly. Chauvin's commission was renewed but, as he shortly afterwards died, his role was taken over by the governor of Dieppe, Aymar de Chaste, who organised another expedition in 1603. Shortly afterwards, however, Chaste also died, and it was then that the king turned to Pierre du Gua, sieur de Monts, under whose direction decisive progress would be made.

Monts was a Huguenot, who after serving Henry in the religious wars had become governor of Pons in Saintonge.[13] He had made a journey with Chauvin, and on 7 November 1603 had an interview with the king, at which he set out his plans for colonisation.[14] The next day he received his commission as 'lieutenant général en Acadie'; he and his associates were to enjoy a monopoly on trade between the 40th and 46th parallels, and were to establish centres of colonisation. Early in 1604 he founded the Compagnie de la Nouvelle France, which in the next few years succeeded in establishing bases at Annapolis (1605) and then Québec (1608). The king continued to support them, and in 1608 agreed to pay for the upkeep of the Jesuit fathers Biard and Massié, sent to the 'mission d'Acadie'.[15] So Monts, with his more famous successor Champlain, laid the foundations of the French presence in what came to be known as Canada.

To what extent was their work directed by the king? Poirson, always eager to emphasise Henry's far-sighted intelligence, affirms that he was 'the soul of all these ventures'.[16] This must be an exaggeration, for there was a long tradition of French adventuring in North America, of which

Chauvin and Monts were the latest leaders. But it does seem that the king took an active interest in the colonial ventures, and that he did his best to protect Monts from enemies in France. In December 1603, for instance, he explained in a circular letter to the *amirautés* that the monopoly would last for ten years.[17] In January 1604 he wrote to the *parlement* of Rouen that it should cease its opposition to Monts.[18] In January 1605 he intervened in his favour against the *officiers des traites*,*[19] keeping up the pressure with further letters that February[20] and an *arrêt* that March.[21] In the end, the combined opposition of Sully – who believed that Frenchmen could never prosper in the northern latitudes – and the mercantile interests forced Henry to revoke Monts' concession. But by then the French were established both at Annapolis and at Québec, and it is hard to deny that this remarkable extension of their power owed much to the support of the king.

(iv) 'Il me tint continuellement la main'

Between 1602 and 1605 the English ambassador in Paris was Sir Thomas Parry, whom Henry mistrusted almost as much as he had disliked his predecessor, Sir Ralph Winwood. But, in the closing months of 1605, Parry was joined by his successor, Sir George Carew, and this emissary proved to be a man after the French king's heart. In January 1606, the two English diplomats went on the customary visit to Saint-Germain to see the Dauphin. Carew, whose reports were almost always more appreciative and optimistic than those of Parry, found the child to be 'of a very strong and vigorous disposition',[22] and the young Louis, taking the letter brought from the Prince of Wales, opened it and asked his physician Héroard to read it for him.

After this first visit, Carew gradually became more and more friendly with the French king. In October 1606, for instance, he went to see him at Fontainebleau, where Henry walked with him for an hour and a half, and their conversation was only interrupted when one of the royal chaplains came to tell him that it was noon, and time for Mass.[23] By July 1607, Carew had become so familiar with Henry that their conversations took place as they sat side by side, and the following August we find them hunting together, and then strolling through the royal park with the queen, Henry holding Marie with one hand and Carew with the other.

This need for physical contact, for expressing himself in what has been called 'body language', had always been a habit with Henry. When, for instance, Claude Groulart came to see him at Montceaux in 1598, he took the *premier président* for a long stroll in the park, holding Gabrielle d'Estrées by one hand and Groulart by the other.[24] He seems in part to have used this 'language' as a mark of particular esteem. When the papal legate, Alexander de Medici, came to see him in March 1597, the king made him sit down with him in a small room where they were so close, as the legate wrote, 'that he constantly took my hand'.[25] The legate noted the same thing at another audience, in July 1598.[26] Bassompierre, too, observed that Henry 'always leaned on somebody',[27] and he seems to have used this frequent bodily contact as a way of expressing his trust and confidence in people. It would be interesting to know if this habit, relatively uncommon in Western Europe today, was peculiar to the king, or if his contemporaries – perhaps particularly the *méridoniaux* – also expressed themselves like that.

(v) 'The King Rejoyceth Much in His Dolphin'

When they were at Saint-Germain, Carew and Parry would have seen something not only of the dauphin, but also of Henry's other children. By the end of 1606 the whole *troupeau*, as it was called, numbered nine: three born of the queen, three of Gabrielle d'Estrées, two of Henriette d'Entragues and one of Charlotte des Essarts. The king, explaining that it was an old French custom – as, indeed, it may have been – had insisted in the face of the queen's resistance that all these children should grow up together, in the charge of the redoubtable Madame de Montglat.

They spent most of their time at Saint-Germain, whose air was reputed to be particularly healthy, and the king often went to see the dauphin there. From his earliest days Henry liked to play with the child,[28] and was a very attentive father. When Louis was little, the king would play the game of hiding and calling his name, or would join him at the table and butter his bread for him, or would take him to see the great carp in the pond. When he got a bit bigger, they would go hunting and play tennis together, and the time eventually came when Louis was introduced to the royal council. The dauphin was a headstrong child, and Henry enjoined Madame de Mont-glat to beat him as often as necessary – which was frequently. On the whole, Louis seems to have loved and respected his father, who certainly gave him a great deal more attention than did his mother.

Marie, of course, must have felt constantly humiliated by the physical evidence of Henry's infidelity, which may in part account for her apparent neglect of her children. For his part, the king found no incongruity in the antics of his *troupeau*. He was particularly fond of the dauphin, and felt that the sequence of his children's birth was providential, since Louis 'would be in the saddle while his brethren remained in their long coates'.[29] The occasion of Louis' baptism in September 1606 was celebrated with particular ostentation, in the *cour du donjon* at Fontainebleau. This courtyard had recently been extensively rebuilt, in the style which survives to this day, and in a ceremony of quite extraordinary splendour Louis was baptised, along with his sisters Elisabeth and Christine (Plate 15).

The king truly rejoiced much in his dauphin, France's insurance against civil war after Henry's death. On one of the friezes along the top of the wall at Fontainebleau, the salamander used in the time of François I gives way in the building of Henry's time to the emblem of the dolphin. No doubt there was a double symbolism here, for the dolphin was not only a creature famous in folklore for its intelligence and goodwill, but also, in Henry's France, the synonym for the ensured succession, a crucial element in her constitutional stability.

(vi)   'Tant j'estois amoureux de Sedan'

The main menace to this stability in 1606 remained the duc de Bouillon, who continued to defy the king from his stronghold at Sedan, handily sited for negotiations with the princelings of Germany. By the beginning of March 1606, Henry had resolved on an expedition to Sedan, and on 15 March he set out, rather thinly accompanied.[30] Sully mobilised forty-five cannon, with a considerable supply of powder and shot,[31] and as Bouillon was thought to be receiving reinforcements it looked as if there might be a regular siege. Henry took care to justify his expedition to the landgrave of Hesse, and through him to the German princes, but in fact the closer the royal army came to Sedan, the less Bouillon felt like fighting, and the capitulation was soon signed, on April Fool's Day.

The king was exultant, writing back that like Caesar he could say 'Veni, vidi, vici'. As he also wrote,[32] he had shown that he knew how to make himself obeyed, and had no doubt discouraged the ambitions of other great nobles. The Spaniards had feared that Henry was mobilising this force in order to go into Flanders,[33] but no such intention may be detected in the king's letters. Bouillon accompanied the king back to Paris, mounted on a plain horse and looking rather downcast, as well he might. Sully, delighted to have cut down to size his main rival among the Protestant nobles, rode in splendour at the king's side. They were seen to be talking together, with Sully pointing out to His Majesty – as if there were any need of that – the 'belles dames' lining the route. One of these was the Countess of Auvergne, whom the king greeted as she looked down from one of the windows of the Bastille. . . .

(vii)   'The Princes of Germany Begin to Bristle Themselves'

The reconciliation of Bouillon with the king had an immediate effect on French policy towards the German princes. As we have seen (Chapter 9, section i), they had been mistrustful of Henry during 1603, 1604 and 1605, when Bouillon was filling their ears with his complaints. After 1606, however, they became much more open to the idea of forming a Protestant union, and were even inclined to overlook the substantial sums of money which Henry still owed some of them.[34] This growth of opinion in favour of a union was greatly encouraged by the affair of Donauwörth, late in 1607. Donauwörth was an Imperial town, with a substantial Protestant majority among its inhabitants. Following an attempt by the town council to suppress a Catholic procession, the town was put to the Ban of the Empire, and was thereupon occupied by Maximilian of Bavaria. This clear evidence of expansionist ambition on the part of the Viennese Habsburgs was extremely alarming to the Protestant powers, and in May 1608 the Evangelical Union was concluded between four of them; its members were pledged to defend each other if attacked. Among the four were the Elector Palatine and the Duke of Würtemberg; they were joined during 1608 and 1609 by several free cities including Nuremberg, Strasbourg and Ulm.

(viii)   'The Placing of These Waters, for the Transporting of All Her Commodities'

The king spent most of the year 1607 in and around Paris, but in October went to Montargis, to see how the canal-works there were coming on. As early as the reign of François I, the French monarchy had encouraged schemes to build canals, and it was a commonplace that France seemed by nature to have been endowed with rivers which, by the closeness of their sources, were predestined to link up the Mediterranean, the Atlantic, the Channel and the North Sea. Henry and Sully vigorously took up these seductive projects, and by 1607 seem to have been thinking in terms of at least three major canals.[35] One would link the Loire and Seine near Montargis, a second would join the Saône to the Seine near Dijon, and a third would connect the Garonne to the Aude south of Toulouse.[36] Work actually went forward on the first two projects, and the Briare Canal, linking Loire and Seine, was very nearly finished in 1610, and was completed in 1638–42 (Map 21).

Other, lesser projects were successfully carried through before 1610. The Vesle, for instance, was canalised between Reims and the Aisne, and the Clain was similarly canalised between Poitiers and the Vienne. Considering that transport by water was three to five times cheaper than transport by land,[37] it is easy to imagine how the opening of these waterways must have stimulated the markets of towns like Reims and Poitiers.

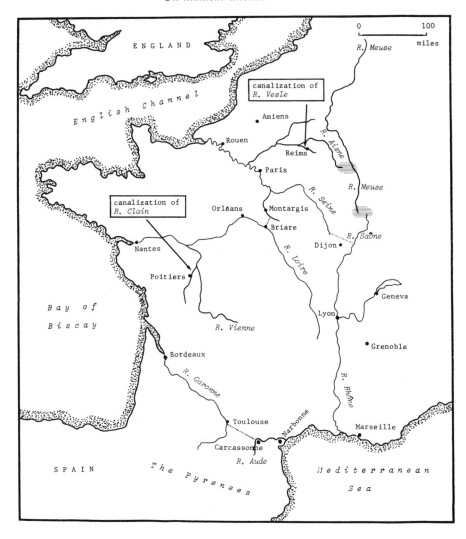

Map 21   *Canals undertaken by Henry and Sully*

Henry and Sully had a variety of motives for undertaking such expensive works. In the case of the Saône–Seine canal, one of the avowed intentions was to cut out the long journey around Spain for goods coming from the Atlantic to the Mediterranean, and so to 'make Spain lose two millions of income and gain them for France'.[38] Other motives were related to specific economic possibilities; an Aisne–Meuse canal, for instance, would enable coal of the Liège district to undercut English coal on the Paris market,[39] and a Saône–Meuse connection could put Marseille in direct touch with the United Provinces. There were, too, strategic considerations. From the Paris Arsenal, heavy equipment could easily be conveyed to threatened points on the eastern frontier; troops, too, could theoretically be shipped in this way, without tiring themselves or ravaging the countryside.

All in all, it is easy to see the attraction of canals for mercantilist kings and statesmen. Once the kingdom was seen as an economic whole, as Henry and Sully undoubtedly saw it, there was everything to be said for breaking down provincial divisions and using the central exchequer to encourage easy communications from one part to another. The work under Henry only lasted about twelve years, but it set a course which would be followed in canal-building throughout the *ancien régime*.

(ix) 'Great Multitudes of Irishmen'

Queen Marguerite had returned to Paris in 1605, bringing with her that alarming news of events in Auvergne. A month or so after her arrival, as she was entering the Jacobin church in Paris, she met at its entrance a destitute Irishwoman who had just given birth to a baby boy. Marguerite picked up the poor child, and saw to his christening.[40] His mother must have been among the first of the Irish refugees who began arriving in France about 1605, victims of the English 'settlement' of their homeland.

By November 1605, these Irish people were beginning to be a serious nuisance in Paris, for at the beginning of that month Chancellor Bellièvre wrote about them both to the king and to Villeroy. There were many men among them, he said, who made the Parisians nervous about what they might get up to at night, and women and children, too, who were so dirty and undernourished that they would surely bring plague to the city.[41] Bellièvre's solution was to charter a boat and send them back either voluntarily or by force; he added that he had tried to palm them off on the sieur de Monts, newly returned from Canada, but 'M. de Monts said that they would be useless and nothing would induce him to receive such worthless people who neither wish nor know how to work'.

Henry's first reaction seems to have been more Christian; he 'offered to take some of them, and to bringe them upp'.[42] But, finding that 'they would doe no manner of work', he, too, began to think that the best thing was to ship them home. One of his almoners was deputed to work among them, in an attempt to provide food for them and to persuade them to work; as L'Estoile said, many people felt that 'to chase the poor people out of Paris ... was to banish God from the city'.[43] But the Irish proved resistant to suggestions that they should work, and gained a reputation for being dishonest wastrels, whose chief skill lay in begetting children.[44]

The Hôtel de Ville had to act. On 18 May 1606 a special levy was made 'for the expulsion of the Irish', and on the following day the gates were guarded while they were rounded up. A boat had been provided, with 2,500 loaves of bread for the voyage, and so the refugees were shipped off to Brest, where the sieur de Sourdéac saw to it that they went on to Ireland. In June 1606 an instruction from James I decreed that they should be diverted to some part of Munster, and there the survivors no doubt resettled as best they might, to be followed before long by another boatload from Paris.

Henry, the Most Christian King, must have felt some compunction about treating the refugees in this way, but he was in a tricky position, given the pressure applied both by the Parisians and by the English ambassador.[45] Something of the same problem arose in October 1607, when the Earl of Tyrone fled to France with his family and followers. Thanks to the opposition of Carew, he was not allowed to come to Paris, though he was permitted to recuperate in Rouen. When Carew tried to press for his arrest, indeed, Henry 'grew into heat and choler, saying "La France est libre, je ne suis esclave ny d'Angleterre ny d'Espagne", and that they were either "Espagnols ou maligns" that would sample the usage of Tyrone in France and in the Low Countries together, and that it was to be known whether he had to doe "avec des hommes ou des bestes"'.[46] Tyrone eventually passed on to the Spanish Netherlands, where he was well received.

11 The Halcyon's Nest, 1607–9

(i) 'The Great Mortification of His Natural Vivacity'

The years 1607 and 1608 mark in most respects the apogee of Henry's reign. By then the various rivals of royal power – in particular the great nobles and the powerful towns – had accepted a certain effacement, and the king had been able to build up a substantial bullion reserve and to complete many public works. On the other hand, he had not yet become involved in that fatal train of events which, beginning with the death of the Duke of Jülich-Cleves, was eventually to lead to the assassination of Henry himself.

Henry's power remained very personal, so that affairs of state could be affected by fluctuations in his health. As we have seen, he had first been troubled by gout in 1602, and had had a more serious attack in 1603. Early in 1604, he had to spend eight days in bed because of it, lying there 'in acute pain and to the great mortification of his natural vivacity', as the Venetian ambassador observed.[1] Gout is a curious affliction, apparently random in its incidence. Throughout 1604 the king was 'forte tourmenté' by it,[2] but in 1605 and 1606 the attacks seem to have been milder.

In 1607 it came back with a vengeance. He had a long attack in June, which according to the English ambassador made him 'chagrin and retyred';[3] L'Estoile noted at the same time that he was so racked by it that he quite changed his appearance and manner.[4] This attack lasted on and off to the end of August, after which he had an intermission. The gout came back in 1608 and again in 1609, but by then Henry seems to have been better able to control, or at any rate to tolerate, it. He would take to his bed at the onset of the pain, but then astonish his courtiers and the ever-vigilant foreign diplomats by suddenly going on a long hunt, or playing some furious sets of tennis. The gout itself was thus used as a political instrument; as the English agent Becher put it, 'the actions of this prince being so full of life and art intermingled, as he doth make his very infirmities to serve for an argument of his vigour of body, a point which he doth much desire should be believed both at home and abroad'.[5]

(ii) 'His Majesty Was Magnificently and Sumptuously Arrayed'

Throughout his reign, Henry had been alert to what Becher calls 'art' in his public actions. Although he was by nature rather informal, not to say dirty and untidy, in his dress, he could on occasion stage-manage magnificent receptions, in which he would appear in the full sartorial splendour of the Most Christian King. The word 'stage-manage' should be taken in the most literal sense; just as he liked to act as master of ceremonies for the royal ballets, so he personally would position and inspect the guards before some solemn ceremony.[6] We have already described one such occasion: the swearing of the abjuration in 1593. Another occurred in October 1602, when the representatives of the Swiss cantons came to France to sign a new treaty of alliance. There were forty-two of these ambassadors, and from the time they entered French territory they were magnificently entertained; at Dijon in the 'maison du roy', at Troyes in the bishop's palace, and at Conflans by Villeroy. They entered Paris on Monday, 14 October, and were escorted by a band of French gentlemen to their assigned lodgings.[7]

On Wednesday the 16th, they dined with the Chancellor, and then went on foot to the Louvre. All its approaches were lined with soldiers, from the French and Scottish guards and from the archers. So the Swiss came into the 'grande salle' and up the main staircase between the serried rows, to be greeted in the antechamber by the king. He was dressed 'very magnificently and sumptuously ... with a priceless diamond-crusted plume in his black and white hat, and a sash of the same colour, also covered with diamonds'. Each of the forty-two Swiss kissed one of the king's hands, while with the other he embraced them round their shoulders. After an exchange of speeches they withdrew, and on the following day went to Saint-Germain to see the dauphin and kiss his hand;[8] here, too, they had a splendid feast.

The actual swearing of the treaty took place in the cathedral of Notre-Dame on Sunday the 20th. The whole church had been decorated with tapestries (the work, no doubt, of the Herbannes and Gaboury families), and the seats were covered with embroidered fleurs-de-lis. Special galleries had been built for the musicians and for the distinguished guests; the king himself heard Mass on a richly ornamented platform. He arrived at about nine in the morning, in a great procession marching to the beat of a drum, and after the Mass, for which the Protestants among the Swiss absented themselves, made a short speech before the actual ceremony of swearing, which the Swiss carried out two by two. After that the music played, and Sully fired numerous salutes from the guns in the nearby Arsenal. More feasts followed, until on Friday the 25th the Swiss left for home. They had impressed the French by their robust appearance, being big-bottomed, ruddy-faced men who 'looked like a crowd of Bacchuses just come from the *vendange*'. In their turn, they had no doubt been dazzled by the king, who had spared no expense to feed and entertain them.

In July 1608 he had a different kind of guest. This time it was a Spanish grandee, Don Pedro of Toledo, come to talk about a Franco-Spanish *rapprochement*. Don Pedro received the usual treatment, being met at Bayonne, Bordeaux, Poitiers, Blois and Orléans by substantial bodies of horse, normally led by the provincial governor.[9] When he arrived at Fontainebleau on 20 July it was about six in the evening, but the maréchal de Brissac escorted him along the *allée des Ormes*, lined by the guards, and to the *cour ovale*, where they dismounted. From there he was taken through great crowds of courtiers to the apartment of Sébastien Zamet, richly furnished.

On the following day, Don Pedro had his first audience with the king, which was followed by several others. The English ambassador observed the audiences closely, reporting that 'the King in his action and gestures was noted to be full of earnestness, walking swiftly and plucking at his shirt often'; no doubt he feared that they were getting along famously.[10] Don Pedro accompanied the court when it returned to Paris, and there he remained until the end of February 1609, often seeing Henry and taking part in the various court festivities like tournaments and ballets, as well as admiring the new buildings, attending church services, and negotiating secretly with spies. The king did his best to impress his guest, and at the end of his stay presented Don Pedro with a great diamond which had cost 18,800 *livres*.[11] For his part, the Spaniard gave many outward signs of respect and even admiration. But the embassy was bound to fail as far as its substance went, for Don Pedro was trying to arrange a marriage between the royal children of France and Spain, in return for Henry's abandonment of the Dutch.[12] As the king remarked after their first meeting, 'I was a little astonished and not much edified' by these proposals,[13] which had no chance of success at that time, given the continuing cold war between France and Spain.

(iii) *'Tandem arbiter orbis'*

Henry's 'policy of magnificence' was not confined to plans for impressing his visitors by sumptuous displays. Throughout the reign, in more or less subtle ways, writers, engravers, medallists and painters were encouraged to develop the theme of Henry as the Gallic Hercules or Jupiter,[14] the king under whom *renovatio* would at last be possible. Both the *Astrée* of Honoré d'Urfé, for instance, and the *Théâtre de l'agriculture*, by Olivier de Serres, look to a new Golden Age made possible by the all-conquering king.[15] Needless to say, Henry kept a tight control over the press, and did not hesitate to suppress writings judged seditious or even over-critical,[16] while rewarding authors who followed a suitable line.

Among the engravers, Gaultier produced many versions of the king as Hercules, and the medals which Sully had struck for each New Year's Day often took up the Hercules theme (see Plate 16). When Sully wanted to work out a set of mythological tapestries for his country house, he chose to represent Henry as Apollo (Sully himself was Saturn, and his wife Venus...).[17] The mythology of the Sun King had distant roots. We might be tempted to take this artistic propaganda lightly, were it not for a very curious episode showing how seriously the king took it himself. In February 1610 he was planning to go to war, and wanted everybody to know about it. So first of all he had himself measured for a new suit of armour with the maximum publicity, and then he caused to be 'set up in his chamber within these few dayes a table, wherein is paynted a man fleeing from Venus, and the image of gaming, and following Hercules after two other images, of hope and fortune'.[18] It was almost as if the king, too, needed this visual propaganda to convince himself of his seriousness.

(iv)   'The Greatest and Goodliest Palace of Europe'

Of course, it is in the royal palaces that we find the most spectacular examples of cultural propaganda. At the Louvre itself, whose very structure was a reverberant affirmation of royal power (see Chapter 9), the most significant decorations were found in the *petite galerie*. The ceiling of this splendid room was painted with allegorical scenes from antiquity, while the walls between the windows were decorated with portraits of the kings and queens of France, from Saint Louis down to Henry IV.[19] Some critics felt that there was not enough relationship between these two themes, but the message of the wall-paintings was unmistakable: Henry was the latest in a long line of distinguished monarchs. This very historical concept, seen as well, for instance, in the series of imperial busts at Innsbruck, owed its origin perhaps to concepts found in antiquity, being an example of what Vitruvius calls megalography.[20] The *petite galerie* certainly seems to have dazzled some visitors, to judge from the reaction of Thomas Coryate, who found it 'so unspeakably faire ... that a man can hardly comprehend it in his minde, that hath not first seene it with his bodily eyes'.[21]

At Saint-Germain-en-Laye the king merely finished off the little palace begun by Catherine de Medici. Sir Anthony Mildmay's impression of this building was very favourable; he found it 'one of ye best conveyed little houses that ever I sawe'.[22] But the most remarkable feature at Saint-Germain was the series of six gardens leading down from the escarpment, on which the *château* stood, to the Seine.[23] These gardens were planned by Etienne du Pérac, who had just come back from Italy, and were constructed by Claude Mollet, royal gardener. Each of them formed part of a general scheme, but each was complete in itself, like the gardens of the Villa d'Este. On several levels there were grottoes and fountains, the work of Thomas and Alexander Francini, whom Henry had brought from Florence, where they served the Grand Duke of Tuscany. The grottoes were decorated with sea-shells and coral, specially brought in from Rouen, and some of the fountains were concealed in the mouths of grotesque beasts, from which a jet of water would come and soak the unwary passer-by, to the delight of the king.[24]

Work had begun both at the Louvre and at Saint-Germain in 1594; two years later, the king began his extensive additions to Fontainebleau.[25] These involved almost every part of the *château* at one time or another, but the most remarkable new structures were the *Porte Dauphine* and the *Cour des Offices*. It is hard to imagine two buildings more different in style; the first has strongly Mannerist features (Plate 17), while the second is very reminiscent of the buildings in Paris around the Place Royale and the Place Dauphine. As usual, it seems to be impossible to determine who were the responsible architects, though we may be sure that they were not the same person. Inside, the most remarkable work was the *belle cheminée*, largely destroyed in 1725. For this, the sculptor Mathieu Jacquet created superb marble bas-reliefs showing some of Henry's victories, as well as a splendid equestrian statue of the king, and various heads of Mercury and of Hercules.[26] Visitors to Fontainebleau in Henry's day were always impressed by this marvellous work, and also by the great extent and variety of the gardens which the king had planted. Here, again, it was the Francinis who were responsible for those fountains and water-works which so delighted the king. He often visited the Fontainebleau gardens with the dauphin, and there is an amusing account of him feeding the great carp which (then as now) inhabited some of the ponds.

The Louvre and Fontainebleau, and to a lesser extent Saint-Germain, were *châteaux* suited for great public occasions, when the king could receive visitors like the papal legate, Maurice the Wise or Don Pedro of Toledo. Montceaux was a different sort of *château*, where Henry went to hunt, sometimes in company with particular friends like the English ambassador Carew. The latter has left an interesting description of the way in which the grounds at Montceaux were laid out in order to make it easy for the king to follow the hunt.[27] Taking advantage of a great curve in the Marne, a very extensive wood had been enclosed, with rides 'all parted out in *patte d'oye*, or *en estoille* as they terme it', so that Henry could from the centre of this star-shaped system of tracks survey the progress of the hunt, and no doubt join it at an opportune moment.

150

(v) 'Spunges to the King'

It was the propaganda role of the great palaces which partly explains the extraordinary place which they occupied in the royal expenditures (see Table 11.1). However, it is evident that the king regarded expenditure on 'buildings' as one of the heads which could be cut in case of emergency.[28] For in 1600, 1605–6, 1608 and 1610 those expenses were reduced from their normal 735 million *livres* to an average of about 550 million. These reductions were in view of the Savoy campaign, the Bouillon expedition, the great floods of 1608 (which necessitated much expenditure on roads and bridges) and the preparations for the 1610 campaign. Of course, under heading 3 these campaigns are reflected in an increased expenditure on *guerres*, a sub-division concerned with payments to fighting men.

Returning to heading 1, it is noticeable that the 'household' in most years consumed more than one-fifth of the total expenditure. Although this has sometimes seemed disproportionate to modern critics, in fact it reflects the importance of the royal household in relation to the rest of the 'administration'; it simply emphasises that to a great extent the king and his immediate entourage *were* the 'government'. This heading also conceals payments which logically ought to go elsewhere; to doctors, for instance, who treated all manner of high personages, to clerics who were awaiting suitable posts, or to secretaries who were employed as periodic *commissaires*. Heading 2, 'guards', remained fairly constant throughout the reign; it referred to the Scottish, Swiss and other guards who protected the king. The progressive increase in expenditure on the Marine du Levant has already been explained in Chapter 8, concerning the Mediterranean galley-fleet. Heading 5 reveals one of the great strategic weaknesses of Henry IV's France: the virtual absence of any naval force in the Atlantic or Channel. In November 1608, Sully apparently told the English ambassador Carew that the French 'were in hand to buy and builde 20 shipps of warre for the Ocean',[29] but this programme never got under way, and it was left to Richelieu to begin building an Atlantic fleet.

Payment to the Ligues des Suisses* was part of a complicated system of contracts, whereby Henry paid off some of the money which he owed to the Swiss soldiers who had fought for him in the early years of the reign.[30] He was forced to take this obligation seriously, since he expected to need the Swiss again one day. Payments for 'artillery' reflect the progress of that arm under Sully.[31] Until 1603 the totals were fairly high, as arms and ammunition were manufactured and stored in the arsenals at Paris and in the provinces (Plate 11). Expenditure fell in 1604, revived in 1606 for the Bouillon expedition, and then tailed off in the end of the reign, before the preparations of 1610. 'Fortifications' show a more stable pattern of expenditure, as we should expect. There was a prolonged effort through-

151

Table 11.1 *Expenditure by the French Crown, 1600–10*

	1600	1601	1602	1603	1604	1605	1606	1607	1608	1609	1610
1 Household[1]	2,074,559	1,998,772	1,950,241	1,942,879	1,934,058	1,857,750	2,445,892	1,867,813	2,303,203	2,262,272	3,514,348
2 Guards[2]	294,322	347,299	310,287	300,082	297,071	296,421	297,901	296,375	294,951	296,351	308,051
3 Guerres[3]	4,946,360	2,581,513	2,792,934	2,602,312	914,580	3,671,391	3,665,414	2,930,083	3,726,003	3,012,746	6,999,690
4 Marine de Levant	194,523	194,912	226,500	293,600	330,400	311,400	384,400	336,175	383,269	426,500	423,420
5 Marine de Ponant	21,000	21,600	28,600	35,300	78,500	24,300	24,000	18,000	37,875	38,675	39,675
6 Ligues des Suisses	1,038,000	2,737,892	2,434,446	1,841,225	1,971,299	1,352,741	1,281,600	3,123,777	1,361,573	1,243,648	1,209,400
7 Artillery	927,622	382,795	487,345	405,332	287,001	374,697	608,565	370,096	286,400	288,995	1,154,218
8 Fortifications	478,727	611,018	465,295	465,542	368,359	423,230	424,577	494,080	532,782	570,593	363,022
9 Buildings	558,352	649,943	796,487	876,926	770,311	598,473	573,511	688,166	536,223	633,298	476,653
10 Ponts et chaussées	6,000	5,765	15,570	4,000	40,600	595,469	740,800	842,227	1,224,153	1,149,150	991,563
11 Etats et pensions	1,812,787	1,767,820	1,794,195	2,009,068	1,768,869	1,941,570	2,010,685	2,024,536	2,117,553	2,184,760	3,130,898
12 Deniers payés par ordonnance	1,055,556	886,803	2,489,556	5,000,537	7,537,801	7,861,303	9,014,772	10,018,700	13,228,318	14,931,917	9,068,414
13 Miscellaneous[4]	551,727	390,019	456,257	440,077	505,417	472,117	376,398	388,357	479,450	384,983	594,661
14 Dons par acquit	475,155	559,100	564,983	680,475	876,790	1,339,470	1,539,032	995,210	1,205,981	1,684,522	1,559,931
15 Deniers payés par acquit	3,865,988	1,405,231	3,063,812	2,134,579	1,282,906	2,685,216	1,600,930	2,191,231	2,203,715	963,057	2,060,269
16 Deniers payés comptants	2,146,141	1,648,901	2,135,058	2,009,413	2,510,500	3,067,827	3,446,079	3,345,192	2,251,175	2,501,982	1,685,853
Total	20,446,819	16,189,333	20,011,606	21,041,347	21,474,462	26,873,375	28,434,556	29,930,018	32,172,624	32,573,449	33,580,066

These figures are derived from Mallet, *Comptes rendus de l'administration des finances*, corrected in some cases by figures found in Sully's papers: see Buisseret, *Sully*, p. 81. For discussions of the figures, which in fact give merely an impression of the level of activity under each head, see Hayden, *France and the Estates General of 1614* and Bonney, *The King's Debts*, pp. 304–9

1 includes *offrandes et aumônes, chambre aux deniers , écurie du roi, argenterie du roi, menus plaisirs, venerie et fauconnerie* and *maison de la reine*.
2 includes *cent gentilshommes, gardes écossaises, gardes du corps du roi, prévôté de l'hôtel* and *cent suisses*.
3 both *ordinaire* and *extraordinaire*.
4 includes *voyages, menus dons* and *ambassades*.

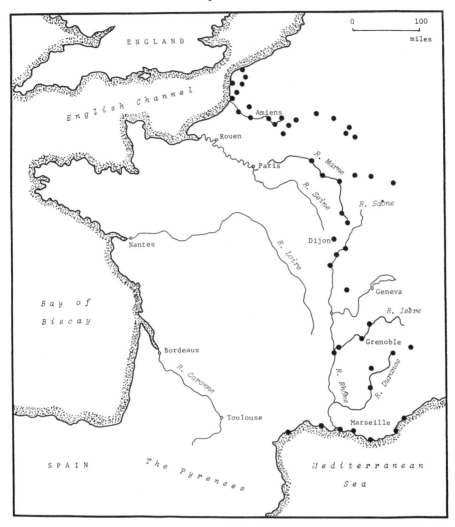

Map 22 *Fortifications constructed by Henry and Sully*
Source: Buisseret, *Sully*, p. 126, with two sites added in Languedoc.

out the decade, as a result of which substantial fortifications eventually covered all the main approaches to France (Map 22). Associated with this work on the fortifications was a great burst of cartographic activity among the royal engineers and their *conducteurs des desseins*.* The provinces of Picardy, Champagne, Burgundy, Dauphiné, Provence and Languedoc came to be much better mapped than had been the case before 1600, and much of this new cartographic knowledge eventually found its way on to the printed maps of France.[32]

153

The entry 'ponts et chaussées' offers an interesting contrast with the previous ones. Whereas in 1600 expenditure on roads and bridges (and canals) was negligible, after 1605, when Sully as *grand voyer* had finally got his administrative structure into place, they yearly took very large sums. We have seen how concerned the king and Sully were to improve communications within France by means of canals (Chapter 10, section viii); another of their great preoccupations was the building and repair of bridges. Map 23 shows how this work was concentrated along the *grands chemins*,* vital not only for trade but also for royal messengers. To put the magnitude of the effort into context, we should consider that the sums spent in the last three years of Henry's reign were not equalled until 1680.

The 'états et pensions' did not fluctuate much over the decade, at least not until Marie de Medici began buying friends in 1610. But the detailed accounts of these *états* are a source of some interest, as they chronicle the rise to favour (and often the decline) of various persons. The 'deniers payés par ordonnance' record a rather bizarre system of accounting, for they in fact summarise the progress of Sully's savings; each year they include not only the yearly surplus, but also the cumulative surplus for previous years. By 1610 roughly 15 million *livres* had been set aside, but this treasure did not long survive the advent of Marie de Medici.

Of the three final entries, the largest and most interesting are those found under the 'deniers payés comptants'. These were secret payments made by the king, and their detailed breakdown shows that throughout the decade immense sums – nearly 2 million *livres* in 1605, 1606 and 1607 – were paid to the Dutch as a war-subsidy. The city of Geneva also received a subsidy each year after 1603, and between 1598 and 1610 monies were channelled through this account to maintain the Protestant garrisons agreed on by the Edict of Nantes. From 1606 onwards, too, large sums went on the 'pensions secrettes à Rome', part of the French diplomatic offensive in the College of Cardinals.[33]

Many of the payments were of a more personal nature. A bewildering variety of mistresses parades through the ledgers: 'La Bourdaisiere', 'Des Fossez', 'Angelique de Longueval', 'Mlle Clin', 'Mme Quelin' (the same?), 'Mlle de La Haye', 'Des Essarts', and even 'Mlle —'. Huge sums of money go to cover the king's gambling debts; in 1609, for instance, the 'sieur Edouard, portugais', received at least 150,000 *livres*. The royal children often received money to go to the fair at Saint-Germain, and special gifts were made to scholars like Casaubon or visiting entertainers like the 'comédiens italiens'. Foreign dignitaries, too, received presents; a great diamond in 1608 for Don Pedro, and in 1603 a harness for the horses given to the king of England.

Often the secret payments have a slightly sinister flavour. The sieur de La Fin, Biron's betrayer, received frequent payments of blood money.

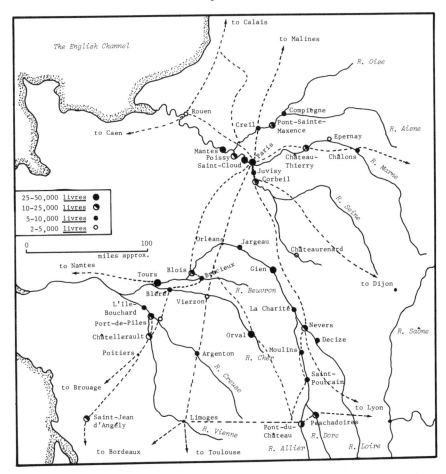

Map 23 *Roads and bridges constructed by Henry and Sully. This is, of course, a partial summary, based only on the accounts of the* trésorier des ponts et chaussées *and applying in general only to the* pays d'élections. *Great towns like Nantes, Bordeaux, Toulouse or Lyon also spent huge sums on their bridges, but this money was not controlled by the* trésorier.

Source: Buisseret, *Sully*, p. 115.

Sometimes there were gifts 'aux denonciateurs', or indeed for the 'pensions secrettes en Angleterre'. Towards the end of the reign, there are increasing numbers of payments 'pour affaires secrettes' – in Burgundy, in Spain, and in unidentified places; no doubt spies were being sent out to gather the information needed before opening a military offensive. All this adds up to a considerable level of clandestine activity, by which the normal processes of diplomacy were supplemented.

155

(vi) 'Someone of Proven Quality, Capacity and Fidelity'

One of the entries for 1596 is a payment of 2,000 *livres* 'au sieur de Bisouze, pour emploier en ung affaire secrette'. Mention of this 'Bisouze', more properly known as Raymond de Viçose, leads us to a consideration of the many agents whom the king used for special purposes, working alongside – and sometimes against – the traditional categories of the historians: the governors, provincial estates, *parlements*, *trésoriers de France* and so on. Very often, when there was tricky or politically sensitive work to be done, the king entrusted it to one of a group of ten or so reliable emissaries. Their names have not generally penetrated into the histories of the reign: men like Pierre Fougeu, sieur d'Escures; Guillaume Fouquet, sieur de La Varenne; André de Froulay, sieur de Gastines; Etienne de La Fond; Antoine Le Camus, sieur de Jambeville; Louis Le Fèvre, sieur de Caumartin; Miles Marion; and Raymond de Viçose.[34]

The career of Viçose is worth examining in detail. His father came from Portugal, but had settled in France 'because of the civil wars in Spain'.[35] Raymond, having been 'nourry et eslevé' alongside the king of Navarre (probably as a Protestant), was in April 1576 sent into Guyenne to tell the king's followers to rally to their master[36] (this, of course, was just after Henry's flight from the royal court). By June 1581 he is called the king's 'secretary',[37] and for the next two or three years he was constantly busy running messages to Henry's allies like the maréchal de Matignon.[38] By 1586 he was emerging from the merely secretarial role, and was sent that June to see and report on what was going on along the Dordogne and Garonne.[39] In October 1586 he fought with the king at Coutras,[40] and two years later was sent to Duplessis-Mornay while the latter was negotiating the truce of April 1589 with Henri III. By this stage the king of Navarre trusted him fully; writing to M. de Lestelle on 19 April 1589 he ends: Adieu; Vicouse vous verra; Vissouse [sic] vous dira tout.'[41] Early in 1590 he was running messages to the Countess of Grammont, who was still the king's mistress,[42] and in March that year he fought at Ivry.[43] During 1591 and the early part of 1592 he bore messages to Henri de Montmorency, busy trying to hold his own in Languedoc,[44] and in March 1592 was sent to encourage the king's supporters in Provence.[45] In the summer of 1592 he was with Duplessis-Mornay, and accompanied the Protestant deputies to court;[46] again the next year he was sent to fetch the Protestant deputies, who were assured that Viçose was 'instruict de nos plus intimes volontez', so that he should be treated as the king himself.[47]

After 1593 the emphasis of Viçose's work shifted somewhat; he was appointed *intendant et contrôleur général des finances* in June 1594,[48] and was increasingly employed in financial negotiations, usually in Guyenne. Here the governor was the maréchal de Matignon, who wrote to the king in October 1594 that since he, Matignon, had returned to the province 'the sieur de Viçose has always remained close by me'.[49] Viçose continued to work alongside Matignon for the next two years, with occasional visits to the royal court; while he was in Guyenne, he kept the king informed about problems like the obstinacy of the Bordeaux *parlement*.[50] He also attended meetings of the representative assemblies, like that of the estates of Rouergue in Rodez in February 1596, from which he reported to the king that the deputies had granted a reasonable sum.[51]

In September 1596 he was sent on a special mission to Poitiers, to try to raise money from the *bureau des finances* there,[52] and the following year was picked to levy the naval force which would have been necessary to reduce Mercœur, had the Duke not surrendered.[53] In July 1598 we find him addressing the Protestant synod in Saint-Jean-d'Angély, who in their message to the king daringly exhorted him not to follow the example of Solomon, who had started well, but was 'destourné à l'occasion des femmes'.[54] Viçose had returned to Guyenne in 1598 specifically to put the province's finances in order,[55] and this kept him busy there for the next two years.

Then in May 1600 he came north again, to be one of the 'judges' at the Fontainebleau conference, where Duplessis-Mornay was so publicly humiliated.[56] The maréchal de Matignon, governor of Guyenne, had died in 1597, and his successor was the mercurial Corsican, Alfonse d'Ornano. From 1601 until about 1606, Viçose worked constantly with Ornano, relaying the king's instructions to him and reporting back to court on affairs in Guyenne. In June 1601, for instance, he was involved in a quarrel between Ornano and the king. On that occasion, Henry wrote of Ornano that he, Henry, has 'never seen such ignorance and stubbornness together ... il faict le Corse à toute oultrance'.[57] Certainly, Ornano was a very difficult man, prone to constant quarrels. In October 1602 he went to Saint-Jean-de-Luz with Viçose, to reconnoitre the harbour there,[58] and they collaborated frequently on problems concerning the province's finances. In the autumn of 1602 Viçose went on a general tour of the Midi, reporting back to the king on the state of Dauphiné, Languedoc and Limousin, and sending details of various dissidents.[59] Again in December 1602 he wrote on the same subject, to say that all was quiet in spite of the efforts of the duc de Bouillon.[60]

In 1603 the chief problem was the quarrel between Ornano and the sieur de Montespan, which Viçose did his best to resolve.[61] At the end of the year he was at Agen, addressing the Agenais concerning the way he was trying to get certain abusive commissions revoked.[62] Viçose does not seem to have been in sympathy with the more rigorous fiscal policy championed by Sully, which was gradually being adopted at this time. In April 1604, for instance, he was giving advice to the municipality of Toulouse on how it might best come to terms with Sully's *chambre de justice*, set up (in theory) to investigate financial abuses. Throughout 1605 he was strongly opposing the establishment of royal *élections*★ in Guyenne, a step crucial to Sully's plan for imposing a uniform fiscal administration on the whole country. Viçose attended the royal councils where this matter was debated, and strongly supported the local delegates' opposition to the establishment of the *élections*. As the chief delegate, Julien de Camberfore, sieur de Selves, wrote back to Agen: 'I have not found any lord [in the council] who will take our side, except M. de Viçose, who since his arrival has greatly strengthened me, and brought all his efforts to bear in this cause.'[63] In the end, the establishment of the *élections* was delayed for a few years.

Returning to Guyenne, Viçose continued at Ornano's side. In December 1605 they were in Nérac together, where, as Viçose reported, the town was in good shape and Ornano well received.[64] Seven months later they again went on a tour, this time to the Pyrenean border; Viçose visited Pau, whence he reported to the king that he thought the royal *château* was looking very good;[65] the grove of French pines (planted by Henry in the 1580s) was, he wrote, incomparable.[66] By now Viçose must have been in his fifties; he had served Henry unremittingly for thirty years, and his name begins to appear less prominently in dispatches from the south-west. Now, too, he was reaping his reward; grants in January 1605 and February 1608, a pension in 1608, and in November 1609 a grant of 15,000 *livres* 'for several journeys, tasks and expenses which he had undertaken for the service of His Majesty during the recent troubles, with great hazard and peril to his life'.[67] In February 1611 he was sent back to Guyenne on a mission by the government of Marie de Medici,[68] but then in November 1612 resigned, for what reason we do not know.

The career of Viçose is very instructive, if we want to understand the way in which Henry's administration actually worked. Although he did not have the formal title of *intendant* (in the later sense), he was in effect for long years Henry's *intendant* in Guyenne. His responsibilities were primarily financial, but they did not stop there; he had also to accompany – and to some degree monitor – successive governors on their rounds, to report back to court both in person and in writing on political developments, and on occasion to intervene in the general affairs of the province. If, as time went by, he tended to sympathise overmuch (as the king might have thought) with provincial aspirations, that was only to be expected; it is a tendency which became common among the *intendants* of the later seventeenth and eighteenth centuries.

There were counterparts to Viçose in many regions of France. In the south-east, it was André de Froulay, sieur de Gastines, who for a time played the same role. Appointed 'député pour la direction des finances en

Provence'[69] around 1600, by March 1601 he had widened his jurisdiction to include Burgundy, Dauphiné and Lyonnais.[70] During that month he was concerned with the smooth demobilising of the forces assembled against the Duke of Savoy[71] and the following year spent the summer with the army of the maréchal de Laverdin, shadowing the Spaniards on the eastern frontier. On this occasion, the king sent him to work alongside Laverdin 'not only to see to the payment of the soldiers, but also in order to help you [Laverdin] in any way you need for my service'.[72] Two years later he represented the king at the Carcassonne meeting of the estates of Languedoc;[73] he performed in his area the same function as Viçose in Guyenne, explaining the royal will to all kinds of local officers.

His counterpart in Normandy was Antoine Le Camus, sieur de Jambeville, who is described as 'little by little preparing people's minds to accept the presence of a permanent official [*fonctionnaire*]'.[74] Le Camus was a *conseiller d'Etat*, Gastines a *maître des comptes*,* and Viçose a *secrétaire du cabinet*; they were all in some way members of the central administration. Sometimes, however, the king sought his agents among the very provincial officials whom they had to control. In Champagne, for instance, the sieur Delorme, *trésorier de France* was chosen to conduct a royal inquiry.[75] In Normandy it was another *trésorier de France*, Guillaume Novince, sieur d'Aubigny, whom the king selected to investigate financial abuses in that province,[76] and in Languedoc yet another, Miles Marion.[77]

It would be tedious to enumerate the activity of all these agents all over France, but it is clear that without them the king would hardly have been able to influence affairs. If he had confined himself to the time-honoured system of *gouverneurs, parlements*, provincial estates and so on, it would have been very difficult to sustain armies, build roads, or enforce unpopular measures like the Edict of Nantes. In effect, agents of the central power like Viçose were the forerunners of the later *intendants*, even if they did not have exactly that title.

(vii) 'The Greatness of His Governors'

Very often these agents operated alongside the provincial governor, both to watch him and to help him. Contemporaries were in no doubt about the importance of the governors, or about the need for the king to be able to control them. For instance, when Captain Ed. Wilton was writing from Crotoy in 1596 to the Earl of Essex, he mentioned that Henry 'seeketh as much as he can to break the greatness of his governors by calling them out of their settled governments into places where neither their friends nor credits can do much'.[78] Certainly, the king could not tolerate any continuation of the kind of feudal autonomy which Mercœur had enjoyed in

159

Brittany, or Mayenne in Burgundy, and when the duc de Montpensier, whom everybody agreed was rather stupid, actually suggested an arrangement of this kind Henry remarked with surprising mildness that he thought Montpensier must have been bewitched by an evil spirit, or perhaps simply be losing his mind.[79]

When it came to actually disposing of the twelve great governments (*gouvernements*), though, Henry's hands were to some extent tied by the events of the 1580s and 1590s. It was not possible to think of dislodging Lesdiguières from the government of Dauphiné, or Montmorency from that of Languedoc; nor would he have wished to remove La Force from Navarre. Around Paris, Montpensier was allowed to remain in Normandy, Saint-Pol in Picardy and Claude de La Châtre in Orléanais. During the wars, Mercœur had been evicted from Brittany, and Mayenne from Burgundy; Brittany went to the young César de Vendôme, with Brissac as lieutenant-governor, and Burgundy went first to Biron and then to the dauphin, with Bellegarde as lieutenant-governor. The young duc de Guise was removed from his area of hereditary influence in the north-east, and sent to Provence; young Condé, too, was sent not to Picardy but to Guyenne, with Ornano as his lieutenant-governor. There was, then, no uniform policy regarding the twelve great governments; Henry simply took advantage of local circumstances in doing his best to retain control of them. The same is true of the governorships of the lesser provinces and of the greater towns. As we have seen in Chapter 7, most of these governors were men who had served Henry well during the wars; in very few cases were the posts as yet hereditary.

The functions of the provincial governors have been the object of much controversy. They were primarily military commanders, but their powers went beyond that; indeed, a recent historian has written that 'some governors [were able] to approach the role of surrogate kings'.[80] During the reign of Henry IV, the only governor of whom this was true was Lesdiguières, in Dauphiné, but many governors played a role beyond the purely military one. Often, they attended the opening of the estates in the province, bringing a message from the king – usually an exhortation to pay more taxes. Of course, they might not be fully in sympathy with royal fiscal demands, and they were often effective agents in getting the tax burden of their province reduced. They were concerned with the way in which the taxes were spent, on roads, bridges and forts, and often circulated in the province with the engineer responsible for it. They also exercised a general control over the greater nobles and the princes, trying to settle their quarrels and on occasion, for instance, rescuing damsels in distress or protecting ecclesiastical property.[81] In the terminology of the time, though they were jealously excluded by the *parlements* from affairs of *justice*, they did play a considerable role in *police*★ and *finances*.

The question of Henry's relations with the governors is bound up with the problem of his attitude towards the *noblesse d'épée* as a whole. As we have repeatedly seen, many of the great nobles were astonishingly ready to dabble with treachery in return for Spanish gold. Henry did his best to keep them happy by the judicious allocation of *pensions* and the promise of posts and advantageous marriages. He also seems, early in the reign, to have planned the foundation in Tours of an 'académie pour la jeunesse noble', which would teach young nobles to 'ride on horseback, handle arms, dance, do gymnastics, read mathematics and perform other virtuous and seemly exercises'.[82] This project does not seem to have come to anything, perhaps because the Jesuits were offering such a successful alternative.

In Henry's France, the role of the noble was to fight, and the king was not willing to do anything which might dampen their ardour. This led him into a great dilemma over the problem of duelling. It has been estimated that between 1598 and 1610 something like 500 to 1,000 nobles perished every year in France through duels.[83] They were of course illegal, not to say un-Christian, and it was Henry's duty to suppress them. Three times, in 1599, 1602 and 1609, he issued strong edicts against them, in 1602 resolving 'to take a solemn oath upon the Evangiles not to pardon hereafter, no not his owne blood, in case of duell'.[84] Alas for good intentions; after the edicts of 1599 and 1602 he was soon pardoning duellists again, and contemporaries had little doubt that the edict of 1609 would be equally ill-observed.

The English ambassador, Sir George Carew, believed that Henry let duels take place so as to divide the nobles and get rid of 'hoate heads'.[85] But we may doubt whether the king was as Machiavellian as that. The fact is that he himself was brave to an almost foolhardy degree in physical encounters, as he had often shown before 1598; he not only admired courage in his nobles, but also had to maintain this 'fount of honour' as a source for the never-ending struggle on the frontiers. As has been well said, the duel problem was 'a dilemma between honour and duty' and, if honour retained the upper hand, we should not be surprised; the reasons were functional as well as personal. It would take a cleric like Richelieu to root out an abuse of this kind.

(viii)   *'L'insolence de ceux dudict parlement'*

One nobility wielded the sword; the other, almost equally redoubtable to an authoritarian king, wielded the pen and wore the robe. The great stronghold of the *noblesse de robe** was the system of *parlements*, with the one in Paris backed by seven in the great provinces. Up to the time of the king's abjuration, in July 1593, five of the eight *parlements* had been split in two, with royalist and League sections. After 1593 these secessions slowly mended themselves; the *parlements* of Paris and Rouen, for instance, were reunited in April 1594, and the two factions in Toulouse came together in 1596. The king had the right to nominate the *premier président* of each *parlement*, and he generally used it to install royalists. In Paris, Achille de Harlay succeeded the League's *premier président* in 1594.[86] In Aix, Guillaume du Vair was established in July 1599.[87] In Toulouse, Nicolas de Verdun was appointed in 1602.[88] In Rouen, Claude Groulart, leader of the royalist rump of Caen, became *premier président* in April 1594.[89] In Dijon, the Leaguer Denis Brûlart was allowed to remain as *premier président*; perhaps the king did not wish for a headlong confrontation with that headstrong *parlement*, in which Benigne Frémiot and Pierre Jeannin could be relied upon to put the royal case.[90]

The reconstituted *parlements* did not see themselves a pliant tools of the Crown, and came into conflict with the king when they were asked to register a variety of edicts. The most sensitive areas were religious and fiscal affairs. Concerning religion, the Edict of Nantes was hard for the *parlements* to swallow. In Paris, remonstrances were entered in January 1599, but the Edict was registered with minor modifications the following month. In Bordeaux there was more resistance; the *parlement*'s deputies were treated to a furious harangue at the Louvre in November 1599,[91] and gave way in February 1600. In Toulouse, too, there was resistance; again the king spoke sharply to the deputies, accusing them still of having 'de l'Espagnol dans le ventre',[92] and they registered the Edict in January 1600. Aix and Rennes followed suit in August of that year, but opposition was stronger in Rouen. There the Edict was registered in September 1599, but with modifications which took away most of its effect; these restrictions were not lifted until May 1609, when the Edict was registered 'purement et simplement'.[93] The other religious matter leading to dispute was the recall of the Jesuits, in September 1603. This time the bitterest opposition came from the very Gallican *parlement* of Paris,[94] for some of the other *parlements* had not by 1603 got round to accepting and enforcing the *arrêt* for the Jesuits' expulsion which had been promulgated in Paris in December 1594.

In fiscal affairs, there was constant tension between the king's desire to raise money and the *parlements'* wish both to safeguard constitutional propriety as they saw it and to protect their own property. Henry constantly tried to levy new taxes, appoint new officers, and alienate fresh portions of the royal domain; in all these areas he was generally resisted by the *parlements*. The conflict could be very prolonged. In 1596, for instance, the king decided to establish a new *prévôt des maréchaux*★ in Brittany. Following the resistance of the *parlement*, the royal letters were registered

162

there in 1601, but it was understood that they would neither be published nor put into effect; we are reminded of the (perhaps legendary) phrase from contemporary Spain: 'His Majesty's orders have been obeyed but not carried out.' The king kept up the pressure, and in 1603 a compromise was reached; no second *prévôt* would be appointed, and the king would be 'reimbursed' for his forbearance. . . .[95]

As Edouard Maugis very well put it in his *Histoire du parlement de Paris*, 'it would be submitting the reader to an extraordinary test to inflict upon him merely an enumeration of the interminable list of edicts. . . . Running over them, one does not know which to admire more; the power of resistance shown by the *parlement*, or the inventive genius of the tax-gatherers, and we begin to wonder if Henry and Sully perhaps saw the whole thing as a game, or as a kind of lottery, in which they would send forward ten edicts so as to get one of them passed.'[96] In conclusion, then, we should not be deceived by the apparently masterful and peremptory tone in which Henry addressed his laggard *parlements*. The fact is that they were corporate bodies of well-entrenched bureaucrats, who knew all the ways of delaying royal legislation – and then could invent some more. As far as the *parlements* went, Henry's power was very far from absolute.

(ix)   'Je vous prie que ce soit Lecomte'

The other great provincial institution with which the king had to contend was the provincial estates. Meeting generally once a year, for a fortnight, they were composed of representatives of the three orders, and existed in many parts of France. But the most powerful provincial estates were the ones corresponding to the seven provincial *parlements*: those of Brittany (Rennes), Burgundy (Dijon), Dauphiné (Grenoble), Guyenne (Bordeaux), Languedoc (Toulouse), Normandy (Rouen) and Provence (Aix). Of these estates, the least powerful was the one in Normandy. As Sully wrote, it was 'but a shadow beside the others',[97] and the historian Henri Prentout confirms this judgement when he writes that its role between 1597 and 1610 was essentially to 'voter l'impôt en protestant'.[98]

These protests were put forward in the traditional *cahier*, which would be received by the provincial governor or some other royal representative when the estates broke up, after their deliberations. In 1609 the Normandy estates observed that 'the routine of making requests has led to a habit of refusing them . . . for it looks as though the replies on the past year's *cahier* are a straightforward copy of those for the previous year'.[99] The estates of Languedoc were less acquiescent. Meeting in November 1604, they angrily noted that 'the replies which monsieur de Rosny and other lords of the Council had put forward on the *cahier* sent to them . . .

did not in any way meet the wishes of the province'.[100] Their position was clear; as they put it in Pézenas in April 1599: 'by the ancient privileges and freedoms of this region, no sums may be imposed or levied on it without the consent of the estates.'[101] Throughout the reign they held to this statement, making it very difficult for the central power to undertake any independent action in Languedoc. Sully would have liked to bypass the estates by establishing in Languedoc the system of *élections* and *élus*★ existing in parts of France not represented by estates. We find among his papers a 'copy of the edict for creating *élus* in Languedoc',[102] but that was never possible, in the face of provincial opposition.

In Guyenne he had the same ambition, and after a long struggle actually succeeded in 1609 in establishing *élus* there.[103] But the estates of Guyenne, like those of Normandy, were relatively tractable. In Brittany, Burgundy and Provence it was another story. In Brittany, the estates refused to contribute money for the upkeep of roads,[104] and particularly refused to recognise Sully's jurisdiction as *grand voyer*.[105] They emphasised that 'no levies of money may be made without the express consent of the estates',[106] and refused to recognise contracts which had been concluded without their knowledge. In Provence there was the same kind of opposition. There, too, the estates insisted on controlling all taxation, and refused to allow the agents of the *grand voyer* to collect taxes for the repair of roads and bridges.[107] Indeed, it was with the greatest of difficulty that Charles de Guise, the governor, persuaded them to permit levies even for the most urgent fortifications of the coast.[108] The estates of Burgundy were perhaps the most independent of all. Sully eventually succeeded in forcing them to pay the salary of Pierre Bourdin, his artillery lieutenant in Dijon,[109] but the most that he could squeeze out of them for roads and bridges, in 1610, was a miserable 20,000 *livres*.[110] In conclusion, we might say that two of the seven great provincial estates – Guyenne and Normandy – showed some sign of collaborating with the king, but that in the five others very little progress was made.

The estates were substantial and often ancient corporate bodies, with a tradition of independence. Some of the towns had an equally ancient tradition of autonomy, but the towns were in general less successful in resisting royal encroachments. This has led some historians, like Gabriel Hanotaux, Ernest Lavisse and Paul Robiquet, to write as if Henry 'destroyed . . . municipal liberties'.[111] Other historians, notably Charles de Lacombe and Auguste Poirson, go as far in the opposite direction, maintaining for instance that the king 'scrupulously respected freedom of choice in the nomination of municipal magistrates'.[112] The history of French kings' involvement in municipal elections certainly goes far back into the Middle Ages. It seems to have been in the reign of Saint Louis that the custom grew up for mayors to be chosen by the king from a list of

164

three candidates, supplied by the municipality.[113] This system was still in use during Henry's reign, but was often overridden by the king. In Langres in 1592, for instance, he requested the election of Jean Roussat.[114] In Bayonne in 1596 he required the municipality to accept the sieur de Grammont as mayor; he was already governor.[115] The same year, in Limoges, he refused to recognise the successful candidates, and strongly influenced elections there on several other occasions.[116] Meanwhile, in Lyon he had reduced the number of *échevins*, thus opening the way to a closer control of the municipality;[117] he used the same tactic in Amiens, after its recovery from the Spaniards in 1597.[118] In Marseille, there was in 1601 so sharp a controversy between the supporters of rival candidates that, as Du Vair wrote, 'they have decided to put the whole affair into the hands of Your Majesty, so that this evil has turned out well, giving you a chance to regain your ancient authority, which your predecessors had – to their great prejudice – allowed to be usurped by the people'.[119] Again in 1607 there was a quarrel between rival interests in the town; this time it was the duc de Guise who established four *consuls* favoured by the king.[120] Much the same thing seems to have happened in Dijon, where throughout the reign there was considerable agitation in municipal affairs. The king was in general opposed to Jean Jacquinot, but could not prevent his election in 1599, 1600 and 1601; in the opinion of the historian Bourcier, royal intervention in Dijon aimed rather at ensuring calm than at ruining the rights of the municipality.[121]

It is very hard to come to a judgement on the king's relations with the Hôtel de Ville in Paris. On the one hand, we have Robiquet's opinion that 'arbitrary royal power was going to allocate all the municipal offices, without any respect for existing rights'.[122] On the other hand, Carsalade du Pont writes that 'Henri IV never tried to influence [*fausser*] the result of the elections'.[123] The truth, as usual, seems to lie somewhere between these extremes. Henry certainly intervened in the elections of 1595, 1596, 1597 and 1600.[124] But three of these were years when it was a matter of survival for him to have a *prévôt des marchands* in Paris who would not be too obstructive to his repeated requests for money to fight the Spaniards; intervention in these circumstances should not be taken as part of an unswerving plan to subvert municipal liberties. In summary, the king seems to have intervened in municipal elections when the requirements of military necessity (Bayonne, Langres), civil order (Marseille, Dijon, Limoges) or fiscal necessity (Paris, Lyon) forced him to do so. He could hardly have been expected to tolerate repeated tumults in a city like Marseille, to have a Leaguer as mayor of Langres, or to allow a well-known opponent to control the finances of the Hôtel de Ville. Outside these limits, his intervention was rare.

Municipal liberties were not only menaced by royal interference in elections. Much more effective was the steady campaign waged by Sully, as *grand voyer* and *surintendant des finances*, to bring municipal finances under his control. In Paris, for instance, the *bureau de la ville* was eventually forced to submit to him their accounts of *octrois*.*[125] In 1604 the Dijon councillor deputed to put the town's case to the king had to send back to Burgundy for a copy of the town's accounts; as he bitterly recorded, 'no business can be done here without M. de Rosny [Sully]'.[126] In 1607, the municipality of Mâcon learned to its dismay that its authorised expenditure had been reduced from 2,404 to 1,870 *livres*.[127]

These were all large towns, with a fiscal resilience which would enable them to outlive Sully's efforts. Among small towns, though, his efforts could be much more effective, as Robert Trullinger has recently shown.[128] From 1605 onwards, all requests by Breton towns to levy new taxes (*octrois*) for public works had to go through the *grand voyer* or his lieutenant. Permission was only granted provided both that past accounts were in order, and that monies were for the future disbursed as they had been authorised. This gave Sully considerable control over the main sources of municipal taxation, and by the end of the reign nine towns had fallen in with the new arrangement. The whole aim, as Sully himself noted on a copy of the royal declaration of 1605, was 'to oblige the towns imposing dues to present their accounts to the *trésoriers de France*, or if necessary to M. de Sully, every three years, and to submit to a check by the *chambre des comptes* every six years'.[129] Evidently, if there had been time to extend this system throughout France, the Crown would have had an effective control over the towns.

(x) *'J'estime que ce ne soyent que querelles particulières'*

There was a good deal of grumbling over these encroachments, but nothing to compare with the tax revolts of Richelieu's later years. In the France of Henry IV, riots, tumults and even revolts were astonishingly common, but they were not normally directed against the Crown. The greatest of these revolts took place in 1594, as we have seen, but others were common down to about 1604. They took three main forms, of which the first was the more or less overtly political plot. The greatest of these were of course Biron's conspiracy in 1602, and the Entragues plot in 1604–5. But there were many other 'remuements', as the king called them; they were regarded as more or less inevitable, products of those 'private quarrels which the idleness of the nobility produces everywhere'.[130] Most remained insignificant, though with Spanish backing always available the king had to watch them all carefully.

The second form which revolt took was the mishandling and even murder of royal officials. Around 1600, for instance, the peasants of Rochechouart killed Simon L'Aumosnier while he was collecting the *taille*. A little later, somebody committed 'acts of rebellion' against the royal official who was investigating evasion of the salt tax at Ingrande.[131] Between 1601 and 1603, as we have seen, resistance to the imposition of the *sol pour livre* was so extensive that the king had to abandon it (Chapter 8, section i). But this kind of opposition was relatively rare after 1600, when the slowly improving condition of the peasants appears to have made their tax burden more or less bearable.[132]

The third form of revolt was the urban tumult; these seem to have been particularly prevalent in the Midi. In Marseille in March 1601, for instance, there was a report of sedition in the town.[133] The Spaniards were always prowling about the off-shore islands, and Marseille had a long tradition of independence which some factions would have liked to revive. But the various groups were always very disunited; as Du Vair wrote in 1603, 'les plus apparens de la ville estoient tellement divisés entre eux que c'estoit pitié'.[134] The struggles do not seem to have had any particular 'class' basis, and were easily suppressed. The same is true of the tumults in Arles in September 1601 and Salon in 1608;[135] the inhabitants of these towns were so accustomed to settling their differences by violence that riots were endemic, and did not have the deeper meaning which we might be inclined to seek in them. In general, the reign of Henry IV marks an interval between the period of civil strife which began in 1562 and the new phase which would come during the Regency.

12 'L'infortune de cet abominable jour'

(i) 'Things Were Now Tending to an Universall Peace'

From the time when he went to Guyenne, in the 1570s, Henry had cultivated diplomatic contacts very widely. Throughout the 1580s and 1590s this diplomatic activity continued, so that his court was rarely lacking foreign visitors, usually from the Protestant east. Charles de Zérotin, as we have seen, came from Bohemia to serve in his armies at the siege of Rouen in 1592. A year later, the son of Edward, Count of Eastern Friesland, was at Henry's court.[1] In 1598, a young man from Lorraine, whose family name was Betstein, also came to the court. He felt so much at home with the king that he remained in France; we know him as François de Bassompierre, the future *maréchal de France*. In 1602, as we have seen, there was a long visit by Maurice of Hesse. We have only to leaf through the lists of 'persons to whom the letters are addressed' in the successive volumes of Henry's *Lettres missives* to form an impression of this intense and intensifying diplomatic activity. As time went by, and the king's religious attitude changed, there was a change of emphasis. Fewer visitors came from Protestant Europe, and more from the Catholic south, particularly Italy; there had, after all, long been a band of Italians resident at the court of the French kings.

Behind these frequent visitors lay a network of diplomatic contacts, hard to unravel fully, but surprisingly extensive, particularly in eastern Europe. With Moscow, contact appears to have been limited to a single letter,[2] but relations with Sweden and Poland were well developed. From 1598 onwards there was war between Sigismund III, king of Poland, and Charles IX of Sweden. These hostilities threatened to disrupt French trade in the Baltic, but Henry was hard pressed to know whom to support. Villeroy and some other members of the council favoured Poland, but Henry and Sully saw in Charles IX of Sweden a surer bulwark against the Habsburgs, and contrived to help him with men for his army and navy.[3] From 1598 onwards, as we have seen, they also sent a yearly subsidy to the Dutch, though this was sharply reduced after the United Provinces began negotiations with the Spaniards in 1608.[4] French relations with the northern Netherlands were becoming distinctly ambiguous towards the end of Henry's reign. They still, of course, shared a common enemy in

Spain, but the Dutch and the French were beginning to come into conflict over maritime and commercial ventures. Henry undoubtedly felt galled that, 'while France and Spain were fighting over townships, forts and hillocks of ground, the Dutch and the English were conquering the world',[5] and he tried to organise his own overseas ventures. In Canada, as we have seen, he was largely successful, but elsewhere he came up against the resistance of the Dutch.[6] Three private ventures to the East Indies having failed, Henry in 1604 formed his own East India Company, using the services of Pieter Lyntgens, an Amsterdam merchant who had fallen out with the Dutch East India Company.

This venture soon ran into problems. In the Netherlands, Lyntgens found it virtually impossible to obtain seamen or supplies, in the face of obstruction by the states-general. In The Hague, the French ambassador (Choart de Buzenval) received a bribe of 1,500 *florins*, and then advised Henry against the project. Meanwhile in Paris the Dutch ambassador, Francis Aerssen, was bribing the queen, Sully and anybody else who might sway the king. Eventually, Lyntgens was forced to give up. But Henry was not to be foiled so easily, and in 1608 began negotiations with another Dutchman, Isaac Lemaire. By April 1609, Lemaire had hired Melchior van den Kerckhove as captain; the following May he set off to seek a north-east passage round the north of Russia. The venture was a failure, for Kerckhove was blocked by ice near the Strait of Kara. But the many difficulties attending Henry's attempts to mount such an expedition show how rooted was Dutch opposition to such French ventures; they never would admit other European powers into their eastern preserve without being forced to it.

With the southern Netherlands relations were almost equally ambiguous. In 1597, as we saw in Chapter 5, the Cardinal-Archduke Albert had led an army south into France, with the aim of relieving Amiens. Baffled, he returned to Brussels, where Henry had an ambassador from 1598. It was difficult to do business with 'the archdukes', as Albert and his wife Isabella were called, for, although nominally independent, they in fact usually followed instructions from Madrid.[7] Sometimes, though, they would act with surprising autonomy; as we shall see, they were at the centre of the storm which would cost Henry his life.

The cold war with Spain itself never let up. The Spaniards did their best to subvert French nobles and key towns, and Henry continued to supply the Dutch rebels with subsidies. On occasion, he went further than that. In 1603, for instance, he wrote to Sully about an ingenious scheme whereby Aerssen, the Dutch ambassador in Paris, would be able to recruit some French veterans; then they were to leave via Dieppe rather than Calais, so as not to arouse suspicion.[8] Curiously enough, Sully did not feel free to fall in with this deception,[9] but the king pressed on with it all the same. Two years later, Henry suggested that it might be good to let Aerssen know when Ambrogio Spinola, the Spanish commander, would be passing near the French eastern frontier, on his way from Milan to the Netherlands; then Prince Maurice, using his French cavalry, could perhaps capture the Genoese general, 'which would be worth a battle gained'.[10] On the other hand, when a little later that year Spinola in fact came through Paris, Henry would not let Aerssen lay 'ambushes for him, to have eyther slayne him or at least to have taken and sent him into Holland'.[11] Dirty tricks like that had to be set up away from French territory.

Within the Iberian peninsula, the French continued to encourage the Moriscoes, even after the failure of Panissault's mission in 1602 (see above, Chapter 9, section vi). When they were eventually expelled, between 1609 and 1612, many fled across the Pyrenees into France.[12] Henry welcomed those who agreed to become Catholics, and some settled in and around the valley of the Dordogne. Most of them made their way across the south of France, where they presented the local authorities with problems like those posed by the Irish in Paris. In Henry's time, they were not impeded from making their way to French ports, from which they could sail to north Africa; Marie de Medici, on the other hand, eventually tried to prevent them from entering France.

As well as encouraging the Moriscoes, Henry would have liked to stir up trouble in Spain's colonies across the Atlantic. It was obvious that bullion from the New World played an important part in sustaining Spain's military power in the Old World, and Sully for one used to urge an attack on the Spanish Indies,[13] which he describes in his memoirs as Spain's vitals, where a fatal blow might be struck against her. No doubt this would have been one of the objectives of the Atlantic fleet. Another objective of the fleet would have been the suppression of English pirates, operating mostly in the Channel. In some ways, the interests of France were closely aligned with those of England, since both were menaced by Spain, and neither was as yet a significant colonial power. Moreover, although Henry disliked Sir Thomas Parry (ambassador 1602–5) very much, he came to be a good friend of his successor, Sir George Carew. But the stumbling-block in relations with England, apart from the disputed debt, was Henry's dislike of James. If he did not actually coin the phrase 'the wisest fool in Christendom' – and it certainly has a Henrician ring – he undoubtedly thought James was an ass, who hunted too much, talked too much and published too much.[14] England, though, was to remain passive in 1610, as she would eight years later, at the 'official' start of the Thirty Years' War.

Around the Mediterranean were powers in whose complex relation-ships Henry often meddled. In the Muslim world, he tried to maintain a

French presence in Morocco,[15] and struggled to ensure that in Constantinople the French were not ousted by the English and the Dutch.[16] As late as January 1601, he had the gall to instruct his ambassador in Constantinople, Savary de Brèves, to encourage the Turks to attack Calabria and Sicily.[17] As we have seen (Chapter 8, section iv), he had never been able to resist the temptation of weakening the Habsburgs by encouraging the Turks, and in this sense he inherited a long-standing French political dilemma, broken in 1688 by the decisive defeat of the Turks at Belgrade and the consequent War of the League of Augsburg.

In Italy, Henry had the great diplomatic advantage that, although the Spaniards were strong, holding Milan, Naples and Genoa, they were much disliked by the rulers of Venice, Florence, Rome and even, eventually, Savoy.[18] The Venetians had been the first to recognise Henry as king of France, in 1589, and he had enjoyed good relations with them ever since. Between 1601 and 1607 they were involved in a long controversy with the Papacy, which was resolved, thanks largely to French mediation, in April 1607. In Rome itself the French party in the College of Cardinals was steadily built up, by judicious pensions and other means, so that when Clement VIII died in 1605 he was succeeded by Leo XI and then Paul V; the first a francophile and the second a benevolent neutral.[19] In Florence, the Grand-Duke Ferdinando, uncle of Henry's wife, ruled on until 1609, and in Savoy, as we shall see, the fickle Duke Charles-Emmanuel was thinking of abandoning the Spaniards. One way and another, at the beginning of 1609 many of the Italian states were friendly towards France.

(ii) 'The Matter of Cleves Is Growen Hote Again'

In Germany at that time, tension was mounting between the Evangelical Union (see Chapter 10, section vii) and the Habsburgs. For many months, Henry's efforts to persuade Maurice of Hesse and the Elector of Brandenburg to join the Union had been vain.[20] In March 1609, however, came an event which, like the affair of Donauwörth in 1607, pushed the Protestant princes into a closer alignment. For in that month occurred the death of John William, Duke of Jülich-Cleves-Berg. This heterogeneous duchy was situated at a particularly sensitive point of Europe's skein of military connections, for it lay between the Dutch and their allies among the German princes, and in imperial hands would pose an immediate threat to the security of the United Provinces (Map 24). The succession to the throne of this duchy was therefore of crucial interest to the general European balance of power.

But the succession was disputed. John William had left no heir, and there were possible claimants from a variety of Protestant and Catholic

171

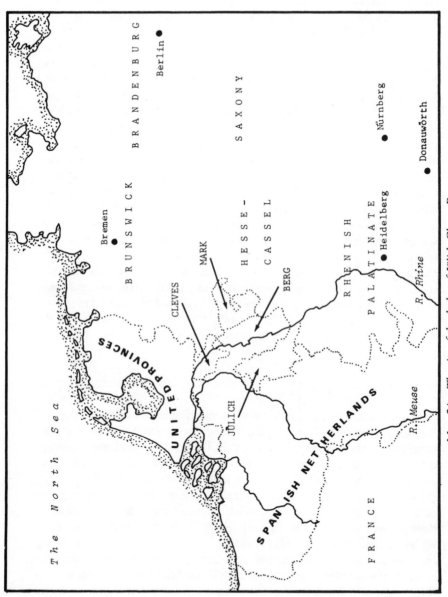

The North Sea

UNITED PROVINCES

BRUNSWICK

BRANDENBURG

Berlin ●

Bremen ●

SAXONY

CLEVES

MARK

HESSE-
CASSEL

BERG

Nürnberg ●

Donauwörth ●

RHENISH

PALATINATE

Heidelberg ●

R. Rhine

JÜLICH

SPANISH NETHERLANDS

FRANCE

R. Meuse

Map 24   *The site of the duchy of Jülich-Cleves-Berg.*

houses. At this juncture, then, the Emperor Rudolph ordered the territory to be sequestrated, pending an imperial decision; Archduke Leopold meanwhile occupied Jülich in July 1609. By the end of the year both Maurice of Hesse and the Elector of Brandenburg had joined the Union, as it became clear to them that only a united front by the Protestant princes might deter the expansion of imperial power. Meanwhile in Paris the opinion of Henry's councillors was divided. As early as August 1609, Sully and Jeannin favoured the use of force, and couriers were sent to the United Provinces, England, Denmark and the German Protestant princes to discover their views.[21] Villeroy, however, favoured caution, and the king himself did not seem able to make up his mind. Various emissaries came to Paris in August and September of 1609 – a certain Teynagel from Archduke Leopold, Richardot from the archdukes, and Count Hohenzollern from the Emperor – but none could propose a compromise acceptable to Henry.[22] On the other hand, he was far from ready for war, particularly when Bongars, after a tour of the German courts, reported back at Fontainebleau in September 1609 that, although their rulers feared Rudolph's intentions, they were not ready to use force in order to dislodge Leopold.[23] So the problem dragged on into the autumn, with neither side able to force a decision in the royal council. As Francis Aerssen wrote back to the United Provinces on 28 November 1609, 'on est fort prompt ici ... nous changeons six fois d'avis en un fait d'importance'.[24]

(iii) 'The Noise of Warre'

The very next day an event occurred which wonderfully cleared Henry's mind; the prince de Condé eloped to Brussels with his young wife Charlotte. This Charlotte was a marvellously beautiful nymph of fifteen, after whom Henry had been lusting since January 1609: he had arranged for her to be married to the prince de Condé, a rather lackadaisical young man, in the hope that he, Henry, could then enjoy her favours. This arrangement, which had both its entertaining and its sordid aspects, quite fell through when Condé fled to Brussels. The king was beside himself, and as early as 1 December 1609 publicly remarked that, if the archdukes would not surrender Condé and the princess, he would go to Flanders and fetch them, at the head of 50,000 men.[25]

So this new Helen, as Aerssen called her, transformed the relatively innocuous controversy over the succession to Jülich-Cleves-Berg into an urgent *causus belli*. To most historians studying the period, this has seemed absurd,[26] but they have had regretfully to admit that it is true; Henry's judgement was always defective when Venus had the upper hand, never more so than in this his last passion. Meanwhile in Germany the princes

173

were assembling in Hall, where in December 1609 and January 1610 they came to the conclusion that Leopold must be resisted, if necessary by force.[27] Their deliberations resulted on 11 February 1610 in the signing of the Treaty of Hall, by which they engaged themselves to provide an army to back the claims of the two Protestant candidates. At the same time, early in February 1610, Henry and his ministers were holding a series of councils at the Louvre and at the Arsenal, out of which emerged the resolution to invade Flanders in the spring. The king's judgement during these deliberations was not improved by the news from Brussels, where Charlotte was being fêted and Condé doing his best to be provocative; invited to drink to the queen of France, he replied that he did not know that there was *one* queen but, rather, four or five. . . .[28]

Henry's spring offensive fell far short of the general alliance envisaged in Sully's chimerical Grand Design.★ The kings of England and Denmark were unwilling to commit themselves, the Venetians counselled caution, many of the German princes were lukewarm, and even the Dutch did not wish to enter into a general offensive. Only the Duke of Savoy seemed enthusiastic to attack the Spaniards in Italy, and his alliance was not what a prudent statesman would normally seek. Nevertheless, late in April 1610 a treaty was signed in Brusol with Charles-Emmanuel, providing that a French army of 14,000 men would be available to attack the Spaniards in north Italy in May 1610.

Even at this stage, Henry's council was far from unanimous. Sully was not at all keen on the Italian campaign, preferring to concentrate on Flanders. Villeroy took the opposite line; perhaps he feared that a campaign on the Rhineland would lead to a general conflagration which would soon be out of hand. As for the king himself, he was still maddened by the 'loss' of Charlotte, and became quite irrational. At an interview with the Spanish ambassador, Don Iñigo de Cárdenas, he grew particularly intemperate, as indeed did Cárdenas. Luckily neither understood the other's language, but the interview terminated with 'each remaining in a towering passion'.[29] By early May all was ready. The main force, of 30,000 men, would advance through Champagne on the Low Countries. In the south-west, the duc de La Force would hold an army of 10,000 men ready to harass Spanish Navarre, and in the south-east Lesdiguières would lead a force of 15,000 men down into Spanish Italy.

(iv) 'La main de cet esprit farouche'

During April and May, the king was busy in Paris, holding conferences and making preparations at the Louvre and at the Arsenal. Early in the afternoon of 14 May he took his carriage to go and see Sully at the Arsenal.

The carriage had a long bench-seat, and Henry sat in the middle of it, with Epernon on his right and the duc de Montbazon on his left; La Force and Laverdin were also there. The day was fine, and the carriage's awnings were taken down, so that the king and his friends could see the decorations in the streets of Paris, ready for the ceremonial entry of Marie de Medici – newly crowned queen – the following day.

On leaving the Louvre, Henry dismissed the captain of the guard, Charles de Praslin, so that the carriage was accompanied only by a dozen or so footmen and some horsemen riding behind it. Soon the vehicle was forced to stop in the rue de La Ferronnerie, where the traffic was heavy and the road narrow. Henry, who had forgotten his glasses, was listening to a letter which Epernon was reading to him. Most of the footmen ran on ahead, to take a short cut; one of the coachmen went on ahead to clear the traffic, and the other bent down to tie his garter. At that moment a large red-headed man sprang up alongside the coach, leaned across Epernon, and stabbed at the king three times. The first blow grazed a rib, the second pierced his lung and cut the aorta, and the third was lost in Montbazon's cloak. Neither Montbazon nor Epernon reacted fast enough to attempt to parry any of the blows; poor Henry, blood gushing from his mouth, soon lost consciousness (Plate 18).

Epernon, Montbazon and Laverdin sprang down from the carriage, and seized the assassin. Ravaillac, for such was his name, offered no resistance, and Epernon ensured that he was taken unharmed. Meanwhile La Force threw his cloak over the king's body, pulled down the awnings, and hurried the coach back to the Louvre, announcing on the way that Henry had been wounded. But the king's blood, dripping through the floorboards on to the street, was an ominous sign, and when they reached the Louvre he was quite dead, and had to be lifted on to his bed, where the queen soon ran, shrieking 'Le roi est mort, le roi est mort'.

He was indeed, and the kingdom entered a state of shock. In Paris, the guards fanned out into the streets to protect the Louvre, and the great nobles who were in town hurried to offer their services to Marie de Medici; Sully barricaded himself into the Bastille. In the provinces, each royal representative handled the news as best he might. In Aix, for instance, Du Vair immediately ordered all the fortifications of Provence to be manned in case of a Spanish attack; then he put out the news that the king had been wounded, and finally assembled the *parlement* to recognise Louis XIII.[30] A week or so after the assassination, Du Vair was visited by Pietro Priuli, who had formerly been Venetian ambassador to France and was now on his way to Spain. Priuli told Du Vair that as he passed through Milan he had spoken to Count Fuentes, who remarked that he had no fear of French preparations for war in Italy, since 'la mort d'un seul abattiroit tout'.[31]

For Peiresc, describing the visit in a letter to Malherbe, this was evidence that Fuentes had set up the plot. But we cannot be so sure about it, as the whole problem of who killed Henry has long been a source of dispute among historians. For Poirson, the murder was simply the unsupported act of an 'abominable fou'. For Michelet, it was the culmination of a long conspiracy involving Epernon and Henriette d'Entragues, with encouragement and money from Spain. For Loiseleur, it was a combination of the two; according to his theory, which certainly takes into account several aspects of the evidence which fit badly with the theories of Poirson and Michelet, Ravaillac in effect pre-empted another assassination-attempt, which had been mounted for the same day by Epernon and Entragues.[32] Roland Mousnier, the most recent historian to deal at length with the case, dwells rather on the way in which Henry's policies, and particularly the war which he was about to wage on the major Catholic powers, were raising a storm of dissension; for him, if Ravaillac had not done the act, then somebody else would have done. It is very unlikely that the truth of the matter will ever be known. The death of Henry IV bears a curious resemblance to that of President Kennedy in 1963. Both were killed, very efficiently, by rather 'marginal' assassins, social misfits who had not previously made their mark in any particular way. Around both murders developed many theories, neither confirmed nor destroyed by apparently intense judicial investigations. In each case, there was more than a suspicion that accomplices were involved, including perhaps the agents of a foreign power. But in neither case has any certainty been reached.

(v) 'C'était un roi, celui-là'

What is certain is that Henry died at the right time for his reputation. Had he succeeded in launching his offensive, it is virtually sure that France would have got bogged down in the kind of struggle which she eventually entered in 1635. But in 1610 there was no equivalent of Gustavus Adolphus to weaken the imperial forces; the issue might well have gone against France, and she certainly would have been reduced to the state of destitution and social disorder which resulted from the fiscal demands of Richelieu's later years. As it was, a small French army marched to Jülich in the spring, the imperialists there capitulated in September 1610, and by the Convention of Xanten, 1614, a compromise was reached over the succession.[33] Had it not been for Henry's infatuation with Charlotte, a similar compromise might have been possible in 1610.

Meanwhile, the early years of the Regency saw a great outpouring of regret for the lost years of 'Henri le Grand', and the foundation of a durable legend.[34] The funeral orations spoke of Henry's many qualities, generally remaining silent about his many vices.[35] After that, each age of French history refashioned him in its likeness. For the *précieux*, he was the refined and elegant king painted by Rubens. For the *précieuses*, he was the *Grand Alcandre*, the epitome of courtly love. For the opposition under Louis XIV, he was the liberal king, always ready to listen to his *parlements*. Under the Regency, he became a Libertine: the *Vert Galant*. For Voltaire, he became an enlightened despot, contemptuous of the church and sceptical of religion. For the Physiocrats, he and Sully became the great protectors of the peasantry, the men of the 'poule au pot' and the 'deux mamelles'. For the political theorists of the later eighteenth century, Henry's Grand Design was the forerunner of similar schemes offering universal peace.

At the time of the Revolution, Henry's corpse was desecrated, his statue on the Pont Neuf pulled down, and his memory vilified. Under Napoleon, and still more under the Restoration, his reputation was refurbished. But during the nineteenth century monarchical symbols gradually lost their potency in France, and it was no longer necessary to justify present policies by an appeal to past monarchs. So Henry gradually fell into the hands of the historians, and they, too, have tended to fashion him in their own image and likeness.

Conclusion: 'Un roy pour estre grand ne doit rien ignorer'

In some ways, the legend was quite true. For example, Henry's reputation as the *Vert Galant* was unimpeachable, as has been shown again and again. So was his renown as a soldier; he was a cavalry leader, and tactical battlefield commander, of the highest order. In most respects, though, the legendary assertions have to be more carefully examined. What, for instance, about the poule au pot? Henry quite often expressed a desire to help the peasants, but did his reign actually see an improvement in their lot?

In merely fiscal terms, there was some slight improvement, as the weight of the *taille* was somewhat reduced,[1] and edicts of 1595, 1596 and 1600 cancelled back-dues and forbade the seizure of peasants' tools or beasts. In more general terms, we have to distinguish between long- and short-term effects. As we saw at the start, France had about 1550 reached the peak of an upswing in the Malthusian demographic cycle. The population was beginning to press unbearably hard on the available food-supplies, and the latter part of the century, if previous experience was any guide, would have been a time of increasing hardship for the mass of the population, and of a reduction in their number. In fact, the outbreak of the wars of religion in the 1560s reinforced this tendency. Some parts of France retained their earlier level of prosperity longer than others, but by the 1590s ruin was evident everywhere; the scrub was again invading fields, and in Brittany wolves were once more becoming common.

While acknowledging that the period between 1500 and 1690 marks a Malthusian downswing, many authors discern a sort of plateau between 1600 and about 1630.[2] On the Paris market, between 1600 and about 1615, the price of wheat stabilised itself at a relatively low level.[3] In Marseille trade picked up again after the disasters of the mid-1590s.[4] In Rouen the population again began to increase.[5] In the salt trade, France was by 1610 almost back to the position of superiority which she had enjoyed in 1560.[6] It is true that these economic indicators are commercial rather than agricultural, but they directly reflect the productive capacity of the peasantry, and all suggest that after about 1595 a substantial recovery took place.

In one area, thanks to a recent study, we can follow this recovery quite closely.[7] The Hurepoix, a little region immediately south-west of Paris, was ravaged by the wars, whose effect worsened with each decade until in the summer of 1590 disastrous harvest-failures were followed by an exceptional death-rate. This was the culminating blow after thirty years of economic decline, coupled eventually with a grave social crisis. As soon as Henry entered Paris, though, in 1594, things began to improve. The peasants began tilling their land and planting again, in a movement which recalls the years after the disasters of the Hundred Years War. The royal measures modifying the incidence of the *taille* had some effect, and so did Sully's encouragement of road- and bridge-builders.[8] But, as Jacquart writes, 'the Crown's most useful contribution to restoring the rural economy was its creation of favourable material conditions, by bringing order back to the country'. All over France it must have been the same story, as the peasants returned to their fields in peace. By 1610, much of the damage had been repaired, even if the levels of 1560 were not generally reached; to use again the words of Jacquart, it was 'a period of remission rather than a cure', and the malady would catch hold again after 1630.

So much for what Chaunu called the 'conjoncture de la poule au pot'.[9] Henry undoubtedly improved the lot of the peasants, directly and indirectly. But it would not be correct to see him and Sully, as the Physiocrats did, as concerned to give priority to agricultural production over industrial enterprise. Sully certainly did write that tillage and pasturage were the 'deux mamelles de la France' but this did not mean that he and the king wished to discourage merchants and manufacturers. On the contrary, as we have seen (Chapter 9), they did their best to encourage a wide variety of industrial enterprises, and in general followed and developed the proto-mercantilist policies of their predecessors.[10]

Mercantilism is nothing more than the expansion of the power of the state by economic means, and the constant threat from Spain meant that, even if he had wanted to, Henry could not reverse the absolutist trend of the earlier part of the century; he had no choice but to strengthen the Crown in every way he could. In many of his policies, he was following the path traced by François I, and even by Louis XI. To ask if he was trying to create an absolute state is in a sense a foolish question; faced with a battle for survival against Spain, he had no choice. In the process, as we saw in Chapter 11, certain long-standing privileges were swept away. Sometimes, of course, he and Sully took actions whose effect could hardly have been foreseen. In 1604, for instance, they promulgated the edict known as the *paulette*, which in effect allowed office-holders, by paying an annual sum to the royal exchequer, freely to dispose of their offices at the time of their death. There has been much controversy over their motives for this measure. Clearly, they hoped to make a great deal of money (and did), and some historians have thought that they also planned to remove office-holders from the control of local magnates, while others have denied

179

this.[11] In fact, the measure did free office-holders to a great degree from the magnates' control, but it also freed them largely from that of the Crown as well, with consequences which were still working themselves out in 1789.

In most aspects of the legend, Henry is endowed with remarkable mental qualities; turn by turn far-sighted, quick to grasp the point, rapid in deciding upon a course of action, skilful at choosing subordinates and so on. In fact, he did have a very remarkable mind, as his voluminous correspondence testifies. But it was curiously limited; his command of languages was not good and, as Du Perron once remarked, 'he knows nothing about either music or poetry'.[12] Thus in 1597 the legate was surprised to find how little Italian and Latin he knew;[13] and, as we have seen, much of what Cárdenas shouted at him in 1610 (in Spanish) went over his head. In music, this was a marvellously fecund age; at Henry's own marriage (by proxy) to Maria de Medici, in Florence, Jacopo Pieri presented *Euridice*, often regarded as the first opera. Marie sometimes brought singers from Italy, but it would seem that she enjoyed them more than the king did. Similarly with poetry; the 'poètes du Louvre' are generally judged to have been execrable versifiers,[14] though it must be said in Henry's defence that he did bring Malherbe from the provinces and sustain him at the French court.

What a difference when we consider Henry's influence on the visual arts! As the R.P. François de Dainville once observed, he and Sully were both 'visuels';[15] they needed to have maps and plans and drawings in order to visualise problems, and they were passionately interested in art, architecture and sculpture. Thus, when as a young man Henry was casting about for a good site for a fort at Maillezais, he himself sat down and made a topographical sketch, calling Sully over to take his advice on it.[16] Having left his beloved gardens at Pau, he twice sent artists to sketch them, so that he could see how they now looked; in 1582 Jacques Villotte undertook this task, and in 1598 Jacques Androuet du Cerceau spent twenty days at it.[17] Wishing to have a record of the battle-sites of his early days, he agreed to pay Agrippa d'Aubigné a 'reasonable sum' for him to visit these places, so that their plans could supplement the written descriptions.[18] The great effort to establish accurate maps of the French provinces was all part of this intellectual bent, for, as Raymond Ritter put it, Henry was 'un homme qui pense tout par images';[19] maybe, in modern jargon, he was a 'right-sided person', one in whom the right-hand side of the brain was dominant.

His reign saw a great abundance of painting; as Janneau puts it, 'l'œuvre accomplie fut . . . colossale'.[20] Alas, most of the works executed for him have perished, so that it is almost impossible today to form an impression of his taste and the direction of his patronage. It would appear, though, that the painter of greatest genius, who might have formed a school, happily bridging Franco-Flemish and Italian influences, was Toussaint

180

Dubreuil, who died young in 1602. All that we have left from him, following the destruction of the paintings of the *petite galerie* at the Louvre in 1661, are two works, both now in the Louvre. His successor in the king's favour was Jacob Bunel, who also succeeded in combining these two influences; alas, even fewer of his works survive, since the destruction of the Tuileries. Bunel and Dubreuil seem to have been Henry's favourite artists, but the Second Fontainebleau School, as it is sometimes called, included others of considerable merit, of whom the most celebrated are Ambroise Dubois and Martin Fréminet. Some of the works of Dubois survive at Fontainebleau, and show him to have been an honest craftsman; as Béguin puts it, his style is that of a 'flamand italianisé'.[21] Fréminet, who also left works at Fontainebleau, painted in a quite different style; his violent and unbalanced works, best seen in the Chapel of the Trinity there, have a strongly Italian feeling, tending towards the baroque.

In architecture, as we have seen, the achievement of the reign was prodigious, and it is clear from letters and anecdotes that Henry supervised the buildings closely, going down in the early morning, for instance, to sit and talk with the masons busy on the Louvre. In architecture, as in painting, there was in early seventeenth-century France a stylistic tension between the fashion of the north, and of Flanders (identified perhaps with Gallicanism), and the style of Italy, associated to some extent with ultramontanism. On the whole, Henry's taste seems to have leaned towards the northern tradition, exemplified in the great squares in Paris (Place Royale, Place Dauphine) and in the stable-block at Fontainebleau. When, as at the Louvre or at Saint-Germain, he had to incorporate his new buildings with the old structures, he tended towards what might be called a 'proto-classical' style, avoiding the baroque extravagances associated with Italy.

Much the same tension is found in the sculpture of the period. Of the two chief sculptors, Pierre de Francqueville was the more 'Italianising'; born in Cambrai, he had gone early to Italy, whence he was recalled about 1602 at the bidding of Marie de Medici. He was installed in the *grande galerie* of the Louvre, where Henry liked to visit him and watch him at work.[22] Francqueville's surviving works, which include the marvellous *David and Goliath* in the Louvre, have a distinctly Mannerist feeling, deriving no doubt from his years in Italy. The other outstanding sculptor, whose work probably conformed more closely to Henry's taste, was Matthieu Jacquet.[23] His masterwork was the *belle cheminée* at Fontainebleau, constructed between 1597 and 1601. It was dismantled in 1725, but several parts of it survive, at the Louvre and at Fontainebleau itself. The king was particularly attached to the *belle cheminée*, whose style owes nothing to the Italian influence of the earlier decades at Fontainebleau; if we wanted to find a label for it, we might call it 'realist', though it has a fantasy and lightness of touch which belie that pedestrian term. In general, Henry's taste in painting, architecture and sculpture, which so powerfully influenced them during his reign, tended towards what we might call 'northern realism'. After his death, with Marie de Medici free to exercise royal patronage, there would be a swing towards the Italian in all the visual arts.

For contemporaries, one of the king's most remarkable qualities was the speed of his mind. Indeed, it sometimes ran ahead too far for his heart, causing him to make quips which he afterwards regretted. But there hardly can be another king to rival him for *bons mots*. All his entourage had to be ready for banter at any time, and to suffer the indignity of nicknames. Henry himself was 'Saumon', and Sully, for more obvious reasons, was 'Cannonier'. Pompous people who talked for too long – or who looked like talking for too long – could be sure of a deflating barb, for Henry hated what he called 'les harangues folâtres'. In Amiens in 1595, for instance, the town's spokesman having begun 'O most benign, greatest and most clement of kings', Henry cut him short with the remark, 'Add as well, the most tired of kings'. Not taking the hint, another orator set out soon afterwards on a harangue beginning 'Agesilaus, king of Sparta, Sire . . . ', whereupon the king, 'feeling that the speech might be a bit long, cut him off with the words: "Ventre-Saint-Gris, I too have heard of that Agesilaus, but he had eaten, and I have not"'.[24] The same swiftness of wit allowed the king to dispatch his daily business speedily, as he walked with his ministers; there was no need for long discussions on most subjects, as he knew his objectives and quickly decided how to attain them.

This very celerity had as its negative counterpart a lack of constancy, a heritage perhaps from his father, the *ondoyant* Antoine, and even from his grandfather, Henri d'Albret. Nowhere was Henry's inconstancy better seen than in his relations with Marie de Medici. When she first came to Paris, he introduced the marquise de Verneuil to her; as we have seen, the queen did her best to put a bold face on it. Marie must have found this relationship strange, to say the least, but she did her best to retain Henry's affection, hoping no doubt that her position would change once she had given France a dauphin. She was under no illusion as to the importance of this, going as far as to say that, if she gave birth to a daughter, 'she wished her bed might be her tombe'.[25] For his part, the king often treated her kindly, writing, for instance, in late January 1601 that her French was coming on well, and that if she could get a line right every day, then at the end of eight days her whole letter would be in French.[26] Marie then carried out her side of the bargain, by giving birth to Louis, and seems to have thought that Henry might now at least keep Verneuil away from the court. Alas, he had no intention of doing that, and in September 1602 they had a frightful quarrel, in which Marie said that after giving birth to one more child she would retire to a nunnery.[27]

That storm passed over, and the king often behaved kindly towards his queen, taking her to the Saint-Germain fair and publicly expressing delight in their children. Always, though, there was *la marquise* in the background, giving the lie to his endearments. Marie never reconciled herself to this situation, any more than the dauphin could bring himself to countenance his bastard brother; as late as 1608, the queen could not hear the name of Verneuil mentioned without blushing.[28] Small wonder that she tended to retire more and more into the circle of her Italian retainers, further annoying the king. In truth, his inability to observe even the form of fidelity would have wrecked any marriage.

In many respects, then, for good and bad, the legend reflects how things actually were. To what degree, though, did Henry succeed in changing his kingdom between 1600 and 1610? In general, the answer must be that he and Sully succeeded in many of their ventures, establishing the monarchy in a position of strength which could hardly have been imagined in 1589. At the base of the work were Sully's finances (Chapter 11, section v). While slightly reducing the *taille*, he succeeded in building up a huge treasure in the Bastille, and in funding a great variety of public works. Canals were started, and in some cases finished (Chapter 10, section viii). The network of roads was improved, and bridges were repaired or built at crucial points (Chapter 11, section v). Industrial ventures were encouraged, and in one or two cases solid enterprises were established (Chapter 9, section ix). A coherent artillery service was organised, with foundries and supply depots and officers not only in Paris but also in the provinces. The most vulnerable points on the frontier were fortified, and a system of engineers and regular inspections was established (Chapter 11 section v). In the course of this work, these engineers also drew maps which eventually led to a much better understanding of the cartography of France. On the Mediterranean coast, a naval port was established at Toulon, and equipped with a fleet of galleys to protect French interests in that area (Chapter 8, section ix).

Some overseas ventures owed nothing to Sully's help; it was the king's intervention, it would seem, that led to the settlements in Canada (Chapter 10, section iii), and which strengthened the French position at Constantinople. The Crown's position in respect to the great magnates was improved by the defeat of many noble plots. A system of proto-*intendants* enabled the king to be informed about events in the provinces and to intervene if necessary (Chapter 11, section vi). Progress was made in curbing the separatist traditions of some towns, and in bringing others into the royal fiscal structure (Chapter 11, section ix). Where possible, the activities of the *parlements* and of the provincial estates were surveyed and controlled (Chapter 11, section vii). It was, of course, a source of continuing weakness that some nobles remained fractious, that many Protestants were discontented, and that the succession was in the hands of a minor. But in most respects the work of the king and of Sully had greatly strengthened the monarchy between 1600 and 1610, and had improved the lot of the bulk of people living in France.

When we come, finally, to try to assess Henry the man, it is very instructive to compare him with his near-contemporary and long-time enemy, Philip II of Spain. They shared more tastes than at first seems apparent.[29] Both were avid huntsmen, from their earliest years. Both had a passion for gardens, and a real flair, it would seem, for designing them. Both were great patrons of art and architecture, leaning rather towards Flemish than towards Italian models. Both took a close interest in the reform of their respective churches, and in the choice of reforming bishops. Both, finally, were cartographic addicts, concerned to visualise their realms by constantly commissioning maps, plans and drawings.

Outside this area of shared intellectual interests, though, the differences were very sharp. Philip was a rather sedentary person, who had taken to heart his father's dictum that 'travelling about one's kingdoms is neither useful nor decent'. He also seems to have followed the paternal advice that too much sexual activity would be bad for his health. Philip in fact hated to touch or to be touched, in sharp contrast to Henry, who needed constant bodily contact with people. Philip liked to put things down on paper, after due consideration; Henry was happiest in verbal exchanges, when his quick wit could pass quickly from one subject to the next. Philip had no taste for gambling, which was a natural part of Henry's frenetic life-style. As we should expect, they suffered from different kinds of illness. Philip did not contract venereal disease or gout, the results of over-indulgence of one sort and another, but, then, Henry did not suffer from arthritis or psychosomatic headaches. It was the difference between two quite different characters; the one sober, solid and rather plodding, the other dynamic, mercurial and – the word recurs – *ondoyant*.

The way they moved among their people was also very different. Whereas Philip could mingle freely with his subjects, Henry always had to be on the lookout for a possible assassin, and his frequent comings and goings must have been a nightmare for his guard-commanders. What happened after their deaths, in 1598 and 1610, is also instructive. When Philip died, there was no political uncertainty in Spain, and the crown passed smoothly to Philip III. When Henry died, on the other hand, there was a period of considerable unrest, and the whole political balance of power within Europe was sharply changed. As in the case of Louis XIV in 1715, the death of the French king removed a most potent piece from the political and constitutional chessboard, and the whole game was changed. Henry may not have been a model husband or a man of great constancy, but he was an extraordinary personality, and when he died things could never again be the same.

Notes

Prologue

1 On these developments see Georges Duby (ed.), *Histoire de la France rurale*.
2 On Jeanne see Nancy Roelker, *Queen of Navarre: Jeanne d'Albret, 1528–1572*.

Chapter 1

1 Palma-Cayet, Vol. I, p. 174.
2 See Raymond Ritter, *Le Château de Pau*.
3 Palma-Cayet, Vol. I, p. 175.
4 This concept is advanced by Irene Mahoney, *Royal Cousin: The Life of Henry IV of France*. I have in the early chapters relied heavily on this work and also on Pierre de Vaissière's *Henri IV*.
5 *Lettres missives*, Vol. I, p. 3.
6 Palma-Cayet, Vol. I, p. 178.
7 *Lettres missives*, Vol. V, pp. 462–3.
8 Pierre de L'Estoile, *Journal*, Vol. I, p. 21.
9 See *Mémoires de Sully*, ed. L'Ecluse, Vol. I, p. 9.
10 Thus Mahoney, *Royal Cousin*, p. 26.
11 See the entry in the *compte d'argenterie* for 1571, listed in *Expositions Henry IV* (Lourdes), p. 41.
12 For a recent, close analysis of these negotiations, see N. M. Sutherland, *The Massacre of Saint Bartholomew and the European Conflict 1559–1572*.
13 *CSP Foreign* 1572–4, art. 464.
14 Sully, *Oeconomies royales*, ed. David Buisseret and Bernard Barbiche, pp. 12–15.
15 On this affair see Mahoney, *Royal Cousin*, p. 68.
16 *CSP Foreign* 1572–4, art. 1364.
17 ibid. 1572–4, art. 1462.
18 ibid. 1575–7, art. 605.
19 For a recent interpretation of this event, see Raymond Ritter, 'Le roi de Navarre et sa prétendue fuite de la Cour en 1576'.
20 *Lettres missives*, Vol. I, pp. 121–2.
21 *CSP Foreign* 1575–7, art. 1314.
22 *Cal. MSS Salisbury*, Vol. II, p. 352.
23 *CSP Foreign* 1578–9, art. 579.
24 *Lettres missives*, Vol. I, p. 265.
25 G. Baguenault de Puchesse, 'Henri IV avant son avènement', pp. 181–2.
26 *CSP Foreign* 1583, art. 734.
27 In 1584 many of them accompanied him when he visited Montaigne; see Jean Marchand (ed.), *Le Livre de raison de Montaigne*, for 19 December.

Chapter 2

1 The work of Aline Karcher has begun a re-assessment of the reign of Henri III; see, for instance, her 'L'assemblée des notables de Saint-Germain-en-Laye (1583)'.
2 On the League movement see J. H. M. Salmon, *Society in Crisis: France in the Sixteenth Century*, pp. 234–75.
3 Jacques-Auguste de Thou, *Histoire universelle*, Vol. VI, p. 392.

4 *Lettres missives*, Vol. I, pp. 502–3.
5 Vaissière, *Henri IV*, p. 262.
6 ibid., p. 265.
7 Quoted in Jean H. Mariéjol, *Henri IV et Louis XIII*, p. 250.
8 *Lettres missives*, Vol. II, pp. 129–30.
9 *CSP Foreign* 1583, art. 734.
10 Described by De Lamar Jensen in *Diplomacy and Dogmatism* . . .
11 Sully, *Oeconomies royales*, pp. 129–30.
12 *CSP Foreign* 1583, art. 734.
13 Quoted in Mariéjol, *Henri IV et Louis XIII*, pp. 252–3.
14 *Lettres missives*, Vol. I, pp. 254–5.
15 In his case, Navarre had made a direct approach; as a Savoyard diplomat wrote back to his Duke in July 1585: 'j'ay veu une lettre que le roy de Navarre escrit à son cousin le prince de Conty de sa main'. See Alain Dufour (ed.), *René de Lucinge: lettres sur les débuts de la Ligue*, p. 159.
16 *Lettres missives*, Vol. II, p. 286.
17 Sully, *Oeconomies royales*, pp. 157–8.
18 For this campaign, see the old but excellent work by Sir Charles Oman, *A History of the Art of War in the Sixteenth Century*, pp. 470–80.
19 Sully, *Oeconomies royales*, pp. 188–9.
20 ibid., p. 193.
21 See, however, the argument justifying Henry's conduct advanced by Garrett Mattingly, *The Spanish Armada*, pp. 177–8.
22 *Lettres missives*, Vol. II, p. 427. On his hereditary tendency towards tuberculosis, and its various manifestations before 1589, see Raymond Ritter, *Henry IV*, pp. 123–39.
23 *Lettres missives*, Vol. II, pp. 443–58.
24 ibid., Vol. II, pp. 480–1.
25 For an interesting account of his last hours, see duc d'Angoulême, *Mémoires*, ed. Michaud and Poujoulat; Charles de Valois, duc d'Angoulême was an eyewitness.

Chapter 3

1 Which, as we shall see in Chapter 7, was very extensive. On Henry's hereditary claim see Ralph Giesey, 'The juristic basis of dynastic right to the French throne', pp. 30–2.
2 Palma-Cayet, Vol. I, p. 54.
3 A fuller list is given in Auguste Poirson, *Histoire du règne de Henri IV*, Vol. I, p. 34.
4 For some time, of course, these services were defective. It was not until November 1590, for instance, that the 'musique de la chapelle du roi' was re-established; see L'Estoile, *Journal*, Vol. I, p. 80.
5 *Lettres missives*, Vol. III, p. 116.
6 See D. Thickett (ed.), *Etienne Pasquier: lettres historiques pour les années 1556–1594*, p. 332.
7 Gabriel Hanotaux, *Tableau de la France en 1614*, p. 116, quoting the Venetian ambassador Pietro Duodo.
8 For Queen Elizabeth's nettled reaction to this over-chivalrous conduct, see *Lettres missives*, Vol. III, p. 285.
9 For a justification of his strategic sense, however, see Howell A. Lloyd, *The Rouen Campaign 1590–1592*, pp. 110–11.
10 L. Léger, 'Le siège de Rouen par Henri IV d'après des documents tchèques', p. 70.
11 Because of rough weather they used barges rather than their pontoon-bridge; see Lloyd, *Rouen Campaign*, pp. 187–8.
12 John H. Elliott, *Europe Divided*, p. 340.
13 See J. H. M. Salmon, 'The Paris Sixteen'.
14 According to Jules Nouaillac, *Villeroy, secrétaire d'État* . . . , pp. 241–2.
15 Quoted in Mariéjol, *Henri IV et Louis XIII*, p. 377.

Chapter 4

1 L'Estoile, *Journal*, Vol. I, p. 193.
2 Palma-Cayet, Vol. I, p. 546, and BN ms. fr. 4016, fo. 19.
3 For a good account, see Palma-Cayet, Vol. I, pp. 546–8.
4 *Lettres missives*, Vol. II, pp. 822–3.
5 ibid., Vol. IV, p. 12.
6 M. de Rommel (ed.), *Correspondance inédite de Henri IV avec Maurice-le-Savant*, pp. 9 etc.
7 *Cal. MSS Salisbury*, Vol. IV, p. 343.
8 L'Estoile, *Journal*, Vol. I, p. 261.
9 ibid., Vol. I, p. 296.
10 *Lettres missives*, Vol, IV. pp. 5–6, 14–15 and 29.
11 L'Estoile, *Journal*, Vol. I, p. 331.
12 ibid., Vol. I, p. 365.
13 ibid., Vol. I, p. 438; it had 'gone over to the distaff side' because the head of the Protestants was now Henry's sister, Catherine de Bourbon.
14 *Lettres missives*, Vol. IV, p. 129.
15 There is a good list of these compositions in L'Estoile, *Journal*, Vol. I, pp. 415–16.
16 *Revue Henri IV*, Vol. I, p. 164.
17 Martin Wolfe, *The Fiscal System of Renaissance France*, pp. 216–22.
18 Winwood, *Negotiations*, Vol. I, p. 120.
19 *CSP Venice* 1592–1603, art. 247.
20 *Lettres missives*, Vol. IV, pp. 236–7; see also Vol. IV, pp. 357–8.
21 Jehan de Vernyes, *Mémoires*, p. 52.
22 Notably Bertrand de Jouvenel, *On Power*.
23 Vaissière, *Henri IV*, p. 439.
24 For a good account, see Palma-Cayet, Vol. I, pp. 613–20.
25 L'Estoile, *Journal*, Vol. I, p. 384; and Palma-Cayet, Vol. I, p. 624.
26 *Lettres missives*, Vol. IV, p. 114.
27 L'Estoile, *Journal*, Vol. I, p. 385.
28 ibid., Vol. I, pp. 405–6; and Palma-Cayet, Vol. I, p. 627.
29 L'Estoile, *Journal*, Vol. I, pp. 386–8.
30 Quoted in Vaissière, *Henri IV*, p. 449.
31 Palma-Cayet, Vol. I, p. 629.
32 *Lettres missives*, Vol. IV, p. 120, a circular letter.
33 L'Estoile, *Journal*, Vol. I, p. 406.
34 Palma-Cayet, Vol. I, p. 634.
35 Thickett, *Pasquier*, p. 337.
36 Paul Robiquet, *Histoire municipale de Paris*, Vol. III, p. 181.
37 ibid., Vol. III, p. 183.
38 L'Estoile, *Journal*, Vol. I, p. 412.
39 For a good summary, see Salmon, *Society in Crisis*, pp. 276–91.
40 See Yves-Marie Bercé, *Croquants et Nu-Pieds*.
41 L'Estoile, *Journal*, Vol. I, p. 420.
42 *Lettres missives*, Vol. IV, p. 184.
43 Roland Mousnier, *La Vénalité des offices sous Henri IV et Louis XIII*, pp. 542–51.
44 Fernand Braudel, *The Mediterranean and the Mediterranean World in the Age of Philip II*, p. 1216.
45 Boris Porchnev, *Les Soulèvements populaires en France de 1623 à 1648*, p. 47.

Chapter 5

1 L'Estoile, *Journal*, Vol. I, p. 443.
2 See, for instance, ibid., Vol. I, pp. 264, 312, 408, 437, 488, 493–4, 560, 570 and 614, and Vol. II, pp. 24 and 97.
3 ibid., Vol. I, p. 437.

4 PRO SP 78/49, fo. 21; this seems to be the same device as the one mentioned in L'Estoile, *Journal*, Vol. II, p. 97.
5 PRO SP 78/53, fo. 108.
6 Raymond Ritter (ed.), *Lettres du cardinal de Florence sur Henri IV et sur la France, 1596–1598*, p. 61, n. 1.
7 On this point see Roland Mousnier, *L'Assassinat d'Henri IV*, pp. 206–8.
8 Printed in Palma-Cayet, Vol. II, pp. 3–5.
9 *Lettres missives*, Vol. IV, pp. 363–5; and Palma-Cayet, Vol. II, p. 17.
10 *Lettres missives*, Vol. IV, p. 375.
11 See the list in Palma-Cayet, Vol. II, p. 17.
12 AN K 108, 106.
13 See the account of the entry in Palma-Cayet, Vol. II, pp. 26–9.
14 L'Estoile, *Journal*, Vol. I, p. 462.
15 *Cal. MSS Salisbury*, Vol. V, p. 289.
16 *Lettres missives*, Vol. IV, p. 400.
17 ibid., Vol. IV, p. 404.
18 L'Estoile, *Journal*, Vol. I, p. 466.
19 Palma-Cayet, Vol. II, p. 5.
20 According to an English report, PRO SP 78/37, fo. 41.
21 *Lettres missives*, Vol. IV, p. 406.
22 Henri Drouot, *Mayenne et la Bourgogne*, Vol. II, p. 472.
23 L'Estoile, *Journal*, Vol. I, p. 448.
24 See Henry's letter of 3 April 1596, *Lettres missives*, Vol. IV, p. 553; he thought they were heading for Péronne or Montreuil.
25 ibid., Vol. IV, p. 574, n. 1.
26 ibid., Vol. IV, p. 574.
27 *CSP Venice* 1592–1603, art. 448; Piero Duodo to Doge and Senate.
28 Thou, *Histoire universelle*, Vol. XII, p. 644.
29 *Lettres missives*, Vol. IV, p. 416.
30 The most recent work on this assembly is J. Russell Major, 'Bellièvre, Sully and the assembly of notables of 1596'.
31 Claude Groulart, *Memoires ou voyages par lui faits en Cour*, ed. Michaud and Poujoulat, p. 565.
32 BN Dupuy 7, fo. 19; facsimile in *Lettres missives*, Vol. IV, p. 657.
33 PRO SP 78/38, fo. 191.
34 ibid., 78/39, fo. 59; letter of 16/26 February 1597. (With regard to dates, 16/26 February was the 16th in England, using the Old Style calendar, and the 26th in France and those countries which had adopted the Gregorian reform of 1582.)
35 See Albert Chamberland, 'Jean Chandon et le conflit entre la cour des aides et le conseil du roi'.
36 *Cal. MSS de L'Isle*, Vol. II, p. 228.
37 L'Estoile, *Journal*, Vol. I, p. 438.
38 ibid., Vol. I, p. 473.
39 Ritter, *Lettres du cardinal de Florence*, p. 91.
40 ibid., p. 111.
41 L'Estoile, *Journal*, Vol. I, p. 408.
42 ibid., Vol. I. pp. 428, 429 and 504.
43 PRO SP 78/38, fo. 99.
44 Groulart, *Mémoires*, p. 577.
45 Sully, *Les Economies royales*, ed. Michaud and Poujoulat, Vol. I, pp. 246–7.
46 *CSP Venice* 1592–1603, art. 260.
47 L'Estoile, *Journal*, Vol. I, p. 497.
48 PRO SP 78/39, fo. 74.
49 *Cal. MSS Salisbury*, Vol. VII, p. 99, Mildmay to the Earl of Essex, Paris, 6/16 March 1596/7.
50 *Lettres missives*, Vol. IV, p. 726.
51 ibid., Vol. IV, p. 826: letter of 11 August 1597 to the Duke of Piney-Luxembourg.

52 ibid., Vol. IV, p. 764.
53 ibid., Vol. IV, p. 764.
54 ibid., Vol. IV, p. 217: letter of 24 September 1597 to the sieur de Noailles.
55 ibid., Vol. IV, p. 777.
56 The figures are not easy to establish, but various estimates may be found in Ritter, *Lettres du cardinal de Florence*, p. 136 (mid-May); PRO SP 78/39, fos 268 (late May), 346 (late June); Palma-Cayet, Vol. I, p. 765 (mid July); Ritter, *Lettres du cardinal de Florence*, p. 171 (late August); and PRO SP 78/40, fo. 90 (September).
57 Palma-Cayet, Vol. I, p. 765.
58 PRO SP 78/40 fo. 14: letter of 9/19 July.
59 See G. Bonnault d'Houet, *La Première Ambulance sous Henri IV*.
60 *Lettres missives*, Vol. IV, p. 861.
61 ibid., Vol. IV, p. 855.
62 ibid., Vol. IV, p. 851.

Chapter 6

1 *Lettres missives*, Vol. IV, p. 1064.
2 ibid., Vol. IV, p. 899; Louis de Berton, sieur de Grillon, was an old comrade-in-arms.
3 On Mercœur's policies, see Louis Grégoire, *La Ligue en Bretagne*.
4 Robert Cecil and J. Herbert, in France to impede if possible the peace negotiations with Spain: PRO SP 78/41, fo. 338.
5 The pair were eventually married in 1609.
6 *Lettres missives*, Vol. IV, p. 918.
7 ibid., Vol. IV, p. 981.
8 See Léonce Anquez, *Histoire des assemblées politiques des réformés de France*.
9 Recently analysed by N. M. Sutherland in 'The Edict of Nantes and the "Protestant state"'.
10 *Lettres missives*, Vol. V, pp. 89–94.
11 ibid., Vol. V, p. 181.
12 ibid., Vol. V, pp. 181–2.
13 For its text, see Palma-Cayet, Vol. II, pp. 171–2.
14 *Lettres missives*, Vol. IV, p. 1010.
15 Palma-Cayet, Vol. II, p. 167.
16 PRO SP 78/42, fo. 54.
17 L'Estoile, *Journal*, Vol. I, pp. 525–6.
18 *Economies royales*, Vol. I, p. 284.
19 *Lettres missives*, Vol. V, pp. 34 and 41–2.
20 For a good survey, see Ritter, *Henry IV*, pp. 134–6.
21 *Lettres missives*, Vol. V, p. 63.
22 Groulart, *Mémoires*, p. 580.
23 *Lettres missives*, Vol. V, p. 63.
24 See David Buisseret, 'Les *ingénieurs du roi* de Henri IV'.
25 *Lettres missives*, Vol. IV, pp. 212 and 254.
26 L'Estoile, *Journal*, Vol. I, p. 563.
27 *Lettres missives*, Vol. IV, p. 999.
28 Groulart, *Mémoires*, p. 581.
29 The best account of her death is in Raymond Ritter, *Charmante Gabrielle*, pp. 538–45.
30 PRO SP 78/43, fo. 86.
31 ibid., fo. 97.
32 AN 120 AP 10, fos 19–20.
33 ibid., fos 23–4.
34 Winwood, *Negotiations*, Vol. I, pp. 20–2.
35 Vaissière, *Henri IV*, p. 522.
36 PRO SP 78/43, fo. 260.
37 Charles Merki, *La Marquise de Verneuil et la mort d'Henri IV*, p. 58.

38 Winwood, *Negotiations*, Vol. I. pp. 115–18.
39 L'Estoile, *Journal*, Vol. I, p. 580.
40 PRO SP 78/43, fo. 127.
41 *Economies royales*, Vol. I, p. 276.
42 On the early course of the negotiations see Louis Batiffol, *La Vie intime d'une reine de France au XVIIe siècle*.
43 Winwood, *Negotiations*, Vol. I, p. 131.
44 See the account in Palma-Cayet, Vol. II, pp. 232–4.
45 L'Estoile, *Journal*, Vol. I, p. 583.
46 Thou, *Histoire universelle*, Vol. XIII, p. 437.
47 Described in L'Estoile, *Journal*, Vol. I, p. 589.
48 *Economies royales*, Vol. I, p. 323.
49 L'Estoile, *Journal*, Vol. I, p. 588.
50 Palma-Cayet, Vol. II, p. 240.
51 L'Estoile, *Journal*, Vol. I, pp. 590–1.
52 Agreement printed in Palma-Cayet, Vol. II, pp. 242–4.
53 Edouard Rott, *Henri IV, les Suisses et la Haute-Italie*, p. 92, n. 3.
54 *Lettres missives*, Vol. V, pp. 212–13.
55 ibid., Vol. V, pp. 215–16.
56 Jules Nouaillac (ed.), *Un Envoyé hollandais à la cour de Henri IV: lettres inédites de François Aerssen à Jacques Valcke (1599–1603)*, p. 78, n. 2.
57 *Lettres missives*, Vol. V, p. 245.
58 For these contracts, see François de Mallevouë (ed.), *Les Actes de Sully*.
59 ibid., pp. 378–80.
60 See, for instance, AC Châlons-sur-Marne, AA 8, fo. 134.
61 See David Buisseret, *Sully*, p. 157, for these details.
62 This is the figure given by Neville in a letter to Cecil of 21 July 1600: PRO SP 78/44, fo. 247.
63 On this work see L'Estoile, *Journal*, Vol. I, pp. 585–6.
64 On this controversy see J. A. Lalot, *Essai historique sur la conférence tenue à Fontainebleau entre Duplessis-Mornay et Duperron le 4 mai 1600*.
65 *Lettres missives*, Vol. V, p. 230.
66 *Economies royales*, Vol. I, p. 330.
67 Palma-Cayet, Vol. II, p. 278.
68 *Lettres missives*, Vol. V, p. 273.
69 L'Estoile, *Journal*, Vol. I, p. 621.
70 *Lettres missives*, Vol. V, p. 291.
71 Palma-Cayet, Vol. II, p. 280.
72 *Lettres missives*, Vol. V, p. 306.
73 PRO SP 78/44, fo. 279.
74 Buisseret, *Sully*, p. 157.
75 *Lettres missives*, Vol. V, p. 319.
76 See Palma-Cayet, Vol. II, pp. 307–10.
77 PRO SP 78/45, fo. 9.
78 Nouaillac, *Villeroy*, p. 392.
79 Poirson, *Histoire*, Vol. I, p. 383.
80 Nouaillac, *Villeroy*, pp. 392–3; and Rott, *Henri IV*, pp. 101–4.
81 *Lettres missives*, Vol. V, p. 373.
82 Rott, *Henri IV*, p. 100.
83 Geoffrey Parker, *The Army of Flanders and the Spanish Road*, pp. 69–70.
84 For these letters, see *Lettres missives*, Vol. V, pp. 314 and 322.
85 For a description of the voyage, see Batiffol, *Vie intime*, Vol. I, pp. 29–31.
86 Described in Palma-Cayet, Vol. II, pp. 290–1.
87 Winwood, *Negotiations*, Vol. I, pp. 276–7.
88 ibid., Vol. I, p. 267; for two sharply differing opinions of Marie's appearance and character, see Mahoney, *Royal Cousin*, pp. 370–1, and Merki, *Verneuil*, pp. 86–7.
89 Palma-Cayet, Vol. II, p. 293.

90 ibid., Vol. II, p. 294.
91 Winwood, *Negotiations*, Vol. I, p. 280.
92 Palma-Cayet, Vol. II, p. 296.
93 *Lettres missives*, Vol. V, p. 375.
94 L'Estoile, *Journal*, Vol. II, p. 6.

Chapter 7

1 Robert Dallington, *The View of Fraunce*, p. G4.
2 The *comptes de bouche* between 1593 and 1627 survive in BN ms. fr. 25761; they make entertaining reading.
3 Vaissière, *Henri IV*, p. 612; and Batiffol, *Vie intime*, Vol. I, p. 196.
4 Cited here as Groulart, *Mémoires*.
5 According to Tallemant des Réaux, *Historiettes*, Vol. I, p. 975, n. 7.
6 For his life, see La Bouillerie, *Un Ami de Henri IV*.
7 See duc de La Force, *Le Maréchal de La Force (1558–1652)*.
8 Preserved in BN ms. fr. 23195–8.
9 See Guyot de Saint-Michel (ed.) *Correspondance . . . de Henry le Grand avec J. Roussat*.
10 He had, for instance, lost Amiens in 1597.
11 The fullest list is in BN Clairambault 837, fo. 3225–3349; this may be supplemented by AN KK 151, 152 and 153, and from BN ms. fr. 7854.
12 PRO SP 78/44, fo. 404; a list of 'officiers de la couronne'.
13 For details of this curious affair, see L'Estoile, *Journal*, Vol. I. pp. 567–9; on La Rivière see the essay by Hugh Trevor-Roper in Allen Debus (ed.), *Science, Medicine and Society in the Renaissance*.
14 According to L'Estoile, *Journal*, Vol. II, p. 375.
15 Eud. Soulié and Ed. de Barthélemy (eds), *Journal de Jean Héroard*; note, however, the qualifications expressed in Elizabeth Marvick, 'The character of Louis XIII: the role of his physician'.
16 He eventually made a distinguished career in England: see his long entry in *The Dictionary of National Biography*.
17 Pineau wrote a work on extracting gallstones, and also engaged himself to instruct young surgeons in this art: see Mallevouë, *Actes de Sully*, pp. 11–13.
18 On his work here, see Buisseret, *Sully*, p. 210.
19 *Journal de Jean Héroard*, Vol. I, p. 428.
20 See AN KK 149, the *comptes de l'argenterie* for 1607; the same accounts survive for 1595 (AN KK 148) and 1591 (AN KK 147). Other interesting household accounts include BN ms. fr. 3994, the king's music for 1595, and AN KK 155, the *écurie* accounts for 1607.
21 On the air-gun see David Rivault, *Les Elemens de l'artillerie*.
22 By that date the formerly geographical division of responsibilities was giving way to a functional division.
23 Quoted in Nouaillac, *Villeroy*, p. 383; on the differences between Sully and Bellièvre, see Raymond Kierstead, *Pomponne de Bellièvre*, pp. 124–36.
24 For an attempt to trace the complicated history of this office, see Bernard Barbiche and David Buisseret, 'Sully et la surintendance des finances'.
25 On their work see Buisseret, 'Les *ingénieurs du roi*'.
26 In his *Relation of the State of France*, printed in Thomas Birch (ed.), *An Historical View of the Negotiations between the Courts of England, France and Brussels, 1592–1617*, p. 489.
27 On his embassy see P. P. Laffleur de Kermaingant (ed.), *Mission de Jean de Thumery* (part of *L'Ambassade de France*).
28 Some of the king's letters to him were published in P. P. Laffleur de Kermaingant (ed.), *Lettres de Henri IV au comte de La Rochepot*.
29 These negotiations are set out in Jacques Bongars, *Lettres latines de M. de Bongars*.
30 On the work of Vic see the various works of Edouard Rott, and in particular *Henri IV*.

31 See Rémy Couzard, *Une Ambassade à Rome sous Henri IV*, and Bernard Barbiche, 'L'influence française à la cour pontificale sous le règne de Henri IV'.

32 A. L. Horniker, 'Anglo-French rivalry in the Levant from 1583 to 1612'.

33 This account of everyday life at the Louvre is based on Louis Batiffol's two works, *Le Louvre sous Henri IV et Louis XIII* and *La Vie intime d'une reine de France au XVIIe siècle*.

34 See the king's letter to Montmorency, *Lettres missives*, Vol. V, pp. 388–90.

35 See Ritter, *Henry IV*, pp. 401–5; and Charles Read (ed.), *Daniel Chamier: journal de son voyage à la cour de Henri IV en 1607*, pp. 51–60.

36 On Henry's food see Robert Le Blant, 'Marchés de pain, de viandes et de poissons pour Henri IV, 21 décembre 1607'.

37 On these musicians see Batiffol, *Vie intime*, Vol. I, p. 101.

38 Epernon's position was ambiguous; although he was personally close to the king, he held no post of great responsibility.

39 See Michel Bareau, 'Manuel Pimentel et le "jeu du roi" en 1608'.

40 Recorded in the secret accounts, BN ms. fr. 4559 and AN 120 AP 10; see Ch. 11, sect. v.

41 On these ballets see Margaret McGowan, *L'Art du ballet de cour en France, 1581–1643*; the author points out that we have few details of the ballets before 1610.

42 Batiffol, *Vie intime*, Vol. I, p. 121.

Chapter 8

1 Antoine Fontanon, *Les Edicts et ordonnances des rois de France*, Vol. II, p. 531.

2 Valois, *Inventaire*, no. 5923; it ought to be added that some of the many *arrêts* concerning the *pancarte* at this time appear to contradict each other.

3 ibid., no. 6156.

4 ibid., no. 6231.

5 ibid., no. 6547.

6 Winwood, *Negotiations*, Vol. I, p. 329.

7 See the interesting account of this council meeting in Groulart, *Mémoires*, p. 586.

8 *Lettres missives*, Vol. V, pp. 417–18.

9 Winwood, *Negotiations*, Vol. I, p. 341.

10 BN ms. fr. 23197, fo. 12.

11 Bernard Barbiche (ed.), *Correspondance du nonce en France Innocenzo del Bufalo, évêque de Camerino (1601–1604)*, p. 277.

12 See, for instance, Valois, *Inventaire*, no. 7036.

13 Gabriel Hanotaux, *Sur les chemins de l'histoire*, pp. 52–4.

14 Salmon, *Society in Crisis*, p. 312.

15 Valois, *Inventaire*, no. 7155.

16 L'Estoile, *Journal*, Vol. II, p. 36.

17 Bernard Barbiche, *Sully*, p. 67.

18 *Lettres missives*, Vol. V, p. 408.

19 ibid., Vol. V, p. 417.

20 For contemporary plans of these towns, see David Buisseret, 'Les fortifications de la Picardie vers 1600'.

21 Palma-Cayet, Vol. II, p. 340.

22 *CSP Venice 1592–1603*, art. 1006.

23 *Lettres missives*, Vol. IX, p. 472.

24 ibid., Vol. V, p. 459.

25 G. Groen van Prinsterer (ed.), *Archives et correspondance inédite de la maison d'Orange-Naussau*, Vol. II, pp. 2–3.

26 Merki, *Verneuil*, pp. 89–90.

27 Winwood, *Negotiations*, Vol. I, p. 293.

28 ibid., Vol. I, p. 367.

29 ibid., Vol. I, p. 331.

30 Louise Bourgeois afterwards published a pamphlet called *Comment et en quel temps la reine accoucha de Monsieur le Dauphin*, from which the following details are taken.
31 Winwood, *Negotiations*, Vol. I, p. 348.
32 Described in L'Estoile, *Journal*, Vol. II, p. 47.
33 Winwood, *Negotiations*, Vol. I, p. 338.
34 L'Estoile, *Journal*, Vol. I, p. 48.
35 ibid., Vol. I, p. 49.
36 Jose Luis Cano de Gardoqui, *Tensiones hispanofranceses en el siglo XVII*, p. 24.
37 Winwood, *Negotiations*, Vol. I, pp. 288–9.
38 Gardoqui, *Tensiones*, p. 64.
39 ibid., p. 28.
40 *Lettres missives*, Vol. V, pp. 666–8.
41 ibid., Vol. V, pp. 413–14.
42 L'Estoile, *Journal*, Vol. II, p. 78; the secret accounts show that this ambassador received a present of a thousand *livres*: AN 120 AP 10, fo. 40.
43 *Lettres missives*, Vol. V, p. 744.
44 See, for instance, ibid., Vol. V, p. 419; for the figures, see Buisseret, *Sully*, p. 82.
45 Kermaingant, *Lettres de Henri IV*, p. 18.
46 BN ms. fr. 23196, fo. 303.
47 Martin Philippson, *Heinrich IV und Philipp III*, Vol. II, p. 173.
48 *Lettres missives*, Vol. V, p. 448.
49 Philippson, *Heinrich und Philipp*, Vol. III, p. 3.
50 Winwood, *Negotiations*, Vol. I, pp. 365–6.
51 Palma-Cayet, Vol. II, p. 363.
52 ibid., Vol. II, p. 383.
53 This barely credible combination seems to have been firmly established by Alain Dufour, 'La paix de Lyon', p. 439.
54 Winwood, *Negotiations*, Vol. I, pp. 384–5.
55 Palma-Cayet, Vol. II, p. 363.
56 See the secret accounts: AN 120 AP 10, fo. 46 (5,000 *livres*).
57 *Lettres missives*, Vol. V, pp. 578–9, 587–8 and 588–9.
58 ibid., Vol. V, p. 594.
59 ibid., Vol. V, pp. 595 and 599.
60 ibid., Vol. V, pp. 601–2 and 602–3.
61 Palma-Cayet, Vol. II, p. 364.
62 See the account of his arrest in Merki, *Verneuil*, p. 109.
63 Palma-Cayet, Vol. II, p. 364.
64 *Lettres missives*, Vol. V, p. 612.
65 ibid., Vol. VIII, p. 836.
66 Palma-Cayet, Vol. II, p. 370.
67 As set out in PRO SP 78/47, fos 151–2.
68 Winwood, *Negotiations*, Vol. I, p. 425.
69 David Buisseret and Bernard Barbiche (eds), 'Lettres inédites de Sully', pp. 94–5.
70 AN 120 AP 10, fo. 46.
71 L'Estoile, *Journal*, Vol. II, p. 76.
72 *Lettres missives*, Vol. V, p. 671.
73 ibid., Vol. V, p. 693.
74 ibid., Vol. V, pp. 696–7.
75 BN ms. fr. 23197: letter from Viçose (see Ch. 11, sect. vi).
76 Winwood, *Negotiations*, Vol. I, p. 439.
77 ibid., Vol. I, p. 447.
78 Valois, *Inventaire*, no. 6134.
79 ibid., no. 6681.
80 *Lettres missives*, Vol. V, pp. 542–3 and 546.
81 Sully, of course, claims the credit: *Economies royales*, Vol. I, p. 404.
82 L'Estoile, *Journal*, Vol. II, p. 79.
83 For what follows, see David Buisseret, 'The French Mediterranean fleet under Henri IV'.

84 See, for instance, BN ms. fr. 23196, fos 37 and 41.
85 Winwood, *Negotiations*, Vol. I, p. 380.
86 BN ms. fr. 4014, fo. 177.
87 Mallevoüe, *Actes de Sully*, p. 9.
88 According to the Venetian ambassador: Nicolò Barozzi and Guglielmo Berchet (eds), *Relazioni degli stati europei . . .* , Vol. I, p. 458.
89 According to Ithier Hobier, *De la construction d'une gallaire*; Hobier was one of Henry's *secrétaires sans gages*.
90 BN Dupuy 154, fos 103–10.
91 Raymond de Bonnefons, whose plan for Toulon is preserved in AN 120 AP 48, fo. 75.
92 BN ms. fr. 23198, fo. 156.
93 Described by Charles de La Roncière in his *Histoire de la marine française*, Vol. IV, pp. 371–87.
94 ibid., Vol. IV, pp. 444–57.

Chapter 9

1 L'Estoile, *Journal*, Vol. II, p. 81.
2 *CSP Venice* 1592–1603, art. 875.
3 Palma-Cayet, Vol. II, pp. 431–2.
4 *CSP Venice* 1592–1603, art. 310.
5 *Lettres missives*, Vol. VI, p. 87.
6 *CSP Venice* 1603–7, art. 64.
7 *Economies royales*, Vol. I, p. 430.
8 L'Estoile, *Journal*, Vol. II, p. 102.
9 ibid., Vol. II, p. 115.
10 *Lettres missives*, Vol. VI, p. 72.
11 For Sully's instructions, see BN ms. fr. 25117, fos 33–44.
12 *CSP Venice* 1603–7, art. 81.
13 *Lettres missives*, Vol. VI, p. 132.
14 BN ms. fr. 10308, fo. 139.
15 *Lettres missives*, Vol. V, p. 554.
16 PRO SP 78/49, fos 40–2.
17 *CSP Venice* 1592–1603, art. 687.
18 ibid., 1603–7, art. 90.
19 ibid., 1603–7, art. 107.
20 *Lettres missives*, Vol. VI, p. 10.
21 See Henri Fouqueray, *Histoire de la Compagnie de Jésus*, Vol. II, p. 535.
22 ibid., Vol. II, p. 632.
23 The remonstrances of the *parlement* and the king's reply are printed in Roland Mousnier, *L'Assassinat d'Henri IV*, pp. 338–43.
24 Fouqueray, *Histoire*, Vol. II, p. 652.
25 See Françoise de Dainville, *La Naissance de l'humanisme moderne*.
26 Fouqueray, *Histoire*, Vol. III, p. 18.
27 See the letter quoted in Charles de Lacombe, *Henri IV et sa politique*, p. 58.
28 Jacques Hennequin, *Henri IV dans ses oraisons funèbres*.
29 Poirson, *Henri IV*, Vol. III, p. 751.
30 Pierre Hélyot, *Histoire des ordres monastiques*, Vol. I, p. 112.
31 Fouqueray, *Histoire*, Vol. III, pp. 176–95.
32 Henri Bremond, *Histoire littéraire du sentiment religieux en France*, Vol. II, p. 105.
33 ibid., Vol. II, p. 402.
34 Poirson, *Henri IV*, Vol. IV, p. 501.
35 For Valladier, and for many of the other churchmen cited as examples, see the *Dictionnaire de biographie française*.
36 Buisseret and Barbiche, 'Lettres de Sully', p. 108.

37 J. Michael Hayden, 'The social origins of the French episcopacy at the beginning of the seventeenth century', pp. 27–40.
38 Frederick Baumgartner, 'Crisis in the French episcopacy'.
39 *Lettres missives*, Vol. VI, p. 565.
40 See also the old book by Louis Prunel, *La Renaissance catholique en France au XVIIe siècle.*
41 The question of Henry's relations with Saint François is very hard to elucidate, but it would not appear that the king had anything to do with the genesis of *Introduction à la vie dévote* (*pace* Jung); Bremond (*Histoire*, Vol. I, p. 93, n. 1) concluded that no judgement was possible here.
42 Hennequin, *Henri IV*, p. 105, n. 78.
43 Mariéjol, *Henri IV et Louis XIII*, p. 92.
44 On this plot see Merki, *Verneuil.*
45 Printed in Palma-Cayet, Vol. II, pp. 475–6.
46 *Lettres missives*, Vol. VI, p. 237.
47 For more details, see David Buisseret, 'A stage in the development of the *intendants*: the reign of Henri IV', pp. 31–2.
48 Palma-Cayet, Vol. II, pp. 507–8.
49 See also Nouaillac, *Villeroy*, pp. 314–23.
50 *CSP Venice* 1603–7, art. 215.
51 See La Force, *Le Maréchal*, Vol. I, pp. 228–35.
52 Philippson, *Heinrich und Philipp*, Vol. I, p. 293.
53 See the letter of 12 August 1604 from Sully to La Force, preserved in the Pierpont Morgan Library, New York.
54 As Andrew C. Hess puts it in 'The Moriscos: an Ottoman Fifth Column in sixteenth-century Spain'.
55 Valois, *Inventaire*, no. 8171.
56 BN ms. fr. 22315, fos 29–40.
57 PRO SP 78/39, fo. 25: Mildmay to Cecil in 1597. See also Groulart, *Mémoires*, p. 570.
58 See BN ms. fr. 4559, fo. 52; Valois, *Inventaire*, no. 5881; and *Lettres missives*, Vol. VIII, p. 733.
59 Buisseret, *Sully*, pp. 153–4.
60 There is a rather inadequate list in Louis Hautecœur, *Histoire de l'architecture classique en France*, Vol. I, pt 3, pp. 345–7.
61 *Le Mercure françois* (1610), p. 485.
62 PRO SP 78/52, fo. 73. For the account of the buildings which follows I have relied not only on Hautecœur's masterly résumé in his *Histoire*, but also on Jean-Pierre Babelon's recent and very thorough 'Les travaux de Henri IV au Louvre et aux Tuileries'.
63 Poirson, *Henri IV*, Vol. III, p. 759.
64 L'Estoile, *Journal*, Vol. II, p. 105.
65 Dallington, *View of Fraunce*, p. D.
66 PRO SP 78/55, fo. 89.
67 *Lettres missives*, Vol. IV, p. 672.
68 René Lebègue (ed.), *Lettres de Peiresc à Malherbe*, 20 January 1608.
69 Batiffol, *Vie intime*, Vol. I, pp. 300–1.
70 Edict of 28 January 1563, quoted in Hautecœur, *Histoire.*
71 Printed in Mallevoüé, *Actes de Sully*, p. 18.
72 See, for example, Jean-Pierre Babelon, *Demeures parisiennes sous Henri IV et Louis XIII*, p. 16.
73 *Lettres missives*, Vol. VII, p. 219.
74 ibid., Vol. VII, p. 238.
75 L'Estoile, *Journal*, Vol. II, p. 561.
76 ibid., Vol. II, p. 259.
77 See the extract from Sauval quoted in Poirson, *Henri IV*, Vol. II, pp. 757–8.
78 For a reproduction of an engraving of the project, see Barbiche, *Sully*, p. 102.
79 L'Estoile, *Journal*, Vol. II, p. 61.
80 This was what L'Estoile meant when he wrote that Laffemas 'did nothing but scribble

and use up perfectly good paper' (*Journal*, Vol. II, p. 221). Laffemas' publications are set out in M. Champollion-Figeac (ed.), *Documents historiques inédits*, Vol. IV, pp. viii–ix.

81 ibid., Vol. IV, pp. 6–282.
82 See, for instance, ibid., Vol. IV, pp. 41–2.
83 On these enterprises see Prosper Boissonade, *Le Socialisme d'État*, and also Gustave Fagniez, *L'Economie sociale de la France au temps de Henri IV*.

Chapter 10

1 *Lettres missives*, Vol. VI, p. 466; and Sully, *Economies royales*, Vol. II, p. 46.
2 *Lettres missives*, Vol. VI, p. 480.
3 ibid., Vol. VI, p. 552.
4 *Mercure françois*, p. 12.
5 ibid., pp. 11–12.
6 Léonce Anquez, *Histoire des assemblées politiques des réformés de France*, pp. 207–12.
7 *Lettres missives*, Vol. VI, p. 353.
8 See Sully's letters in Buisseret and Barbiche, 'Lettres de Sully'.
9 *Journal de Héroard*, Vol. I, p. 160.
10 For the other objects brought back, see La Roncière, *Histoire*, Vol. IV, p. 321.
11 On these early efforts see Poirson, *Henri IV*, Vol. II, pp. 283–7.
12 On these developments see the biography of Chauvin in the *Dictionary of Canadian Biography*, Vol. I, pp. 209–10.
13 See also ibid., Vol. I, p. 290.
14 La Roncière, *Histoire*, Vol. IV, p. 320.
15 Fouqueray, *Histoire*, Vol. III, pp. 196–215.
16 Poirson, *Henri IV*, Vol. II, p. 289.
17 Fagniez, *Economie sociale*, p. 283.
18 *Lettres missives*, Vol. VIII, p. 899.
19 Valois, *Inventaire*, no. 8909.
20 Fagniez, *Economie sociale*, p. 284.
21 Valois, *Inventaire*, no. 9271.
22 PRO SP 78/53, fo. 5.
23 ibid., fo. 176.
24 Groulart, *Mémoires*, p. 579.
25 Ritter, *Lettres du cardinal de Florence*, p. 113.
26 ibid., p. 229.
27 Marquis de Chantérac (ed.), *Journal de ma vie: mémoires du maréchal de Bassompierre*, p. 270.
28 Many of these games are described in the *Journal de Héroard*. For the injunction to have Louis beaten often, see *Lettres missives*, Vol. VII, p. 385.
29 PRO SP 78/54, fo. 65.
30 L'Estoile, *Journal*, Vol. II, p. 186.
31 On these preparations see Buisseret, *Sully*, p. 159.
32 *Lettres missives*, Vol. VI, pp. 601–2.
33 *CSP Venice* 1603–7, art. 336.
34 These sums are listed in Léonce Anquez, *Henri IV et l'Allemagne*, p. 63; the largest creditor was the Duke of Würtemberg.
35 PRO SP 78/53, fo. 262: Carew to Salisbury, 2 April 1607.
36 On these projects see Fagniez, *Economie sociale*, pp. 188–201.
37 See the figures in Buisseret, *Sully*, p. 118.
38 Sully, *Economies royales*, Vol. I, p. 558.
39 For these motives, see Buisseret, *Sully*, pp. 117–18.
40 L'Estoile, *Journal*, Vol. II, p. 172.
41 For these letters, see David Buisseret, 'The Irish at Paris in 1605'.
42 PRO SP 78/53, fo. 5.
43 L'Estoile, *Journal*, Vol. II, p. 181.

44 ibid., Vol. II, p. 191.
45 As late as August 1609, though, the Irish were still a problem: see François-Tommy Perrens, *L'Eglise et l'État en France*, Vol. II, p. 169.
46 PRO SP 78/53, fo. 361.

Chapter 11

1 *CSP Venice* 1603–7, art. 126.
2 See, for instance, *Lettres missives*, Vol. VI, p. 266.
3 PRO SP 78/53, fo. 284.
4 L'Estoile, *Journal*, Vol. II, p. 255.
5 PRO SP 78/55, fo. 223.
6 *Cal. MSS Salisbury*, Vol. XVII, p. 563.
7 On this visit see L'Estoile, *Journal*, Vol. II, pp. 81–6, and Palma-Cayet, Vol. II, pp. 394–8.
8 A visit recorded in *Journal de Héroard*, Vol. I, p. 36.
9 On this embassy see E. Fréville, 'Ambassade de Don Pèdre de Tolède'.
10 PRO CSP 78/54, fo. 134.
11 BN ms. fr. 4559, fo. 91.
12 See François-Tommy Perrens, *Les Mariages espagnols*, pp. 93–207.
13 *Lettres missives*, Vol. VII, p. 580.
14 See particularly Françoise Bordon, *Le Portrait mythologique à la cour de France sous Henri IV et Louis XIII*.
15 Corrado Vivanti, 'Henri IV, the Gallic Hercules', p. 194.
16 Though he did not, of course, go as far as Richelieu would; see Alfred Soman, 'Press, pulpit and censorship in France before Richelieu'.
17 Jean-Pierre Babelon, 'La tenture des Dieux brodée pour Sully'.
18 PRO SP 78/56, fo. 30.
19 Jacques Thuillier, 'Peinture et politique: une théorie de la galerie royale sous Henri IV'.
20 Quoted in Babelon, 'Les travaux de Henri IV', p. 98.
21 Thomas Coryate, *Coryate's Crudities*, p. 25.
22 PRO SP 78/39, fo. 189.
23 See Louis Hautecœur, *Les Jardins des Dieux et des hommes*, pp. 134–6.
24 Albert Mousset, 'Les Francine', p. 37.
25 On this work see J.-P. Samoyault and C. Samoyault-Verlet, *Le Château de Fontaine-bleau sous Henri IV*.
26 For an account of the *belle cheminée*, and a list of its surviving parts, see Edouard-Jacques Ciprut, *Mathieu Jacquet*, pp. 55–60.
27 PRO SP 78/53, fo. 313.
28 See Françoise Bayard, 'Le secret du roi: étude des comptants ès mains du roi sous Henri IV'.
29 PRO SP 78/54, fo. 195.
30 See Barbiche, *Sully*, pp. 78–80.
31 Summarised in Buisseret, *Sully*, pp. 141–55.
32 On this work see Buisseret, 'Les *ingénieurs du roi*'.
33 On this offensive see Barbiche, 'L'influence française'.
34 See Buisseret, 'A stage in the development'.
35 BN Cabinet d'Hozier, 107.
36 *Lettres missives*, Vol. I, p. 91.
37 ibid., Vol. I, p. 376.
38 ibid., Vol. I, pp. 414, 481, 565, 587 and 603.
39 ibid., Vol. II, p. 220.
40 BN Cabinet d'Hozier, 107.
41 *Lettres missives*, Vol. II, p. 475.
42 ibid., Vol. III, p. 122.
43 BN Cabinet d'Hozier, 107.

44 *Lettres missives*, Vol. III, pp. 337 and 539.
45 ibid., Vol. III, pp. 580–1.
46 ibid., Vol. III, p. 663.
47 ibid., Vol. III, p. 780.
48 BN Cabinet des Titres, PO 2984.
49 *Archives de la Gironde*, Vol. XIV, p. 330.
50 BN Dupuy 100, fo. 21.
51 ibid., fo. 11.
52 Albert Chamberland, 'La tournée de Sully et de Rybault dans les généralités en 1596', p. 5.
53 BN Cabinet d'Hozier, 332.
54 BN ms. fr. 23195, fo. 407.
55 Sully, *Economies royales*, Vol. I, p. 295.
56 Palma-Cayet, Vol. II, p. 257.
57 *Lettres missives*, Vol. V, p. 428.
58 *Archives de la Gironde*, Vol. XIV, p. 371.
59 BN Dupuy 61, fo. 294.
60 BN ms. fr. 23197, fos 205–6.
61 *Archives de la Gironde*, Vol. XIV, pp. 418–21.
62 BN ms. fr. 23198, fo. 507.
63 AM Agen, CC 123; see also J. Russell Major, 'Henry IV and Guyenne: a study concerning origins of royal absolutism'.
64 BN ms. fr. 23198, fo. 507.
65 BN ms. fr. 23054, fo. 240.
66 Ritter, *Château de Pau*, p. 252.
67 Valois, *Inventaire*, no. 14595.
68 *Archives de la Gironde*, Vol. XIV, p. 454.
69 Valois, *Inventaire*, no. 5967.
70 ibid., no. 6305.
71 Sully, *Economies royales*, Vol. I, p. 376; and *Lettres missives*, Vol. V, p. 396.
72 ibid., Vol. VII, p. 836.
73 AN H 748/20, fo. 7.
74 Henri de Frondeville, 'Antoine Le Camus de Jambeville (1551–1619)', p. 4.
75 On his activity see Buisseret, 'A stage in the development', p. 32.
76 ibid., pp. 32–3.
77 ibid., pp. 34–5.
78 *Cal. MSS Salisbury*, Vol. V, p. 289.
79 According to Sully, *Economies royales*, Vol. I, p. 201.
80 Robert Harding, *The Anatomy of a Power Elite: The Provincial Governors of Early Modern France*, p. 14.
81 See *Lettres missives*, Vol. IV, p. 872, and Vol. V, p. 217.
82 Buisseret, *Sully*, p. 194.
83 Edmund Dickerman, 'Henry IV of France, the duel and the battle within'.
84 PRO SP 78/46, fo. 43.
85 Dickerman, 'Henry IV', p. 209.
86 Ernest Glasson, *Le Parlement de Paris*, Vol. I, p. 78.
87 Charles Alexandre Sapey, *Etudes biographiques*, p. 63; and Valois, *Inventaire*, no. 5739.
88 J.-B. Dubédat, *Histoire du parlement de Toulouse*, Vol. I, p. 638.
89 Amable Floquet, *Histoire du parlement de Normandie*, Vol. IV, p. 2.
90 N. de La Cuisine, *Le Parlement de Bourgogne*, Vol. II, pp. 87–128.
91 *Lettres missives*, Vol. III, pp. 180–1.
92 ibid., Vol. III, p. 182.
93 Floquet, *Normandie*, Vol. IV, pp. 252–5.
94 Glasson, *Le Parlement de Paris*, Vol. I, p. 240.
95 Henri Carré, *Le Parlement de Bretagne après la Ligue*, pp. 471–2.
96 Edouard Maugis, *Histoire du parlement de Paris*, Vol. III, p. 266.
97 BN ms. fr. 23042, fo. 135.

98 Henri Prentout, *Les Etats provinciaux de Normandie*, Vol. I, p. 338.
99 Robillard de Beaurepaire (ed.), *Cahiers des états de Normandie sous le règne de Henri IV*, Vol. II, p. 160.
100 AN H 748/20, fos 7–8.
101 AD Lozère, C 536, fo. 562.
102 AN 120 AP 31, fos 25–30.
103 J. Russell Major, 'Henry IV and Guyenne', and also *Representative Government in Early Modern France*.
104 BN ms. fr. 22315, fo. 92.
105 BN ms. fr. 22315, fos 109–10.
106 BN ms. fr. 22314, fo. 592.
107 BN ms. fr. 22315, fo. 99.
108 AD Bouches-du-Rhône, C 11.
109 AD Côte d'Or, C 3075, fo. 273.
110 AD Côte d'Or, C 3076, fo. 206.
111 Gabriel Hanotaux, *Sur les chemins de l'histoire*, p. 45.
112 Poirson, *Henri IV*, Vol. I, p. 424.
113 Albert Babeau, *La Ville sous l'ancien régime*, p. 71.
114 *Lettres missives*, Vol. III, p. 663.
115 ibid., Vol. IV, p. 550.
116 Salmon, *Society in Crisis*, p. 312.
117 A. Kleinclausz, *Histoire de Lyon*, Vol. II, pp. 22–3.
118 Pierre Deyon, *Amiens, capitale provinciale*, p. 431.
119 BN ms. fr. 23196, fo. 305.
120 René Pillorget, 'Luttes de factions et intérêts économiques à Marseille de 1598 à 1618', p. 715.
121 François Bourcier, 'Le régime municipal à Dijon sous Henri IV'.
122 Robiquet, *Histoire municipale de Paris*, Vol. III, p. 196.
123 Henri de Carsalade du Pont, *La Municipalité parisienne à l'époque d'Henri IV*, p. 39.
124 For the latter year, see his curious letter in the autograph file at the Houghton Library, Harvard University.
125 *Registres des délibérations du bureau de la ville de Paris*, Vol. XII, pp. 238–9, Vol. XIII, pp. 26–7.
126 Jules Garnier (ed.), *Correspondance de la mairie de Dijon*, Vol. III, p. 84.
127 AC Mâcon, CC 103, no. 31.
128 Robert Trullinger, 'The *grand voyer* as an instrument of royal centralization in Brittany under Henry IV'.
129 AN 120 AP 1, fo. 210.
130 *Lettres missives*, Vol. V, p. 486.
131 For these events, see Valois, *Inventaire*, nos 5950 and 5987.
132 According to Porchnev, *Soulèvements*, p. 48.
133 BN ms. fr. 23196, fo. 362.
134 Pillorget, 'Luttes de factions', p. 721.
135 BN ms. fr. 23196, fos 423, 443 and 448.

Chapter 12

1 *Exposition Henri IV* (Archives Nationales) AD Nord B 19291.
2 *Lettres missives*, Vol. VII, p. 444.
3 See Alexandre Schürr, 'La politique de Henri IV en Suède et en Pologne', and also, it is said, 'Henri IV, correspondance avec Jean Sobieski', *Figaro littéraire*, 28 October–11 November 1939.
4 Buisseret, *Sully*, p. 82.
5 Braudel, *Mediterranean*, p. 1220.
6 This whole conflict is well summarised in Robert Lindsay, 'Henry IV and the northeast passage to the Indies'.

7 Charles H. Carter, 'Belgian "autonomy" under the archdukes, 1598–1621'.
8 *Lettres missives*, Vol. VI, pp. 40–2.
9 ibid., Vol. VI, p. 47.
10 ibid., Vol. VI, p. 378.
11 PRO SP 78/52, fo. 379.
12 Louis Cardaillac, 'Le passage des Morisques en Languedoc'.
13 *CSP Venice* 1603–7, art. 688.
14 See, for instance, ibid., art. 710.
15 *Lettres missives*, Vol. VII, p. 212.
16 Horniker, 'Anglo-French rivalry'.
17 *Lettres missives*, Vol. V, p. 744.
18 See the old article by Félix Robiou, 'La politique de Henri IV en Italie'.
19 Barbiche, 'L'influence française'.
20 Rommel, *Correspondance de Henri IV*, pp. 394, etc.
21 *CSP Venice* 1603–7, art. 568.
22 John L. Motley, *The Life and Death of John of Barneveldt, Advocate of Holland*, Vol. I, pp. 78–88.
23 Anquez, *Henri IV et l'Allemagne*, p. 167.
24 Quoted in Nouaillac, *Villeroy*, p. 493.
25 ibid., p. 500.
26 See, for instance, Paul Henrard, *Henri IV et la princesse de Condé 1609–10*.
27 Anquez, *Henri IV et l'Allemagne*, p. 177.
28 *CSP Venice* 1603–7, art. 783.
29 Motley, *Barneveldt*, Vol. I, p. 182.
30 Lebègue, *Lettres de Peiresc*, pp. 48–52.
31 ibid., pp. 50–1.
32 Jules Loiseleur, *Ravaillac et ses complices*.
33 Anquez, *Henri IV et l'Allemagne*, pp. 193–8.
34 Described in detail in Marcel Reinhard, *La Légende de Henri IV*.
35 Hennequin, *Henri IV*.

Conclusion

1 See the graph in Buisseret, *Sully*, p. 78.
2 See, for instance, Duby, *Histoire de la France rurale*, Vol. II, p. 192.
3 Micheline Baulant and Jean Meuvret (eds), *Prix des céréales extraits de la Mercuriale de Paris, 1520–1620*, Vol. II, p. 152.
4 Micheline Baulant, *Lettres de négociants marseillais: les Frères Hermite (1570–1612)*, p. xi.
5 Philip Benedict, 'Catholics and Huguenots in sixteenth-century Rouen', p. 218; note also his section, pp. 209–10, summarising the literature arguing that the religious wars had little effect.
6 Alain Delumeau, 'Le commerce extérieur français au XVIIe siècle', pp. 84–5.
7 Jacquart, *Crise rurale*.
8 See also the article by Prosper Boissonade, 'Les voies de communication terrestres et fluviales en Poitou sous le règne de Henri IV'.
9 Pierre Chaunu, 'Au dix-septième siècle, rythmes et coupures', p. 1176.
10 For this argument, see Buisseret, *Sully*, pp. 171–5.
11 For a recent summary of the various positions, see Major, *Representative Government*, pp. 389–92.
12 Quoted in Antoine Adam, *Histoire de la littérature française au XVIIe siècle*, Vol. I, p. 25.
13 Ritter, *Lettres du cardinal de Florence*, pp. 102 and 141.
14 Antoine Adam, *Grandeur and Illusion*, pp. 167–8.
15 François de Dainville, *Le Dauphiné et ses confins*, p. 9.
16 Sully, *Oeconomies royales*, pp. 167–8.
17 Ritter, *Le Château de Pau*, p. 248.

18 Jean Plattard, *Une Figure de premier plan dans nos lettres de la renaissance: Agrippa d'Aubigné*, p. 94.
19 Ritter, *Charmante Gabrielle*, p. 35.
20 Janneau, *La Peinture française*, p. 10.
21 Sylvie Béguin, *L'Ecole de Fontainebleau*, p. 125.
22 On the work of Francqueville, see the biography by Pierre de Francqueville.
23 On his life and work, see E. J. Ciprut.
24 L'Estoile, *Journal*, Vol. I, p. 467.
25 Winwood, *Negotiations*, Vol. I, p. 293.
26 *Lettres missives*, Vol. V, pp. 272–3.
27 Barbiche, *Correspondance du nonce*, p. 353.
28 *Lettres missives*, Vol. VII, p. 606.
29 On Philip II my guide has been the recent biography by Geoffrey Parker.

Sources and Bibliography

(i) Henry's Letters

The prime source for Henry's reign is his correspondence, the *Recueil des lettres missives*, published in nine volumes, following extensive and officially backed investigations, between 1843 and 1876. Alas, this substantial publication has proved over the past hundred years to be 'notablement incomplet', as Bernard Barbiche puts it, and has had to be supplemented by many other published collections of his letters. These have eventually become very numerous, so that a mere listing of them covers twenty closely packed pages (Bernard Barbiche, (ed.), *Lettres de Henri IV* (Vatican City, 1968), in *Studi e testi* 250). Combining these sources, we may reasonably assume that we have recovered a substantial proportion of the letters. One point merits attention, and it is that not all the letters apparently written by the king are in fact in his hand. As Berger de Xivrey observed (*Lettres missives*, Vol. I, pp. xx–xxi), he had a *secrétaire de la main*, a certain Jacques L'Allier, sieur du Pin, whose task it was to imitate Henry's handwriting, and this secretary was so skilful that it is only occasionally that his work betrays itself. However, it seems reasonable to assume that, even if the king did not write all the letters which are apparently in his hand, they at any rate represent what he wished to say.

(ii) Diplomatic Correspondence

The letters of foreign diplomats stationed at Henry's court can also be a useful source of information. Many have been published, or calendared. Between 1601 and 1604, for instance, the papal nuncio wrote often to Rome, and his letters may be found in the *Correspondance du nonce en France*, edited by Bernard Barbiche (Paris/Rome, 1964). Earlier, the Cardinal of Florence visited France, and his letters were published by Raymond Ritter in *Lettres du cardinal de Florence* (Paris, 1955); no doubt further such publications will emerge from the papal archives. From 1594 onwards, the Grand Duke of Tuscany had a representative at the French court, and extracts from the correspondence of these agents were published by Abel Desjardins in *Négociations diplomatiques de la France avec la Toscane*, Vol. V (Paris, 1875). Even earlier, the Venetians had an ambassador in Paris; his letters and *relazioni*, as well as those of his successors, may be found in the *Relazioni degli stati europei . . .*, ed. Nicolò Barozzi and Guglielmo Berchet, 10 vols (Venice, 1856–78). Similar material, not all of it overlapping, is printed in the *CSP Venice*, Vols 9–11 (London, 1897–1904), edited by H. F. Brown. In Turin the archives contain much useful material, described in Jean-Jacques-Marc Armingaud's 'Documents relatifs à l'histoire de France recueillis dans les archives de Turin', *Revue des sociétés savantes*, 6e série, Vol. V (1877), pp. 126–60. But it has not been published, and I have not been able to see it.

The Swiss cantons had no permanent representative at the French court, but there was a series of visiting Genevan agents, whose reports are preserved at Geneva. They are enumerated by Jules Flammermont in his *Rapport ... sur les correspondances des agents diplomatiques étrangers en France* (Paris, 1896), pp. 297–8. I have not seen them, but they were extensively used in Rott's *Henri IV, les Suisses et la Haute-Italie*. In the same remarkable report by Flammermont are listed the few documents which were produced by various agents of the German princes (pp. 139–40); when he undertook his mission, these papers were in the 'archives secrètes d'état du royaume de Prusse', but I do not know if they are still in existence. A few are printed in Rommel, *Correspondance inédite de Henri IV avec Maurice-le-Savant* (Paris, 1840): in the Viennese archives, nothing appears to survive.

The English agents and ambassadors in France form a particularly useful source of information for Henry's reign. Their letters and reports are preserved mostly at the Public Record Office in the State Papers 78 series, from which many documents have been published in the *Negotiations* of Sir Ralph Winwood, in the *Historical View of the Negotiations*, edited by Thomas Birch, and in *The Edmondes Papers*, edited by Geoffrey Butler. Other diplomatic letters and reports may be found in the publications of the Historical Manuscripts Commission for the collections of Lord de L'Isle and Dudley and of the Marquis of Salisbury. The correspondence of the ambassadors whom Spain kept at Paris after 1599 is less interesting, because neither Tassis nor Cárdenas entered into any familiarity with the king. Copies of their correspondence are preserved at the Archives Nationales (KK 1585 to 1608, etc.); the original documents have been returned to Simancas, and have formed the basis of the remarkable studies by Cano de Gardoqui. The only part which appears to have been published is the letters from Cárdenas to be found in Volume V (Madrid, 1844) of the *Collección de documentos inéditos para la historia de España*.

Letters coming in to Paris from French agents overseas are, of course, normally of interest rather for diplomatic history than for the general history of the reign. Many of these letters are to be found at the Bibliothèque Nationale; I have used only those which have been printed. They include letters from: Christophe de Harlay, sieur de Beaumont; Philippe de Béthune, sieur de Charost; Jacques Bongars; Philippe Canaye, sieur de Fresnes; Paul Choart, sieur de Buzenval; Jacques Davy du Perron; Pierre Jeannin; and Jean de Thumery, sieur de Boissize (see Bibliography for details). Finally, the Archives Nationales have recently acquired a whole collection of 'documents relatifs aux règnes de Henri IV et de Louis XIII', many of which concern foreign affairs (AN 90 AP 32). But this collection became available too late for me to use it in this book.

(iii) Minutes of Various Bodies

Quite a few of the minutes of corporate bodies exist, and they are both more informative and more entertaining than might be supposed. The *registres* of the *parlements* survive as follows:

Brittany   BN nouvelles acquisitions françaises 733–5
Burgundy BM Dijon, fonds Saverot, ms. 1499
Guyenne   BM Bordeaux, ms. 371
Normandy BN ms. fr. 11,919 and 22,462.

The *délibérations* of the provincial estates have been fully catalogued in Russell Major's *Representative Government in Early Modern France*, pp. 673–713. The *plumitif** of the Paris *chambre des comptes* is at AN P 2665–70; the surviving *registres secrets* of the Paris *cour des aides* are in AN Z^1A 158–9. The remaining *registres* of the various *bureaux des finances* are enumerated in Buisseret, *Sully*, pp. 214–20. I have not found in the archives many interesting series of municipal minutes, but for Paris there are the splendid volumes of *Registres des délibérations du bureau de la ville de Paris*; volumes 12 (1909), 13 (1905) and 14 (1908) are of most interest for Henry's reign.

(iv)   Accounts

The acquisition by the Archives Nationales in 1955 of the 'Papiers de Sully' made available the Crown's chief fiscal documents for the period 1598–1610. I have relied heavily on these in Chapter 11, supplementing them chiefly with BN ms. fr. 4559, for the king's secret discretionary payments. There are also a good many miscellaneous accounts which survive from the various departments of the royal household. These are useful for identifying the chief officials, and for details of domestic life:

AN KK 147 'argenterie'* 1591
AN KK 148 'argenterie' 1595
BN ms. fr. 25761 'comptes de bouche' 1593–1627
BN ms. fr. 3994 'chappelle de musique' 1595
AN KK 151 'officiers domestiques' 1599–1608
Archives du Département des Affaires Etrangères France 764 'maison du Dauphin' 1602
AN O^1 2387 officers for the royal palaces 1605–8
AN KK 149 'argenterie' 1607
AN KK 155 'écurié* 1607
BN ms. fr. 7854 'officiers domestiques', c.1610
BN Clairambault 837 'officiers domestiques' 1589–1665
BN Clairambault 1216 changes among the 'officiers domestiques'
AN KK 152 'officiers domestiques' 1609
AN KK 153 'officiers domestiques' 1610

(v)   Memoirs and Contemporary History

I have tried, in the words of Philippson, not to 'look at Henry's reign through Sully's spectacles'. Still, his memoirs, the oddly named *Oeconomies royales*, remain a central source for the study of the reign, and the Société de l'Histoire de France is in the process of (rather slowly) publishing a new edition of them. The *Journal de ma vie* of Bassompierre is much more limited, but he, too, was close to the king, and gives us an intimate view of life at his court. Claude Groulart only came to court periodically, but he seems to have been particularly trusted by the king, so that his *Mémoires* and *Voyages par lui faits en cour* are unusually revealing. So are the *Historiettes* of Tallemant des Réaux, recently re-edited with very extensive notes by Antoine Adam. The *Journal* of Jean Héroard, doctor to the dauphin, is a remarkable source for the infancy of Louis XIII, and for his relations with his parents, but we ought to note that this is merely a publication of extracts; it would probably be profitable to read the manuscripts in full. Finally, there are the old standbys, Palma-Cayet and L'Estoile. In his *Chronologie novenaire* (1589–98) and his *Chronologie septenaire* (1598–1604), Palma-Cayet adopts the annalist form, giving a remarkable variety of accurate information, year by year; his is a sort of scaffolding inside which any history of the reign must be built. The information in L'Estoile's *Journal* is less far-ranging and less accurate; Hauser goes so far as to write that 'we can almost say that, to fix the date of a pamphlet's appearance, we should never believe L'Estoile' (*Les Sources de l'histoire de France*, p. 36). However, L'Estoile is an indispensable source of information for events in Paris, about which he was unusually well informed.

(vi)   Notarial Documents

Notarial documents form the basis of Mallevoüe's *Actes de Sully*, and of Ciprut's *Nouveaux documents*; there is no doubt much fresh information still to be found in the Minutier Central at the Archives Nationales, particularly on the history of the arts. But I have not been able to work there very much, apart from a brief foray to discover what had emerged from the *études** covered by Mallevoüe since his time.

(vii)   Bibliography

(A)   CONTEMPORARY PRINTED BOOKS

d'Angoulême, Charles de Valois, duc, *Mémoires*, ed. Michaud and Poujoulat, Vol. 11 (Paris, 1857).

d'Aubigné, Théodore-Agrippa, *Histoire universelle*, ed. A. de Ruble, 10 vols (Paris, 1886–97).

Bongars, Jacques, *Letters latines de M. de Bongars* (Paris, 1681).

Bourgeois, Louise, *Comment et en quel temps la reine accoucha de M. le Dauphin*, ed. Michaud and Poujoulat, Vol. 11 (Paris, 1857).

Chastillon, Claude de, *Topographie française* (Paris, 1648).

Coryate, Thomas, *Coryate's Crudities* (1611), ed. W. M. Schutte (London, 1978).

Dallington, Robert, *The View of Fraunce* (London, 1604).

Du Perron, Jacques Davy, Cardinal, *Les Ambassades et négotiations* ... (Paris, 1633).

Fontanon, Antoine, *Les Edicts et ordonnances des rois de France*, 3 vols (Paris, 1611).

Hobier, Ithier, *De la construction d'une gallaire* (Paris, 1622).

Hurault, Philippe, comte de Cheverny, *Mémoires*, ed. J. A. Buchon (Paris, 1836).

L'Estoile, Pierre de, *Journal*, ed. L. R. Lefèvre, 3 vols (Paris, 1948–60).

Le Mercure françois (Paris, 1611).

Palma-Cayet, Pierre-Victor, *Chronologie novenaire* and *Chronologie septenaire*, ed. J. A. Buchon (Paris, 1836).

Rivault, David, sieur de Fleurance, *Les Elemens de l'artillerie* (Paris, 1608).

Sully, Maximilien de Béthune, duc de, Oeconomies royales, ed. David Buisseret and Bernard Barbiche, Vol. I (Paris, 1970). See also, for the latter part of these memoirs, the earlier edition: *Les Economies royales*, ed. Michaud and Poujoulat, Vols I and II (Paris, 1837). There is also an eighteenth-century paraphrase of the memoirs, edited by the abbé de L'Ecluse: *Mémoires de Sully*, 3 vols (Paris, 1747).

Tallemant des Réaux, *Historiettes*, ed. Antoine Adam, 2 vols (Paris, 1960–1).

Thou, Jacques-Auguste de, *Histoire universelle*, 16 vols (London, 1734).

(B) EDITIONS OF MANUSCRIPTS AND COLLECTIONS OF DOCUMENTS

Albèri, Eugenio, *Relazioni degli ambasciatori veneti al senato*, 15 vols (Florence, 1839–63).

Archives curieuses de l'histoire de France, ed. M. L. Cimber and F. Danjou, 27 vols (Paris, 1837).

Barbiche, Bernard (ed.), *Correspondance du nonce en France Innocenzo del Bufalo, évêque de Camerino (1601–1604)* (Rome/Paris, 1964).

Barbiche, Bernard (ed.), *Lettres de Henri IV* ... (Vatican City, 1968).

Barozzi, Nicolò and Berchet, Guglielmo (eds), *Relazioni degli stati europei* ... , 10 vols (Venice, 1856–78).

Bassompierre, *see* Chantérac.

Baulant, Micheline and Meuvret, Jean (eds), *Prix des céréales extraits de la Mercuriale de Paris, 1520–1620* (Paris, 1960).

Beaurepaire, Robillard de (ed.), *Cahiers des Etats de Normandie sous le règne de Henri IV*, 2 vols (Rouen, 1880–2).

Berger de Xivrey, *see* Xivrey.

Birch, Thomas (ed.), *An Historical View of the Negotiations between the Courts of England, France and Brussels, 1592–1617* (London, 1740).

Buisseret, David and Barbiche, Bernard, 'Lettres inédites de Sully', *Annuaire-bulletin de la Société de l'Histoire de France* (1974–5), pp. 81–117.

Butler, G. G. (ed.), *The Edmondes Papers* (London, 1913).

Buzenval, *see* Vreede.

Calendar of Manuscripts of the Most Honourable the Marquis of Salisbury at Hatfield House, 24 vols (London, 1883–1976).

Calendar of State Papers, Foreign Series of the Reign of Elizabeth, 23 vols (London, 1863–1950).

Calendar of State Papers and Manuscripts . . . *in the Archives and Collections of Venice*, 38 vols (London, 1864–1947).

Carew, Sir George, *A Relation of the State of France*, *see* Birch.

Chamier, Daniel, *see* Read.

Champion, Pierre (ed.), *Sommaire mémorial de Jules Gassot* (Paris, 1934).

Champollion-Figeac, M. (ed.), *Documents historiques inédits* (*Documents inédits sur l'histoire de France*), 4 vols (Paris, 1848).

Chantérac, marquis de (ed.), *Journal de ma vie: mémoires du maréchal de Bassompierre*, 4 vols (Paris, 1870–7).

Choart, *see* Vreede.

Cimber, M. L. and Danjou, F., *see Archives curieuses* . . . .

Collard, Louis-Henri and Ciprut, Edouard-Jacques (eds), *Nouveaux documents sur le Louvre* (Paris, 1963).

Desjardins, Abel (ed.), *Négociations diplomatiques de la France avec la Toscane*, 6 vols (Paris, 1859–86).

Dufour, Alain (ed.), *René de Lucinge: lettres sur les débuts de la Ligue* (Paris/Geneva, 1964).

Galitzin, Augustin (ed.), *Lettres inédites de Henri IV* (Paris, 1860).

Garnier, Jules (ed.), *Correspondance de la mairie de Dijon*, 3 vols (Dijon, 1870).

Groen van Prinsterer, G. (ed.), *Archives du correspondance inédite de la maison d'Orange-Nassau*, Vol. II, *1600–1625* (Utrecht, 1858).

Groulart, Claude, *Mémoires ou voyages par lui faits en Cour*, ed. Michaud and Poujoulat, Vol. II (Paris, 1857).

Guyot de Saint-Michel (ed.), *Correspondance politique et militaire de Henry le Grand avec J. Roussat, maire de Langres* (Paris, 1816).

Henry IV, *see* Galitzin, Guyot de Saint-Michel, Kermaingant, Lajeunie, Rommel and Xivrey.

Héroard, *see* Soulié.

Isambert, François-A. (ed.), *Recueil général des anciennes lois françaises*, 29 vols (Paris, 1821–33).

Isnard, Albert (ed.), *Actes royaux*, Vol. I (Paris, 1910).

Kermaingant, P. P. Laffleur de (ed.), *L'Ambassade de France en Angleterre sous Henri IV*, 2 vols (Paris, 1886–95).

Kermaingant, P. P. Laffleur de (ed.), *Lettres de Henri IV au comte de La Rochepot* (Paris, 1889).

Lajeunie, J. E. M. (ed.), 'Correspondance entre Henri IV et Béthune . . . 1602–1604', *Mémoires et documents publiées par la société d'histoire et d'archéologie de Genève*, vol. XXXVIII (1952), pp. 189–474.

Lalanne, Ludovic (ed.), *Oeuvres de Malherbe*, 4 vols (Paris, 1862).

Lebègue, René (ed.), *Lettres de Peiresc à Malherbe* (Paris, 1976).

Léger, L. (ed.), 'Le siège de Rouen par Henri IV d'après des documents tchèques', *Revue historique*, vol. VII (1878), pp. 66–77.

Lettres missives, see Xivrey.

Malherbe, *see* Lalanne.

Mallet, J. R. (ed.), *Comptes rendus de l'administration des finances du royaume de France* (London, 1789).

Mallevouë, François de (ed.), *Les Actes de Sully* (Paris, 1911).

Marchand, Jean (ed.), *Le Livre de raison de Montaigne* (Paris, 1948).

Memorials of Affairs of State in the Reigns of Queen Elizabeth and King James I . . ., ed. Edmund Sawyer, 3 vols (London, 1725).

Montaigne, *see* Marchand.

Nouaillac, Jules (ed.), *Un Envoyé hollandais à la cour de Henri IV: lettres inédites de François Aerssen à Jacques Valcke (1599–1603)* (Paris, 1908).

Osborne, Thomas (ed.), *A Collection of Voyages and Travels*, 2 vols (London, 1745).

Pasquier, *see* Thickett.

Peiresc, *see* Lebègue.

Péricaud, Antoine (ed.), *Notes et documents pour servir à l'histoire de Lyon (1594–1610)* (Lyon, 1845).

Poirson, Auguste (ed.), *Mémoires de Sancy et de Villeroy, documents divers . . .* (Paris, 1868).

Read, Charles (ed.), *Daniel Chamier: journal de son voyage à la cour de Henri IV en 1607* (Paris, 1858).

Registres des délibérations du bureau de la ville de Paris, ed. François Bonnardot, Alexandre Tuetey, Paul Guérin *et al.*, 15 vols (Paris, 1883–).

Report on the Manuscripts of Lord de L'Isle and Dudley Preserved at Penshurst Place, 6 vols (London, 1926–66).

Ritter, Raymond (ed.), *Lettres du cardinal de Florence sur Henri IV et sur la France, 1596–1598* (Paris, 1955).

Robillard de Beaurepaire, *see* Beaurepaire.

Romier, Lucien (ed.), *Lettres et chevauchées du bureau des finances de Caen sous Henri IV* (Paris, 1910).

Rommel, M. de (ed.), *Correspondance inédite de Henri IV avec Maurice-le-Savant* (Paris, 1840).

Soulié, Eud. and Barthélemy, Ed. de (eds), *Journal de Jean Héroard*, 2 vols (Paris, 1868).

Sturler, Jacques de, 'Documents diplomatiques et administratifs relatifs aux différends commerciaux et maritimes survenus entre les Pays-Bas et la France, 1599–1607', *Bulletin de la Commission Royale d'Histoire de la Belgique* (1939).

Thickett, D. (ed.), *Etienne Pasquier: lettres historiques pour les années 1556–1594* (Geneva, 1966).

Valois, Noël (ed.), *Inventaire des arrêts du conseil d'état (règne de Henri IV)*, 2 vols (Paris, 1886–93).

Vernyes, Jehan de, *Mémoires* (Paris, 1874).

Vreede, George W. (ed.), *Lettres et négociations de Paul Choart, seigneur de Buzanval et de François d'Aerssen* (Leiden, 1848).

Xivrey, Berger de and Guadet, Jules (eds), *Lettres missives de Henri IV*, 9 vols (Paris, 1843–76).

(C) SECONDARY WORKS

Adam, Antoine, *Grandeur and Illusion* (London, 1974).

Anquez, Léonce, *Henri IV et l'Allemagne* (Paris, 1887).

Anquez, Léonce, *Histoire des assemblées politiques des Réformés de France* (Paris, 1859).

Babeau, Albert, *La Ville sous l'ancien régime* (Paris, 1880).

Babelon, Jean-Pierre, *Demeures parisiennes sous Henri IV et Louis XIII* (Paris, 1965).

Babelon, Jean-Pierre, 'La tenture des Dieux brodée pour Sully', *Gazette des beaux-arts* (1967), pp. 365–72.

Babelon, Jean-Pierre, 'Les travaux de Henri IV au Louvre et aux Tuileries', *Paris et Ile-de-France: mémoires*, vol. XXIX (1978), pp. 55–130.

Baguenault de Puchesse, G., 'Henri IV avant son avènement', *Revue Henri IV*, vol. II (1907–8), pp. 1–8 and 161–83, and vol. III (1909), pp. 1–27.

Barbiche, Bernard, 'L'influence française à la cour pontificale sous le règne de Henri IV', *Mélanges d'archéologie et d'histoire*, vol. LXXVII (Ecole Française de Rome, 1965), pp. 277–99.

Barbiche, Bernard, *Sully* (Paris, 1978).

Barbiche, Bernard, 'Une tentative de réforme monétaire à la fin du règne d'Henri IV', *XVIIe siècle*, vol. LXI (1963), pp. 3–17.

Barbiche, Bernard and Buisseret, David, 'Sully et la surintendance des finances', *Bibliothèque de l'Ecole des Chartes*, vol. CXXI (1965), pp. 538–43.

Bareau, Michel, 'Manuel Pimentel et le "jeu du roi" en 1608', *Bibliothèque d'Humanisme et Renaissance*, vol. XXXVII (1975), pp. 201–12.

Baschet, Armand, *Les Comédiens italiens à la cour de France* (Paris, 1882).

Batiffol, Louis, *Le Louvre sous Henri IV et Louis XIII* (Paris, 1930).

Batiffol, Louis, 'Le trésor de la Bastille de 1605 à 1611', *Revue Henri IV*, vol. III (1909–12), pp. 200–9.

Batiffol, Louis, *La Vie intime d'une reine de France au XVIIe siècle*, 2 vols (Paris, 1931).

Baulant, Micheline, *Lettres de négociants marseillais: les Frères Hermite (1570–1612)* (Paris, 1953).

Baumgartner, Frederick, 'Crisis in the French episcopacy,' *Archiv für Reformations geschichte*, vol. LXX (1979), pp. 278–301.

Bayard, Françoise, 'Le secret du roi: étude des comptants ès mains du roi sous Henri IV', *Bulletin du Centre d'Histoire Economique et Sociale de la Région Lyonnaise* (1974), pp. 1–27.

Béguin, Sylvie, *L'Ecole de Fontainebleau* (Paris, 1960).

Benedict, Philip, 'Catholics and Huguenots in sixteenth-century Rouen', *French Historical Studies*, vol. IX (1975), pp. 209–34.

Benedict, Philip, *Rouen during the Wars of Religion* (Cambridge, 1981).

Bercé, Yves-Marie, *Croquants et Nu-Pieds* (Paris, 1974).

Berty, Alphonse, *Topographie historique du vieux Paris*, 8 vols (Paris, 1885–97).

Beyer, Victor (ed.), *Au Musée du Louvre: la sculpture française du XVIIe siècle* (Paris, 1977).

Bishop, Maurice, *Champlain: The Life of Fortitude* (London, 1949).

Boissonade, Prosper, *Le Socialisme d'état* (Paris, 1927).

Boissonade, Prosper, 'Les voies de communication terrestres et fluviales en Poitou sous le règne de Henri IV', *Revue Henri IV*, vol. II (1907–8), pp. 193–228 and 295–311, and vol. III (1909), pp. 65–102.

Bonnault d'Houet, G., *La Première Ambulance sous Henri IV* (Paris, 1919).

Bonney, Richard, *The King's Debts: Finance and Politics in France, 1598–1661* (Oxford, 1981).

Bordon, Françoise, *Le Portrait mythologique à la cour de France sous Henri IV et Louis XIII* (Paris, 1974).

Bourcier, François, 'Le régime municipal à Dijon sous Henri IV' *Revue d'histoire moderne*, vol. VIII (1930), pp. 85–117.

Boussinesq, G., 'Sommes promises aux chefs de la Ligue', *Revue Henri IV*, vol. I (1905–6), p. 164.

Braudel, Fernand, *The Mediterranean and the Mediterranean World in the Age of Philip II* (New York, 1972).

Bremond, Henri, *Histoire littéraire du sentiment religieux en France*, 11 vols (Paris, 1920–38).

Buisseret, David, 'Les Fortifications de la Picardie vers 1600', *Mémoires de photo-interprétation*, vol. 3 (1966), pp. 4–39.

Buisseret, David, 'The French Mediterranean fleet under Henri IV', *The Mariner's Mirror*, vol. 1 (1964), pp. 297–306.

Buisseret, David, 'Les *ingénieurs du roi* de Henri IV', *Bulletin de géographie*, vol. LXXVII (1964), pp. 13–84.

Buisseret, David, 'The Irish at Paris in 1605', *Irish Historical Studies*, vol. XIV (1964), pp. 58–9.

Buisseret, David, 'The legend of Sully', *The Historical Journal*, vol. V (1962), pp. 181–8.

Buisseret, David, 'A stage in the development of the *intendants*; the reign of Henri IV', *The Historical Journal*, vol. IX (1966), pp. 27–38.

Buisseret, David, *Sully* (London, 1968).

Canal, Séverin, *Les Origines de l'intendance de Bretagne* (Paris, 1911).

Cardaillac, Louis, 'Le passage des Morisques en Languedoc', *Annales du Midi* (1971), pp. 259–69.

Carné, Louis Joseph de, *Les Etats de Bretagne*, 2 vols (Paris, 1875).

Carré, Henri, *Le Parlement de Bretagne après la Ligue* (Paris, 1888).

Carré, Henri, *Recherches sur l'administration municipale de Rennes au temps de Henri IV* (Paris, 1888).

Carsalade du Pont, Henri de, *La Municipalité parisienne à l'époque d'Henri IV* (Paris, 1971).

Carter, Charles H., 'Belgian "autonomy" under the archdukes, 1598–1621', *Journal of Modern History*, vol. XXXVI (1964), pp. 245–59.

Chamberland, Albert, 'Le conseil des finances en 1596 et 1597 et les *Economies Royales*', *Revue Henri IV*, vol. I (1905–6), pp. 21–32, 152–63, 250–60 and 275–84.

Chamberland, Albert, 'Jean Chandon et le conflit entre la cour des aides et le conseil du roi', *Revue Henri IV*, vol. II (1907–8), pp. 113–25.

Chamberland, Albert, 'La tournée de Sully et de Rybault dans les généralités en 1596', *Revue Henri IV*, vol. III (1909), supplement.

Charlier-Meniolle, R., *L'Assemblée des notables tenue à Rouen en 1596* (Paris, 1911).

Chaunu, Pierre, 'Au dix-septième siècle, rythmes et coupures', *Annales*, vol. XIX (1964), pp. 1171–81.

211

Church, William Farr, *Constitutional Thought in Sixteenth-Century France* (Cambridge, Mass., 1941).

Ciprut, Edouard-Jacques, *Mathieu Jacquet* (Paris, 1967).

Couzard, Rémy, *Une Ambassade à Rome sous Henri IV* (Paris, 1901).

Couzard, Rémy, 'Le rétablissement des Jésuites', *Revue Henri IV*, vol. II (1907–8), pp. 94–110.

Crue, François de, *Les Derniers Desseins de Henri IV* (Paris, 1902).

Crue, François de, *Henri IV et les députés de Genève* (Geneva/Paris, 1901).

Dainville, le R.P. François de, *Le Dauphiné et ses confins* (Paris/Geneva, 1968).

Dainville, le R.P. François de, *Les Jésuites et l'éducation de la société française*, 2 vols (Paris, 1940).

Dainville, le R.P. François de, *La Naissance de l'humanisme moderne* (Paris, 1940).

Debus, Allen (ed.), *Science, Medicine and Society in the Renaissance*, 2 vols (New York, 1972).

Delumeau, Alain, 'Le commerce extérieur française au XVIIe siècle', *XVIIe*, vols 70–1 (1966), pp. 81–105.

Des Cilleuls, A., *Henri IV et la chambre de justice de 1606* (Nancy, n.d.).

Deyon, Pierre, *Amiens, capitale provinciale* (Paris/The Hague, 1967).

Dickerman, Edmund, *Bellièvre and Villeroy* (Providence, RI, 1971).

Dickerman, Edmund, 'The conversion of Henry IV', *The Catholic Historical Review*, vol. LXIII (1977), pp. 1–13.

Dickerman, Edmund, 'Henry IV of France, the duel and the battle within', *Societas*, vol. III (1973), pp. 207–20.

Dillen, J. G. van, 'Isaac Le Maire et le commerce des actions de la compagnie des Indes Orientales', *Revue d'histoire moderne*, vol. X (1935).

Dimier, Louis, *French Painting in the Sixteenth Century* (London, 1904).

Doucet, Roger, 'Les finances de la France en 1614', *Revue d'histoire économique et sociale*, vol. XVIII (1930), pp. 133–63.

Doucet, Roger, *Les Institutions de la France au XVIe siècle*, 2 vols (Paris, 1948).

Drouot, Henri, *Mayenne et la Bourgogne*, 2 vols (Paris, 1937).

Du Colombier, Pierre, *Le Style Henri IV–Louis XIII* (Paris, 1941).

Dubédat, J.-B., *Histoire du parlement de Toulouse*, 2 vols (Paris, 1885).

Duby, Georges (ed.), *Histoire de la France rurale*, 4 vols (Paris, 1975–6).

Dufayard, Charles, *Le Connétable de Lesdiguières* (Paris, 1892).

Dufour, Alain, 'La paix de Lyon', *Journal des savants* (1965), pp. 428–55.

Elliott, John H., *Europe Divided* (New York/Evanston, Ill., 1968).

Fagniez, Gustave, *L'Economie sociale de la France au temps de Henri IV* (Paris, 1897).

Febvre, Lucien, 'Aspects méconnus d'un renouveau religieux en France entre 1590 et 1620', *Annales*, vol. XIII (1958), pp. 639–50.

Flammermont, Jules, *Rapport . . . sur les correspondances des agents diplomatiques étrangers en France* (Paris, 1896).

Floquet, Amable, *Histoire du parlement de Normandie*, 7 vols (Rouen, 1840–2).

Fouqueray, Henri, *Histoire de la compagnie de Jésus*, 5 vols (1910–25).

Francqueville, Robert de, *Pierre de Francqueville* (Paris, 1968).

Fréville, E., 'Ambassade de Don Pèdre de Tolède', *Bibliothèque de l'Ecole de Chartes*, vol. I (1839), pp. 344–66.

Frondeville, Henri de, 'Antoine Le Camus de Jambeville (1551–1619)', *Normannia* (1936), pp. 1–15.

Gardoqui, Jose Luis Cano de, *La cuestion de Saluzzo en las communicaciones del Imperio español, 1588–1601* (Valladolid, 1962).

Gardoqui, Jose Luis Cano de, *Tensiones hispanofranceses en el siglo XVII* (Valladolid, 1970).

Giesey, Ralph, 'The juristic basis of dynastic right to the French throne', *Transactions of the American Philosophical Society*, n.s., vol. LI (1961), pp. 1–47.

Glasson, Ernest, *Le Parlement de Paris*, 2 vols (Paris, 1901).

Grégoire, Louis, *La Ligue en Bretagne* (Paris/Nantes, 1856).

Guiffrey, Jules, 'Logements d'artistes au Louvre', *Nouvelles archives de l'art français*, vol. II (1873), pp. 1–163.

Hanotaux, Gabriel, *Etudes historiques sur le XVIe et le XVIIe siècle en France* (Paris, 1886).

Hanotaux, Gabriel, *Sur les chemins de l'histoire*, 2 vols (Paris, 1924).

Hanotaux, Gabriel, *Tableau de la France en 1614* (Paris, n.d.).

Harding, Robert, *The Anatomy of a Power Elite: The Provincial Governors of Early Modern France* (New Haven, Conn./London, 1978).

Hauser, Henri, *Les Sources de l'histoire de France*, vol. IV, *Henri IV* (Paris, 1916).

Hautecœur, Louis, *Histoire de l'architecture classique en France*, 3 vols (Paris, 1963–7).

Hautecœur, Louis, *Les Jardins des Dieux et des hommes* (Paris, 1959).

Hayden, J. Michael, *France and the Estates General of 1614* (Cambridge, 1974).

Hayden, J. Michael, 'The social origins of the French episcopacy at the beginning of the seventeenth century', *French Historical Studies*, vol. X (1977), pp. 27–40.

Hélyot, Pierre, *Histoire des ordres monastiques*, 8 vols (Paris, 1721).

Hennequin, Jacques, *Henri IV dans ses oraisons funèbres* (Paris, 1977).

Henrard, Paul, *Henri IV et la princesse de Condé 1609–10* (Brussels, 1870).

Hess, Andrew C., 'The Moriscos: an Ottoman Fifth Column in sixteenth-century Spain', *American Historical Review*, vol. LXXIV (1968), pp. 1–25.

Horniker, A. L., 'Anglo-French rivalry in the Levant from 1583 to 1612', *Journal of Modern History*, vol. XVIII (1946), pp. 289–305.

Jacquart, Jean, *La Crise rurale en Ile-de-France 1550–1670* (Paris, 1974).

Jensen, De Lamar, *Diplomacy and Dogmatism . . .* (Cambridge, Mass., 1964).

Jung, Emile, *Henri IV écrivain* (Paris, 1855).

Karcher, Aline, 'L'assemblée des notables de Saint-Germain-en-Laye (1583)', *Bibliothèque de l'Ecole de Chartes*, vol. CXIV (1956), pp. 115–62.

Kierstead, Raymond, *Pomponne de Bellièvre* (Evanston, Ill., 1968).

Kleinclausz, A., *Histoire de Lyon*, vol. II (Lyon, 1948).

La Bouillerie, Sébastien de, *Un Ami de Henri IV: Guillaume Fouquet, marquis de La Varenne* (Mamers, 1906).

La Cuisine, N. de, *Le Parlement de Bourgogne*, 3 vols (Dijon/Paris, 1864).

La Force, le duc de, *Le Maréchal de La Force (1558–1652)*, 2 vols (Paris, 1928).

La Roncière, Charles de, *Histoire de la marine française*, Vol. IV (Paris, 1923).

La Roncière, Charles de, 'Les routes de l'Inde', *Revue des questions historiques*, vol. LXXVI (1904), pp. 157–209.

La Tourasse, B. de, 'Le château neuf de Saint-Germain-en-Laye', *Gazette des beaux-arts* (1924), pp. 68–95.

213

Lacombe, Charles de, *Henri IV et sa politique* (Paris, 1877).

Lacroix, Paul, 'La porte et place de France sous le règne de Henri IV', *Gazette des beaux-arts* (1870), pp. 561–6.

Lalot, J. A., *Essai historique sur la conférence tenue à Fontainebleau entre Duplessis-Mornay et Duperron le 4 mai 1600* (Paris, 1889).

Le Blant, Robert, 'Marchés de pains, de viandes et de poissons pour Henri IV, 21 décembre 1607', *Bulletin philologique et historique* (1969), pp. 685–96.

Lee, Maurice, *James I and Henri IV* (Urbana, Ill., 1970).

Lhuillier, Théophile, *L'Ancien château royal de Montceaux-en-Brie* (Paris, 1885).

Lindsay, Robert, 'Henry IV and the northeast passage to the Indies', *Terrae incognitae*, vol. II (1970), pp. 1–14.

Lloyd, Howell A., *The Rouen Campaign 1590–1592* (Oxford, 1973).

Loiseleur, Jules, *Ravaillac et ses complices* (Paris, 1873).

McGowan, Margaret, *L'Art du ballet de cour en France, 1581–1643* (Paris, 1963).

Mahoney, Irene, *Royal Cousin: The Life of Henry IV of France* (New York, 1970).

Major, J. Russell, 'Bellièvre, Sully and the assembly of notables of 1596', *Transactions of the American Philosophical Society*, new series, vol. 64 (1974), pp. 1–34.

Major, J. Russell, 'Henry IV and Guyenne: a study concerning origins of royal absolutism', *French Historical Studies*, vol. IV (1966), pp. 363–83.

Major, J. Russell, *Representative Government in Early Modern France* (New Haven, Conn./London, 1980).

Mariéjol, Jean H., *Henri IV et Louis XIII* (Paris, 1905). (Vol. VI of *Histoire de France*, ed. Ernest Lavisse.)

Marvick, Elizabeth, 'The character of Louis XIII: the role of his physician', *Journal of Interdisciplinary History*, vol. IV, no. 3 (1974), pp. 347–74.

Masson, Paul, *Les Galères de France 1481–1781* (Paris, 1938).

Mattingly, Garrett, *The Defeat of the Spanish Armada* (London, 1962).

Maugis, Edouard, *Histoire du parlement de Paris*, 3 vols (Paris, 1913–16).

Merki, Charles, *La Marquise de Verneuil et la mort d'Henri IV* (Paris, 1912).

Miron de l'Espinay, Albert, *François Miron et l'administration municipale de Paris sous Henri IV de 1604 à 1606* (Paris, 1885).

Motley, John I., *The Life and Death of John of Barneveldt, Advocate of Holland*, 2 vols (London, 1874).

Mousnier, Roland, *L'Assassinat d'Henri IV* (Paris, 1964).

Mousnier, Roland, 'Etat et commissaire . . . ' in *Forschungen zu Staat und Verfassung: Festgabe für Fritz Hartung* (Berlin, 1958).

Mousnier, Roland, *Les Institutions de la France sous la monarchie absolue*, 2 vols (Paris, 1974–80).

Mousnier, Roland, 'L'opposition politique bourgeoise à la fin du XVIe siècle et au début du XVIIe siècle', *Revue historique*, vol. CCXIII (1955), pp. 1–20.

Mousnier, Roland, *La Vénalité des offices sous Henri IV et Louis XIII*, 2nd edn (Paris, 1971).

Mousset, Albert, 'Les Francine', *Mémoires de la Société d'Histoire de Paris et de l'Ile-de-France*, vol. LI (1930), pp. 1–53.

Nouaillac, Jules, 'Henri IV et les Croquants du Limousin', *Bulletin historique et philologique* (1912), pp. 321–50.

Nouaillac, Jules, 'Le règne de Henri IV', *Revue d'histoire moderne et contemporaine* (1907–8), pp. 104–23 and 348–63.

Nouaillac, Jules, *Villeroy, secrétaire d'etat* ... (Paris, 1909).

Oman, Sir Charles, *A History of the Art of War in the Sixteenth Century* (London, 1937).

Pagès, Georges, 'Essai sur l'évolution des institutions administratives en France', *Revue d'histoire moderne*, vol. VII (1932), pp. 8–57 and 113–37.

Palm, Franklin C., *Politics and Religion in Sixteenth-Century France* (Boston, Mass./New York, 1927).

Pannier, Jacques, *L'Eglise réformée de Paris sous Henri IV* (Paris, 1911).

Parker, Geoffrey, *The Army of Flanders and the Spanish Road* (Cambridge, 1972).

Perrens, François-Tommy, *L'Eglise et l'état en France* (Paris, 1872).

Perrens, François-Tommy, *Les Mariages espagnols* (Paris, 1869).

Philippson, Martin, *Heinrich IV und Philipp III*, 3 vols (Berlin, 1870–6).

Pigeonneau, Henri, *Histoire du commerce de la France*, 2 vols (Paris, 1885–97).

Pillorget, René, 'Luttes de factions et intérêts économiques à Marseille de 1598 à 1618', *Annales* (1972), pp. 705–30.

Pingaud, Léon, 'Henri IV et Louis XIV', *Revue des questions historiques*, vol. XLVI (1889), pp. 169–204.

Pinsseau, Henri, *Le Canal Henri IV ou canal de Briare* (Paris/Orléans, 1943).

Plattard, Jean, *Une Figure de premier plan dans nos lettres de la renaissance: Agrippa d'Aubigné* (Paris, 1931).

Poète, Marcel, *Paris durant la grande époque classique* (Paris, 1911).

Poirson, Auguste, *Histoire du règne de Henri IV*, 4 vols (Paris, 1865).

Porchnev, Boris, *Les Soulèvements populaires en France de 1623 à 1648* (Paris, 1963).

Prentout, Henri, *Les Etats provinciaux de Normandie*, 3 vols (Caen, 1925–7).

Prunel, Louis, *La Renaissance catholique en France au XVIIe siècle* (Paris, 1921).

Reinhard, Marcel, *La Légende de Henri IV* (Paris, n.d.).

Ritter, Raymond, *Charmante Gabrielle* (Paris, 1947).

Ritter, Raymond, *Le Château de Pau* (Paris, 1919).

Ritter, Raymond, *Henry IV* (Paris, 1944).

Ritter, Raymond, 'Le roi de Navarre et sa prétendue fuite de la Cour en 1576', *Bulletin philologique et historique* (1969), pp. 667–84.

Robiou, Félix, 'La politique de Henri IV en Italie', *Revue des questions historiques*, vol. XXI (1877), pp. 5–34.

Robiquet, Paul, *Histoire municipale de Paris*, 3 vols (Paris, 1880–1904).

Roelker, Nancy, *Queen of Navarre: Jeanne d'Albret, 1528–1572* (Cambridge, Mass., 1968).

Rott, Edouard, *Henri IV, les Suisses et la Haute-Italie* (Paris, 1882).

Salmon, J. H. M., *Society in Crisis: France in the Sixteenth Century* (New York, 1975).

Samaran, Charles, 'Henri IV et Charlotte de Montmorency', *Annuaire-bulletin de la Société de l'Histoire de France* (1951), pp. 53–109.

Samoyault, J.-P. and Samoyault-Verlet, C., *Le Château de Fontainebleau sous Henri IV (pamphlet available at the château).*

Sapey, Charles Alexandre, *Etudes biographiques* (Paris, 1858).

Saulnier, Eugène, *Le Rôle politique du cardinal de Bourbon* (Paris, 1912).

Schürr, Alexandre, 'La politique de Henri IV en Suède et en Pologne', *Revue Henri IV*, vol. II (1907–8), pp. 25–33.

Shennan, J. H., *The Parlement of Paris* (London, 1968).

Simpson, Lesley B., *The Struggle for Provence, 1593–6* (Berkeley, Cal., 1929).

Soman, Alfred, 'Press, pulpit and censorship in France before Richelieu', *Proceedings of the American Philosophical Society*, vol. CXX (1976), pp. 439–63.

Sutherland, N. M., 'The Edict of Nantes and the "Protestant state"', *Annali della fondazione italiana per la storia amministrativa*, vol. II (1965), pp. 199–236.

Sutherland, N. M., *The French Secretaries of State in the Age of Catherine de Medici* (London, 1962).

Sutherland, N. M., *The Massacre of Saint Bartholomew and the European Conflict 1559–1572* (London, 1973).

Thuillier, Jacques, 'Peinture et politique: une théorie de la galerie royale sous Henri IV', in *Etudes d'art français offertes à Charles Sterling* (Paris, 1975).

Trullinger, Robert, 'The *grand voyer* as an instrument of royal centralization in Brittany under Henry IV', *Proceedings of the Western Society for French History*, vol. III (1975), pp. 26–34.

Usher, Abbot P., *The History of the Grain Trade in France, 1400–1710* (Cambridge, Mass., 1913).

Vaissière, Pierre de, *Henri IV* (Paris, 1925).

Viollet, Paul, *Le Roi et ses ministres* (Paris, 1912).

Vivanti, Corrado, 'Henri IV, the Gallic Hercules', *Journal of the Warburg and Courtauld Institutes*, vol. XXX (1967), 176–97.

Wilkinson, Maurice, *The Last Phase of the League in Provence, 1588–1593* (London, 1909).

Wolfe, Martin, *The Fiscal System of Renaissance France* (New Haven, Conn., 1972).

Zeller, Berthold, *La Minorité de Louis XIII: Marie de Médici et Sully* (Paris, 1892).

Zeller, Gaston, 'L'administration monarchique avant les intendants', *Revue historique*, vol. CXCVII (1947), pp. 180–215.

Zeller, Gaston, 'L'industrie en France avant Colbert', *Revue d'histoire économique et sociale*, vol. XXVIII (1950), pp. 3–20.

Zeller, Gaston, *Les Institutions de la France au XVIe siècle* (Paris, 1948).

Chronological Table

1547		Death of François I and accession of Henri II
1553	December	Birth of the future Henry IV
1557	February	Henry with his parents at the French court
1557–60		Peaceful years in Béarn
1560	August	Henry with Jeanne back to the French court
1562	March	Jeanne banished to Béarn; Henry left at court
		The 'massacre of Vassy'
	June	Henry obliged to adopt Catholicism
	November	Death of Henry's father, Antoine de Navarre
1564	March–	
1566	May	The Grand Tour through France
1567	January	Henry and Jeanne leave the French court for Béarn
1567–71		Henry's 'apprenticeship' in Béarn
1572	April	Marriage between Henry and Marguerite de Valois agreed
	June	Death of Jeanne d'Albret
	July	Henry enters Paris
	August	The marriage, and the Massacre of Saint Bartholomew
	September	Henry again obliged to adopt Catholicism
1572–5		Henry at the royal court
1574	May	Death of Charles IX and accession of Henri III
1576	February	Henry leaves court for Béarn
	June	Henry abjures Catholicism
		Formation of Catholic League in Picardy
1576–80		Henry acts independently as king of Navarre
1580	May	Capture of Cahors by forces under Henry's command
1581	May	Assembly of Montauban endorses Henry's policies
1584	June	Death of duc d'Alençon; Henry now heir to French throne
	December	Treaty of Joinville between the Guises and the king of Spain
1585	March	Declaration of Castres; Montmorency, Condé and Henry accuse the Guises of planning to usurp the throne of France
	July	Treaty of Nemours between the Guises and Henri III
1587	October	Battle of Coutras
1588	May	Day of Barricades in Paris: Henri III expelled
	December	Murder of the Guises by Henri III
1589	April	Truce between Henri III and Henry of Navarre
	July	Murder of Henri III; Henry of Navarre becomes king of France
	September	Battle of Arques

1589	September–	
	November	First attack on Paris
1590	March	Battle of Ivry
	May–September	Second attack on Paris
	November	First meeting between Henry and Gabrielle d'Estrées
1591	February–April	Siege and capture of Chartres
	November–	
1592	April	Unsuccessful siege of Rouen
1593	January	Assembly of estates-general
	May	Henry announces his intention to reconvert to Catholicism
	July	Ceremony of the abjuration at Saint-Denis
1594	February	Ceremony of the coronation at Chartres
	March	Entry into Paris and expulsion of the Spaniards
	July	Revolt of the *Croquants* in Limousin
	December	Châtel incident and edict for the expulsion of Jesuits
1595	January	Declaration of war upon Spain
	June	Battle of Fontaine-Française; Spaniards capture Doullens
	September	Henry enters Lyon; Spaniards capture Cambrai
	October–	
1596	May	Siege and capture of La Fère
	April	Spaniards capture Calais
	November–	
1597	January	Assembly of Notables in Rouen
	March	Spaniards capture Amiens
	March–	
	September	Siege and recovery of Amiens
1598	February–	
	May	Henry's voyage into Brittany
	February	Treaty with Mercœur
	April	Edict of Nantes
	May	Treaty of Vervins
	September	Death of Philip II of Spain
	October	Henry's severe attack of fever
1599	April	Death of Gabrielle d'Estrées
	October	Provisional promise of marriage given to Henriette d'Entragues
	December	Henry's marriage with Marguerite annulled
	December–	
1600	March	Visit to France by the Duke of Savoy
	April	Signature of marriage contract between Henry and Maria de Medici
	May	The 'Fontainebleau Conference'
	August–	
	November	War against the Duke of Savoy
	November	Marie lands at Marseille

	December	Henry meets Marie in Lyon
1601	January	Treaty of Lyon ends war with Duke of Savoy
	May	Resistance to the *pancarte* in Poitiers
	July	La Rochepot incident in Valladolid
	August–	
	September	Henry visits the north-eastern provinces
	September	Birth of the dauphin Louis
1602	March	La Fin reveals Biron's conspiracy
	April	Henry suffers his first attack of gout
	July	Biron decapitated in the Bastille
	September	Visit to France by Maurice of Hesse; reception of delegation from the Swiss cantons
	December	Bouillon retreats to Languedoc
1603	February–March	Henry visits the eastern frontier
	April	Death of Elizabeth of England
	May	Henry suffers from severe fever at Fontainebleau
	September	Edict of Rouen, permitting return of Jesuits
1604	February	General interdict on trade with Spain
	April	L'Hoste drowned in the Marne
	October	Interdict cancelled
	November	Trial of Auvergne and Entragues
1605	July	Protestant assembly in Châtellerault
	September–	
	October	Henry visits Limousin and south-west
	November	Gunpowder Plot in England
1606	March	Successful expedition to Sedan
	May	Expulsion of the Irish from Paris
	September	Baptism of the dauphin at Fontainebleau
1607	July	Foundation-stone laid at Hôpital Saint-Louis
	October	Henry goes to view the *canal de Briare*
	December	Donauwörth occupied by Maximilian of Bavaria
1608	March	Formation of Evangelical Union in Germany
	July–	
1609	February	Visit to France by Don Pedro of Toledo
	March	Death of Duke of Jülich-Cleves-Berg
	April	Truce between Spain and the United Provinces
	July	Archduke Leopold occupies Jülich
	November	Charlotte de Montmorency takes off for the Netherlands
	December–	
1610	February	Assembly of German princes in Hall
	April	Treaty of Brusol with Duke of Savoy
	May	Assassination of Henry IV

Glossary

Acquits de comptant: Orders sent to the royal treasury by the king, ordering payment of certain sums without receipts and without the normal checking by the *chambre des comptes* (see below).

Alcalde: Spanish municipal magistrate.

Amiral des mers du Levant: Each of the maritime provinces united to France – Provence, Brittany and Guyenne – had its *amiral*, with jurisdiction over coasts and fleets. The *amiral de Provence* was also *amiral des mers du Levant*, responsible for the Mediterranean fleet.

Argenterie: Service of the royal household responsible for providing clothes and furniture.

Arquebusiers: Infantry armed with the harquebus, the portable fire-arm in use in French armies between about 1525 and 1630.

Arrêt: A legislative ruling, which might or might not emanate from the Crown.

Aumônier: The *grand aumônier* was responsible for religious affairs at court; he gave communion to the king, baptised the royal children, married the princes and saw to charitable works.

Béarnais: Inhabitant of Béarn.

Brevet: An act by which the king concedes a certain privilege.

Bureau des finances: The fifteen *bureaux des finances* were the provincial centres through which taxes were gathered and monies disbursed (see also *trésoriers de France, élections* and *élus*). In general, they existed only where there was no *provincial estates* (see below).

Cahiers (de doléances): The members of the estates-general and of the provincial estates used to draw up a *cahier* (literally a note-book) which contained their wishes and grievances, for presentation to the king or his representative.

Capitaines des gardes: Four officers who, serving quarterly, guarded the king's person.

Chambellan (grand): Officer responsible for the royal *gentilshommes de la chambre* and *valets de chambre*.

Chambre de justice: A special court, assembled to inquire into some particular abuse, normally in the fiscal system.

Chambre des comptes: The Paris *chambre des comptes* was, historically speaking, simply a branch of the royal council, sitting with particular jurisdiction over fiscal affairs. It was responsible for approving the accounts of the *bureaux des finances*; eventually there were a dozen provincial *chambres*, each performing the same function for its region.

Chambre mi-partie: A court staffed by both Protestant and Catholic judges, re-affirmed by the Edict of Nantes to offer some possibility of justice to the minority religion. Such courts existed in Paris, Castres, Nérac and Grenoble; they disappeared in the course of the seventeenth century.

Chevalier de l'accolade: A person dubbed knight by the king, normally for valour on the battlefield.

Commissaires: A *commissaire* was a person granted a *commission* to carry out some judicial or fiscal function; *commissaires* were thus distinct from those who carried out similar functions by virtue of their *office*.

Conducteur des desseins: Many of the *ingénieurs du roi* (see below) were accompanied by *conducteurs des desseins*, whose task was to draw maps and plans of places where work was envisaged.

Connétable: The *connétable*, whose office went back to the origins of the monarchy, was the operational head of the armed forces in the absence of the king; he also had (lucrative) rights in the courts for which he was responsible.

Conseil d'Etat: Council concerned with the administrative direction of the realm's affairs, particularly but not exclusively in fiscal matters.

Conseil des finances: In principle, this council was responsible for the day-to-day management of fiscal affairs, but during the reign of Henry IV it was largely superseded by the activity of Sully as *surintendant des finances* (see Chapter 7, section iii).

Conseiller: One of the chief legal officers in a *parlement*.

Conseiller d'Etat: Person who might be called to the deliberations of the *conseil d'Etat*.

Consuls: Name given to municipal officers, or aldermen, in the south.

Contrôleur-général des postes: Officer who, during the reign of Henry IV, came to supervise the systems for distributing both royal and private mail.

Council of Trent: Ecumenical council which, sitting between 1545 and 1563, promulgated decrees which reformed certain abuses in the ancient church, and defined its doctrines more closely.

Cour des aides: A court with jurisdiction over problems arising from the levy of taxes; there was a *cour des aides* in Paris, and up to a dozen of them in the provinces.

Cour des monnoies: A court based in Paris with responsibility for monetary affairs: the detection of counterfeiters, assaying of currency and so forth.

Déclaration: A legislative act modifying or interpreting some previous *edict* or *ordonnance* (see below).

Echevin: A municipal officer; the northern equivalent of the southern *consul*.

Ecu: Silver coin, worth three *livres* (see below); after September 1602, accounting was by *livres* rather than by *écus*.

Ecurie: The royal stables, divided into the *petite écurie* and the *grande écurie*.

Edict (édit): A new royal law concerning some circumscribed matter (cf. *ordonnance*).

Elections: Fiscal sub-divisions, roughly ten to each *bureau des finances*.

Elus: The officers serving the *élections*.

Estates-general: Representative assemblies of the three estates, periodically convoked by the king. In fact, none was called by Henry IV.

Etudes: Literally a legal office, hence the *étude* under which legal documents are now classified in the archives.

Fleurs de lis: The lily symbol found on the arms of the French kings.

Gallican: The Gallican party in the French church stood for the defence of the 'liberties' of that church, over against the pretensions of Rome (see *ultramontane*).

Gouverneur (governor): Provincial representative of the king, at the head of one of twelve *gouvernements*. I have sometimes translated this as 'governor'; note, however, that his function was not to 'govern' in the modern sense.

Grand Design: A great plan for establishing political equilibrium and perpetual peace throughout Christendom, attributed to Henry IV by Sully in the least factual version of his memoirs.

Grand écuyer: Officer in charge of the royal stables; a post of great importance under a king who enjoyed hunting, like Henry IV.

Grand maître: Officer in charge of the royal household.

Grand maître de l'artillerie: Grand master of the artillery, an office fully explained in Chapter 7, section iii.

Grand prévôt: Officer responsible for the maintenance of order at court.

Grand voyer: In effect, the minister of communications; see Chapter 7, section iii.

Grands chemins: Also called *chemins royaux*; they were the roads along which there was a regular service of royal messengers.

Hôtel de ville: Town hall.

Ingénieur du roi: Royal engineer, one of a dozen or so such officers, each normally assigned to a province; see Chapter 11, section v.

Intendant: Provincial representative of royal power, with wide attributions and a permanent post. Such officers do not appear in a systematic way before the time of Richelieu, in the 1630s.

Intendant de justice: Person equipped with a special commission to enforce justice in a specified area.

Intendant des finances: Here, it means a certain officer working in Paris under the *surintendant des finances*; the term may also designate a person equipped with a special commission to reform the royal finances in a certain region.

Intendant des meubles de la Couronne: Officer responsible for the royal furnishings, a post of some importance in the days of itinerant courts.

Intendant des turcies et levées: Officer responsible for the dikes alongside certain rivers.

Keeper of the seals (garde des sceaux): The keeper of the seals had to seal edicts and royal letters when the chancellor was absent or indisposed.

King's Evil: Scrofula, a disease brought on by dietary insufficiency.

Knights of Malta: Members of an ancient religious order, committed to the defence of Christendom against the Turk.

Lance: Long metal-tipped wooden spear.

Landsknechts: German infantry, armed with the pike, originally organised towards the end of the fifteenth century.

Langue d'oc: Dialect of the south of France, where *oui* is pronounced 'oc'.

Langue d'oïl: Dialect of the north of France, and eventually of the whole country.

Largesse: Royal bounty.

Lèse-majesté: Act infringing the royal sovereignty.

Lieutenant-général: Deputy to the king; effective ruler in the time of a minor or incapable monarch.

Lieutenant-governor: Deputy to the governor; in fact, the term *lieutenant-général* was widely used for this post, but I have avoided it so as not to cause confusion with the 'lieutenant-général [du roi]'.

222

Glossary

Ligues des Suisses: Association of cantons whose soldiers had served the kings of France, and who were still owed money by them.

Lit de justice: The *lit de justice* was a special session of the *parlement* in which the king made known his sovereign will.

Livre: Financial unit, worth one-third of an *écu* (see above).

Maître de la garderobe: Keeper of the royal wardrobe.

Maître des comptes: Officer of the *chambre des comptes* (see above).

Maréchal: The highest military rank.

Maréchal des logis: Low-ranking cavalry officer, responsible for the stables.

Maréchal-général des camps et armées: Officer responsible for assigning each unit its place in the camp on campaign.

Marine du Levant: The Mediterranean fleet.

Millier: Archaic measure of weight, one thousand *livres*, or pounds (something like half a ton?).

Moriscoes: Descendants of the Moors in Spain.

Noblesse d'épée: Literally, 'nobility of the sword'; that part of the nobility owing its status to military prowess and rank.

Noblesse de robe: The 'nobility of the robe', comprising those whose claim to nobility rested on office in the *parlements* and elsewhere.

Octrois: Taxes levied by royal authority in the towns, mostly on foodstuffs.

Officiers des traites: Officers of the customs service, both internal and external.

Orangist: Supporter of the House of Orange, under whose leadership the Dutch were in the process of winning their independence from Spain.

Ordonnance: Body of royal law concerning some general matter (cf. *édit*).

Pancarte: The *sol pour livre*, a 5-per-cent sales tax whose rates were set out on a billboard, or *pancarte*.

Parlement: The sovereign court responsible for registering royal edicts; in addition to the one in Paris, there were seven provincial *parlements*.

Picorreurs: Lightly armed infantry, or skirmishers.

Pionnier: Soldier specialising in heavy labour for the army, digging trenches, hauling cannon and so forth. Anglicised to 'pioneer'.

Places de sûreté: Towns held by the Protestants under the guarantee of royal edicts and whose garrisons were paid by the Crown.

Plumitif: Minutes of a meeting.

Police: The maintenance of public order in a very wide sense, including the enforcement of law, the suppression of criminals and so forth.

Premier maître d'hôtel: Officer in charge of the royal table, the *bouche du roi*.

Premier pannetier: Officer responsible for the royal bread, under the *premier maître d'hôtel*.

Premier président: The chief officer of a *parlement*.

Premier tranchant: Officer in charge of serving the royal table with meat.

Prévôt des marchands: In Paris and Lyon, title borne by the mayor.

Prévôt des maréchaux: Military magistrate appointed to control vagabonds, deserters and so forth.

Procès-verbal: Document setting out what has been discussed on some occasion.

Provincial estates: Representative assemblies, normally meeting annually, in the ancient great provinces: Auvergne, Brittany, Burgundy, Dauphiné, Lan-

223

guedoc, Normandy and Provence. These were the *pays d'états*, or regions with estates, often and not quite accurately contrasted with the *pays d'élections*, or regions having *élections* (for which see above).

Quartier: Quarter in a town.

Robin: Pejorative term for a member of the *noblesse de robe* (see above).

Secrétaire d'Etat: Secretary of state, whose functions are described in Chapter 7, section iii.

Serviteur: A favourite term of Henry's for those who were in his service.

Setier: Archaic measure of volume (of grain), roughly half a litre.

Sorbonne: In the sixteenth century, this term applied to the faculty of theology of the University of Paris.

Surintendant en la justice et police: See *intendant de justice*; the terms were interchangeable.

Taille: The chief direct tax, levied on the *taillables* of the third estate.

Topographe du roi: Post whose duties involved making plans and drawings of buildings and sites.

Trésorier (général) de France: One of the ten fiscal officers staffing each *bureau des finances* (see above).

Trésorier de l'Épargne: Officer in charge of receiving and distributing funds from the central treasury.

Trésorier des gabelles: Treasurer of funds from the salt tax.

Trésorier des parties casuelles: Treasurer of funds deriving chiefly from the sale of offices.

Ultramontane: Literally, 'beyond the montains'; meaning in accordance with the aims and interests of Rome and the Papacy.

Ventre-Saint-Gris: Henry's favourite expletive; it has never been satisfactorily explained.

Villes de sûreté: See *places de sûreté*.

Voiturier par eau/terre: A carter, or person undertaking transport.

Walloons: French-speaking inhabitants of the southern part of the Spanish Netherlands.

Index

Abbadie, Jean Pierre d', bishop of Lescar 4
Abbeville (Somme) 58, 67, 108
Abjuration of Henry 44–5, 70, 147, 162
Acarie, Madame Barbe Avrillot 123
Aerssen, Francis, Dutch ambassador 169–73
Agen (Lot-et-Garonne) 10, 157
Ailleboust, Jehan d', doctor 95
Aisne, river 142, 143
Aix (Bouches-du-Rhône) 29, 86, 162, 175
Albert, cardinal-archduke 67, 75, 100, 103, 108, 110, 113, 169, 173
Albret, province 13
Albret, Henri d', king of Navarre 2–3, 182
Albret, Henri d', sieur de Miossens 14
Albret, Jeanne d' 2–7, 26
Aldobrandini, Pietro, cardinal 85, 87
Alençon (Orne) 9, 33
Alençon, see Anjou
Alibour, see Ailleboust
Amiens (Somme) 58, 64–6, 69, 70, 74, 92, 99, 118, 135, 165, 169, 182
Amours, Pierre d' 164
Amsterdam (Netherlands) 100
Andelot, see Châtillon-Coligny
Andoins, Corisande d' 25–6
Androuet du Cerceau, Jacques, architect 180
Angennes, Nicolas de, sieur de Rambouillet 41, 58
Angers (Maine-et-Loire) 69, 90
Anglure, Anne d', sieur de Givry 28, 29
Anhalt, Christian of 38, 100
Anjou, province 9
Anjou, François d', duc d'Alençon 8, 9, 12, 14
Annapolis (Nova Scotia) 139
Annecy (Haute-Savoie) 124
Annulment of Henry's marriage 77, 79
Antibes (Alpes-Maritimes) 111
Appian Alexander 7
Aragón, province of Spain 127
Arambure, see Harambure
Arc, river 83
Architecture 128–33, 140–1, 180–2
Ardres (Pas-de-Calais) 61, 62, 74, 108
Argouges, Florent d', treasurer 95
Arles (Bouches-de-Rhône) 79, 167
Armand, père 122
Army 61, 66–7, 81–5, 97, 99
Arques-la-Bataille (Seine-Maritime) 29, 31, 33, 37, 58, 90
Arquien, see La Grange
Arras (Pas-de-Calais) 65, 67
Arros, N. d' 8

Artillery 31, 33, 61, 67–8, 80, 81, 83–5, 97–8, 104, 116, 141, 147, 151, 164, 183
Assembly of Notables 48, 62, 64, 106, 128, 134
Aubigné, Théodore-Agrippa d' 33, 46, 180
Auchy, see Conflans
Aude, river 142
Augustinians, monastic order 123
Aumale (Seine-Maritime) 39
Aumale, see Guise
Aumont, Jean d' 28, 29, 31, 33
Auneau (Eure-et-Loir) 25
Auvergne, province 37, 112, 144
Auvergne, see Valois
Auxerre (Yonne) 124
Avignon (Vaucluse) 87, 107

Babelon, Jean-Pierre, historian viii
Babou de La Bourdaisière, Isabelle 38
Babou de la Bourdaisière, Marie 79
Badoer, Angelo, Venetian ambassador 121
Balagny, see Monluc
Balagny, Madame de 56
Ballets 105, 147
Baltic Sea 168
Barbiche, Bernard, historian 203
Barcelona (Spain) 116
Barnabites, religious order 123
Barrault, see Jaubert
Barricades 25, 63, 72
Bassompiere, François de 105, 140, 168
Batz, N. de 14
Baugy, N. de 100
Baumgartner, Frederick, historian 124
Bavaria, Maximilian, duke of 142
Bayonne (Basses-Pyrénées) 5, 91, 148, 165
Béarn, province 3–5, 7, 8, 13, 25, 54, 91, 123
Beaulieu (Corrèze) 9
Beaulieu, see Ruzé
Beaumanoir, Jean de, sieur de Laverdin 24, 113, 159, 174
Beaumont-lez-Tours (Indre-et-Loir), nunnery 126
Beaumont, see Harlay
Beaune (Côte-d'Or) 18
Beaune, Renaud de 43–5, 94
Beaurepaire, see Langlois
Beautor (Aisne) 61
Beauvais (Oise) 108
Beauvais-Nangis, see Brichanteau
Beauvoir, see Goulard
Beauxoncles, Charles-Timoléon de, sieur de Sigognes 90

225

Becher, English agent 146
Béguin, Sylvie, art historian 181
Belgrade (Yugoslavia) 171
Belin, *see* Sérillac
Bellegarde, *see* Saint-Lary
Bellièvre, Pomponne de, chancellor 43, 74, 97, 99, 103, 144
Benoist, René, churchman 44, 50, 94
Bergerac (Dordogne) 11, 22
Berry, province 37
Bertaut, Jean, poet 126
Bérulle, Pierre cardinal de 123
Besse, Pierre de, preacher 123
Béthune, river 29
Béthune, Philippe de, sieur de Charost 100, 122, 204
Béthune, *see* Sully
Betstein, *see* Bassompierre
Biard, Pierre, sculptor 96, 138
Bigorre, region 13
Biron, *see* Gontaut
Blavet (Morbihan) 69, 74, 128
Blaye (Gironde) 91
Blois (Loir-et-Cher) 10, 25, 26, 27, 112, 120, 148
Bohemia 38, 168
Boisdauphin, *see* Laval
Boisrozay, *see* Goustemesnil
Boissize, see Thumery
Bongars, Jacques, diplomat 95, 100, 173, 204
Bonne, François de, duc de Lesdiguières 12, 14, 18, 20, 37, 41, 46, 67, 83, 84, 85, 92, 103, 125, 160, 174
Bordeaux (Gironde) 6, 11, 56, 91, 128, 148
parlement 73, 157, 162
Bouillon, *see* La Tour d'Auvergne
Bourbon, Antoine de 2–4, 8, 10, 182
Bourbon, Catherine de 10, 67
Bourbon, Charles de, comte de Soissons 21, 22, 50, 94, 109, 112, 113
Bourbon, François de, prince de Conty 7, 8, 14, 21, 109
Bourbon, Henri de, duc de Montpensier 28, 33, 90, 109, 112, 160
Bourbon-Bausset, Suzanne de 3, 4
Bourcier, François, historian 165
Bourdeille, N. de 55
Bourdin, Pierre, artillery lieutenant 164
Bourg (Ain) 83, 84, 113
Bourgeois, Louise, midwife 109
Bourgeois, Marin, gunsmith 96
Bourges (Cher), 90, 106, 107
Boussinesq, Georges, historian 48
Brancas, André de, sieur de Villars 39, 90
Brancas, Georges de, sieur de Villars 90
Brandenburg, Elector of 79, 172

Braudel, Fernand, historian 55
Bray-sur-Seine (Seine-et-Marne) 35
Bremond, Henri, historian 123
Breslay, René de, bishop of Troyes 124
Bresse, province 80, 85, 92
Brest (Finistère) 90, 145
Brèves, *see* Savary
Briare (Loiret) canal 142
Brichanteau, Nicolas de, sieur de Beauvais-Nangis 103
Bridges, 96, 98, 151, 154, 160, 164, 166, 179, 183
Brissac, *see* Cossé
Brittany, province 37, 41, 49, 60, 68, 69, 74, 90, 134, 160, 163, 164, 166, 178
estates 127–8
parlement 162–3
Brive (Corrèze) 22
Brossier, Marthe, supposed witch 95
Brouage (Charente-Maritime) 91
Brûlart, Denis, *premier président* 92, 162
Brûlart, Nicolas, sieur de Sillery 74, 97
Brusol, treaty of 174
Brussels (Belgium) 67, 80, 103, 110, 169, 173, 174
Budget 151–5
Bueil, Jacqueline de, comtesse de Moret 56
Bufalo, Innocenzo del, nuncio 203
Bugey, region 85
Bunel, Jacob, painter 181
Burgundy, province 15, 57, 58, 92, 110, 113, 123, 153, 154, 159, 160, 163, 164, 166
Buzenval, *see* Choart

Caboche, N. 8
Caen (Calvados) 29, 162
Cahors (Lot) 11
Calais (Pas-de-Calais) 61, 62, 74, 92, 108, 109, 135, 169
Caltagirone, Bonaventura da, patriarch of Constantinople 80
Calvin, Jean 2
Camberfore, Julien de, sieur de Selves 158
Cambrai (Nord) 16, 47, 48, 59, 60, 74, 181
Camus, Geoffrey de, sieur de Pontcarré 43
Canada 123, 138, 144, 169, 183
Canals 98, 142–4, 154, 183
Canaye, Philippe de, sieur de Fresnes 100, 204
Capuchins, religious order 123–4
Carcassonne (Aude) 29, 159
Cárdenas, Don Iñigo de, Spanish ambassador 174, 180, 204
Carew, Sir George, English ambassador 56, 99, 139, 140, 145, 148, 150, 151, 161, 170

Carlat (Cantal) 128
Carmelites, religious order 123
Carsalade du Pont, Henri de, historian 165
Cartography 76, 88, 99, 153, 180, 183–4
Casaubon, Isaac, scholar 154
Castille, Spanish province 127
Castres (Tarn) 17, 114
Cateau-Cambrésis, treaty of 74
Catherine de Medici 5, 7, 8, 11, 21, 26, 79, 129, 130, 149
Caumont, Jacques Nompar de, sieur de La Force 14, 91, 99, 112, 113, 127, 136, 160, 174, 175
Cavalli, Marin, Venetian ambassador 119
Cecil, Sir Robert, English secretary of state 56, 63, 64, 74, 78, 79, 112, 121
Chalais (Charente) 22
Chalon-sur-Saône (Saône-et-Loire) 81
Châlons-sur-Marne (Marne) 18, 29, 53, 57, 92
Chambéry (Savoie) 80, 83
Chambord (Loir-et-Cher) 119
Chamier, Daniel, Protestant divine 103
Champagne, province 15, 28, 29, 92, 153, 159, 174
Champlain, Samuel de, explorer 138
Charbonnières (Doubs) 83–4
Charles V, emperor 1, 2
Charles V, king of France 130
Charles IX, king of France 8, 17
Charles X 42
Charles IX, king of Sweden 168
Charles-Emmanuel I, duke of Savoy 37, 41, 74, 80, 83, 92, 110, 112, 113, 114, 115, 159, 171, 174
Charost, see Béthune
Charpentier, Claude, eye specialist 95
Chartres (Eure-et-Loir) 37, 38, 50, 81
Chaste, Aymar de 90, 138
Chastillon, Claude de, engineer 61, 76
Châtel, Jean, would-be assassin 54, 56, 57, 121
Château-Thierry (Aisne) 39
Châteauvieux, Joachim de, guard-commander 28, 99
Châtellerault (Vienne) 26, 65, 137
Châtillon, François de 14
Châtillon-Coligny, N. de, marquis d'Andelot 14
Chaunay (Vienne) 7
Chaunu, Pierre, historian 179
Chauvin, Pierre de, sieur de Tonnetuit 138–9
Chavigny, see Le Roy
Chelles (Seine-et-Marne) 36, 123
Cheverny, see Hurault
Chizé-sur-Boutonne (Deux-Sèvres) 22

Choart, Paul de, sieur de Buzenval 14, 100, 169, 204
Choiseul, Charles de, sieur de Praslin guard-commander 92, 99, 113, 175
Chourses, Jean de, sieur de Malicorne 91
Christine, daughter of Henry IV 141
Clain, river 142
Claude, belle garce 78, 109
Clément, Jacques, assassin 27
Clement VIII, pope 41, 54, 80, 171
Clermont (Puy-de-Dôme) 29, 125
Clervant, N. de 22
Clin, see Quelin
Coarraze (Basses-Pyrénées) 3, 4
Coeffeteau, Nicolas, preacher 123
Coeuvres (Aisne) 37, 64
Cognac (Charente) 7, 21
Coligny, Gaspard de 7–8
Comedians 105, 154
Comminges, Roger de, sieur de Sobole 118
Communications, see roads and bridges
Compiègne (Oise) 29
Condé, Henri prince de 7, 8, 10, 11, 14, 17, 18, 22, 24, 25, 26
Condé, Henri II prince de 160, 173–4
Condé, Louis prince de 6
Conflans (Savoie) 83
Conflans (Marne) 147
Conflans, Eustache de, sieur d'Auchy 92
Constantinople 60, 80, 81, 101, 110, 123, 127, 171, 183
Contarini, Francesco, Venetian diplomat 121
Conty, see Bourbon
Corbeil (Seine-et-Oise) 35
Corbie (Somme) 51
Coryate, Thomas, author 149
Cossé, Charles de, comte de Brissac 48, 51, 53, 148, 160
Coton, père Pierre 94, 122, 123
Coucy (Aisne) 60
Coutras (Gironde) 21, 22, 33, 37, 58, 156
Craon (Mayenne) 41, 127
Crillon, Louis de Berton de 69
Croquants, the 54–5, 99
Crozon (Finistère) 128

Dainville, le R. P. François de, historian 180
Dale, Valentine, English agent 9
Dallington, Robert, author 88, 129
Damville, see Montmorency
Danfrie, Philippe, engraver 96
Danube, river 70
Dauphiné, province 12, 18, 20, 37, 41, 92, 103, 133, 134, 153, 157, 159, 160, 163
Defunctis, N., *grand prévôt* 125
Delorme, N. 159

Denmark 18, 79, 173, 174
Descartes, René 122
Des Essarts, Mlle 140, 154
Des Fosses, Mlle 78, 154
Devereux, Robert, Earl of Essex 38, 58, 103, 108, 159
Dieppe (Seine-Maritime) 29, 31, 38, 58, 90, 110, 138, 169
Dijon (Côte-d'Or) 18, 29, 57, 142, 147, 164, 165, 166
    parlement 73, 92, 112, 162
Dinet, Gaspard, bishop of Mâcon 124
Diplomacy 99–101, 110–111, 168–171
Donauwörth, Imperial town 142, 171
Donnadieu, François de, bishop of Auxerre 124
Dordogne, river 156, 170
Douarnenez (Finistère) 128
Douet, Claude, painter 96
Douet, Claude, galley-officer 116
Doullens (Somme) 58, 74, 90, 92
Dronne, river 22
Drouot, Henri, historian 60
Dubois, Ambroise, painter 181
Dubreuil, Toussaint, painter 181
Duels 161
Du Gua, Pierre de, sieur de Monts, explorer 138–9, 144
Du Laurens, André, doctor 95
Du Pérac, Etienne, architect 130, 149
Du Perron, Jacques Davy, theologian 44, 54, 82, 83, 94, 95, 122, 204, 207
Duplessis, Philippe, sieur de Mornay 12, 14, 19, 33, 46, 68, 81–3, 90, 95, 120, 125, 156, 157
Dutch, *see* United Provinces
Du Vair, Guillaume, *premier président* 53, 86, 91, 103, 111, 116, 162, 165, 167, 175

East India Company 169
Eauze (Gers) 11
Economic structures 1, 135, 144, 178–9
Edmondes, Sir Thomas, English agent 64, 78
Edouard, *see* Fernandez
Egmont, Philip, count of 33
Elbeuf, *see* Lorraine
Elector Palatine 100, 142
Elisabeth, daughter of Henry IV 141
Elizabeth, Queen of England 21, 38, 45, 49, 61, 99, 108, 120
Elliott, J. H., historian 41
Empire, Holy Roman 100, 118, 119, 142
Engineers 68, 99, 153, 160, 183
England, English 18, 21, 31, 38, 40, 61, 66, 67, 74, 100, 134, 155, 169, 170, 173–4

English agents 7, 12, 19, 20, 37, 58, 69, 78, 94, 146
Enríquez, Pedro de Acevedo, count of Fuentes 58–60, 110, 112, 113, 114, 175
Entragues, Henriette d', marquise de Verneuil 78, 86, 90, 108, 109, 114, 122, 125, 126, 140, 166, 176, 182
Epernay (Marne) 39
Epernon, *see* Nogaret
Epinac, Pierre d', Archbishop of Lyon 43
Errard, Jean, engineer 66
Escures, *see* Fougeu
Esparbez, Jean Paul d', sieur de Lussan 91
Espinay, Timoléon d', sieur de Saint-Luc 51, 91
Essex, *see* Devereux
Estates-general 10, 25–6, 27, 42–3, 62
Estrées, Gabrielle d', Henry's mistress 37–8, 56, 60, 64, 69, 75, 77–9, 90, 140
Evreux (Eure) 33

Falaise (Calvados) 33
Farnese, Alexander, Duke of Parma 36, 37, 39, 42
Fécamp (Sine-Maritime) 47, 128
Fenouillet, Pierre, bishop of Montpellier 124
Feria, *see* Suárez
Ferndinando, Grand Duke of Tuscany 45, 79, 86, 150, 171
Fernandez, Edouard, Portuguese gambler 105, 154
Feuillants, religious order 123
Flament, Jehan, courier 115
Flavigny (Côte-d'Or) 29
Florence, Italy 79, 86, 150, 171, 180
Florence, cardinal of, *see* Medici
Foissy, Philibert de, galley-captain 116
Foix (Ariège) 13
Folembray (Aisne) 60
Folleville (Eure) 39
Fontaine-Française (Côte-d'Or) 57, 58, 90
Fontainebleau (Seine-et-Marne) 75, 77, 80, 82, 87, 95, 101, 104, 107, 108, 109, 112, 119, 122, 130, 139, 140, 141, 148, 150, 157, 173, 181
Fontenay-le-Comte (Vendée) 22, 46
Fontevrault (Maine-et-Loire) 123
Forget, Pierre, sieur de Fresnes 97
Fortia, *see* Pilles
Fortifications 76, 98–9, 103, 107–8, 151–3, 160, 164
Fougeu, Pierre, sieur d'Escures 95, 112, 125, 131, 156
Foullon, Martin, painter 96
Fouquet, Guillaume, sieur de La Varenne 58, 90, 94, 105, 156

Fourcade, Jeanne, wet-nurse 3
Francini, Thomas and Alexander, hydraulic engineers 150
François I 1, 48, 110, 129, 141, 142, 179
Francqueville, Pierre de, sculptor 181
Frankfurt, Germany 38
Frederick V, Elector Palatine, *see* Elector
Fréminet, Martin, painter 96, 181
Frémiot, Bénigne, *parlementaire* 162
Fresnes, *see* Canaye and Forget
Friesland, Edward, count of 168
Froissart, chronicler 7
Froulay, André de, sieur de Gastines 156, 158, 159
Fuentes, *see* Enríquez

Gaboury family of tapestry-makers, 96, 147
Gaillon (Eure) 64
Gambling by Henry 64, 88, 105, 149, 154
Gardens 130, 180, 184
Garonne, river 6, 142, 156
Gascony, province 112
Gastines, *see* Froulay
Gaultier, Léonard, engraver 149
Geneva, Switzerland 2, 6, 95, 114, 154
Genoa, Genoese 116, 170, 171
German princes 18, 21, 22, 25, 31, 38, 40, 45, 95, 100, 118, 119, 141, 171, 174
Gesvres, *see* Potier
Gévaudan, region 21
Gex, region 85
Gironde, estuary of the Garonne and Dordogne 91, 126
Givry, *see* Anglure
Gondi, Jérôme de, banker 87
Gontaut, Armand de, maréchal de Biron 21, 28, 33, 38, 39, 57, 67
Gontaut, Charles de, maréchal de Biron 75, 80, 83, 92, 96, 99, 108, 110, 111, 112–15, 121, 125, 136, 160, 166
Gontaut, Jean de, sieur de Salignac 14
Gonzague, Louis de, duc de Nevers 28, 54, 92
Goulard, Louis de, sieur de Beauvoir 8
Goustemesnil, Jean (or Charles) de, sieur de Boisrosé 47
Governors and *gouvernements* 1, 9, 110, 126, 137, 148, 156, 158, 159–61
Grammont, Antoine de 91, 165
Grand Design 174
Gregory XIV, pope 41
Gremonville, Nicolas de, sieur de Larchant 4
Grenoble (Isère) 81, 84, 92
  parlement 73
Grillon, *see* Crillon
Grisons, the 86

Groulart, Claude, *premier président* 48, 76, 88, 91, 104, 139, 162, 204
Gué-de-Sénac (Gironde) 22
Guicciardini, Jacopo, Italian author 7
Guise family 2, 9, 15–17, 18, 41, 47
Guise, *see* Lorraine
Guise, Mme de, Catherine de Clèves 75, 104
Guitry, N. de 22
Gustavus Adolphus of Sweden 176
Guyenne, province 7, 9, 10–12, 17, 18, 20–2, 91, 103, 136, 156, 157–8, 163–4, 168

Habsburgs, the 110, 142, 168, 171
Hall, Germany 174
Hanotaux, Gabriel, historian 164
Harambure, Jean d', sieur de Romefort 57, 92
Harlay, Achille de, *premier président* 162
Harlay, Christophe de, sieur de Beaumont 204
Harlay, Nicolas de, sieur de Sancy 28, 94
Harlay, Robert de, sieur de Montglat 94
Harlay, N. de, Mme de Montglat 140
Hayden, Michael, historian 124
Hédé (Ille-et-Vilaine) 128
Heidelberg, Germany 22, 118
Hennequin, Jacques, historian 123
Henri II 1, 2, 3, 79, 109, 116, 129
Henri III 5, 8, 11, 15, 17, 18, 20, 22, 25, 26, 27, 28, 34, 90, 92, 124, 129, 156
Herbannes, family of tapestry-makers 96, 147
Héroard, Jean, doctor 95, 139, 206
Hesse, Maurice landgrave of 45, 118, 141, 150, 168, 171, 173
Hohenzollern, N., count 173
Honfleur (Calvados) 33
Hotman, François, treasurer 95
Humières, Charles d' 28
Hungary 119
Hunting by the king 64, 75, 88, 104, 120, 139, 140, 146, 150
Hurault, Philippe, sieur de Cheverny 38, 50, 53
Hurepoix, region 178
Hyères (Var) 116

Ile-de-France, province 1, 28
Illnesses of the king 26, 76, 88, 95, 119–20, 146
Infanta, the, Isabella Clara Eugenia 42–3
Ingrande (Maine-et-Loire) 167
Innsbruck, Austria 149
Intendants, etc. 55, 97, 98, 126, 151, 156–9, 183
Ireland, Irish 44–5, 170
Isabella, 'archduke' 100

Isère, river 84
Isle, river 22
Issoire (Puy-de-Dôme) 37
Italy, Italians 74, 76, 85, 103, 110, 111, 123, 129, 131, 133, 134, 135, 149, 168, 171, 180, 181, 182, 183
Ivry (Eure) 32, 58, 90, 92, 156

Jacquet, Mathieu, sculptor 96, 150, 181
Jacquinot, Jean, of Dijon 165
Jambeville, *see* Le Camus
James (VI of Scotland and I of England) 120, 121, 145, 154, 170
Jargeau (Loiret) 137
Jarnac (Charente) 6
Jaubert, Aimeri de, sieur de Barrault 127
Jeannin, Pierre 92, 112, 131, 162, 173, 204
Jesuits 54, 56, 57, 82, 118, 121, 123, 124, 161, 162
Joinville, *see* Lorraine
Jouvenel, Bertrand de 68
Joyeuse, Henri de (frère Ange de Joyeuse) 49
Joyeuse, duc Anne de 21–4, 27, 60
Jülich-Cleves-Berg, John William, duke of 146, 171
Jusseaume, François, financier 115

Kerckhove, Melchior van den 169

La Boderie, *see* Le Fèvre
La Boidissière, Mlle de 109, 154
La Camere, Isabelle de, singer 104
La Capelle (Aisne) 58, 74
La Charité (Nièvre) 7
La Châtre, Claude de 37, 90, 160
La Chevalerie, N. de 51
La Clielle, Brochard de 54
Lacombe, Charles de, historian 164
La Faye, Antoine de, minister 46
La Force, *see* Caumont
Laffemas, Barthélemy de 131, 134
La Fère (Aisne) 60–2, 67–8
La Fin, Jacques de 80, 112, 154
La Flèche (Sarthe) 6, 122
La Fond, Etienne de 98, 126, 131, 156
La Gaucherie, Françoise de, tutor 5
Lagny (Seine-et-Marne) 37
La Grange, Antoine de, sieur d'Arquien 118
La Guesle, Jacques de 79
La Haye, Mlle de 123, 154
La Mothe-Fénelon (Deux-Sèvres) 76
Langlois, Martin, sieur de Beaurepaire 51
Langres (Haute-Marne) 29, 92, 165
Languedoc, province 12, 18, 20, 41, 91, 114, 134, 153, 156, 157, 159, 160, 163, 164

parlement 91
estates 159
La Noue, François de 21, 29, 60
Larchant, *see* Gremonville
La Rivière, *see* Ribit
La Roche, N. de 138
La Roche-Chalais (Dordogne) 22
La Rochelle (Charente-Maritime) 6, 7, 8, 10, 20, 21, 22, 25, 26, 91, 107
La Rochepot, N. de 100, 111, 126
Lasso, Don Roderigo 103
La Tour d'Auvergne, Henri de, duc de Bouillon 14, 20, 22, 46, 94, 110, 112, 114, 118, 119, 120, 125, 136, 137, 141, 142, 150, 157
La Trémoille, Claude de 21, 22, 24, 28, 33, 46, 58, 125
L'Ausmonier, Simon, tax-gatherer 167
Laval (Mayenne) 33
Laval, Urbain de, sieur de Boisdauphin 59
La Valette, Bernard de Nogaret, sieur de 37
La Varenne, *see* Fouquet
Laverdin, *see* Beaumanoir
Lavisse, Ernest, historian 21, 164
League, the Holy 16–18, 20, 25, 26, 42, 49, 51, 54, 57, 62, 90, 116, 119, 126
Le Camus, Antoine de, sieur de Jambeville 107, 156, 159
Le Catelet (Aisne) 58, 74
Le Conquet (Finistère) 18
Le Fèvre, Antoine de, sieur de La Boderie 100
Le Fèvre, Louis de, sieur de Caumartin 156
Le Havre (Seine-Maritime) 33, 90
Leighton, Mr, English agent 9
Lello, Henry, English diplomat 101
Lemaire, Isaac, explorer 169
Le Mans (Sarthe) 33
Le Nôtre, Pierre, gardener 130
Le Polet, suburb of Dieppe 29–30
Le Roy, François, sieur de Chavigny 43
Leo XI, pope 171
Leopold, archduke of Austria 173
Lescar, bishop of, *see* Abbadie
Lescot, Pierre, architect 129
Lesdiguières, *see* Bonne
L'Estoile, Pierre de, historian 5, 44, 53, 58, 60, 64, 65, 75, 109, 133, 206
Leucate (Aude) 111
Levis, Charles de 125
L'Hôpital, Louis de, sieur de Vitry 28, 47, 99, 113
L'Hoste, Nicolas, spy 121, 126
Lhuillier, Jean, *prévôt des marchands* 51
Libertat, Barthélemy de 48
Liège, Belgium 143
Lillebonne (Seine-Maritime) 47

Limoges, Limousin 29, 106–7, 121, 123, 136, 157, 165
Lintlaer, Jean, engineer 130
Lisieux (Calvados) 33
L'Isle-Bouchard (Vienne) 26
Literature, Henry's style and taste in 5, 7, 33, 62
Livorno, Italy 107, 123, 157
Lodève (Hérault) 125
Loire, river 29, 69, 90, 126, 142
Lomellini, Ambrogio, Genoese 116
Longpré (Somme) 67
Longuejoue, *see* Montglat
Longueval, Angélique de 154
Longueville, *see* Orléans
Lorraine, duchy 168
Lorraine, Charles de, duc d'Aiguillon 94
Lorraine, Charles de, duc d'Aumale 15, 18
Lorraine, Charles de, duc d'Elbeuf 15, 48
Lorraine, Charles de, duc de Guise 48, 49, 50, 61, 91, 103, 105, 110, 111, 160, 164, 165
Lorraine, Charles Cardinal de 15, 18, 26
Lorraine, Claude de, prince de Joinville 2, 112
Lorraine, François de, duc de Guise 2
Lorraine, Henri de, duc de Guise 5, 8, 15, 18, 22, 25, 26, 72
Lorraine, Marie de, abbess 123
Lorraine, Philippe-Emmanuel de, duc de Mercoeur 18, 37, 41, 49, 60, 61, 68, 69, 70, 74, 90, 157, 159
Lorraine, Renée de, abbess 123
Louis XI 1, 179
Louis XIII (*dauphin*) 96, 109, 119, 125, 128, 130, 139, 140, 141, 147, 160, 175, 183
Louis XIV 130, 149, 177, 184
Lourdes (Hautes-Pyrénées) 3
Lussan, *see* d'Esparbez
Luther, Martin 2
Lyon (Rhône), Lyonnais 1, 58, 59, 80, 81, 83, 85, 86, 103, 106, 111, 112, 121, 134, 159, 165

Mâcon (Saône-et-Loire) 5, 124, 166
Madrid, Spain 81, 127
Maggio, le père, Jesuit 121
Maillejais (Vendée) 180
Malesherbes (Loiret) 79
Malherbe, François de 91, 130, 133, 136, 176, 180
Malta 86, 116
Malthus Francis, economist 1, 178
Manou, *see* O
Mansfelt, Charles count of 58
Mantes (Seine-et-Oise) 31, 35, 41, 135
Manufactures 131, 133–5, 179, 183

Maps, *see* cartography
Marans (Charente-Maritime) 21
Marescot, Michel, doctor 95
Maria/Marie de Medici 79, 84, 86, 88, 101, 105, 108, 116, 119, 123, 139, 140, 154, 158, 170, 174, 175, 180–2
Marion, Miles, treasurer 156, 159
Marne, river 36, 77, 121, 127, 150
Marseille (Bouches-du-Rhône) 48, 86, 116, 143, 165, 167
Mathew, Toby, author 128–31
Matignon, Charles de, *maréchal* 50
Maupeou, Gilles, treasurer 95
Maurevert, Charles de Louviers, sieur de, assassin 7
Maurice, prince of Orange 170
Maurienne, region 83, 84
Mayenne, *see* Lorraine
Mayerne, *see* Turquet
Meaux (Seine-et-Marne) 36, 47, 99
Medici, Alexander of, Cardinal of Florence 64, 74, 140, 180, 203
Melun (Seine-et-Marne) 35, 51, 77
Mendoza, Bernardino de 42
Mercoeur, *see* Lorraine
Merki, Charles, historian 78
Mersenne, Marin 122
Metz (Moselle) 118, 123, 125
Meudon (Seine-et-Oise) 27
Meuse, river 143
Michelet, Jules, historian 176
Milan, Milanese 57, 101, 114, 170, 171, 175
Mildmay, Sir Anthony 63, 65
Minimes, religious order 123
Miossens, *see* Albret
Mirebeau (Vienne) 26
Mistresses of the king 8, 9, 11, 12, 37–8, 56, 64, 78, 79, 86, 88, 108, 109, 122, 149, 154, 178, 182–3
Mocenigo, Giovanni, Venetian ambassador 32, 49, 118
Mollet, Claude, gardener 150
Montglat, *see* Harlay
Monluc, Jean de, sieur de Balagny 47, 48, 60
Montaigne, Michel de 4
Montargis (Loiret) 142
Montauban (Tarn-et-Garonne) 7, 12
Montbazon, Hercule de Rohan, duc de 90, 175
Montceaux (Seine-et-Marne) 60, 64, 75, 76, 104, 108, 139, 150
Montereau (Seine-et-Marne) 35
Montspan, N. de 157
Montferrand (Puy-de-Dôme) 49
Montguyon (Charente-Maritime) 22
Montholon, François de 28
Monthulin (Pas-de-Calais) 74

Montmélian (Savoie) 83–4
Montmorency, duc Anne de 2
Montmorency, Charlotte de 173–6
Montmorency, François de 2
Montmorency, Henri de, sieur de Damville, constable 2, 14, 17, 18, 20, 75, 87, 91, 97, 99, 103, 112, 114, 120, 156, 160
Montmorency, Louise de 99
Montpellier (Hérault) 95, 124
Montpensier, Mme Catherine de 53
Montpensier, *see* Bourbon
Montreuil (Pas-de-Calais) 108
Monts, *see* Du Gua
Moret, *see* Bueil
Moriscoes 110, 127, 170
Morocco 171
Moscow, Russia 168
Moulins (Allier) 95, 106
Mousnier, Roland, historian 55, 176
Moussoullens, *see* Saint-Jean
Munster, Ireland 145

Nantes (Loire-Atlantique) 69, 70, 87, 90, 96, 98, 114, 137, 154, 159, 162
Nanteuil, *see* Schomberg
Naples, Neapolitans 53, 58, 171
Narbonne (Aude) 111
Nassau, Justin of 60, 74
Navarre, kingdom 2, 6, 8, 13, 91, 130, 136, 160
Navarre, *see* Bourbon, Savoie
Navy 86, 90, 91, 115–17, 151, 170
Nemours (Seine-et-Marne) 18, 25
Nemours, Mme Marie de 53
Nérac (Lot-et-Garonne) 11, 12, 63, 158
Netherlands, Spanish 16, 36, 39, 58, 74, 75, 85, 111, 121, 127, 145, 169, 170
Neufville, Nicolas de, sieur de Villeroy 43, 81, 85, 97, 99, 101, 103, 119, 121, 126, 127, 144, 147, 168, 173, 174
Nevers, *see* Gonzague
Neville, Sir Henry, English ambassador 78, 79, 84
Nirot (Dux-Sèvres) 10, 26
Nobility 2, 20, 28, 42, 55, 61, 77, 87, 114, 134–7, 146, 161
Nogaret, Jean-Louis de, duc d'Epernon 17, 28, 61, 82, 105, 112–14, 118, 136, 174–6
Nogent-sur-Seine (Aube) 81
Normandy, province 15, 28, 29, 32, 33, 41, 64, 88, 90, 134, 159, 160, 163, 164
Nostredame, Michel de, soothsayer 5
Nouaillac, Jules, historian 85
Novince, Guillaume, sieur d'Aubigny 159
Noyon (Oise) 38
Nuremberg, Germany 70, 142

O, François d' 28, 51, 53, 64
O, Jean d', sieur de Manou 28
Oise, river 31, 61
Oratorians, religious order 124
Orléans (Loiret), Orléannais 80, 81, 90, 95, 106, 134, 148, 160
Orléans, François de, comte de Saint-Pol 50, 92, 160
Orléans, Henri d', duc de Longueville 28, 29, 31, 50
Orléans, Louis d', pamphleteer 21
Ornano, Alphonse d' 91, 103, 136, 157, 158, 160
Ossat, Arnaud d' 54
Ostend, Belgium 108
Overseas ventures 90, 123, 138–9, 169, 183

Painting 180–3
Pallar, stream 22
Palma-Cayet, Pierre-Victor, historian 5, 44, 133, 206
Panissault, N., secret agent 127, 170
Papacy, *see* Rome
Paris 1, 5, 7, 8, 9, 11, 12, 25, 29, 31, 33, 35, 36, 39, 40, 42, 44, 48, 53, 60, 62, 63, 65, 75, 78, 80, 81, 87, 95, 101, 103, 105, 106, 108, 109, 118, 123, 128, 129, 133, 142, 143, 144, 145, 148, 160, 169, 172, 178, 179
  Archives Nationales 48
  Arsenal 51, 80, 87, 98, 103, 104, 144, 147, 174
  Bastille 98, 113, 114, 135, 136, 141, 175, 183
  Bibliothèque Nationale 8, 48, 62
  Champs-Elysées 130
  Collège de Navarre 54
  cour des aides 106
  Faubourg Saint-Martin 35
  Feuillants 103
  Grand Châtelet 51
  Hôpital Saint-Louis 133
  Hôtel de Ville 75, 129, 145, 165, 166
  Louvre 42, 51, 53, 72, 76, 87, 101, 104, 105, 109, 128, 129, 130, 133, 147, 149, 150, 162, 174, 175, 181
  Notre-Dame 51, 53, 74, 147
  parlement 41, 42, 53, 54, 57, 59, 60, 62, 65, 72, 79, 80, 97, 113, 121, 122, 125, 161, 162
  Place Dauphine 132–3, 150, 181
  Place Royale 96, 128, 131, 133, 135, 150, 181
  Pont Neuf 129, 133
  Porte Neuve 51
  Porte Saint-Denis 51, 53
  Rue Dauphine 131, 133

Saint-Benoist 124
Saint-Eustache 44
Saint-Germain-l'Auxerrois 77
Saint-Séverin 123
Sorbonne 53, 54, 57
Tuileries 104, 128–30, 133, 181
Parlements, see Paris, Toulouse, Grenoble,
 Bordeaux, Dijon, Rouen and Rennes
Parma, *see* Farnese
Parry, Sir Thomas 56, 121, 139, 140, 170
Pau (Basses-Pyrénées) 2–4, 11, 127, 130,
 158, 180
Paul V, pope 171
Paulet, Amyas, English ambassador 11
Peiresc, Nicolas Fabri de 133, 176
Pellevé, cardinal Nicolas de 43
Périgord, region 55, 136
Périgueux (Dordogne) 22
Pertuis (Vaucluse) 29
Pézenas (Hérault) 163
Philip II of Spain 12, 16, 33, 36, 41, 43, 100,
 184
Philip III of Spain 85, 100, 111, 112, 114,
 125, 126, 184
Philippe-Auguste, king of France 31, 180
Philippson, Martin, historian 111, 205
Picardy, province 2, 6, 9, 15, 28, 29, 31, 37,
 59, 65, 66, 92, 107, 133, 134, 153, 60
Picoté, N., courier 113
Piero, Jacopo, composer 180
Pilles, Pierre-Paul de Fortia, sieur de 69
Pimentel, Manuel, dice-maker 105
Pineau, Séverin, surgeon 95
Piney-Luxembourg, Henry duc de 74
Plessis-lès-Tours (Indre-et-Loire) 27
Pliny, ancient author 7
Plots and insurrections 54–5, 87, 91, 106–7,
 111–15, 125–6, 136–7, 166–7
Plutarch, ancient author 5
Pluvinel, Antoine de, riding master 96
Poirson, Auguste, historian 48, 85, 123,
 164, 176
Poitiers (Vienne) 41, 48, 107, 134, 142, 148,
 157
Poitiers, Diane de, duchesse de Valentinois,
 mistress of Henri II 109
Poitou, province 21, 22, 28, 91, 112, 134,
 137
Poland 8, 79, 168
Pontcarré, *see* Camus
Pontoise (Seine-et-Oise) 9
Pont-Sainte-Maxence (Oise) 31
Porchnev, Boris, historian 55
Portocarrero, Hernantello 65–7
Portugal 156
Potier, Isabelle 79
Potier, Louis, sieur de Gesvres 97

Praslin, *see* Choiseul
Prieur, Barthélemy, sculptor 96
Primel (Finistère) 128
Priuli, Pietro, Venetian diplomat 175
Propaganda, cultural 58, 74–5, 86–7, 133,
 146–50
Protestants 65, 68, 69, 70–4, 76, 79, 83, 90,
 92, 107, 137, 175
Provence, province 37, 41, 86, 91, 103, 111,
 133, 134, 153, 156, 159, 160, 163–4
Provincial estates, *see* under Province
Provins (Seine-et-Marne) 35

Québec, Canada 139
Quelin, Mme 79, 154
Quercy, region 136

Raffis, N., refugee 127
Rambouillet, *see* Angennes
Ravaillac, François, assassin 175–6
Razing of castles 127–8
Refugees 144–5, 170
Reims (Marne) 15, 50, 123, 142
Religious sentiment and attitudes of the king
 17, 28, 44, 51, 53–4, 75, 82–3, 122–5
Rennes (Ille-et-Vilaine) 128
 parlement 73
Revol, Louis 43
Rhône, river 91
Ribit, Jean, sieur de La Rivière, doctor 82, 95
Richelieu, Armand Du Plessis, cardinal de
 86, 100, 119, 151, 161, 166, 176
Rieux, René de, sieur de Sourdéac 90, 145
Riom (Puy-de-Dôme) 107
Ritter, Raymond, historian 180, 203
Roads 98, 151, 154, 160, 179, 183
Roanne (Loire) 80
Robin, Jehan, *herboriste* 95
Robiquet, Paul, historian 54, 164, 165
Rochechouart (Haute-Vienne) 167
Rochefort-sur-Loire (Maine-et-Loire) 128
Rocroi (Ardennes) 92
Rodez (Aveyron) 157
Rohan, *see* Montbazon
Romano, Julio, singer 104
Rome (papacy) 41, 43, 54, 62, 72, 77, 100,
 103, 154, 171
Romefort, *see* Harambure
Roquelaure, Antoine de 14, 17, 94, 105
Rosny, *see* Sully
Rott, Edouard, historian 85
Rouen (Seine-Maritime) 5, 29, 33, 37, 38, 40,
 58, 62, 64, 78, 122, 138, 145, 150, 168
 archbishop 17
 parlement 48, 62, 73, 76, 77, 88, 91, 139,
 162
Rouergue, region 157

Roussat, Jean, mayor of Langres 92, 165
Rubens, Pierre-Paul, painter 177
Rudolph II, emperor 70, 103, 118, 173
Rue (Somme) 18
Russia 169
Ruzé, Martin, sieur de Beaulieu 97

Saint Bartholomew, Massacre of 7, 14, 72, 91
Saint-Bernard, pass 85
Saint-Brice (Charente) 21
Saint-Cloud (Hauts-de-Seine) 27, 31, 39
Saint-Denis (Seine-Saint-Denis) 35, 44, 51, 54
Saint-Dizier (Haute-Marne) 18, 92
Saint-Geniès, N. de 12
Saint-Germain (Yvelines) 7, 8, 56, 73, 75, 80, 87, 108, 109, 130, 138, 139, 140, 147, 149, 150, 154, 181, 183
Saint-Germain-Beaupré, N. de 66
Saint-Hérem, N. de 49
Saint-Jean, François de, sieur de Moussoullens 49
Saint-Jean-d'Angély (Charente-Maritime) 157
Saint-Jean-de-Luz (Pyrénées-Atlantiques) 157
Saint-Jean-Pied-de-Port (Pyrénées-Atlantiques) 6
Saint-Lary, Roger de, sieur de Bellegarde 28, 50, 79, 86, 92, 94, 105, 160
Saint-Luc, *see* Espinay
Saint-Maixent (Deux-Sèvres) 22
Saint-Martin-de-Ré (Ile-de-Ré) 117
Saint-Pol, *see* Orléans
Saint-Quentin (Aisne) 92
Sainte-Foy (Gironde) 70, 137
Saintonge, region 21
Sales, Saint François de 124
Salignac, *see* Gontaut
Salon de Crau (Bouches-du-Rhône) 5, 167
Salluzo, Italy 74, 79, 80, 81, 85
Sanzay (Deux-Sèvres) 22
Saône, river 57, 87, 142, 143
Saumur (Maine-et-Loire) 46, 70, 83, 90
Sauve, Charlotte de 8, 9
Savage, Sir Arthur 66
Savary, Jean, sieur de Brèves 60, 81, 101, 110, 171
Savoie, Henri de, duc de Nemours 33, 49
Savoy 81, 103, 111, 117, 151, 171
Savoy, Charles-Emmanuel, duke of 37, 41, 74, 80, 83, 92, 110, 112, 113, 114, 115, 159, 171, 174
Saxony, Germany 79
Scaramelli, Giovanni, Venetian diplomat 121

Schomberg, Gaspard de, comte de Nanteuil 43, 65, 68
Scotland, Scots 18, 44, 50, 91, 99, 147, 151
Sedan (Ardennes) 38, 114, 141
Seine, river 39, 51, 81, 129, 142, 143, 149
Selves, *see* Camberfore
Sérillac, François de, comte de Belin 61
Serres, Olivier de, agriculturalist 148
Shrewsbury, earl of 64
Sigismund II, King of Poland 168
Sigogne, *see* Beauxoncles
Sillery, *see* Brûlart
Sixtus V, pope 41
Smyth, Ottywell, English agent 58
Sobole, *see* Comminge
Soissons (Aisne) 18, 60
Soissons, *see* Bourbon
Somme, river 58–9, 60, 66
Sourdéac, *see* Rieux
Sourdis, François de 37
Spain, Spaniards 20, 25, 26, 36, 37, 41, 42, 51, 53, 57, 61, 62, 64, 65, 66, 69, 70, 74, 76, 85, 86, 91, 92, 98, 99, 103, 110, 111, 114, 116, 126–7, 136, 141, 143, 154, 159, 163, 165, 166, 167, 168, 169, 171, 173
Spanish Road, the 111, 113
Spies 121, 126–7, 148, 155
Spinola, Ambrogio de, Spanish general 170
Stafford, Sir Edward, English ambassador 37
Strasbourg (Bas-Rhin) 118, 119, 142
Suárez de Figueroa, Lorenzo, duke of Feria 43, 51, 53
Sublet, Michel, treasurer 95
Sully, Maximilien de Béthune, duc de 8, 14, 20, 22, 25, 33, 46, 48, 49, 51, 58, 60, 64, 68, 76, 79, 80, 81, 83, 85, 90, 91, 97, 98, 99, 101, 103, 104, 106, 113, 114, 115, 116, 119, 120–6, 131–4, 139, 141–4, 149, 151, 154, 157, 158, 163, 164, 166, 168–70, 173–5, 177, 179, 180, 182–4
Suresnes (hauts-de-Seine) 43, 91, 96
Sweden 18, 168
Switzerland, Swiss 21, 27, 28, 31, 33, 44, 50, 60, 66, 100, 101, 147, 151
Synods (Protestant assemblies) 25–6, 65, 70, 137

Tarentaise, region 84
Tarquin, Pierre, gardener 130
Tassis, Juan Bautista de, Spanish ambassador 111, 125, 127, 204
Taxes 1, 54, 75, 98–9, 160, 163, 167, 178, 183
Teynagel, imperial ambassador 173
Thou, Jacques Auguste de 43, 96, 133

Thumery, Jean de, sieur de Boissise 55, 99, 204
Toledo, Don Pedro of 148, 150, 154
Tonnetuit, *see* Chauvin
Toul (Meurthe-et-Moselle) 18
Toulon (Var) 91, 116, 183
Toulouse (Haute-Garonne) 18, 29, 121, 142, 158, 162
 parlement 73
Tours (Indre-et-Loire) 29, 31, 53, 112, 115, 134, 135, 161
Towns 42, 55, 92, 106–7, 113, 146, 160, 164–6, 183
Travecy (Aisne) 61
Trent, Council of 44, 54, 62, 108, 124
Troyes (Aube) 81, 92, 99, 124, 135, 147
Trullinger, Robert, historian 166
Turenne (Corrèze) 114
Turin, Italy 80, 115
Turks 86, 105
Turquet, Théodore, sieur de Mayerne 95
Tuscany, duke of, *see* Ferdinando
Tyrone, earl of 145

Ulm, Germany 142
United Provinces, Dutch 40, 59, 60, 69, 74, 99, 100, 101, 110, 120, 126, 129, 134, 135, 144, 148, 154, 168, 169, 170, 171, 173, 174
Unton, Sir Henry, English ambassador 38
Urfé, Honoré d', novelist 148
Ursulines, religious order 123–4

Vaissiére, Pierre, historian 51
Valence (Drôme) 81
Valencia, Spain 127
Valentinois, *see* Poitiers
Valladier, André, preacher 123
Valladolid, Spain 111
Valois, house of 2, 3, 17, 18, 27, 68, 105
Valois, Charles de, comte d'Auvergne 106, 112, 113, 125, 126, 136
Valois, Marguerite de, Henry's wife 7, 11, 12, 77, 128, 130, 136, 144
Valromey, region 85
Valtelline, Italian pass 100
Vassallo, Genoese galley-captain 116
Velasco, Don Luis de 57
Vendôme, *see* Bourbon
Vendôme, César de, Henry's son with Gabrielle d'Estrées 69, 90, 160

Vendômois, region 6
Venice, Venetians 32, 65, 100, 110, 121, 146, 171, 174, 203
Verdun (Meuse) 18, 118
Verdun, Nicolas de, *premier président* 91, 162
Verneuil (Oise) 109, 126
Verneuil, *see* d'Entragues
Verneuil, Henri de, Henry's son by Henriette d'Entragues 125
Vernyes, Jean de, president 49
Vervins (Aisne) 74, 79, 99, 100, 111, 118, 121
Vesle, river 142
Vic, Dominique de 92
Vic, Méry de 100
Viçose, Raymond de 94, 156, 157, 159
Vienne, river 142
Villars, *see* Brancas
Villemur (Hautes-Pyrénées) 41
Villeroy, *see* Neufville
Villotte, Jacques, artist 180
Vimory (Loiret) 25
Vincheguerre, Jacques, galley-captain 116
Vitruvius, Roman architect 149
Vitry-le-François (Marne) 92
Vitry, *see* l'Hôpital
Vivarais, region 134
Vivonne (Vienne) 26
Vizille (Isère) 192
Voltaire, François-Marie Arouet, dit 177
Vouzailles (Vienne) 22

Walloons 33, 53, 58
Walsingham, Sir Francis 11
Wilton, Captain Edward, English soldier 159
Winwood, Sir Ralph, English diplomat 84, 85, 86, 109, 111, 112, 115, 116, 121, 139, 204
Wolfe, Martin, historian 49
Würtemberg, Frederick duke of 100, 142

Xanten, the Convention of 176

Yvetot (Seine-Maritime) 39

Zamet, Sébastien, financier 64, 78, 87, 104, 109, 148
Zérotin, Charles de, volunteer from Bohemia 38, 168

235